Advancing Global Bioethics

Volume 6

Series editors

Henk A.M.J. ten Have
Pittsburgh, USA

Bert Gordijn
Dublin, Ireland

The book series Global Bioethics provides a forum for normative analysis of a vast range of important new issues in bioethics from a truly global perspective and with a cross-cultural approach. The issues covered by the series include among other things sponsorship of research and education, scientific misconduct and research integrity, exploitation of research participants in resource-poor settings, brain drain and migration of healthcare workers, organ trafficking and transplant tourism, indigenous medicine, biodiversity, commodification of human tissue, benefit sharing, bio-industry and food, malnutrition and hunger, human rights, and climate change.

More information about this series at http://www.springer.com/series/10420

Joseph Tham • Kai Man Kwan • Alberto Garcia
Editors

Religious Perspectives on Bioethics and Human Rights

Springer

Editors
Joseph Tham
Ateneo Pontificio Regina Apostolorum
Rome, Italy

Alberto Garcia
Bioethics and Human Rights
UNESCO
Rome, Italy

Kai Man Kwan
Department of Religion and Philosophy
Hong Kong Baptist University
Kowloon Tong, Hong Kong

ISSN 2212-652X ISSN 2212-6538 (electronic)
Advancing Global Bioethics
ISBN 978-3-319-58429-4 ISBN 978-3-319-58431-7 (eBook)
DOI 10.1007/978-3-319-58431-7

Library of Congress Control Number: 2017951127

Printed on acid-free paper

This Springer imprint is published by Springer Nature
The registered company is Springer International Publishing AG
The registered company address is: Gewerbestrasse 11, 6330 Cham, Switzerland

Preface

When colleagues agreed to hold the international conference related to bioethics, religious life, and human rights at our Hong Kong Baptist University, I was immediately drawn to the complexities that could be involved. Having taught in both religious and philosophical studies within primarily a Chinese context for nearly three decades, I had been focused on other religious and philosophical traditions but imagined that the international level of this particular conference would include many new perspectives that I had not regularly engaged. Motivated by that imagined hope, I became involved and sat through the whole conference except for the final roundup session (because I had other obligations at that time), and I was not at all disappointed, though I was surprised a few times, and seriously concerned about certain matters by the time the conference was completed.

As could be expected, the intellectual tenor of the level of discussion was generally very high, and so there was much to be learned and many questions that flowed from nearly each session. As will be manifest in this volume, the main approach to the complex theme was through representatives of the varying religious traditions. Because I have continued to have interest in Chinese expressions of Islam throughout my career, and knowing the tensions and fears that had developed especially since the destruction of the World Trade Center Towers in New York City in 2001, I requested to serve as the chairperson for the panel on Islam. It proved to be the most provocative and difficult panel of all those presented at the conference, and so it was very memorable. But more significantly, it was only one of a variety of responses from so many of the religious representatives that produced one of the big surprises of the whole conference: most religious intellectuals involved have some particular problems with how human rights could be applied to any number of experienced problems, and so very little was consequently done to focus on bioethics and its problems.

One notable exception in this regard was the Jewish contribution, because it was offered by a pair of medical doctors and was presented from the angle of their actual medical practice. Still, the majority of the participants spent most of their energy and concerns on seeking to align their own religious convictions with the more general concerns surrounding the justifications required to present a viable understanding of human rights that could be undergirded not only by the Universal Declaration of Human Rights but also their own religious community.

Fortunately, most religious traditions had more than one representative present during the conference sessions, and so another surprise came in the diversity of perspectives that were expressed among various religious traditions. One new addition to this heady intellectual pluralogue that was held was a representative from Daoist traditions, and the representative from that tradition did not lose the opportunity to capitalize on that fact. Much was learned from Roman Catholic and Protestant differences, while, in contrast, the voices of colleagues who spoke from Ruist ("Confucian") and Buddhist traditions were relatively muted. I believe the latter occurred primarily because there were not as many others within the conference who identified with those two traditions, and so when they took up their relatively more skeptical attitudes toward human rights, it tended to mesh with the questions that other religious intellectuals expressed as well.

Nevertheless, with all these significant surprises that did occur during the conference, the general concern that impressed me deeply was this: there is still very much to do in order to understand how religious communities can address both human rights and the technical problems of bioethics in our current age. Because this volume is dedicated to that purpose, I laud the participants, editors, and commentators in moving forward toward this timely and important goal.

Centre for Sino-Christian Studies
Hong Kong Baptist University
Kowloon Tong, Hong Kong

Lauren F. Pfister

Acknowledgments

First of all, we honor the memory of Dr. Prakash Desai, who passed away in 2015 having attended two of our workshops in the past and has contributed to this volume. We thank the WoFoo Social Enterprises of Hong Kong which has sponsored this workshop through the Hong Kong Baptist University. We also thank other donors including the Hong Kong Medical Guild of St. Luke, St. Cosmas, and St. Damian; Denis Chang's Chambers; and other anonymous donors who have contributed to the activities surrounding the workshop. The staffs of the Center for Applied Ethics and the Department of Religious and Philosophy of the Hong Kong Baptist University were most helpful in organizing the logistics of the event and cultural activities, including the Bioethics Art Competition held around those dates. Our sincere gratitude goes to Lovina Hui for organizing the cultural trip to China for the speakers and participants before the workshop. We also thank the supporting staff, fellows, and volunteers of the UNESCO Chair in Bioethics and Human Rights for their presence and assistance. Other than expressing our deep gratitude to those who wrote these papers in the workshop, we thank a team of reviewers who helped with external feedback to these writings. Their names include: Bede Bidlack, Roland Chia, Jinil Cho, Dominic Farrell, Alberto Garcia, Nouzha Guessous, David Heyd, Soraj Hongladarom, Paul Lee, Peter Mango, Cecile O'Connor, Aasim Padela, Beate Rossmanith, Martha Tarasco, Alex Yeung, and Ellen Zhang. We also thank Sameer Advani and Michael Baggot for proofreading, as well as Geoffrey Sem and Matthew Sem for copyediting and arranging the final draft for the submission. Last but not least, we thank the team at Springer for their professional dedication in making this publication a reality.

United Nations
Educational, Scientific and
Cultural Organization

UNESCO Chair in
Bioethics and Human Rights
Roma, Italy

The UNESCO Chair in Bioethics and Human Rights (www.unescobiochair.org) organized a workshop on "Bioethics, Multiculturalism and Religion" and the papers submitted here form the collection of this edited volume.

This UNESCO Chair was established in 2009 with two Roman universities. It offers a university framework of reflection and study, providing information and fostering the application of bioethical principles in science, medicine, and new technologies based on the Universal Declaration on Bioethics and Human Rights. Through integral education, research, and information, it seeks to contribute toward the recognition and promotion of a global and integral vision of bioethics, bringing to light universal values and principles as well as social and legal implications in relation to human rights. By creating a community of persons who are interested in these values, it seeks to promote cultural dialogues and encounters in a spirit of solidarity.

Contents

Contributors

Dariusch Atighetchi Faculty of Theology, Lugano, Switzerland

Bede Benjamin Bidlack Department of Theology, Saint Anselm College, Manchester, NH, USA

Jonathan Chan Religion and Philosophy Department and Centre for Applied Ethics, Hong Kong Baptist University, Hong Kong, China

Denis Chang Denis Chang's Chambers, Hong Kong, SAR, China

Roland Chia Trinity Theological College, Singapore, Singapore

Prakash N. Desai UICMC, University of Illinois at Chicago, Chicago, IL, USA

Ruiping Fan Department of Public Policy, City University of Hong Kong, Kowloon Tong, Hong Kong

Colleen M. Gallagher Section of Integrated Ethics in Cancer Care, Department of Critical Care and Respiratory Care, University of Texas MD Anderson Cancer Center, Houston, TX, USA

Alberto Garcia UNESCO Chair in Bioethics and Human Rights, Rome, Italy

Nouzha Guessous Hassan II University, Casablanca, Morocco

Adina Halevy Psychotherapist, Jerusalem

Jonathan Halevy Shaare Zedek Medical Center, Jerusalem

David Heyd The Hebrew University, Jerusalem

Soraj Hongladarom Department of Philosophy, Faculty of Arts, Chulalongkorn University, Bangkok, Thailand

Kai Man Kwan Department of Religion and Philosophy, Hong Kong Baptist University, Kowloon Tong, Hong Kong

John Lunstroth Research Professor, Health Law & Policy Institute, University of Houston Law Center, Houston, TX, USA

Gonzalo Miranda School of Bioethics, Ateneo Pontificio Regina Apostolorum, Rome, Italy

Dominique J. Monlezun Tulane School of Medicine, New Orleans, LA, USA

Ateneo Pontificio Regina Apostolorum, Rome, Italy

Aasim I. Padela Initiative on Islam & Medicine, University of Chicago, Chicago, IL, USA

Laura Palazzani National Bioethics Committee of Italy, Rome, Italy

Department of Law, LUMSA, Rome, Italy

David A. Palmer Department of Sociology, The University of Hong Kong, Pokfulam, Hong Kong

Claudia R. Sotomayor UNESCO Chair in Bioethics and Human Rights, Rome, Italy

Martha Tarasco School of Bioethics, University of Anahuac, Mexico City, Mexico

Henk ten Have Center for Healthcare Ethics, Duquesne University, Pittsburgh, PA, USA

Joseph Tham School of Bioethics, Ateneo Pontificio Regina Apostolorum, Rome, Italy

Hans Ucko Interreligious Relations and Dialogue of the World Council of Churches, Geneva, Switzerland

Alex Yeung School of Philosophy, Ateneo Pontificio Regina Apostolorum, Rome, Italy

Ellen Y. Zhang Religion and Philosophy Department, Centre for Applied Ethics, Hong Kong Baptist University, Kowloon Tong, Hong Kong

Wenqing Zhao Center for Comparative Philosophy, Duke University, Durham, NC, USA

About the Authors

Dariusch Atighetchi was born in Italy, and he obtained his degree in philosophy at the University of Milan. Subsequently, he received a diploma from the Italian Institute for Middle Eastern and Far Eastern Studies (ISMEO) in Iranian language and culture and a Ph.D. in comparative law at the Second University of Naples. For a number of years, he has been teaching Islamic bioethics at the Second University of Naples and at other Italian and foreign universities. At present, he is professor of Islamic bioethics at the Faculty of Theology, Lugano (Switzerland). His writings include *Islam e Bioetica*, *Islamic Bioethics: Problems and Perspectives*, and *Islam, Musulmani e Bioetica*.

Bede Benjamin Bidlack is assistant professor of theology at Saint Anselm College. He publishes in the areas of comparative theology, Daoist studies, theological anthropology, interreligious dialogue, and philosophy. He is the author of *In Good Company: The Body and Divinization in Pierre Teilhard de Chardin, SJ, and Daoist Xiao Yingsou* (Brill 2015).

Jonathan Chan received his Ph.D. from the Chinese University of Hong Kong. He is currently associate professor at the Department of Religion and Philosophy, Faculty of Arts, and associate director of the Centre for Applied Ethics, Hong Kong Baptist University. He is editor of the *International Journal of Chinese and Comparative Philosophy of Medicine*. His research interests include bioethics, war ethics, Chinese philosophy (Confucianism and Daoism), informal logic, and comparative philosophy. He is the author of numerous articles on war ethics, bioethics, human rights, and informal logic.

Denis Chang is senior counsel and head of chambers in Hong Kong comprising human rights lawyers and other barristers. He is a past chairman of the HK Bar Association and former member of the Basic Law Consultative Committee formed in connection with the drafting of the Basic Law of the HK SARs. He was formerly on the Executive Council of the HK Government. He received his academic and professional qualifications in England, was called to the bar both in England and in Hong Kong, and was appointed Queen's counsel in 1981 and senior counsel in 1997. He is a member of Lincoln's Inn and is chairman of the *Hong Kong Law Journal*.

Roland Chia is Chew Hock Hin professor of Christian doctrine at Trinity Theological College and theological and research advisor of the ETHOS Institute for Public Christianity, Singapore. He is author and editor of many books including *The Ethics of Human Organ Trading* (2009) and *Hybrids, Cybrids and Chimeras: The Ethics of Interspecies Research* (2011).

Prakash N. Desai was born and raised in India. He obtained his medical education at the Faculty of Medicine of the M.S. University of Baroda and completed his psychiatric residency at Northwestern University Medical School in Chicago, Illinois. His extensive work experience includes positions at the B. M. Institute in Ahmedabad in areas of academic psychiatry and community, social, and cultural psychiatry, director of the Department of Mental Health and Developmental Disabilities of the State of Illinois, a position at a veterans healthcare facility on the west side of Chicago, a professorial appointment at the University of Illinois at Chicago, director of education for the University of Illinois Hospital, and associate member of the Committee on Southern Asian Studies at the University of Chicago. Among his many publications are *Health and Medicine in the Hindu Tradition* and *Triumph and Tragedy: Psychohistorical Decisions of Mahatma Gandhi*, several book chapters, and over a dozen papers in professional journals. He has received numerous awards for his work including the Oskar Pfister Award, the George Tarjan Award, and the Bruce Boyer Award. He was also actively involved in the governance of the American Psychiatric Association. He is married and is the father of two daughters and grandfather of three small children.

Ruiping Fan is a professor of philosophy in the Department of Public Policy at the City University of Hong Kong. He serves as associate editor of the *Journal of Medicine and Philosophy*, co-editor of the *International Journal of Chinese and Comparative Philosophy of Medicine*, and editor of Asian Studies in Bioethics and the Philosophy of Medicine book series. His research focuses on Confucian bioethics, Chinese and comparative philosophy, and public policy and ethics. In addition to numerous journal articles and book chapters published, he has also authored *Reconstructionist Confucianism: Rethinking Morality After the West* (in English, 2010) and *Contemporary Confucian Bioethics* (in Chinese, 2011). He was the editor or co-editor of *Confucian Bioethics* (in English, 1999), *Confucian Society and the Revival of Dao* (in Chinese, 2008), *The Renaissance of Confucianism in Contemporary China* (in English, 2011), *Confucian Constitution and China's Future* (in Chinese, 2012), *Ritual and the Moral Life* (in English, 2012), *A Confucian Constitutional Order* (in English, 2013), and *Family-Oriented Informed Consent: East Asian and American Perspectives* (in English, 2015).

Colleen M. Gallagher has worked in the fields of social work and healthcare ethics since 1985. Dr. Gallagher is currently the chief and executive director of the Section of Integrated Ethics in Cancer Care and an associate professor in the Department of Critical Care for the University of Texas MD Anderson Cancer Center where she has worked since 2008. Prior to this, she served as system director of clinical ethics for Resurrection Health Care in Chicago, Illinois, and before this worked for the Catholic Diocese of Cleveland and Catholic Charities Health and Human Services in Ohio. Throughout her career, she has worked as a social worker and program director for programs serving the mentally ill and their families, persons with HIV/AIDS, and the bereaved and other vulnerable populations. She received her doctoral degree in bioethics in healthcare professions and social work from the Union Institute and University, Cincinnati, Ohio, in 2004. She completed an ethics fellowship in 1997 at Georgetown University, Washington DC. She has also served in assisting the growth of both the social work and bioethics fields having held several positions in professional organizations.

Alberto Garcia is the director of the UNESCO Chair in Bioethics and Human Rights (Rome, Italy). He graduated in law at Autonomous University Law School and is a doctor of law from Complutense University of Madrid. Presently, he is professor of philosophy of law and international law at the School of Bioethics of Ateneo Pontificio Regina Apostolorum in Rome. Furthermore he is a researcher of the Human Rights Institute at Complutense University. For 5 years, he has been member of the Steering Committee of Bioethics in the Council of Europe, and in 2005, he has been honored with the National Prize of the Spanish Royal Academy of Doctors in the field of legal and social sciences.

Nouzha Guessous is a medical biologist and professor at Casablanca Hassan II University (Morocco). As researcher in bioethics and women's/human rights, she is associated to the Social Science Research Center Jacques Berque in Rabat. She is former member and chair of the UNESCO IBC (2000–2007) and is currently member of the ALECSO Science and Technology Ethics Committee. She is also co-author of books and encyclopedias as well as regular author of newspaper tribunes on bioethics and women's/human rights.

Adina Halevy has a master's degree in social work and is a psychotherapist in private practice and a consultant to ICELP (the International Center for the Enhancement of Learning Potential) in Jerusalem.

Jonathan Halevy is a physician and associate clinical professor of internal medicine at the Hebrew University Medical School in Jerusalem, and director general of Shaare Zedek Medical Center in Jerusalem.

David Heyd is Chaim Perelman professor of philosophy at the Hebrew University of Jerusalem. His main fields of interest are political philosophy, ethics, and bioethics. He is the author of *Supererogation* (Cambridge, 1982), *Genethics* (Berkeley, 1992), and *Medical Ethics* (Tel Aviv, 1990) and the editor of *Toleration* (Princeton, 1996). Among his numerous articles, many are concerned with bioethical issues such as procreation, genetic technologies, euthanasia, sex selection, wrongful life, surrogacy, and experimentation on human subjects. He served as a member of many ethical committees on surrogacy, on end-of-life issues, and on ethics and genetics and the university's Helsinki committee.

Soraj Hongladarom is an associate professor of philosophy and director of the Center for Ethics of Science and Technology at Chulalongkorn University in

Bangkok, Thailand. He has published books and articles on such diverse issues as bioethics, computer ethics, and the roles that science and technology play in the culture of developing countries. His concern is mainly on how science and technology can be integrated into the life-world of the people in the so-called Third World countries and what kind of ethical considerations can be obtained from such relation. A large part of this question concerns how information technology is integrated in the life-world of the Thai people and especially how such integration is expressed in the use of information technology in education. He is the co-editor of *Information Technology Ethics: Cultural Perspectives*. His works have also appeared in *Bioethics*, *The Information Society*, *AI & Society*, *Philosophy in the Contemporary World*, and *Social Epistemology*.

Kai Man Kwan is a distinguished professor teaching in the Department of Religion and Philosophy at Hong Kong Baptist University. He graduated with an M.Phil. in philosophical theology (1991) and a Ph.D. in philosophy of religion (1993) both from Oxford University while holding a plethora of other degrees from the University of Hong Kong and University of Aberdeen. Professor Kwan has a stellar record of over 30 years of teaching experience in over 15 courses, with a specialization in topics of philosophy and religion. Courses he taught include the "Philosophy and the Meaning of Life," "Quest for Truth and Meaning," and "Approaches to the Study of Religion," to name a few. He has an extensive list of well-received publications such as the journal article "Replication and Theory Development in Organizational Science: A Critical Realist Perspective" (1999). He is also the author of a number of books including *Christian Ethics and the Secular Free Society* (2007) and *The Rainbow of Experiences, Critical Trust, and God: A Defense of Holistic Empiricism* (October 2011).

John Lunstroth is a fellow of the UNESCO Chair in Bioethics and Human Rights (Rome, Italy). He is an ethicist in the broad, non-naturalist sense. He practiced commercial law for about 20 years before returning to school in 2002, first for an LL.M. in health law and policy at the University of Houston Law Center (2004) and then for an M.P.H. from Columbia University (2007). He has published on the regulation of alternative medicine, the ethics of human experimentation, neuroethics, the law of war, the theory of public international law and human rights, and the intellectual history of the Western tradition (focusing on law). He has taught health and human rights, public health law, history of the law of war, and historicist legal theory. He has studied the history and philosophy of medicine (Chinese medicine, homeopathy, and scientific medicine) and science.

Gonzalo Miranda is a professor of the School of Bioethics, Ateneo Pontificio Regina Apostolorum. He serves as board member and treasurer of the International Federation of Centres and Institutes of Bioethics of a Personalist Inspiration (FIBIP). He is the director of the journal *Studia Bioethica*; he is also member of the Board of Directors of the journals *Medicina e Morale* (Rome), *Medicina y Ética* (Mexico), and *Vida y Ética* (Argentina). He is author and editor of and contributed to several books on bioethics, including *The Stem Cell Dilemma: For the Good of All Human*

Beings? (2002), *Bioética e Eutanásia* (2000), *Risposta d'Amore: Manuale di Teologia Morale Fondamentale* (2001), *Le Radici Della Bioetica* (1998), and *Eutanasia: La Antropología Pro-eutanasia y la Antropología Cristiana* (2008).

Dominique J. Monlezun serves as director of global systems research for UNESCO's Chair in Bioethics and Human Rights (Rome, Italy), chief executive officer for global system analytics and structures (Rome, Italy), and director of research and development for the Goldring Center for Culinary Medicine (New Orleans, USA). A close family member's diagnosis of a near fatal disease, worsened by a weak health system, radically redirected his passion for genetic engineering and predictive analytics. He now uses predictive analytics and system strategies to reduce social inequities and empower his collaborators and clients on five continents to optimize their health, business, and nonprofit organizations. His research in biomedical informatics at Harvard Medical School/Massachusetts General Hospital and bioengineering at Brigham and Women's Hospital guided his larger research focus in his first Ph.D. on global health system informatics and his second Ph.D. in global bioethics and international law.

Aasim I. Padela is the director of the Initiative on Islam and Medicine, an associate professor of medicine, and a faculty member of the MacLean Center for Clinical Medical Ethics, all at the University of Chicago. He holds an M.D. from Weill Cornell Medical College, completed residency in emergency medicine at the University of Rochester, and received an M.Sc. in healthcare research from the University of Michigan. His Islamic studies expertise comes via a B.S. in classical Arabic from the University of Rochester, seminary studies during his formative years, and continued tutorials with Islamic authorities. Dr. Padela is a clinician-researcher and bioethicist whose scholarship lies at the intersection of community health and religion. He utilizes diverse methodologies from health services research, religious studies, and comparative ethics to examine the encounter of Islam with contemporary biomedicine through the lives of Muslim patients and clinicians and in the scholarly writings of Islamic authorities. Through systematic research and strategic interventions, he seeks (1) to improve American Muslim health outcomes and healthcare experiences and (2) to construct a multidisciplinary field of Islamic bioethics. As a Robert Wood Johnson Foundation clinical scholar from 2008 to 2011, he developed a community-based research methodology to study and intervene upon American Muslim health disparities. In 2010, as a visiting fellow at the Oxford Centre of Islamic Studies, he studied Islamic moral and theological frameworks, and from 2013 to 2015, as a Templeton Foundation scholar, he led a national survey of Muslim physicians' bioethical attitudes and professional experiences. His current projects span Muslim attitudes and behaviors related to cancer screening and end-of-life care and the intersection of science and Islamic theology and law and are funded by the Templeton Foundation and the American Cancer Society.

Laura Palazzani is professor of philosophy of law at Libera Università degli Studi Maria SS. Assunta (LUMSA University) in Rome, vice-chair of the Italian National Bioethics Committee, and member of the European Group on Ethics in Science and New Technologies (European Commission, Brussels).

David A. Palmer is an associate professor and head of the Department of Sociology at the University of Hong Kong, which he joined in 2008. A native of Toronto, he graduated from McGill University in anthropology and East Asian studies. After completing his Ph.D. in the anthropology of religion at the Ecole Pratique des Hautes Etudes, he was the Eileen Barker fellow in religion and contemporary society at the London School of Economics and Political Science and, from 2004 to 2008, director of the Hong Kong Centre of the French School of Asian Studies (Ecole Française d'Extrême-Orient), located at the Institute for Chinese Studies at the Chinese University of Hong Kong. He is the author of the award-winning *Qigong Fever: Body, Science and Utopia in China* (Columbia University Press, 2007), co-author with Vincent Goossaert of *The Religious Question in Modern China* (University of Chicago Press, 2011; awarded the Levenson Book Prize of the Association for Asian Studies), and co-editor of *Daoism in the Twentieth Century: Between Eternity and Modernity* (University of California Press, 2012). He is currently finishing the book manuscript *Dream Trippers: Global Daoism and the Predicament of Modern Spirituality* (co-authored with Elijah Siegler). He has published several articles, journal issues, and edited volumes on Chinese religion, modern Daoism, the Baha'i Faith, and modern religious movements. His current research projects focus on local ritual traditions, transnational religious movements, and faith-based volunteering and NGOs in the Chinese world and Southeast Asia.

Claudia R. Sotomayor born in Mexico City, holds an M.D. from Universidad Autonoma de Chihuahua in Chihuahua, Mexico. She also graduated with a master's degree in bioethics from Anahuac University with the highest honor. She was the health coordinator for FUNDESPEN A.C., an NGO helping the rural areas of the Mayan Region. She has worked as a professor at Anahuac University, and currently she is working as a research associate and clinical bioethics consultant at different hospitals in Atlanta, GA.

Martha Tarasco received her medical degree from Anahuac University in Mexico and obtained medical specialization in phoniatry in the National Institute of Human Communication of Mexico. She later received training in the UNAM Program for Clinical Medical Resident Researchers and sub-specialization in phoniatry in the University of Salamanca in Spain. Since 1986, she has worked privately in her medical office. She has worked in the Medical School of Anahuac University coordinating the clinical cycles of students. In 1991, she organized a multi-religious symposium on abortion for medical students. During 1992, she was trained in Istituto di Bioetica of Università Cattolica del Sacro Cuore in Rome. In 1993, she opened the first master's degree of bioethics in Mexico. In 2002, she was the first executive director of the newly founded School of Bioethics at Anahuac University, where she now works as a professor and researcher and leads the Institute of Humanism in Health Sciences. In 2005, she obtained her doctoral degree with summa cum laude at the University of Santiago de Compostela, Spain. She has published 8 books, 27 chapters in different books, and 37 articles in different journals.

Henk ten Have studied medicine and philosophy at Leiden University, the Netherlands. He received his medical degree in 1976 from Leiden University and his philosophy degree in 1983. He worked as a researcher in the Pathology Laboratory, University of Leiden (1976–1977); as a practicing physician in the Municipal Health Services, city of Rotterdam (1978–1979); and as a professor of philosophy in the Faculty of Medicine and Faculty of Health Sciences, University of Limburg, Maastricht (1982–1991). From 1991, he was a professor of medical ethics and the director of the Department of Ethics, Philosophy and History of Medicine in the University Medical Centre Nijmegen, the Netherlands. In September 2003, he joined UNESCO as director of the Division of Ethics of Science and Technology. Since July 2010, he is director of the Center for Healthcare Ethics at Duquesne University in Pittsburgh, USA.

Joseph Tham was born in Hong Kong and immigrated to Canada at the age of fifteen. At the University of Toronto, he first majored in mathematical sciences and then graduated from medical school. After several years of work as a family physician, he entered the seminary of the Legionaries of Christ and was ordained a priest in 2004. As a part of this preparation, he has obtained his degrees in philosophy and theology at Rome's Ateneo Pontificio Regina Apostolorum, where he also completed his postgraduate studies in bioethics. He successfully defended his doctoral dissertation with high honors on "The Secularization of Bioethics: A Critical History" under the direction of Dr. Edmund Pellegrino, former chairman of the President's Council on Bioethics. He presently teaches bioethics in Ateneo Pontificio Regina Apostolorum and is the dean of the School of Bioethics. He is the author of *The Missing Cornerstone* (2004, 2009), *The Secularization of Bioethics* (2007), and *Bioetica al Futuro* (2010). He is the editorial coordinator of *Studia Bioethica* and a fellow of the UNESCO Chair in Bioethics and Human Rights.

Hans Ucko studied theology in Lund, Sweden, and is an ordained minister of the Church of Sweden. In his professional career, he has focused on the area of interreligious relations and dialogue and holds a Dr.Th. from the Senate of Serampore College, Kolkata, India. He is the former program executive of the Office on Interreligious Relations and Dialogue of the World Council of Churches, Geneva (1989–2008), with portfolios in Jewish-Christian relations, in multilateral interreligious dialogues, and in the theological assessments of interreligious dialogue. He is the former president of Religions for Peace Europe and served on the Board of Trustees of Hartford Seminary for several years. He is involved in the various programs of Arigatou International, which is headquartered in Tokyo, is the co-chair of the Council for Prayer and Action for Children, and is a board member of Arigatou International New York. He also serves as the president of the Nordic Gülen Institute. Rev. Dr. Ucko is a recipient of the Maja Koene Peace Award for the Promotion of Inter-religious Harmony, Madurai, India, and the Fethullah Gülen International Dialogue Prize, Copenhagen, Denmark. He lives in France and in Sweden.

Alex Yeung was born in Illinois, USA, and ordained a priest in 2003. Previous bachelor's degrees were obtained in the fields of mathematics and music at the University of Waterloo, Canada. His ecclesiastical studies led to a doctorate in philosophy in 2011 with Ateneo Pontificio Regina Apostolorum, Rome, with a thesis entitled "*Imago Dei Creatoris*: Étienne Gilson's 'Essay on the Interior Life' and Its Seminal Influence." He taught courses in philosophy of man, philosophy of culture, and philosophy of religion at the Legion of Christ's Center for Higher Studies in New York for 13 years and at Ateneo Pontificio Regina Apostolorum in Rome for 3 years. He is presently dean of the Faculty of Philosophy at Ateneo Pontificio Regina Apostolorum in Rome.

Ellen Y. Zhang holds a Ph.D. in philosophy of religion from Rice University (Houston, TX). She is now an associate professor in the Department of Religion and Philosophy at Hong Kong Baptist University. She is also a research fellow at the Centre for Applied Ethics at HKBU. Her research projects are related to Chinese philosophy, ethics, and comparative studies. Her publications in ethics include "'Weapons Are Nothing but Ominous Instruments': The *Daodejing*'s View on War and Peace" (2012), "The Ethic of Givenness: An Ethical Dimension of Jean-Luc Marion's Theology of *Gift* and the Buddhist Principle of *Dana*" (2011), "Community, the Common Good, and Public Healthcare: Confucianism and Its Relevance to Contemporary China" (2010), "What Is Personhood? Kant and Huayan Buddhism" (2010), "The Unity of Corporeality and Spirituality: Love in Daoism" (2012), and "The Neo-Confucian Concept of Body and Its Ethical Sensibility" (1999). She is now the editor-in-chief for the *International Journal of Chinese and Comparative Philosophy of Medicine*. She is a member of the APA (American Philosophical Association), the AAR (American Academy of Religion), and the APCA (Association of Chinese Philosophers in America).

Wenqing Zhao is an emerging comparative ethicist. She holds a Ph.D. in public policy and ethics from the City University of Hong Kong. She is now a postdoctoral research fellow at the Center for Comparative Philosophy, Duke University, USA. She is the author of "Is Contemporary Chinese Society Inhumane? What Mencius and Modern Empirical Psychology Have to Say?" (2014) and "A Confucian Worldview and Family-Based Informed Consent: A Case of Concealing Illness from the Patient in China" (2015).

Introduction

Are human rights really universal? Aren't they a product of Western individualistic liberalism? Can they trump local practices and traditions, especially religious ones? These interrogatives will be the subject of this book.

In 2009, the UNESCO Chair in Bioethics and Human Rights (Rome) held the first "Bioethics, Multiculturalism and Religion" workshop in Jerusalem as a forum for representatives of the major religions to discuss a particular bioethical issue from their diverse perspectives. The intention was to hold subsequent workshops on different bioethical issues under the same umbrella of "Bioethics, Multiculturalism and Religion" with the goal of "fostering the art of convergence and cooperation in global ethics." The plan was met with enthusiasm, and workshops have been held in Rome (2011), Hong Kong (2013), and Mexico City (2014). Houston, Texas, will be the site of the 2016 workshop.

After the first workshop, the chair approached Springer with the idea of publishing the proceedings of the workshops as part of the Advancing Global Bioethics series. The Rome papers were published as *Religious Perspectives on Human Vulnerability in Bioethics* (Tham et al. 2014).This book project gathers together the papers prepared for and presented at the Hong Kong workshop.

While the 2011 workshop focused on the principle of vulnerability, the discussions revealed that many conceptual problems remained unresolved with regard to human rights. Many participants found the human rights language too individualistic and somewhat foreign to major religions where the self does not exist in isolation but is normally immersed in a web of relations—family, friends, religious community, and society. Some of these tensions are evident in the aforementioned publication.

We cannot ignore the critique that the concept of human rights is predominantly derived from the Western liberal ideal, in which bioethics is often translated to mean patient autonomy and free choice. This contrasts acutely with Eastern religions which tend to focus more on duties than on rights. Some authors even questioned the existence of universal rights. They are uncertain at what moment universal rights supersede respect for local cultural diversity and customs. For this reason, we thought it opportune to tackle in our next meeting Article 12 of the UNESCO

Declaration on Bioethics and Human Rights (2005) which states: "The importance of cultural diversity and pluralism should be given due regard. However, such considerations are not to be invoked to infringe upon human dignity, human rights and fundamental freedoms, nor upon the principles set out in this Declaration, nor to limit their scope."

The 2013 "Human Rights and Multiculturalism" workshop was held in Hong Kong from December 3 to 5 at Hong Kong Baptist University and was co-organized by that university's Department of Religion and Philosophy and its Centre for Applied Ethics and Centre for Sino-Christian Studies. The workshop theme focused on the relation between human rights and cultural diversity in bioethics. In particular, the participants analyzed this relationship in the life sciences, healthcare, and the appropriate use of technology. The stakeholders involved in these issues are primarily researchers and physicians as well as patients and research subjects. As in previous workshops, participants discussed how these rights conflict with local diversity from the different religious perspectives.

Bioethics scholars from Buddhism, Christianity, Confucianism, Daoism, Hinduism, Islam, and Judaism were commissioned to write either a main paper from their respective traditions or a response. The main paper was to address the following points based on the major tenets of the author's tradition in relation to the UNESCO Declaration on Bioethics and Human Rights: (a) its understanding of human rights and duties, (b) possible conflicts of human rights claims and accepted practices in the tradition, and (c) the possibility human rights could supersede traditional norms with regard to healthcare and life sciences. For each main paper on the seven religious traditions, there were two expert responses, one from the same tradition and one from a different one. The main papers were received about 2 months before the actual workshop and the responses about a month before.

The authors were from 12 countries. However, the reality is much more diversified due to our globalized world. If one were to take into account the cultural backgrounds of the presenters and participants, the following countries were represented: Canada, the Caribbean, China, France, Germany, Greece, Holland, Hong Kong, India, Iran, Israel, Italy, Korea, Mexico, Morocco, Pakistan, Singapore, Spain, Switzerland, Thailand, and the USA. In fact, there are also diversities within the different religious traditions themselves: Catholics, Protestants, and Orthodox Christians, Secular and Orthodox Jews, and Sunni and Shiite Muslims conversed in this setting.

Participants were encouraged to read all the other papers before attending the workshop. Each workshop session focuses on one tradition and lasts about 3 h. Authors of the main paper are allowed some time to summarize their papers followed by two short commentaries from the respondents. This is followed by an ample period of discussion, clarification, and questions from all the participants of the event. These lively discussions and debates seek to clarify the different religious or tradition views on human rights. As many of the speakers and participants were present in previous meetings, there was an atmosphere of respect and friendship that allowed for frank exchanges. Such intellectually stimulating dialogue and encounters allow a rare glimpse of how people of good faith can work together and foster dialogue. After the meeting, the authors were asked to modify their papers based on the feedbacks and peer reviews. These final drafts are collected here.

In one main narrative, the use of human rights in international relations and law dates to the end of WW2. The international community was horrified by "the scourge of war" and, in another attempt to outlaw war, formed the United Nations (UN) in June 1945, just months after the end of the war. Earlier attempts to end war altogether were made after WW1, but neither the League of Nations nor the Kellogg-Briand Pact was successful. Discussions about a UN-type arrangement started relatively early during the war and involved a discussion about what came to be known as human rights. Once the UN was formed, it took another 3 years before the General Assembly could agree on a positive expression of what human rights could be. This was published in 1948 as the Universal Declaration of Human Rights (UDHR). The UDHR was not intended to be a legal document; rather it was understood to be a framework for a subsequent treaty or law on human rights.

The effort to make positive human rights law from the UDHR took 28 years. It was only in 1966 that the International Covenant on Civil and Political Rights (ICCPR) and the International Covenant on Economic, Social and Cultural Rights (ICESCR) would be put out for signature, and they did not enter into force until 1976. Apart from difficulties in the drafting and inclusion of specific norms, the drafters had to grapple with conflicts in the values from which the norms were to be derived. The drafters of both the UN Charter and the UDHR had tried to avoid grounding the ethical imperatives of human rights norms in any philosophical, theological, or cultural system by focusing attention on the word and concept of *dignity*. Human dignity was the textual source of human rights, the source of the attempts through international law to end "the scourge of war."

While *dignity* would remain the textual source of rights, the drafters began their task just as the Cold War was beginning to dominate post-WW2 international relations. Since the drafters were from both liberal and socialist member states, the creation of the new positive international normative system was hampered by the differences in values. How were the drafters to create a hierarchy of politico-legal norms when the norms conflicted? On the one hand was the liberal West, to whom human rights in large part were associated with democracy (suffrage, individualism, due process) and a kind of American model of rights. On the other hand was the socialist East, to whom the community was more important than the individual and the state was to own and provide the necessities of life. The main objection liberal countries had toward the socialist vision was that the implementation of, say, a right to health would force the state to spend money to alleviate poverty and deliver health services. While the state might desire to do that, it might not have the money. And many states were poor. In poor states, the West then argued, the solution was to give the citizens the right to vote and democratically control the state and then let the popular sovereign sort out the problems of resource allocation. Although this simplifies 18 years of complex negotiation, the covenants reflect this argument. The ICCPR embodies civil and political rights that envision a democratic or republican state, and that do not require much of the state other than recognition of the rights. The ICESCR prescribes rights (e.g., the right to health, the right to work) that require the states to take positive civil action. In recognition of the fact that many states do not have the resources to provide those rights, the ICESCR demands only that its rights be "progressively realized" by the state.

In retrospect, we see that although human rights were conceived as a possible political and legal instrument to prevent future atrocities, such as those perpetrated by the Nazi regime against the Jews and other minorities, by the Japanese against the Chinese, and by other powers (including the USA), the way the drafters managed the source values left a legacy of inconsistency in international ethical/legal order. While they pointed to dignity in all of the texts as the unitary source of human rights norms, they in fact produced two covenants that are philosophically at odds with each other. Moreover, they did not give any guidance as how to resolve conflicts between norms, even conflicts *within* each covenant.

The failure to identify a unitary source for human rights, an extremely complex philosophical/political problem for which the drafters are not to be criticized, has certain negative effects. Human rights have proliferated, including greater ambits in subsequent generations of rights. Because of its power to bind nations and win arguments, human rights may fall victim to ideological manipulations and political maneuvers. Religionists and secularists, jurists and politicians, and lobbyists and activists all want a piece of moral high ground under the banner of human rights to further their claims. When that is multiplied by the 193 members of the United Nations, the diversity of voices and opinions can create a sense of cacophony.

Certainly, the tension between universalism and particularism in ethics is an old one, but it has become more urgent in today's global context touching a multitude of bioethical issues. Does the claim of global ethics' or rights' universality necessarily stifle the right to local particularism and thus suppress cultural and religious patrimonies? Does the reality of cultural diversity necessarily infer the inevitability of moral pluralism? The answers are not readily available.

The philosopher and ethicist Alasdair MacIntyre has offered one solution that allows for the expression of cultural diversity and yet eschews moral pluralism. Accordingly, different moral traditions can confront each another on equal footing. In this engagement of culture and traditions, it is possible to enter the conversation with intellectual honesty and "maximal vulnerability" without hiding one's own defects. In this painstaking, slow, and difficult process of soul searching, exchanges and comparisons would allow the rival traditions to see their weaknesses and strengths and rationally recognize their own incoherence and the superiority of their rival, with the possibility of abandonment of their own tradition (MacIntyre 1989). Like our previous publication, this book provides a rare opportunity to compare religious views on human rights from major world religions.

The Chapters

The first part of the book consists in several articles discussing the principle in general and especially the tension between universal human rights and local particular customs that can come into conflict with this, with examples taken from bioethics.

The following chapters provide thought-provoking insights on the relationship between universal human rights and local cultural and religious diversity. In the discussions on the basis of human rights and its universality, it became apparent that there are two visions or approaches. The "thick" or substantive approach wishes to base human rights on natural reason found in our common nature. This vision claims that while the origin of human rights discourse could take its origin from the West, its validity is nonetheless universal in scope and not limited to geography. It recognizes the fact that human rights discourse is an unfinished product and is undergoing evolution and further elucidation. Some traditions find it compatible with a religious base such as being created in the image of God or the metaphysical conception of a common human nature.

On the other hand, the "thin" approach would see human rights as a practical or pragmatic solution that was conceived in the first place to lessen the occurrence of abuses against humanity, as evidenced in recent history. Hence, it willingly accepts the lack of a common basis for human rights and may even find the diversity of cultures precluding such a possibility. In this thin version, there is awareness that the human rights discourse can be manipulated or hijacked by different ideologies when it is not based on a thicker basis. It is this approach that generates the positive legal norms that give human rights their bite in the real world, removing them from the world of abstract right.

These articles set the background to the debate on human rights and cultural diversity according to different cultures and religious traditions. The way different traditions approach this debate depends on how they envision the interplay between faith and reason. On the one hand, universalism is prominent in the secular and liberal post-Enlightenment approach that exalts rationality as the common basis of humanity that allows for dialogue and agreement on shared beliefs in human rights. This common rationality is traced especially to the Judeo-Christian conception of humans being creatures and not the Creator, thus all being equal in the eyes of God. On the other hand, we find particularism in some religious traditions that stress revealed truths to the exclusion of human rationality and that sees this diversity as an important value. However, this "fundamentalist" and voluntarist vision can be troubling as it can lead to violence against those who are different. However, in between these two positions is a middle approach that embraces both faith and reason, either in the natural law tradition or in an appeal to human dignity based on imago Dei, on the recognition of the "Other" as a person, or on the recognition of compassion as the central defining characteristic and mother of all virtues.

When examining the different papers from the seven religio-cultural groups, differences of ethical sensitivities are found not only among the different groups but also within each group. What makes this discussion interesting is that religious traditions are not static but are constantly evolving in their engagement with other religions, philosophies, cultural variances, and challenges from science, technology, and modernity in a globalized reality.

These considerations lead to further examination of a complex web of different issues—culture, religion, politics, philosophy, law, theology, and ethics—that intersect, interact, and cross-pollinate. The debate of the "thick" vs. "thin" approach to ethics and human rights in fact overlaps with the discussions on duties vs. rights, religious vs. secular, faith vs. science, individual vs. societal, nature vs. nurture, and the perennial metaphysical tension of the one vs. many.

Scholars and students interested in religious ethics, human rights, bioethics, cultural diversity, and multiculturalism will find this collection of original articles an important contribution in these cultural debates of our time.

Joseph Tham

Bibliography

MacIntyre, A. 1989. *Whose justice? Which rationality?* 1st ed. Notre Dame: University of Notre Dame Press.

Tham, J., A. Garcia, and G. Miranda (eds.). 2014. *Religious perspectives on human vulnerability in bioethics,* 2014 ed. New York: Springer.

Part I
Theoretical Discussions

Chapter 1
Respect for Cultural Diversity and Pluralism

Henk ten Have

1.1 Introduction

In October 2005, the Universal Declaration on Bioethics and Human Rights was unanimously adopted by the 191 Member States of UNESCO in Paris. The Declaration formulates 15 general principles to guide decisions and practices in bioethics. Article 12 presents the principle of respect for cultural diversity and pluralism: "The importance of cultural diversity and pluralism should be given due regard. However, such considerations are not to be invoked to infringe upon human dignity, human rights, and fundamental freedoms, nor upon the principles set out in this Declaration, not to limit their scope" (UNESCO 2005, Art 12). The aim of this contribution is to clarify the background as well as the significance and limitations of this principle. To better understand why this principle is included in the Declaration as one of the fundamental principles of today's bioethics, it is necessary to explain the specific context in which it has emerged. This context is determined on the one hand by the mission and perspective of UNESCO, as the only United Nations organization concerned with culture, education and science, on the other hand by the development of bioethics as a global endeavor that is no longer only a concern of more developed and resource-rich countries.

1.2 The Context of UNESCO

Since its founding in November 1945, just after the Second World War, UNESCO is committed to the intellectual and moral solidarity of humankind. Its major concern was: how can future wars, violence and atrocities been prevented? Promoting a

H. ten Have (✉)
Center for Healthcare Ethics, Duquesne University, Pittsburgh, PA, USA
e-mail: tenhaveh@duq.edu

J. Tham et al. (eds.), *Religious Perspectives on Bioethics and Human Rights*,
Advancing Global Bioethics 6, DOI 10.1007/978-3-319-58431-7_1

culture of peace requires a focus on international cooperation and shared values. The Constitution of UNESCO states that "since wars begin in the minds of men, it is in the minds of men that the defences of peace must be constructed" (UNESCO 1945). The founding members of the organization also have assured that the advances of science and technology will take place within the framework of universal respect for justice, for the rule of law and for human rights.

1.2.1 Huxley, Teilhard de Chardin, and Potter

Philosopher and biologist Julian Huxley, its first Director-General, had a clear vision for the Organization. If scientific progress wants to contribute to peace, security and human flourishing, it is not only necessary to collaborate, but also to know each other's cultures and traditions. It is furthermore imperative to relate science to values that are promoting the benefit of humanity. Huxley was the promoter of *evolutionary humanism*, the idea that human progress is primarily driven by cultural evolution. Human beings are special since they are not determined by biological processes, not subjected to mechanisms of natural selection. They are able to determine their own destiny, and to direct the development of the world and human existence. They should use their rationality, guided by ethical principles, to improve the human condition. Progress can be made through convergence of cultures. Education is of primary importance since it means learning from each other; science is equally important since knowledge helps to better daily life for everybody. Recognizing differences is crucial but at the same time it should lead to identifying what is fundamental for every human being. UNESCO, working in the areas of education, science and culture, can therefore pre-eminently contribute to mutual understanding among human beings, as a mechanism of cultural evolution. It can counter the forces of divisiveness and conflict through exchange and collaboration, and help to create a world community. In this stage of evolution, progress is primarily focused on values: intellectual, esthetic, emotional, and moral values. The main task of UNESCO, in the words of Huxley, is to "help the emergence of a single world culture with its own philosophy and background of ideas and with its own broad purpose" (Huxley 1946). The dialectics of cultural evolution will overcome the political and cultural antithesis between East and West, individualism and collectivism, capitalism and communism within an encompassing synthesis.

Huxley's views were influenced by the ideas of the French philosopher, geologist, palaeontologist and Jesuit Pierre Teilhard de Chardin. His message was that humanity will develop into a global community. Due to the processes of *planetary compression* (intensified communication, travel, exchanges through economic networks) and *psychic interpenetration* (increased interconnectedness and a growing sense of universal solidarity) humankind will be involved in an irresistible process of unification, according to Teilhard de Chardin (1975, 2004). The emergence of a global community is not happening, in the terminology of Teilhard, because human beings will accept one single truth or will desire one single thing but because they recognize a single being-as-human. They are becoming increasingly aware of their interdependency and their common destiny. Shortly after the Second World War, Teilhard wrote that even incidental recurrences of racism and nationalism do not have importance in the overall process of cultural and social evolution of the planet; they are disastrous for individuals but compel us sooner or later to come together on the basis of human solidarity. This is what he has called the "planetization of Mankind" (Teilhard de Chardin 2004, p. 108). The driving force is evolution. This notion is no longer only relevant for biology but it can clarify all dimensions of the human condition: matter, life and mind. The process of evolution furthermore is ongoing. It progresses through humankind, not in the sense that there will be a new biological species of super-humans but that it creates more complexity and consciousness among human beings, an 'ultra-human' phase. In Teilhard's view, humanity is becoming more unified, more interdependent, and increasingly cooperative. In humankind, evolution has become converging instead of diverging. Humankind would evolve into a coherent whole, a cosmopolitan community. Nowadays, human beings have significant means at their disposal to facilitate communication, distances can be easily overcome, borders between nations are becoming futile; they have many more ways to get to know other people. Growing unification within complex diversities and an increasing feeling of solidarity between human beings are stages in the process of evolution that will lead to a moral community of citizens of the world. The world population is growing while the surface of the earth remains the same; therefore, people are obliged to cooperate even more intensely: "We can progress only by uniting" (Teilhard de Chardin 2004, p. 66).

In 1988, Van Rensselaer Potter argued that we need a global bioethics to broaden the scope of bioethics into real concerns about the environment and the future of humankind (Potter 1988). An important intellectual source of inspiration for Potter, especially in his early publications, was the work of Teilhard de Chardin. Potter made a reference to this work in the Preface of his 1971 book, explaining that he started to study it in 1964 (Potter 1971). He also mentioned some of Teilhard's books at the end of his 1970 article (Potter 1970). In 1968 Potter published an article on Teilhard, later included as Chap. 2 in his 1971 book (Potter 1968). He recognized that Teilhard like him was interested in the problem of human progress. They shared the view that human progress is the goal of the universe, that we should try to bring about the best possible future and that the best way to do this is to combine the science of biology with human values (Ten Have 2012). Potter took it for granted therefore that he could regard the work of Teilhard as a corroboration of some of his basic ideas. In fact, the image of a global ethical community connects the views of Potter, Teilhard de Chardin and Huxley.

1.2.2 The Bioethics Program

Since its foundation, UNESCO has been concerned with moral issues in relation to science. From the 1970s onwards, the emergence of the life sciences, in particular, has led to international examination of bioethical questions. This global focus on bioethics was institutionalized in 1993 with the establishment of the International Bioethics Committee (IBC) together with a work program and budget for international activities. The program was expanded in 1998 with the foundation of the World Commission on the Ethics of Scientific Knowledge and Technology (COMEST), which is addressing other areas of applied ethics such as environmental ethics, science ethics and technology ethics, following the successful example of the IBC in bioethics. Since 2002, UNESCO has also been coordinating the activities of international bodies in the area of bioethics through the Inter-Agency Committee on Bioethics of the United Nations (with, among others, FAO, OECD and WHO). In the same year, the 191 Member States decided that ethics should be one of the five priorities of the Organization.

1.2.3 The Notion of Common Heritage

The idea of a global community is closely connected to the notion of "common heritage of humankind" that plays a significant role in the activities of UNESCO. This notion was introduced in international law in the late 1960s to regulate common resources such as the ocean bed and outer space (Herber 1991; Strati 1991; Holmila 2005). A milestone has been the speech of Maltese ambassador Arvid Pardo to the General Assembly of the United Nations in November 1967 in which he argued that the sea-bed and the ocean floor are a common heritage of mankind and therefore should be used and exploited for peaceful purposes and to the benefit of humankind as a whole (United Nations 1967). Seventy percent of the surface of the earth consists of ocean. The sea-bed harbors significant amounts of minerals while immense supplies of oil and gas are under the ocean floor. New technologies are rapidly developing to explore the oceans, but they are owned by richer countries that will profit from them. Technological progress will therefore mean that developed countries will increasingly exploit the oceans and consider the ocean floor as their territory. Countries that are landlocked and countries without the necessary technology will be excluded from the benefits of ocean exploration and exploitation. At the same time, oceans play a growing military role with fleets of nuclear submarines and the possibility of military installations on the ocean floor. Another threat is increasing pollution of oceans, particularly through dumping of radioactive waste and contamination with oil and heavy metals. A few months before Pardo's speech the tanker Torrey Canyon shipwrecked on the British coast causing an environmental disaster in England and France. Pardo argues that these threats are no longer potential but real. We have a choice to continue to leave the management of oceans to separate nations with their individual interests, or to allocate it to international supervision for the benefit of humanity as a whole. He proposes to regard the oceans as common heritage. It is obvious that Pardo's proposal was initially rejected by developed countries but much welcomed by developing countries. For the latter group of countries, this notion was a useful instrument to effectuate a more equal distribution of natural resources in the world. Pardo's efforts eventually led to the UN Convention on the Law of the Sea (adopted in 1982) that recognized the deep sea bed and ocean floor and its resources as the common heritage of humankind.

The new concept in fact went back to the older tradition of Roman law that distinguished the separate category of *res extra commercium,* for example common property and public property (such as rivers). This category defines objects of law that cannot be economically exchanged, thus not sold or owned by anybody. The distinction between private and common property was famously used in 1609 by Hugo Grotius in his book *Mare Liberum* where he argued that the sea is *res omnium communes* like the air and the sun: these are things that are used and enjoyed by everyone but they cannot be owned by anyone (Joyner 1986; Bovenberg 2006).

The notion of common heritage initially is used for areas with material resources that are outside the borders of nation states, "common space areas" such as ocean floor but also the moon, outer space and Antarctica. But the use of the notion gradually expanded to vital resources within the territory of individual nations, such as tropical rainforest. Individual countries manage these resources (often spread over several countries) but by considering them as common heritage a shared interest is constructed. They need to be preserved in such a way that it benefits humanity rather than merely the citizens of one or more countries; its significance for future generations should be recognized. Resources labeled as common heritage are vital for the survival of humankind; proper management and stewardship therefore transcends any national interests.

In the 1970s, the concept came to be used to include culture and cultural heritage. The member states of UNESCO adopted in 1972 the World Heritage Convention. It determines that cultural accomplishments can be regarded as common heritage when they have outstanding universal value (exemplary, unique, and irreplaceable) and when they are exceptionally important for the sustainability and quality of life on earth. It is true of course that these cultural accomplishment are owned by a particular state or a people but they nonetheless have special juridical status and therefore require protection since they have at the same time universal value. Declaring that certain cultural accomplishments are common heritage of humankind therefore implies a symbolic expropriation. It also introduces a tension between universality and particularity. All cultural heritage is produced within a specific context, history and tradition; that makes it unique. At the same time, it is the expression of the creativity of humankind, and this gives it universal value. Cultural heritage is no longer only representative of a particular culture but of human culture in general.

Widening the use of the concept of common heritage has led to the construction of a new global geography of symbols indicating that humanity itself can be regarded as a community. At the initiative of UNESCO, the temples in Abu Simbel in Egypt were entirely relocated in 1968 to avoid their destruction after the building of the

Aswan Dam in the Nile River. This relocation showed that the international community regarded the temples not merely as a product of the Egyptian civilization from the thirteenth century B.C. Although built by Pharaoh Ramses, they were the common property of humankind and needed to be preserved. Labeling some cultural products as a world heritage produces therefore a global grammar in which diverse and local phenomena receive a universal significance and require global management. These cultural treasures are expressions of human identity at a global level; they are part of the quest of citizens of the world; they become indicators of world culture. Regarding and categorizing cultural property as world heritage implies a global civilization project that seeks to create a new planetary community representing humanity as a whole, enable the identification of world citizens, and evoke a sense of global solidarity and responsibility. On the one hand, it places high regard on cultural diversity but demonstrates on the other hand that it can only be preserved within a global perspective underlining its importance for all human beings.

1.2.4 Cultural Diversity

One of the missions of UNESCO, as defined in its Constitution, is protection of cultural heritage ("the world's inheritance of books, works of art and monuments of history and science"). The Convention adopted in 1972 resulted in the creation of the World Heritage List that now includes 759 cultural properties (plus 193 natural and 29 mixed properties) in 160 countries. The Convention covers tangible heritage, i.e. material manifestations such as monuments and objects. But culture is also expressed in living or intangible heritage that manifest the identity and continuity of traditions that groups and communities have inherited from ancestors and transmit to future generations. In order to protect this kind of heritage (such as oral traditions, rituals, artistic practices, and festive events) the Convention for the Safeguarding of the Intangible Cultural Heritage was adopted in 2003.

The underlying idea of both Conventions is a universal vision on culture and a shared heritage (Musitelli 2002). The concept of culture is taken very broadly. In the Universal Declaration on Cultural Diversity (adopted in 2001) culture is regarded as "the set of distinctive spiritual, material, intellectual and emotional features of society or a social group, and … it encompasses, in addition to art and literature, lifestyles, ways of living together, value systems, traditions and beliefs" (UNESCO 2001, Preamble). Though it does not articulate the common distinction between nature and culture, it assumes that culture is produced by human beings, so that it reflects patterns of human activity as well as symbolic structures and systems. Culture therefore is a defining feature of human beings. But at the same time, culture is always specific; it is produced within a particular context and tradition, and therefore reflects diverging characteristics of human beings. The tension between universality and particularity in culture is recognized in the 2001 Convention in the first article: "Culture takes diverse forms across time and space. This diversity is embodied in the uniqueness and plurality of the identities of the groups and societies making up humankind. As a source of exchange, innovation and creativity, cultural diversity is as necessary for humankind as biodiversity is for nature. In this sense, it is the common heritage of humanity and should be recognized and affirmed for the benefit of present and future generations" (UNESCO 2001, Art 1). The paradoxical strategy therefore is that cultural diversity is recognized as the common heritage of humanity. This notion is used to bridge universal and particular dimensions. Cultural heritage is not a "common area" such as the ocean or outer space but it is located within a national territory (or several territories). This means that it requires respect for national sovereignty but at the same time it is under international supervision. Cultural heritage is also the expression of a particular identity but at the same time it expresses a value for humanity. A cultural object will only be recognized as world heritage if its particularity can be universalized so that it will fit into a universal framework. But it must also combine universal value with uniqueness; it can only be regarded as world heritage if it is strongly different from other cultural heritage. The universalization of the particular must therefore be joined with the particularization of the universal. If the notion of common heritage succeeds in bridging these dimensions it will have significant normative implications. First, it should be safeguarded for the benefit of present and future generations. Second, it is a positive asset of humanity; it is a source of exchange, innovation and creativity, and as necessary for the future of humankind as biodiversity for nature. Third, it is more than an economic resource; it widens the range of options for everyone; policies for the inclusion and participation of all cultural groups and citizens are guarantees of vitality, social cohesion and peace.

Explaining cultural diversity in terms of common heritage of humanity productively unites the local and global levels. Cultural heritage is essential for generating social order and identity. At local levels, it is the expression of the specific identity of a nation or people, in continuity with tradition and history. It is heritage precisely because it is essential for community-building. When the same idea of cultural heritage is applied at global level, and considered as heritage of humanity, it creates a global geography of universal symbols. By identifying tangible and intangible heritage that has value for all people in the world, the idea of heritage not only suggests a world as one single space for human activity and creativity; but it also constructs humankind as an imagined moral community, it provides a general structure for organizing and expressing differences, a global grammar for local contexts. The notion of common heritage is thus an instrument of a cosmopolitan project employed to create a political community that does not yet exist, and premised upon a shared symbolic universe, common interests and global solidarity.

1.3 The Context of Global Bioethics

The second context to understand the emergence of the principle of respect for cultural diversity is the rise of global bioethics. The global perspective of bioethics today is not a matter of geographical expansion, but rather it refers to phenomena that have a global dimension—i.e., they are no longer dependent on the specifics of a particular culture or society. This is not the same as arguing that global bioethics is a unified field of inquiry in which bioethicists behave in similar ways everywhere in the world or that there is international agreement on fundamental values. That there are similar bioethical problems in different countries does not imply that the same ethical approach exists everywhere. The global dimension, however, invites us to rethink our usual approaches and ethical frameworks. It makes us aware of the "locality" of our own moral views while, at the same time, encouraging us to search for moral views that are shared globally. In this challenge, bioethics is increasingly connected with international law, particularly human rights law, which has a similar global vision (Veatch 2012; Ten Have and Gordijn 2013).

1.3.1 Moral Diversity at Global Level

The growing importance of global bioethics has reactivated the significance of the notion of moral diversity. The development of global bioethics demands a broader framework of normative interpretation and assessment. Is it justified to apply the principle of informed consent in Nigeria where there is a significantly different culture? Should we respect the Chinese practice of harvesting organs from executed persons? In a global perspective, the ethical systems of different cultures need to be examined and moral values analyzed and applied in specific contexts. This is generally recognized as necessary. It has opened up new and fascinating fields of research. But the next step brings us into the old controversy of universal values and local values. Is there a universal framework of principles and values or are principles and values different, depending on the local, cultural and religious normative systems?

For some, global bioethics as such is an attempt to universalize a specific set of bioethical principles and to export or impose them in the rest of the world. They claim that the four principles formulated by Beauchamp and Childress (2013) are typically North-American principles that are not valid in other parts of the world. Others maintain that global bioethics necessarily reaches beyond the Western individualist perspective of traditional bioethics (Kelly et al. 2013). It is true that these principles have been formulated in Western countries but that does not imply that they have no validity outside of these countries. We should make a distinction between origin and validity. The fact that our numerical notation originated from the Arab culture (while they inherited it from the Hindu culture), does not mean that Arab colleagues can still claim it as theirs or that we can blame them for having their figures imposed on us. The same is true for ethical principles. Whether or not global bioethics is considered to be *ethical imperialism*, it has increased sensitivity regarding the application of basic concepts such as individual autonomy and informed consent across the globe. In many non-Western cultures, the autonomy of individuals is not privileged over communities. Global bioethics, therefore, should recognize that in these countries responsibilities towards family, community, and society can have more significance than individual rights, but that does not mean that individual rights are insignificant. This was a major issue in the development of the UNESCO *Universal Declaration on Bioethics and Human Rights* (Ten Have and Jean 2009).

The search for global ethical principles focuses on the values that we share as human beings. For some bioethicists this will be a futile endeavor since different and contradictory ethics systems exist. If there is no basis for rational verification of ethical judgments, then all efforts to formulate ethical principles as universal means in practice that the dominating system attempts to impose its principles as the universal ones. But this is a mistaken view. It is demonstrated in the activities of the Parliament of the World's Religions. In 1993 approximately 200 leaders from more than 40 religious and spiritual traditions signed the 'Declaration Toward a Global Ethic' (Parliament of the World's Religions 1993). This statement, drafted by German theologian Hans Küng, declared that all traditions share common values such as respect for life, solidarity, tolerance, and equal rights (Küng 1997). The document emphasizes that it is important to show what world religions have in common rather than how they differ. A similar spirit is reflected in the UNESCO Bioethics Declaration but motivated by the notion of common heritage.

1.3.2 Global Bioethics and Common Heritage

If the challenge for global bioethics is to recognize moral diversity and at the same time emphasize globally shared values and principles it has to assume a global community as a moral community. Global bioethics then refers not merely to extent (a worldwide scope involving "citizens of the world" who are increasingly connected and related due to processes of globalization) but also to content (the identification of global values and responsibilities as well as the establishment of global traditions and institutions). The concept of common heritage of humankind is an appropriate intellectual and practical tool to construct the idea of a global community as the real focus of global bioethics. It was applied first in the late 1990s in the field of genetics, followed in the 2000s by the adoption of a global framework of bioethical principles.

The HUGO Ethics Committee was the first to apply the notion of common heritage on the human genome. The HUGO Statement on the Principled Conduct of Genetics Research in 1996 declares that the human genome is part of the common heritage of humanity (HUGO 1996; Knoppers and Joly 2007). The Universal Declaration on the Human Genome and Human Rights, adopted by UNESCO in 1997 already in Article 1 states; "In a symbolic sense, it [the human genome] is the heritage of humanity" (UNESCO 1997) This point of view is reiterated by the Council of Europe in 2001 in Recommendation 1512 (Council of Europe 2001).

Applying the notion in the field of bioethics expands its scope significantly. While initially used for "common areas" that were nobody's property, applying the notion on cultural heritage already accepted that it can be located within a specific territory but nonetheless it requires management for the benefit of humankind. Applying the concept on the human genome locates heritage within an individual body, making it at the same time private and common property. However, using the notion in these different areas is accompanied with the same normative implications: free and open access, peaceful use, benefit sharing, and protection of future generations (Byk 1998; Bovenberg 2006).

The next step is even more interesting. Although the notion itself is not mentioned it can be argued that the Bioethics Declaration is developed within the mindset of common heritage. It identifies ethical principles that must be considered as heritage of humanity. These principles are located within individual minds but part of everybody's world of ideas. The principles are universal but always applied within the context of particularity and diversity. They exemplify the adage that is often used in discourse of globalization: think globally, act locally.

With such a universal framework, global bioethics can now claim to represent a global geography of moral values that enables humanity itself to be regarded as a moral community (George 1996). It implies that citizens of high-income countries can no longer be indifferent to clinical research practices or organ trade in low-income countries since the same moral values and standards apply within the global community, although the application is always modified according to local circumstances and local communities. Membership in the global community furthermore draws on a growing number of global institutions and movements (e.g., Doctors without Borders, Bioethics Beyond Borders, Oxfam, fair trade, UNESCO). In other words, there is no longer a necessary conflict between universal and particular approaches. There is a global community of shared values. These values are the product of intensive and continuous negotiation, deliberation, and dialogue. They are reflected in a universal framework that overrides the diversity of principles and values in different parts of the world and in various religions and cultural traditions. But this framework proceeds without the articulation of absolute principles and values since there is not one supreme principle that trumps the others. Bioethics will continue to proceed with rational deliberation through interpreting, weighing and applying multiple ethical principles at the same time. The existence of a global framework of ethical principles will not eliminate ethical disagreements.

1.3.3 Continuous Negotiation and Consultation

Immediately after the adoption of the *Universal Declaration on Bioethics and Human Rights* a vigorous debate emerged, especially in regard to the conception of universality underlying the document. Some questioned the possibility of a trans-cultural moral approach and universal principles. Others repeated the old argument that so-called universal principles are merely the reiteration of specific, i.e. Western, principles and their imposition to the rest of the world. Interestingly, non-Western scholars exposed different views. Jing-Bao (2005) argued that it is necessary to explore non-Western cultures to discover that they advocate universal principles. It is a mistake to assume that such principles (e.g. human dignity) are alien to and incompatible with these cultures. It is an example of *moral protectionism* to assume that ethical principles, even after having emerged and being formulated in Western culture, continue to remain the property of such specific cultures, and therefore not universal but only valid within this specific context. This is exactly the experience within UNESCO. It was explicitly at the request of developing countries that the Organization undertook the drafting of the Universal Declaration since these countries wanted to have a framework of universal principles, in order to put limitations to the tendency of introducing double standards with a reference to cultural diversity. Cultures differ but this does not imply that common standards and universal principles do not exist.

1.3.4 The Interstitial Space of Bioethical Discourse

In response to these criticisms it is pointed out that global bioethics, in the spirit of the notion of common heritage, is not simply advocating universal values or acknowledging moral diversity. It is a dialectical effort to bridge universalism and particularism. Global bioethics is not a finished product but a project that has not yet resulted in a clear normative approach, comparable to principlism in first generation bioethics. The main challenge is to combine convergence and divergence. How can recognition of differences in moral views and approaches be reconciled with the convergence towards commonly shared values? Criticisms of global bioethics often presuppose simplistic views of globalization. While worldwide interconnectedness bridges the gap between distance and proximity, some scholars assume a radical contrast between moral strangers and friends, while others fear the growth of a bioethical monoculture. But it is not correct that globalization produces either uniformity or multiplicity; it does both. People nowadays are part of multiple cultures. It is not clear where their roots exactly are. They consider themselves at the same time Dutch, European, and citizen of the world. The same is true for the notion of culture itself. No culture today is monolithic and pure. All cultural traditions are dynamic; they have changed and are changeable; they are necessarily a mélange of different components. Differences do not exclude that there is a common core. The term *interculturalism* is therefore more appropriate than multiculturalism since it acknowledges diversity while at the same time insisting on universal values. The term 'interculturality' emphasizes interaction. 'Inter' refers to separation but also linkage and communication. The supposition is that we can position ourselves between two cultures; we can occupy a place between the universal and the particular. It means that we recognise similarities between self and other that can be the basis for dialogues between cultures, and at the same time that we can maintain difference and sustain boundaries between self and other. In other words, conceptually and practically, we are "in-between," moving beyond dualistic, binary thinking, adopting universalising as well particularizing practices simultaneously (Lobo et al. 2011).

While multiculturalism emphasizes respect for diversity, individual freedom, justice and equal treatment, interculturalism introduces a moral vocabulary of interaction, dialogue, participation, trust, cooperation and solidarity. It is not sufficient to have multiple co-existent value systems and respect them; rather, the challenge is to produce and cultivate practices that can create community. If there is common ground it needs to be cultivated through interaction and communication. Convergence is not given but the result of an ongoing activity of deliberation, consultation and negotiation. It is exactly this "interstitial perspective" that motivates the development of global bioethics.

Wallace (2009) has suggested that there is an association between the possibility of moral reform, moral progress and human fallibility. Global bioethics can be improved because as human beings we can never be sure about our moral beliefs. Charles Sanders Peirce' notion of fallibilism implies that none of our moral judgments are absolutely certain; there is always a chance that we might be mistaken. Fallibilism does not exclude universality. As long as universal principles have not turned out to be wrong we continue to work with them as action-guides. This is also the reason why we continuously have to evaluate and possibly revise our moral beliefs. For morality, the famous analogy of Otto Neurath applies: knowledge is like a vessel on the open sea; we cannot bring it ashore in order to caulk and reconstruct it afresh from the bottom; we must repair the ship while sailing and moving on our way. The normative enterprise therefore requires dialectic evolution in order to approach but never to reach an ideal limit. This fallibilistic perspective with the implied need for continuous testing and assessing is close to the initial ideas of Van Rensselaer Potter when he defined bioethics as "a new discipline that combines biological knowledge with a knowledge of human value systems in an open-ended biocybernetic system of self-assessment…" (Potter 1975, p. 2299).

1.4 Development of the Declaration

In the past, UNESCO has adopted two declarations in the field of bioethics: the *Universal Declaration on the Human Genome and Human Rights* (1997) and the *International Declaration on Human Genetic Data* (2003). The scope of standard-setting was expanded significantly with the mandate given by the Member States to develop a universal declaration on bioethics. The previous declarations had focused on the specialized area of genetics and genomics. When the new mandate was given, all topics relevant to bioethics were placed on the table for negotiation.

1.4.1 Building Consensus on International Bioethics

In October 2001, the General Conference, supported by the Round Table of Ministers of Science, invited the Director-General of UNESCO to examine the possibility of developing a universal instrument on bioethics. The feasibility study drafted by the International Bioethics Committee (IBC) concluded that it was possible to find common ground in divergent bioethical positions by focusing on basic principles (IBC 2003). Some of these principles had already been identified in previous declarations. The study also stressed the necessity to develop a universal instrument because scientific practices are now developing rapidly and extending beyond national borders. Developed and developing countries should therefore achieve broad consistency in regulations and policies. In October 2003, the General Conference provided a mandate to submit a draft declaration in 2 years. In the meeting, the French President (Jacques Chirac) made a vigorous plea for a universal normative framework, preferably a Convention, to guide the progress of the life sciences and to protect the integrity and dignity of human beings.

The subsequent process of drafting, entrusted to the IBC, taking into account the short time frame, the variety of ethical cultures and traditions, and the controversial nature of many bioethical issues, had four characteristics.

1.4.1.1 Gradual Elaboration

To explore ideas about the scope and the structure of a possible declaration, all Member States were consulted in writing between January and March 2004. The IBC organized a meeting in April 2004, inviting Intergovernmental Organizations (e.g. FAO, WIPO, Council of Europe), NGOs (e.g. WMA, HUGO), National Bioethics Committees (e.g. from Japan, Korea, New Zealand, Mexico, Republic of Congo) and international bioethics societies. Questions debated at this stage included whether the focus should be on human beings or broader; which fundamental bioethical principles could be identified; and whether specific areas of application of the principles should be explored.

1.4.1.2 Extensive Consultations

Drafting the text between April 2004 and January 2005, the IBC extensively consulted many stakeholders. The UN Inter-Agency Committee on Bioethics discussed drafts during two of its meetings. Consultations with regional experts took place in Buenos Aires and Moscow. National consultations were held in the Netherlands, Iran, Lithuania, Turkey, Korea, Mexico, Indonesia and Portugal. In August 2004, the IBC organized a public hearing in Paris, with representatives of religious and spiritual perspectives. Finally, the draft text was subjected to a written consultation with all Member States between October and December 2004.

1.4.1.3 Transparent Process

During the elaboration of the text, drafts, at various stages of the elaboration process, were published on the website of UNESCO. The work of the IBC drafting group was therefore conducted in as public a way as possible in order to facilitate consensus formation and early identification of any dissenting views. During the 2005 General Conference many member states underlined the quality of the consultation process put in place for the elaboration of the Declaration.

1.4.1.4 Multifarious Expertise and Negotiations

Dealing with bioethics in an intergovernmental organization such as UNESCO implies a linkage between science and politics. Any normative instrument needs to reflect the scientific and ethical state of the art. But in the end it is submitted for approval to the Member States which then decide if they want to adopt it. The draft text developed by independent scientific experts of the IBC was necessarily subjected to political negotiations amongst the governmental experts who represented the governments of Member States. The result is that the cogency of the final text, in some respects, may be diminished in order to create maximum adherence by all of the governments involved. In order to facilitate the opportunities for compromise, the work of the independent IBC was connected at an early stage with that of governmental experts. Several amendments to the IBC text were made by the governmental experts. The Declaration, as adopted, represents the IBC draft as so amended.

1.4.2 The Contents of the New Declaration

One of the contentious issues in the elaboration was the scope of bioethics. At least three views were advanced. These were that bioethics has to do with (1) medicine and health care, (2) the social context, such as access to health, and (3) the environment. In different parts of the world, different conceptions, definitions and histories of bioethics are evident. The scope of the adopted text of the Declaration is an obvious compromise between these views. It addresses "ethical issues related to medicine, life sciences and associated technologies as applied to human beings, taking into account their social, legal and environmental dimensions" (UNESCO 2005, Art 1a).

The aims of the Declaration are multiple. However, the most important aim is to provide "a universal framework of principles and procedures to guide States in the formulation of their legislation, policies or other instruments in the field of bioethics" (UNESCO 2005. Art 2i). One characteristic of present-day bioethics is that it is not merely an academic discipline; it is also an area of public debate and policy-making. This is why the Declaration primarily addresses states. But at the same time, since the bioethical principles identified are founded on human rights and fundamental freedoms, every individual is involved in bioethics. The Declaration, therefore, also aims "to guide the actions of individuals, groups, communities, institutions and corporations, public and private" (UNESCO 2005, Art 2).

The heart of the Declaration is to be found in the 15 principles that are listed. The principles determine the different obligations and responsibilities of the moral subject (*moral agent*) in relation to different categories of moral objects (*moral patients*). The principles are arranged according to a gradual widening of the range of moral objects: the individual human being itself (human dignity; benefit and harm; autonomy), other human beings (consent; privacy; equality), human communities (respect for cultural diversity), humankind as a whole (solidarity; social responsibility; sharing of benefits) and all living beings and their environment (protecting future generations and protection of the environment, the biosphere and biodiversity).

Some of the principles are already widely accepted (e.g. consent). Others have been endorsed in previous Declarations (e.g. sharing of benefits). What is innovative in the set of principles in the new Declaration is the balance struck between individualist and communitarian moral perspectives. The Declaration recognizes the principle of autonomy (Art.5) as well as the principle of solidarity (Art.13). It emphasizes the principle of social responsibility and health (Art. 14) which aims at re-orienting bioethical decision-making towards issues urgent to many countries (such as access to quality health care and essential medicines especially for women and children, adequate nutrition and water, reduction of poverty and illiteracy, improvement of living conditions and the environment). Finally, the Declaration anchors the bioethical principles firmly in the rules governing human dignity, human rights and fundamental freedoms. The section on the application of the principles (Arts 18 to 21) is also innovative because it provides the spirit in which the principles ought to be applied. It calls for professionalism, honesty, integrity and transparency in the decision making process; the setting up of ethics committees; appropriate assessment and management of risk; and ethical transnational practices that help in avoiding exploitation of countries that do not have an ethical infrastructure.

1.4.3 The Status of the Declaration

Unlike the Oviedo Convention adopted by the Council of Europe, the Universal Declaration of UNESCO does not constitute a binding normative instrument in international law. However, the unanimous adoption by the Member States is not merely symbolic but gives the Declaration moral authority and creates a moral commitment. For the first time in the history of bioethics, all states of the international community are committed to respect and implement the basic principles of bioethics, set forth within a single text. The innovative dimension of the Declaration is that it constitutes a commitment of governments to a set of bioethical principles. Previous international declarations, although sometimes very influential (such as the *Declaration of Helsinki*) have been adopted by professional organizations (such as the World Medical Association). The adoption of the Declaration also illustrates that there is now agreement about principles that form the basis of global bioethics, itself firmly founded on international human rights. After several decades, bioethics has developed into an established and recognized discipline. During this process of maturation, consensus on fundamental principles has gradually emerged. It is important to note that the rather limited core of four principles that are always recited (the so called 'Georgetown mantra') is now evolving into a coherent set of fifteen principles, taking into account not only individual and interpersonal perspectives but also community, social, environmental and even global perspectives. This new constellation of fundamental principles is not only the outcome of a process of internationalization of bioethics, taking into account a wider range of ethical principles that goes beyond the perspective of particular cultures and specific societies. It is also the starting point for a true globalization of bioethics – a global bioethics that cares about issues and problems in all areas of the world and that responds to the needs and concerns of all human beings on this planet.

1.5 Significance of the Principle of Respect for Cultural Diversity and Pluralism

One of the accomplishments of global bioethics is that respect for cultural diversity and pluralism is regarded as an ethical principle in itself. However, the status of this principle when balanced against other ethical principles is controversial. It is also unclear how respect for cultural diversity should be situated in the delicate balance between universalism and particularism (Ten Have and Gordijn 2011). The UNESCO Declaration presents a clear view. For the first time in bioethics, respect for diversity has been formulated as a specific principle that should be taken into account in the assessment of ethical issues and problems. But at the same time, it is the only principle of the Declaration for which the hierarchical status is determined. Article 12 explicitly states that considerations of diversity cannot be invoked to justify infringements of human dignity and human rights, or any other principle of the Declaration (UNESCO 2005, Art 12). In the balancing of principles, this particular principle therefore is the weakest one. It is the only principle that could not overrule the other principles. Naturally, this view is not uncontested. During the deliberations and negotiations the controversy was clear in the debate about informed consent. Although there was wide consensus that consent is a fundamental principle in global bioethics, it was also argued that in other cultures the emphasis is different. In African countries, a communitarian approach underlines the importance of the group or tribe. In healthcare and research decisions the group discusses the issue and the community leader is the one taking the lead in decision-making. In Arab countries the head of the family is crucial, and the husband makes decisions rather than the spouse(s). Nonetheless, the principle requires that in the end the concerned individual needs to provide informed consent. Such different approaches to implementation of principles are common but they do not affect the validity of the principles. Informed consent in North-America requires a great deal of bureaucracy; patients are required to sign extensive documentation. In many other countries, however, one's word is one's bond, and asking for a signature is a sign of distrust. Balancing and weighting different principles is a continuous challenge in bioethical debate. But how the principle of respect for cultural diversity and pluralism should be balanced with other principles, has a more fundamental implication for the status of global bioethics itself.

1.5.1 Need for Normative Assessment

Taking seriously the bioethical questions and answers in different countries, cultures and religions implies not to impose a particular normative framework but to do as much justice as possible to the normative considerations and concerns existing in these different contexts. This is why cross-cultural studies in bioethics are important. We need to know in detail and with precision what are the ethical problems in other communities and regions, what are the strategies of argumentation and justification used, and what are the approaches and solutions to address these problems. But bioethics is not anthropology. This phase of exploration and clarification is just the starting-point for the real work in bioethics: normative analysis. In many cases, the research never reaches this point; it is jammed in the empirical domain. It provides excellent descriptions but no normative judgment. What seems to be presented as bioethics is in reality anthropology. An example is an interesting study of Adriana Petryna (2009). She provides an excellent narrative of internationalization of clinical trials but she does not make a critical judgment. In fact her book is a long history of exploitation, social injustice and manipulation of regulations. Another risk surfaces when normative judgments are indeed made on the basis of empirical research: ethical relativism. What is considered as right or wrong in the healthcare setting is assumed to depend on the socio-cultural context. An example offer Subrata Chattopadhay and De Vries (2008). They argue that modern bioethics is a typical Western phenomenon. It is born in the West and therefore will always have the birthmarks of western civilization. When it is globalised, it has become the agent of moral imperialism. This argument seems to demonstrate modesty and respect for cultural diversity. Who are we to impose our judgment on another culture? Nobody wants to be considered a bioethical imperialist. But in real practice the argument is fallacious and unjust. It is a fallacy because the genesis of an activity is not identical to its validity. The argument is also unjust. It is 'doublespeak' to justify conditions and circumstances that are reproachable from the point of view of universal values. *Asian values* for example have often been promoted to justify authoritarian regimes. But, as Amartya Sen (1997) has shown, the so-called Asian values are not especially Asian in any significant sense. It is a kind of moral protectionism to continue to regard basic ethical notions and human rights as Western values that cannot be exported to other cultures. It is necessary to study and analyse moral values in different parts of the world but there is nothing that support the thesis of a grand dichotomy or 'clash of civilisations'. It is useful to quote Sen's conclusion: "Our ideas of political and personal rights have taken their particular form relatively recently, and it is hard to see them as "traditional" commitments of Western cultures. There are important antecedents of those commitments, but those antecedents can be found plentifully in Asian cultures as well as Western cultures" (Sen 1997, p. 38).

1.5.2 The Alleged Harm of Universal Principles

The claim that respect for cultural diversity is an ethical imperative is sometimes combined with the critique that the universalist approach to bioethics is harmful (Chattopadhyay and De Vries 2013). The harm is threefold. First, mainstream bioethics has a Western bias; because of its specific origin it is focusing on particular issues and interests only. Second, confronted with other cultures, bioethics poorly addresses moral diversity. Third, bioethics is simply exported to other cultures without sensitivity to moral diversity. The conclusion is that this leads to ethical imperialism. Bioethics is 'imposed' on non-western cultures. Such a point of view apparently assumes that bioethics in 2014 is similar to the one of 1974 or 1984. Bioethics is taken as a stable product of American culture that can simply be exported like a smart phone. It does not take into account that principlism no longer is the uncontested theoretical framework; that other methodological approaches have developed; that a wide range of theories have been formulated; and heterogeneous practices have emerged. No worries about care ethics, narrative ethics, or interpretive bioethics; they are all modifications of the same basic pattern. Not only does this static view not recognize scientific advances; it also does not appreciate cultural change and transformation. Apparently, the non-western countries have remained the same despite globalization. In this view contributions of scholars from India, South Africa, Brazil or China have not significantly contributed to the development and expansion of global bioethics, or have under-articulated the specific character of their contributions, or perhaps they have even been too much involved in the intellectual realm that perpetuates the imposition of Western bioethics.

1.6 Conclusion

It is time to leave the static view of bioethics behind and to acknowledge that ethics itself is changing as a result of processes of globalization. The confrontation with different ethical traditions and cultures is challenging ethics to rethink and transform its content, character, methods and sources of validation (Dower 2013). Respect for cultural diversity therefore requests to go beyond the dichotomy of imposition or acceptance, universality or particularity, ethical imperialism or protectionism. Taking diversity seriously may result in the emergence of a new global bioethics with a new vocabulary and content from many traditions. Or it may result in a two-level approach: a global bioethics emphasizing the shared principles and values, and a localized bioethics articulating the norms of different cultural settings. We do not know yet what kind of global bioethics will eventually result. But the dichotomies that are often made on the basis of respect for cultural diversity and pluralism are too simplistic. The further elaboration of global bioethics must be inclusive rather than exclusive. This is one of the fundamental contributions that international organizations such as UNESCO have brought to bioethics, and hopefully will continue to bring. It serves as a impartial but highly committed platform to exchange moral experiences and foster international cooperation. Western scholars have in fact been in the minority during the process of drafting and negotiating that has led to the Universal Declaration on Bioethics and Human Rights and it is not their views that have prevailed in the document.

Bibliography

Beauchamp, Tom L., and James F. Childress. 2013. *Principles of biomedical ethics*. 7th ed. New York: Oxford University Press.

Bovenberg, Jasper. 2006. *Mining the common heritage of our DNA: Lessons learned from Grotius and Pardo*. Duke Law & Technology Review 8. http://www.law.duke.edu/journals/dltr/articles/2006dltr0008.html. Accessed 28 Mar 2014.

Byk, Christian. 1998. A map to a new treasure island: The human genome and the concept of common heritage. *Journal of Medicine and Philosophy* 23 (3): 234–246.

Chattopadhyay, Subrata, and Raymond De Vries. 2008. Bioethical concerns are global, bioethics is Western. *Eubios J Asian Int Bioeth* 18 (4): 106–109.

———. 2013. Respect for cultural diversity in bioethics is an ethical imperative. *Medicine, Health Care and Philosophy* 16 (4): 639–645.

Council of Europe. 2001. *Recommendation 1512*. Protection of the human genome by the Council or Europe. http://assembly.coe.int/Documents/AdoptedText/ta01/EREC1512.htm. Accessed 28 Mar 2014.

Dower, Nigel. 2013. Globalization. In *The international encyclopedia of ethics*, ed. Hugh LaFollette, 2174–2186. Oxford: Blackwell Publishing.

George, William P. 1996. Looking for a global ethic? Try international law. *The Journal of Religion* 76 (3): 359–382.

Herber, Bernard. 1991. The common heritage principle: Antarctica and the developing nations. *American Journal of Economics and Sociology* 50 (4): 391–406.

Holmila, Erkki. 2005. Common heritage of mankind in the law of the sea. *Acta Societatis Martensis* 1 (1): 187–205.

HUGO Ethical, Legal, and Social Issues Committee. 1996. *Statement on the Principled Conduct of Genetics Research*. http://www1.umn.edu/humanrts/instree/geneticsresearch.html. Accessed 28 Mar 2014.

Huxley, Julian. 1946. *Unesco, its purpose and its philosophy*. Preparatory Commission of the United Nations Educational, Scientific and Cultural Organisation. http://unescodoc.unesco.org/images/0006/000681/068197eo.pdf. Accessed 27 Mar 2014.

IBC. 2003. Report of the IBC on the possibility of elaborating a universal instrument in bioethics. Paris.

Jing-Bao, N. 2005. Cultural values embodying universal norms: A critique of a popular assumption about cultures and human rights. *Developing World Bioethics* 5 (3): 251–257.
Joyner, Christopher. 1986. Legal implications of the concept of the common heritage of mankind. *International and Comparative Law Quarterly* 35: 190–199.
Kelly, David F., Gerard Magill, and Henk ten Have. 2013. *Contemporary catholic healthcare ethics*. Washington, DC: Georgetown University Press.
Knoppers, Bartha, and Yann Joly. 2007. Our social genome? *Trends in Biotechnology* 25 (7): 284–288.
Küng, Hans. 1997. *Weltethos für Weltpolitik und Weltwirtschaft*. München: Piper Verlag.
Lobo, Michele, Vince Marotta, and Nicole Oke, eds. 2011. *Intercultural relations in a global world*. Champaign: Common Ground Publishing.
Musitelli, Jean. 2002. World heritage, between universalism and globalization. *International Journal of Cultural Property* 11 (2): 323–336.
Parliament of the World's Religions. 1993. *Declaration toward a global ethics*. See: http://www.parliamentofreligions.org/_includes/FCKcontent/File/TowardsAGlobalEthic.pdf
Petryna, Adriana. 2009. *When experiments travel. Clinical trials and the global search for human subjects*. Princeton/Oxford: Princeton University Press.
Potter, Van Rensselaer. 1968. Teilhard de Chardin and the concept of purpose. *Zygon* 3: 367–376.
———. 1970. Bioethics, the science of survival. *Perspectives in Biology and Medicine* 14: 127–153.
———. 1971. *Bioethics: Bridge to the future*. Englewood Cliffs: Prentice-Hall.
———. 1975. Humility with responsibility – A bioethic for oncologists: Presidential Address. *Cancer Research* 35: 2297–2306.
———. 1988. *Global bioethics: Building on the Leopold legacy*. East Lansing: Michigan State University Press.
Sen, Amartya. 1997. *Human rights and Asian values: What Kee Kuan Yew and Le Peng don't understand about Asia*. The New Republic, July 14: 217(2–3): 33–38 (http://www.hmb.utoronto.ca/HMB303H/weekly_supp/week-02/Sen_Asian_Values.pdf). Accessed 28 Mar 2014.
Strati, Anastasia. 1991. Deep seabed cultural property and the common heritage of mankind. *The International and Comparative Law Quarterly* 40 (4): 859–894.
Teilhard de Chardin, Pierre. 1975. *The phenomenon of man*. New York: Harper Collins Publishers.
———. 2004. *The future of man*. New York: Doubleday. (original English translation 1964).
Ten Have, Henk. 2012. Potter's notion of bioethics. *Kennedy Institute of Ethics Journal* 22 (1): 59–82.
Ten Have, Henk, and Bert Gordijn. 2011. Diversity and bioethics. *Medicine Health Care and Philosophy* 14 (3): 227–228.
Ten Have, Henk, and Bert Gordijn. 2013. *Handbook of global bioethics*. Dordrecht: Springer.
Ten Have, Henk, and Michele S. Jean, eds. 2009. *The UNESCO universal declaration on bioethics and human rights: Background, principles, and application*. Paris: UNESCO Publishing.
UNESCO. 1945. *Constitution*. http://portal.unesco.org/en/ev.php-URL_ID=15244&URL_DO=DO_TOPIC&URL_SECTION=201.html. Accessed 28 Mar 2014.
———. 1997. *Universal declaration on the human genome and human rights*. Paris. http://portal.unesco.org/en/ev.php-URL_ID=13177&URL_DO=DO_TOPIC&URL_SECTION=201.html. Accessed 28 Mar 2014.
———. 2001. *Universal declaration on cultural diversity*. Paris. http://portal.unesco.org/en/ev.php-URL_ID=13179&URL_DO=DO_TOPIC&URL_SECTION=201.html. Accessed 28 Mar 2014.
———. 2005. *The universal declaration on bioethics and human rights*. Paris. http://unesdoc.unesco.org/images/0014/001461/146180E.pdf. Accessed 28 Mar 2014.
United Nations General Assembly. 1967. Twenty-second Session, First Committee, 1515th meeting. New York. https://www.un.org/depts/los/convention_agreements/texts/pardo_ga1967.pdf. Accessed 28 Mar 2014.

Veatch, Robert M. 2012. *Hippocratic, religious, and secular medical ethics. The points of conflict*. Washington, DC: Georgetown University Press.
Wallace, K.A. 2009. Common morality and moral reform. *Theoretical Medicine and Bioethics* 30: 55–68.

Chapter 2
Human Rights and Cultural Diversity in UNESCO Bioethics

John Lunstroth

2.1 Introduction

In October 2005 UNESCO adopted by acclamation the Universal Declaration on Bioethics and Human Rights (Declaration or UDB). It purports to "enshrine bioethics in human rights" and ensure "respect for the life of human beings", so that "human beings everywhere can benefit from the advances of science and technology within the framework of respect for human rights and fundamental freedoms."[1]

The UDB was systematically critiqued, with some withering criticism, even before it was adopted. The journal *Developing World Bioethics* devoted its September 2005 issue to the draft UDB. The editors of that issue, Willem Landman and Udo Schuklenk, in their editorial introduction, slammed both UNESCO and the Declaration. UNESCO was accused, among other things, of "meddling in the professional domain of another United Nations (UN) agency, WHO."[2] Although their assessment that "many unexpected universal truths" were "unearthed" in the Declaration was sarcastic, the commentators chosen for inclusion in that issue made reasonable critiques of the form and content of the Declaration.[3]

---

[1] Koïchiro Matsuura, *Forward*, UNESCO Universal Declaration of Human Rights (2005), hereinafter "UDB."

[2] Willem Landman & Udo Schuklenk, *UNESCO "declares" universals on bioethics and human rights - many universal truths unearther by UN body*, 5 Developing World Bioethics iii(2005). Their view of the UN and its agencies is naïve.

[3] See e.g., Matti Hayry & Tuija Takala, *Human Dignity, Bioethics, and Human Rights*, see id. at;Mary C. Rawlinson & Anne Donchin, *The Quest for Universality: Reflections on the Universal Draft Declaration on Bioethics and Human Rights*, see id. at 258;John R. Williams, *UNESCO"s Proposed Declaration on Bioethics and Human Rights - A Bland Compromise*, see id. at 210.

J. Lunstroth (✉)
Health Law & Policy Institute, University of Houston Law Center, Houston, TX, USA
e-mail: lunstroth@gmail.com

J. Tham et al. (eds.), *Religious Perspectives on Bioethics and Human Rights*,
Advancing Global Bioethics 6, DOI 10.1007/978-3-319-58431-7_2

After it was adopted it generated mixed reviews.[4] In 2009 the *Journal of Medicine and Philosophy* devoted an issue to examining its "potential merits and pitfalls."[5] In general these assessments were longer and more thoughtful.[6] There has not been much subsequent scholarly commentary.[7]

Proponents of the Declaration tend to take it, and the representations made about it by UNESCO, at face value. For example, Faunce and Nasu find it links bioethics and human rights, and Adorno finds it extends and strengthens notions of human dignity.[8]

At a more general level, the Declaration can be read as more evidence of the ongoing struggle within UNESCO policy between universalism and relativism.[9]

It is Kopelman though, I think, who best hints at the framework with which to make sense of the Declaration and its manifest problems. Kopelman is an academic bioethicist trained in philosophy. Her work focuses narrowly on bioethics.

Kopelman argues, citing Jonsen, another bioethicist, that bioethics functions at two levels.[10] It is both "public discourse" and an academic "discipline." Public discourse is the discussion between members of the public, including experts, about moral issues disclosed by the more technical analyses that occur in inter-disciplinary talk. Its goal may be to "promote moral reflection" and policy development. It differs from interdisciplinary talk because it does not comprehend the nuanced arguments of the experts, rather it is the way the public digests technical discourse. There is, consequently, a sometimes serious disconnect between what the experts really say and what the public understands and makes decisions about. Kopelman's conclusion is that the Declaration succeeds as public discourse, but is problematic as academic ethics.

---

[4] Cheryl Cox Macpherson, *Global bioethics: did the universal declaration on bioethics and human rights miss the boat?*, 33 Journal of Medical Ethics 588(2007);Harald Schmidt, *Whose Dignity? Resolving Ambiguities in the Scope of "Human Dignity" in the Universal Declaration on Bioethics and Human Rights*, see id. at 578;Roberto Andorno, *Global bioethics at UNESCO: in defence of the Universal Declaration on Bioethics and Human Rights*, see id. at 150.

[5] Griffin Trotter, *The UNESCO Declaration on Bioethics and Human Rights: A Canon for the Ages?*, 34 Journal of Medicine and Philosophy 195, 195 (2009).

[6] Roberto Andorno, *Human Dignity and Human Rights as a Common Ground for Global Bioethics*, see id. at 223;Mark J. Cherry, *UNESCO, "Universal Bioethics," and State Regulation of Health Risks: A Philosophical Critique*, see id. at 274;Thomas Alured Faunce & Hitoshi Nasu, *Normative Foundations of Technology Transfer and Transnational Benefit Principles in the UNESCO Universal Declaration on Bioethics and Human Rights*, see id. at 296;Darryl Gunson, *Solidarity and the Universal Declaration on Bioethics and Human Rights*, see id. at 241;Loretta M. Kopelman, *Bioethics as Public Discourse and Second-Order Discipline*, see id. at 261;O. Carter Snead, *Bioethics and Self-Governance: The Lessons of the Universal Declaration on Bioethics and Human Rights*, see id. at 204.

[7] See e.g., Adele Langlois, *The Global Governance of Bioethics: Negotiating UNESCO"s Universal Declaration on Bioethics and Human Rights*, 5 Global Health Governance 1(2011).

[8] See Andorno, *Global bioethics at UNESCO: in defence of the Universal Declaration on Bioethics and Human Rights*;Faunce & Nasu.

[9] Eriksen, Thomas Hylland. 2008. Between universalism and relativism: A critique of the UNESCO concepts of culture. In Culture and rights: Anthropological perspectives, ed. Jane Cowan et al. Cambridge: Cambridge University Press, p. 1.

[10] Kopelman, 263.

I think Kopelmen is right, although her bioethics lens is too restrictive to recognize the vast international issues UNESCO purports to take on in the Declaration.

2.2 The Declaration and International Norms

The Declaration is complex formally and substantively. Formally it is complex because it is neither a straight forward statement of "ethical" norms, in which it is understood that "ethical" is distinguished categorically from legal (and perhaps moral) norms, nor is it municipal or international law. Kopelman reads the Declaration as "ethics," whereas most other commentators read it as "soft law."[11] The intention of UNESCO was to provide a framework to states for the consideration and adoption of uniform bioethical laws. It is very clear that UNESCO defines a "declaration" as soft law.[12] It is intended by UNESCO that the norms it is promulgating become law through natural and customary law and historical processes. These types of norms acquire a kind of legitimacy that exceeds mere ethical standards by the intention, formality and solemnity of their issuance and content. Thus, their status as soft laws, norms the international community has accepted into the formal processes by which norms become law. Acceptance into the process does not guarantee the norms will become positive law, but it is a clear grant of legitimacy.

The substantive complexity of the Declaration is perhaps less complexity than confusion. In order to add legitimacy to its norms, to make them stronger in the international law pipeline, the Declaration refers repeatedly to several buzz-words: universal, science, human rights, dignity, and fundamental freedoms. All of these words have powerful meanings in the discourse of international law and UNESCO's references to them are meant to incorporate them into the Declaration. Incorporation by reference is standard legal fare, so on its face this will not be problematic to some, but to others, including myself, the way the incorporation is attempted renders the Declaration almost useless.

To understand this one must survey the actual normative environment of international law, the realm to which the Declaration aspires, and that which it seeks to incorporate by reference. In short the incorporation fails because the thing(s) the Declaration seeks to incorporate do not exist as things that can be used like that, and because those things themselves exist in a normative environment that determines their meanings and that higher level of determinative normative meaning is not referred to, but when considered plays an important role.

The following table illustrates a taxonomy of the normative environment of international law:

---

[11] ANDORNO, *Global bioethics at UNESCO: in defence of the Universal Declaration on Bioethics and Human Rights.*

[12] UNESCO Basic Documents: *General introduction to the standard-setting instruments of UNESCO*

Level 1: Dominant value, constitution:	Oligarchy
Level 2: Competing values	
(2)a ideologies	Science, human rights (morality), neoliberalism, democracy, socialism
(2)b institutions	Development, public health, humanitarianism, sovereignty
Level 3: Positive law:	Int'l human rights; other int'l public law; constitutional law

One can see multiple normative orders all ordered more or less by a *de facto* oligarchic constitution. When UNESCO used the word "universal" it dragged in all the normative regimes in the Table. It would have had fewer problems had it restricted itself to references to human rights, and even fewer problems had it only referred to dignity, but all of those references are to contested concepts or normative regimes.

Each node or label in the Table refers to a normative system that has claims to universality. Unfortunately, those universalisms compete with each other, they cannot all be universal, and their uneasy co-existence is incontrovertible evidence none of them is universal. Although there is a de facto Aristotelian constitution,[13] of oligarchical character, it can only be said to be universal by virtue of its power, not its ethical authority, as it is considered illegitimate by several of the nodes.

Human rights refers to at least three different kinds of law and to a rhetorical order. Human rights law consists of norms *ius cogens*, the only laws that have real claims to universality, first generation rights (democratic norms), and second generation rights (socialist norms).[14] An appeal to human rights as law is inherently incoherent; and appeal to human rights as rhetorical or moral norm is understandable it is so vague the same appeal could be made by a tyrant, a democrat and a socialist. It has no inherent moral meaning other than justice, and justice is legendarily difficult to pin down.

Dignity, while appearing to easily be a single moral norm, itself has been used in two vastly different and materially relevant ways. It refers to upper class notions of mutual respect in Europe, while in America it refers to lower class notions.[15] "Fundamental freedoms" is simply another way of referring to the most important civil and political human rights, usually in the liberal order.

The reference to higher order norms by groups seeking to establish soft law norms is commonplace, but the most successful accept the primacy of first generation human rights, and refer simply to one or more specific rights as the legal foun-

---

[13] ARISTOTLE, The Politics of Aristotle (Ernest Barker trans., Clarendon Press 1946). 1253a19-28.

[14] It also refers to a great many different hard and soft treaty regimes, and third and fourth generation rights. See e.g., BURNS H. WESTON, *Human Rights*, 6 Human Rights Quarterly 257(1984). See generally, PHILIP ALSTON & RYAN GOODMAN, International Human Rights (Oxford University Press. 2013).

[15] JAMES Q. WHITMAN, *The Two Western Cultures of Privacy: Dignity versus Liberty*, 113 Yale Law Journal 1151(2004).

dation for their projects. For example, the human rights community developed the right of free, prior and informed consent (FPIC) as a normative structure designed to give people "a say about development projects, such as dams, mines and, logging and other large infrastructure projects, which affect them in some way."[16] Instead of invoking the entire normative universe, the promoters anchor the right concretely and simply in ICCPR art. 1:

> This principle is protected by international human rights law as "all peoples have the right to self-determination" and linked to the right to self determination, "all peoples have the right to freely pursue their economic, social and cultural development".[17]

2.3 The Normative Order of Science (and Bioethics)

The normative order of science is radically different than the other normative orders, and bears its own explanation. Bioethics is a school of ethics that is pendant on science. Science is so different that for purposes of its peer nodes in the Table, and the nodes under it, the Table could be divided into only two kinds of norms: scientific norms and moral (ethical/legal/political) norms. UNESCO seeks to establish universal "bioethical" norms, and refers extensively to the moral/legal order to do so. Not only is the appeal to international law problematic for the reasons above, there is a categorical incommensurability between norms of science and moral/legal norms.

Belief that science provides the best way to understand the world is called naturalism.[18] Naturalism includes a belief in materialism, the dogma that all things consist only of matter.[19] On this theory, the basis of the life sciences is that all living things are accidental biochemical machines. There is no possibility for free will on this theory, and thus its incommensurability with the moral/legal order, since the basis of political order is the capacity to make decisions and be responsible.

Science is institutionally very powerful, and beginning in the 1950s began to behave badly towards humans. By the late 1960s it was clear that science needed to be guided, if not simply reined in.[20] This was the period during which science enjoyed the most credibility it would ever have, and all of the critics were naturalists believing in the other main dogma of science, its promise to bring peace and security to the world at large.

---

[16] Christina Hill, et al., Guide to Free, Prior and Informed Consent (Oxfam Australia 2010).

[17] Id. at, 1.

[18] Brian Leiter, *Rethinking Legal Realism: Towards a Naturalized Jurisprudence*, 76 Texas Law Review 267(1997).

[19] For a fuller description, see Thomas Nagel, Mind & Cosmos: Why the Materialist Neo-Darwinian Conception of Nature is Almost Certainly False (Oxford University Press. 2012).

[20] M. Hogan, A Cross of Iron: Harry S. Truman and the Origins of the National Security State, 1945–1954 (1998);David J. Rothman, Strangers at the Bedside: A History of How Law and Bioethics Transformed Medical Decision Making (Basic Books. 1991).

Bioethics is the socio-political response to the excesses of science, and this purpose is clearly enunciated in the Declaration. Although the original ethical response in the 1960s included critique from philosophers, theologians, lawyers, and judges, it was dominated by social and medical scientists. Almost all of them were and continue to be naturalists.[21] There was and continues to be a strong emphasis from within the naturalist community to self-regulate, although with major disasters, such as Tuskegee in the United States, governments step in with legislation.

The federal U.S. legislation adopted in 1981, now known as Federal Policy for the Protection of Human Subjects,[22] established the system of ethical peer review within the research community that continues to serve as a model for ethical review around the world. Social and medical scientists dominated the multi-year project of drafting the report and recommendations to Congress that informed the legislation. One of the core notions of the legislation is that scientists review their own projects and decide whether they are "ethical" or not. Another is that subjects of research, i.e., citizens, do not have the right to sue for violations of their human rights in the event science/scientists hurt them. Instead, the statute established a federal oversight agency, the Office of Human Subject Protection, that has the authority to remove the permission of scientists and institutions to do research (if the research is federally funded in some way). The oversight agency was deemed by Congress to represent the interests of all research subjects sufficiently as a group.

The description of the U.S. government's response to scientific "misconduct" is illustrative of how the scientific community can distort an ethics and human rights response to science. The medical and life sciences need human bodies for various reasons, chief among them to develop information that can be structured as oligarchic intellectual property, and as consumers of medical and scientific products. When naturalists seek to control their scientist colleagues they are pressured to do as little as possible by the oligarchic structures and the desire to appease their colleagues.

In some ways then, it may be that when the naturalists at UNESCO, the UN agency devoted to the advancement of science, want to focus on bioethics, they follow the American model of treading carefully around the scientists, giving them as much freedom as possible. If the proposed ethical guidance is incoherent, this means the oligarchic ends and the scientific community can dominate in the outcome since they are the ones with the power. I discuss the alternative in the conclusion.

---

[21] See e.g., National Commission for the Protection of Human Subjects of Biomedical and Behavioral Research, The Belmont Report: Ethical Principles and Guidelines for the Protection of Human Subjects of Research (Department of Health, Education, and Welfare. 1979). (including Appendices); Rothman.

[22] National Research Act. PL 93–348 (HR 7724), 93rd Congress. (1974). 4 CFR 46 (1981–2009).

2.4 Article 12

> Article 12 – Respect for cultural diversity and pluralism
>
> The importance of cultural diversity and pluralism should be given due regard. However, such considerations are not to be invoked to infringe upon human dignity, human rights and fundamental freedoms, nor upon the principles set out in this Declaration, nor to limit their scope.

Article 12 is troubling on its face. It begins, in the title, by announcing that it addresses "respect for cultural diversity and pluralism," suggesting it will be open and respectful of them. However, in its first sentence, it says merely that states ought to give multiculturalism and pluralism "due regard." Giving something "due regard" is certainly less than giving it "respect." The kind of downgrading in importance of multiculturalism and pluralism continues in the second of its two sentences.

The second sentence prohibits the use of multiculturalist and pluralist arguments to limit the scope of the bioethical principles of the Declaration. If multicultural and pluralist arguments are to be made, then of what use can they be? Just to promote the principles of the Declaration? Article 12 seems to simply foreclose a certain kind of critique. We can ignore that the Declaration manages to forbid multicultural and pluralist critique of the concepts of "human dignity, human rights and the fundamental freedoms." That seems far beyond the UNESCO's remit, added perhaps for rhetorical value only, or to align the principles with far more powerful normative regimes. The whole point, the ethicist and human rights advocate would say, of multicultural and pluralist arguments is exactly to limit or modify the application of externally imposed norms. That the Declaration requires states to ignore such critiques, or to pay them mere lip service, requires states to derogate from the civil and political rights accorded all citizens under positive international human rights law. The international order widely recognizes democracy as the fundamental political value encoded in the International Bill of Human Rights, and this norm explicitly violates that norm by prohibiting states from permitting citizens to have a functional voice in making certain decisions. It would seem, on that reading, to be an unjustifiable norm, not legitimate on its face.

It also appears to be inconsistent, in its severe limitation of the use of multicultural and pluralist arguments, with the core purposes of the Declaration, which are expressed in the following four "aims"[23]:

> Article 2 – Aims
>
> The aims of this Declaration are:
>
> (a) to provide a universal framework of principles and procedures to guide States in the formulation of their legislation, policies or other instruments in the field of bioethics; …
>
> (b) to promote respect for human dignity and protect human rights, by ensuring respect for the life of human beings, and fundamental freedoms, consistent with international human rights law;

---

[23] I read the other four aims to gloss these main aims.

(c) to recognize the importance of freedom of scientific research and the benefits derived from scientific and technological developments, while stressing the need for such research and developments to occur within the framework of ethical principles set out in this Declaration and to respect human dignity, human rights and fundamental freedoms;
(d) to foster multidisciplinary and pluralistic dialogue about bioethical issues between all stakeholders and within society as a whole; …

Article 12 appears to disrespect human rights and fundamental freedoms, and to quell multidisciplinary and pluralist dialogue.

The history of Article 12 reveals the underlying problem and the reason it became so restrictive.[24] The Declaration was adopted in October, 2005. In April of that year the first meeting of experts was held aimed at finalizing the draft.[25] A February 2005 memo indicates that at that time Article 12 was Article 7. Paragraphs 48–52 addressed the issues intended to be covered by this article. Of special importance is Paragraph 51:

> 51. During the written consultation process, some countries expressed their fear that respect for cultural diversity could easily be used to override any other moral consideration. The text of the declaration therefore adds the proviso (as in the Universal Declaration of Cultural Diversity) that this principle cannot be used to limit the application of the other universal principles: "such considerations shall not be invoked to infringe upon human dignity, human rights and fundamental freedoms nor upon the principles set out in this Declaration, nor to limit their scope".

By May, 2005 Article 7 read as follows:

> Article 7 – Respect for Cultural Diversity and Pluralism
>
> Any decision or practice shall take into account the cultural backgrounds, schools of thought, value systems, traditions, religious and spiritual beliefs and other relevant features of society. However, such considerations shall not be invoked to infringe upon human dignity, human rights and fundamental freedoms nor upon the principles set out in this Declaration, nor to limit their scope.[26]

Here the first sentence clearly requires respect for cultural diversity and pluralism, although it still has the over-restrictive language disabling the political power of the pluralist discourse. But the final version of the first sentence shows a complete capitulation to those states that fear that the protection of minority and ethnic discourse will lead to some kind of political disorder. Not only was it rewritten, the entire article was moved to a less prominent position as Article 12:

> The importance of cultural diversity and pluralism should be given due regard.

---

[24] There is no space in this paper to provide a thorough history either of the conflict underlying Article 12, nor of the UDB itself. Here I refer only to enough documents to identify the problem.

[25] UNESCO, First Intergovernmental Meeting of Experts Aimed at Finalizing a Draft Declaration on Universal Norms on Bioethics, EXPLANATORY MEMORANDUM ON THE ELABORATION OF THE PRELIMINARY DRAFT DECLARATION ON UNIVERSAL NORMS ON BIOETHICS, SHS/EST/05/CONF.203/4, Paris, 21 February 2005.

[26] UNESCO, Second session of the intergovernmental meeting of experts aimed at finalizing a draft of a declaration on universal norms on bioethics, AGENDA, SHS/EST/05/CONF.204/1, Paris, 4 May 2005.

There is no question ethnically oriented discourse can be used for purposes inconsistent with human rights norms, nonetheless the right to freedom of conscience (ICCPR Art 18) and freedom of expression (ICCPR 19) clearly disable Article 12. Moreover, human rights norms themselves can be used to the detriment of human rights. But stifling politically enabled discourse is always detrimental to democratic principles. The solution is not to stifle discourse, but lies elsewhere, perhaps in strengthened and educated ethics committees, or in broader educational programs.

In any event, the real problem embodied in [the new] Article 12 revolves around the idea of universality. It clearly intends to establish the justice norms (dignity, freedom), human rights, and the Declaration as universal norms that in all cases supersede "cultural diversity and pluralism." Since the main purpose of human rights, especially the ICCPR, is to protect "cultural diversity and pluralism", the very heart of democracy, we must question how such a provision could have been conceived in the middle of so many explicit injunctions to respect human rights.

ICCPR, Article 27

In those States in which ethnic, religious or linguistic minorities exist, persons belonging to such minorities shall not be denied the right, in community with the other members of their group, to enjoy their own culture, to profess and practise their own religion, or to use their own language.

As explained above, the ICCPR contains the most universal international human rights norms there are, and the Declaration, while in one breath invoking human rights, in the next blithely removes them. On the Declaration's own terms, in which it asserts no provision shall be read in derogation of human rights, Article 12 is void.

I suggest this is symptomatic of bioethics in the American model, in which bioethical norms are drafted by scientists and other naturalists who are tone-deaf to dignity and inexperienced and unschooled in the history, details and necessities of international human rights norms. That these norms are then approved by the political order says little about their quality as norms, because the political order will depend on the representations of the naturalist drafters that these norms are "bioethics', something the political order will read as specialty, and in any event, the political order will not be too concerned if the experts get it wrong because they are signing on only to a declaration. At a more abstract level, the political order will bless the acts of scientist experts because it knows the life sciences are excellent at protecting the marketplace.

I do not mean to cast aspersions on the intentions of the drafters, who I must assume act under the good faith belief they are doing something good. But I am suggesting that naturalists who find themselves drafting international legal norms that have universalist aspirations have a responsibility to (i) examine their own metaphysical commitments and their ethical implications, and (ii) learn enough about the history and necessity of human rights to produce documents that actually respect them.

2.5 Conclusion

The general message of the Declaration, that the life and health sciences should be used responsibly and without taking advantage or harming people, is easy and needs to be repeated. The Declaration does a good thing in this sense. But we have seen that when looked at carefully it seems not to commit itself to anything more than a general statement, although it purports to invoke universal principles. I suggested the general problem arises from the American model of doing bioethics, in which bioethics is created, maintained and enforced by the scientific community and its sympathizers. If this is so, then *quis custodiet ipsos custodes*?

There is no need to start from scratch, as though bioethics are some kind of special normative system. That sense of bioethics is characteristic of the state, or hubris, of science. From the perspective of political order, science is another ethical institution in the socio-political firmament, and as such it should be subject to the same norms as all other ethical institutions. But science sees itself as a non-political entity, outside of the larger socio-political order, and subject to its own norms. Since science is *sui generis*, its norms should be *sui generis*. Bioethics is based on that assumption about science. But if that assumption is rejected, as it should be, then the ethics of scientific practice and of science are not *sui generis*, rather they are coordinate with the larger political and ethical system. The norms that should govern science are readily found in the human rights regime.

Bioethics should begin with one or more already defined human rights as did the proponents of the right of free, prior and informed consent (FPIC).[27]

The Declaration is concerned with the effect of the life sciences, including medicine and public health, on people and communities, especially the vulnerable. In the following Table I list each article, its ethical concern and the human right or rights that apply:

UDBHR Art	Issue	Human right(s)
3, 8	Human dignity, rights, freedoms	Int'l Bill of Human Rights
4	Benefit and harm	ICCPR 7
5, 6, 7	Autonomy and other consent issues	ICCPR 7
9	Privacy	ICCPR 17
10, 11, 12	Equality, non-discrimination, diversity	ICCPR 2, 3, 27 and others
14	Social rights	ICESCR substantive rights
15	Sharing benefits	ICCPR art 1.2
13,16	Protect future and environment, solidarity	Solidarity rights[a]

[a]Weston, 266. See also, Gunson

[27] Christina Hill, et al., Guide to Free, Prior and Informed Consent (Oxfam Australia 2010), p. 12.

Bioethics should be elaborated and theorized by explicit linkage to higher order norms, such as these. General, confusing, vague and impractical linkages and references to "fundamental freedoms", human rights and human dignity can be avoided.

Thinking it through illustrates why this approach would be difficult to implement in the oligarchic order.

ICCPR 1 confers property rights on people and peoples. For example, when companies get information from human experimentation, or collection of genetic material, and use it to make products, drugs, or other products, human rights norms confer a property right in that substance or information. The information and substances taken from people is often hard to identify, or people are unaware it is being taken, or they are not properly advised as to how it will be used to make profits, and how much those profits might be. A rights-based approach to the relationship between people and communities and science would result in a more equitable negotiation. A fair negotiation would entail that both parties were represented by competent counsel; that the negotiation would take place prior to the intervention; that consideration for the property interest that would be created be fair and reasonably related to the potential profits; and that consideration include compensation to communities. This would interpose a barrier between science and human beings, reversing the current presumption that science should have free access to people but for consent. Consent as it is currently structured is well-known to be almost meaningless.

At a more structural level, corporations could be re-rationalized. They, like science, are ethical institutions and as such should have not only rights but duties to the entire ethical order. Currently we create corporations as fictitious beings whose only internal purpose is to return profits to the owners. States enact various restrictions and regulations, but the general principle for the nature of a corporation is profit-seeking. In fact, this norm is so entrenched the corporation can be sued by its owners if it strays from this mandate. The same community that seeks to enact bioethical norms could focus its energy on re-visioning the inherent nature of the corporation, its ethical nature. Such fictitious persons should be required by law to have internal norms of respect for humans and other living things; norms that recognize there is only one biosphere, that its resources are limited, that property is created and maintained by states out of those common resources, that property is necessary for individual wellbeing but the need of fictitious persons for property can reasonably be limited, that fictitious persons owe duties of care and responsibility to all humans, and those duties of care and responsibility can impose real limits on the powers and freedoms of corporations to intervene in markets and communities. In this way the "bioethics" goals of the UNESCO Declaration could be institutionalized through a treaty that requires states who create corporations to only create corporations that have these internal norms.

The various critiques of the Declaration outlined above should stimulate a different kind of discussion, a more realistic one. It should begin in the same way, with the recognition science needs to be limited. But then, instead of accepting the internal narrative of science, science should be seen as an ethical institution and its misleading representations that it is somehow apolitical and ahistorical have simply to be put aside. Science should be regulated on the same terms every other socio-political institution is. Once the acts of science are put on par with the ethical acts of all other socio-political institutions, then mystifications about how it should be regulated, arising from the various ideologies of science, will disappear. Science should be for people, but not people as science sees them, as dehumanized aggregated individuals, but people as they are parts of political and constitutional order.

Beyond this the discussion should at least recognize the distorting effect oligarchy has on the ideology of science in socio-political order, and should attempt some normative push-back. When the conflict between the oligarchic and the democratic constitutions is addressed, then it will be possible to clarify the norms that are needed, based on a clearer vision of higher-order values and power. If the discussion recognizes its role in the conflict, then perhaps we can move closer to resolving this internal contradiction until, in Hegelian fashion, the next one emerges.

Bibliography

Alston, Philip, and Ryan Goodman. 2013. *International human rights*. Oxford: Oxford University Press

Andorno, Roberto. 2007. Global bioethics at UNESCO: In defence of the Universal Declaration on Bioethics and Human Rights. *Journal of Medical Ethics* 33: 150.

———. 2009. Human dignity and human rights as a common ground for global bioethics. *Journal of Medicine and Philosophy* 34: 223.

Aristotle. 1946. *The Politics of Aristotle*. Trans. Ernest Barker. Oxford: Clarendon Press.

Carter Snead, O. 2009. Bioethics and self-governance: The lessons of the universal declaration on bioethics and human rights. *Journal of Medicine and Philosophy* 34: 204.

Cherry, Mark J. 2009. UNESC, "Universal Bioethics," and State Regulation of Health Risks: A philosophical critique. *Journal of Medicine and Philosophy* 34: 274.

Eriksen, Thomas Hylland. 2008. Between universalism and relativism: A critique of the UNESCO concepts of culture. In *Culture and rights: Anthropological perspectives*, ed. Jane Cowan et al. Cambridge: Cambridge University Press.

Faunce, Thomas Alured, and Hitoshi Nasu. 2009. Normative foundations of technology transfer and transnational benefit principles in the UNESCO universal declaration on bioethics and human rights. *Journal of Medicine and Philosophy* 34: 296.

Gunson, Darryl. 2009. Solidarity and the universal declaration on bioethics and human rights. *Journal of Medicine and Philosophy* 34: 241.

Hayry, Matti, and Tuija Takala. 2005. Human dignity, bioethics, and human rights. *Developing World Bioethics* 5.

Hogan, M. 1998. *A cross of iron: Harry S. truman and the origins of the national security state, 1945–1954*. Cambridge: Cambridge University Press.

Hill, Christina et al. 2010. *Guide to free, prior and informed consent*. Melbourne: Oxfam.

Kopelman, Loretta M. 2009. Bioethics as public discourse and second-order discipline. *Journal of Medicine and Philosophy* 34: 261.

Landman Willem, and Udo Schuklenk. 2005. *UNESCO "declares" universals on bioethics and human rights – Many universal truths unearther by UN body*, 5 Developing World Bioethics iii.

Langlois, Adele. 2011. The global governance of bioethics: Negotiating UNESCO's universal declaration on bioethics and human rights. *Global Health Governance* 5: 1.

Leiter, Brian. 1997. Rethinking legal realism: Towards a naturalized jurisprudence. *Texas Law Review* 76: 267.

Macpherson, Cheryl Cox. 2007. Global bioethics: Did the universal declaration on bioethics and human rights miss the boat? *Journal of Medical Ethics* 33: 588.
Nagel, Thomas. 2012. *Mind & Cosmos: Why the materialist neo-darwinian conception of nature is almost certainly false*. Oxford: Oxford University Press.
National Commission for the Protection of Human Subjects of Biomedical and Behavioral Research. 1979. *The belmont report: Ethical principles and guidelines for the protection of human subjects of research.* Department of Health, Education, and Welfare.
National Research Act. 1974. PL 93-348 (HR 7724), 93rd Congress.
Rawlinson, Mary C., and Anne Donchin. 2005. The quest for universality: Reflections on the universal draft declaration on bioethics and human rights. *Developing World Bioethics* 5: 258.
Rothman, David J. 1991. *Strangers at the bedside: A history of how law and bioethics transformed medical decision making*. New York: Basic Books.
Schmidt, Harald. 2007. Whose dignity? Resolving ambiguities in the scope of "Human Dignity" in the universal declaration on bioethics and human rights. *Journal of Medical Ethics* 33: 578.
Trotter, Griffin. 2009. The UNESCO declaration on bioethics and human rights: A canon for the ages? *Journal of Medicine and Philosophy* 34: 195.
Weston, Burns H. 1984. Human rights. *Human Rights Quarterly* 6: 257.
Whitman, James Q. 2004. *The two western cultures of privacy: Dignity versus liberty. Yale Law Journal* 113: 1151.
Williams, John R. 2005. UNESCO's proposed declaration on bioethics and human rights – A bland compromise. *Developing World Bioethics* 5: 210.

Chapter 3
Human Rights and the Relational Self: A Personalist Approach

Denis Chang

Abstract Drawing on insights from both secular and religious sources, including the Aristotelian-Thomistic tradition and the Confucian Relational Self, the author presents a heuristic framework for a personalist relational philosophy (**"PRP"**) of human rights that can serve as a basis for global values and universal norms in a culturally diverse and pluralistic world. Human beings are both particular and universal, the one and the many, the self and the other, the subject and object of human rights and duties, of love and responsibility. The **PRP** presented here, underpinned by a realist anthropology and a critical-realist axiology, suggests how a holistic shift to the embodied relational self within a virtue-based personalist ethic of care can profoundly affect the clinical practice of bio-medicine and bio-ethics but also, inter alia, the ways in which the law structures rights and rights structure relationships and vice versa. This is part of an on-going search for an integral ecology, hermeneutics and praxis of human rights.

3.1 Introduction

The primary objective of this paper is to give a sketch of a heuristic framework for a *personalist relational philosophy* ("**PRP**") that will indicate how global values and universal human rights norms can be reasonably justified in a culturally diverse and pluralistic world.

As is made clear in Art. 12 of the UNESCO Universal Declaration of Bioethics and Human Rights, 2005 (the "**UDBHR**"), whilst "due regard" should be given to the importance of cultural diversity and pluralism, "such considerations are not to be invoked to infringe upon human dignity, human rights and fundamental freedoms, nor upon the principles set out in this Declaration, nor to limit their scope".

D. Chang (✉)
Denis Chang's Chambers, Hong Kong, SAR, China
e-mail: dlawchang@aol.com

J. Tham et al. (eds.), *Religious Perspectives on Bioethics and Human Rights*, Advancing Global Bioethics 6, DOI 10.1007/978-3-319-58431-7_3

The second, and related objective, is to suggest how a holistic shift to the embodied relational self within a personalist ethic of care can help mitigate the excessive individualism often associated with modern "Western" secular liberalism and, at the same time, the fragmentation and loss of identity that can result by the post-modern "splintering of the self".

Such a shift can have far-reaching implications not only with regard to the clinical practice of medicine and bioethics but can also, and more broadly, help to transform, *inter alia*, the ways in which the law structures rights and rights structure relationships. The relational lens, it is hoped, will bring into proper focus the "human" in "human rights" as part of an on-going search for an ecology, hermeneutics and praxis of human rights that best accord with the truth of the human condition and contribute to integral human development.

3.2 Self-Construals

Let me, then, take from social and cultural psychology three fundamental types or modes of "self-construal" (i.e. self-definition or self-representation), namely the individual self, the collective self and the relational self. These modes are sometimes also expressed in terms of "independent", "interdependent-collective" and "relational" self-construals.[1]

It is not suggested that one mode of self-definition or presentation necessarily excludes another; or that these are the only modes.[2] Nor is it suggested that we should limit ourselves to the data and insights gleaned from the social sciences alone. As is rightly noted in the Preamble of the UDBHR "*a person's identity includes biological, psychological, social, cultural and spiritual dimensions*".

I argue for an inter-disciplinary holistic approach that attests to the dynamic unity-in-diversity and multi-dimensional character of the *human person as a relational being* existing in a world which, despite human suffering and structures of alienation and of evil, is still mediated by meaning and capable of being trans-valued by love.

In inter-cultural mediation and trans-cultural understanding, an integral creative vision or shared horizon of civilizing values is called for but without falling into an easy eclecticism or a moral relativism under the guise of a pluralism that all-too readily allows "the substance of justice [to be] held hostage to the brute facts of global diversity. ".[3]

[1] Cross et al., *Handbook of Individual Differences in Social Behaviour*, eds. Mark R Leary & Rick Hoyle, 512–526, New York: Guilford (2009); and see also Cross in *Social and Personality Psychology Compass*, Vol. 3, Issue 6, pages 949 et seq. (December 2009).

[2] Sedikides, Gaertner, O'Mara, *Individual Self, Relational Self, Collective Self: - Hierarchical Ordering of the Tripartite Self,* Psychological Studies, 2011, Vol. 56, Number 1, Page 98.

[3] S. Macedo, *What Self-governing Peoples Owe to One Another: Universalism, Diversity, and the Law of Peoples,* Fordham Law Review (2004) 72(5) pp.1721–1738

3.3 What *Is* the Relational Self?

The motivational primacy of the "individual self" is an atomistic or monadic "I" at the centre of the moral universe whereas the "relational self" is motivated by an empathetic "I–and-Thou" in significant relationships, typically dyadic though not necessarily so. The "collective self" is chiefly driven by an undifferentiated "We" and "Us" of the collectivity.[4]

Relationships are constitutive of a person's character and very identity. A person, however, is not simply the sum total of his or her relationships. Notwithstanding contemporary hermeneutics of the self that speaks, for example, of the self existing only within "webs of interlocution",[5] there is an ontology of the self, or perhaps more accurately an ontology of the human person, with a reality that goes beyond partial perspectives offered by the empirical and social sciences.

The "relational self" that we speak of is "embodied, affective and relational,"[6] in other words it is that of a flesh-and-blood human being socially embedded in a web of relationships which crucially include close "nested" relationships but also extend or are capable of extending to and beyond those of family, friends, faith communities or other groups to which the person actually or potentially belongs. Indeed, it has a spiritual and a universal dimension, including the ecological, with an awareness and care of and concern for other selves and of the lifeworld and stewardship of the environment.[7]

3.4 What *Are* Basic Human Rights?

Human rights are entitlements or claims which everyone possesses simply by virtue of our nature as human beings.[8] I have used both the singular "everyone" and the plural "our" because we are both singular as well as plural. Each one of us, from the first moment of existence, is unique but all of us are members of the human race. As I see it, human rights are the expression of normative values based on basic human needs or goods and equal intrinsic human worth and dignity translated into claims of

[4] Sedikides and Brewer, *Individual Self, Relational Self, Collective Self*, Psychology Press, 01/gen/2001.

[5] Charles Taylor, *The Sources of the Self: The Making of Modern Identity*, Cambridge, MA: Harvard University Press, 1989 p 36.

[6] Jennifer Nedelsky, *Laws Relations*, Oxford University Press, New York, 2011 at p 33 et seq.

[7] See DeCicco & Stroink on the "*Meta-Personal Self*" in International Journal of Transpersonal Studies, 26, 2007. The characteristics of the "Meta-Personal Self" suggest that they can also be aspects of the relational self as presented here.

[8] Cf Jack Donnelly, *Universal Human Rights in Theory and Practice*, (Ithaca & London: Cornell University Press, 1989), 2nd edn, p 7 *et seq*. But see Michael Freeman, *Human Rights*, (UK & USA: Polity Press, 2002), pp. 60–62.

right and universal norms,[9] or at the very least "a right to have rights"[10] with co-relative duties, rooted in our shared humanity. The modern idiom for what historically was implied in the term "natural right" in the singular, and later better articulated in the plural, is transformed into what is to-day commonly called "human rights".[11]

The account I am giving does not deny the possibility of human transcendence or exclude religious or theistic underpinnings and dimensions of human sacredness and worth (e.g. by reference to *Imago Dei*) (Genesis 1:26). Such underpinnings provide ontological grounding for human sacredness and intrinsic dignity in a manner which the Kantian "autonomous self" or a purely immanent frame does not purport to nor can ever guarantee or supply on its own.

However, "both trajectories of anthropology, religious and secular, are necessary in fostering community in the 21st Century…. Most people live between two worlds, secular and religious, both of which inform their decisions and behaviour. Both discourses speak to our modern dilemma of how to be human in the face of the Other"[12]

The proposition that human beings have certain basic rights simply by virtue of our shared humanity implies that "*the basic rights of the human person…have always existed with the human being…independently of, and before, the State*"[13]

This means that basic human rights are not state-conferred but it does *not* mean that positive law has no role to play in their protection and realization. Positive law does have an important and in many cases a necessary role. There is the practical task of fleshing out and translating general principles into specific policies. The process *includes* what is called "*determinatio*" in Thomistic methodology, illustrated by the way in which practical reason resolves co-ordination problems by

---

[9] Denis Chang. *Human Rights: 'So They are Not for the State To Make' or Unmake? A Short Meta-Legal Meditation on the 'Human" in "Human Rights* (2010) HKLJ Vol. 40, Part 2 at p.154 et seq.

[10] An expression borrowed from Hannah Arendt, *The Origins of Totalitarianism*, N.Y., Schocken Books (1951)2004 Ed. with Edition with Introduction by Samantha Power), p 379. It is *not* suggested that H. Arendt, in the context of her reflections on statelessness, was using the expression in the same sense as it is used here or that it was based on the same rationale.

[11] Denis Chang, ibid. (see footnote 9). See also Brian Tierney, *The Idea of Natural Rights: Studies on Natural Rights, Natural Law and Church Law*, (Atlanta, Ga: Scholars Press, 1997),at pp. 1150–1625 and Nicholas Wolterstorff, *Justice – Rights and Wrongs*, (Princeton and Oxford: Princeton University Press, 2008), p45 et seq. For the view that the idea of natural rights originated neither in the Enlightenment nor in the individualistic philosophy of the late Middle Ages, but was already employed by the canon lawyers of the twelfth century.

[12] Michele Saracino, "*On Being Human*: *A Conversation with Lonergan and Levinas*", Marquette University Press (2003), Milwaukee, Wisconsin, at pp. 13 and 14.

[13] Judge Tanaka in the *South West Africa Cases* (Second Phase) ICJ Rep (1966) 5 at p 296, cited with approval in the decision of the Hong Kong Court of Final Appeal in the case of *Secretary of Justice v Yau Yuk Lung* (2007) 7 HKCFAR 385.

choosing between two options which are incompatible with each other but which are both consistent with the basic requirements of practical reasonableness.[14]

3.5 Are Particularity and Universality Incompatible?

Particularity and universality are not incompatible categories and can be mutually reinforcing.[15] As I see it in the present context, this is because human beings are both particular and universal, the one and the many, the self and the other, the subject and object of human rights and duties, of love and responsibility (*infra*).

In short, a human being is here to be taken both as *existential referent* and *concrete universal*, thus giving a basis for mediating between *particular* cultures and *universal* normative values. In my view, a human rights norm is universal not because of its abstractness but because of its potential completeness, not by stripping objects of their particularities but by envisaging human subjects in their necessities and situated-relatedness.[16]

Such "necessities" are conceived broadly in terms of the basic human goods needed for *eudaimonia* or flourishing of the human person as a relational being. They include, for example, respect for human life and dignity that is part of the intrinsic worth of each and every human being and what in justice is due to everyone simply by virtue of our shared humanity.

In this context, it has been rightly observed by John Finnis "…when we come to explain the requirements of justice, which we do by referring to the needs of the common good at its various levels, then we find that there is reason for treating the concept of duty, obligation or requirement as having a more strategic explanatory role than the concept of rights. The concept of rights is not on that account of less importance or dignity: for the common good is precisely the good of the individuals whose *benefit*, from fulfillment of duty by others, is their *right* because *required in justice* of those others".[17]

Of course not all values are normative and not all normative values are universal or translatable into human rights and duties. However, as noted in the opening words of the Preamble to the UDBHR, human beings have the "*unique capacity…to reflect upon their own existence and on their environment, to perceive injustice, to avoid danger, to assume responsibility, to seek cooperation and to exhibit the moral sense that gives expression to ethical principles*".

---

[14] Robert P. George, *Kelsen and Aquinas on the Natural-law Doctrine,* 75 Notre Dame L. Rev. 1625(2000). Available at: http://scholarship.law.nd.edu/ndlr/vol75/iss5/3

[15] Jacqueline A. Laing and Russell Wilcox, *The Natural Law Reader* (Wiley Blackwell, 2014) at p.342.

[16] Compare this with the definition of "universal viewpoint" by Bernard Lonergan in "Insight", *A Study of Human Understanding,* Fifth Edition (1992), Vol 3, at p. 590 in *Collected Works of Bernard Lonergan* ed. Crowe and Doran, University of Toronto Press, Toronto Buffalo London.

[17] John Finnis, 2011, *Natural Law and Natural Rights* (2nd Edition), Oxford, at p. 210.

3.6 A Critical- Realist Axiology: Realist Anthropology & the Ontic Value of Human Persons

It is precisely because of the unique capacity and moral sense that we have as human beings, possessed of both "speculative" (i.e. theoretical) reason and "practical reason" as well as inter-subjective feelings, emotions and empathy as part of our embodied human nature, that we are able to arrive at a firm grasp of values with the aid of human intuition and insights[18] and through a *combination* of experiencing, understanding, judging and deciding.

What I have just referred to above is the four-level dynamic structure of human knowing and acting as discussed extensively by Lonergan in his works.[19] The first three, relating to "data, concept, judgment", constitute the "critical-realist" component; the fourth level consists of *evaluation* and responsible action-oriented *decision,* the axiological and ethical component.

"Critical realism" insists that true knowledge can be achieved of the world, including the truth of the human condition in its embodied reality – hence "realist" – but that such knowledge is reached not just by taking an unreflective look (as in naïve realism) but through insight and grasp of what *is* (ontology) and what *ought* to be (values, ethics) through a process of experiencing, conceiving, judging and deciding.

Inasmuch as a knowledge of reality and especially human reality, is required in a judgment of value, the critical-realist component plays an essential part in the grasp of values. In my view, the values grasped include the ontic value of persons[20] and other normative values that are translatable into universal human rights and duties.

In other words, the *whole* person - with the capacity to make rational *and* affective judgments and responsible decisions– is engaged in the grasp of normative values[21] that pertain to what is true, right and good in the search for authentic human good and happiness not just for oneself but for others and indeed for "All-under-Heaven" (including the "future generations" referred to in Articles 2(g) and 16 of the UDBHR).

---

[18] These include what is called *synderesis* in Aquinas – a stock of effortless insights into basic reasons for action which help or direct the virtue of practical reasonableness – and *phronesis* (practical wisdom) in Aristotle. In Confucius, the *functional* equivalent of Aristotle's *phronesis* is *yi* (義) (which includes the notion of what is right and fitting) at least if *yi* is coupled with *zhi* (智), meaning wisdom.

[19] Bernard Lonergan, *Insight: A Study of Human Understanding*, eds. Frederick Crowe and Robert Doran, vol.3, *Collected Works of Bernard Lonergan* (Toronto: University of Toronto Press, 1992), chapter 18.2.3; see also a fuller analysis of the operations involved in the work referred to in Footnote 20 below.

[20] Bernard Lonergan, *Method in Theology (Toronto: University of Toronto Press, 1971),* at pp. 34–41.

[21] Insofar as ethical *decision* is oriented towards action and goes beyond mere *evaluation*, it can be regarded in Lonergan's schema as tending towards or forming part of a 5th level of consciousness and intentionality, namely that of responsible action or ethical living in which the *whole* acting person is likewise engaged.

The human faculties of "will" and "reason", so to speak, meet in the unity of the embodied subject as a feeling, willing, thinking and acting person whose intersubjective consciousness, structured by insight, is transformed into a conscience that can be both intensely personal and no less intensely social. It is also a conscience that can powerfully speak and act *through* as well as *transcend* the cultures and ethos of particular times and places.

The *realist anthropology* adopted here requires that we be attentive to all relevant data, including those facts as apprehended at the empirical, experiential and phenomenological levels, which speak to our human condition, including identity, singularity as well as solidarity.

This is of particular importance when we find it necessary to formulate concepts, discover or establish objective markers or criteria and make judgments and decisions relating, for example, to such matters as the beginning and end of human life and other questions regularly encountered in biomedicine and bioethics.[22]

An approach which is not rooted in a realist anthropology runs the risk of moral subjectivism and relativism and of introducing unjust and arbitrary discriminatory practices in violation of such fundamental principles as are encapsulated, for example, in the UDBHR and other human rights instruments which declare *all* human beings to have the right to life and to be equal in inherent dignity and fundamental rights.

3.7 Seeing Oneself as Another

The relational lens helps to bring into sharp focus the truth that care of the self necessarily includes care for others; although oneself is not the same as the other, it enables one to see oneself *as* another (to borrow the title of one of Paul Ricoeur's works, "*Oneself as Another*"[23]) and thus to see in the self the figure of "the other" such that the other must be treated alike as a fellow human being equal in intrinsic worth and inherent dignity despite difference, deprivation or distance.[24]

---

[22] Whilst practical reasoning proceeds from its own first principles (which Aquinas regarded as the basic precepts of natural law) and whilst the "ought" is not derived from the "is" in the manner of deductive or syllogistic reasoning (Hume), the information drawn from such disciplines as anthropology and sociology can be highly relevant and often indispensable to sound judgments of right and wrong e.g. a knowledge of human embryogenesis and intrauterine human development is critical to a proper application of moral principles to the question of abortion: Robert P. George, "*Kelsen & Aquinas on Natural Law,* ibid., *supra,* at p. 1627.

[23] Paul Ricoeur, *Oneself as Another, trans. Katheen Blamsey,* Chicago: University of Chicago Press, 1992 (1990).

[24] Denis Chang, ibid. at *p.256.*

"To kill a human being", says Jean-Francois Lyotard, "is not just to kill an animal of the species *Homo sapiens* but the human community present in the other as both capacity and promise".[25]

Those who believe that both the self and the other are made in the image of God (*Imago Dei*) will readily see a theistic grounding for the sacredness, inherent worth and inviolability of each and every human being. At the same time the relational lens used in PRP should help to correct some of the individualistic distortions of modern secular liberalism as well as the nihilistic tendencies of a postmodern centre-less splintering of the self.[26]

3.8 What *Is* Personalism?

"Personalism", which speaks of the central importance of the person, has many forms, as pointed out by Jacques Maritain in *the Person and the Common Good*[27] and other works. Maritain and Emmanuel Mounier were among the leading personalists of his day schooled in the Thomistic tradition. Mounier wrote: "…if the first condition of individualism is the centralization of the individual in himself, the first condition of personalism is his decentralization, in order to set him in the open perspectives of personal life".[28]

Another leading contemporary personalist, schooled both in Thomism and in the phenomenology of Max Scheler, was none other than Karol Wojtyla who delivered an important paper on "Thomistic Personalism" in 1961 at the Catholic University of Lublin and elaborated on the subject in his subsequent works before he became Pope John Paul II (and made various authoritative pronouncements on personalism after he became Pope).[29] One of the things that he attempted to do was to synthesize

---

[25] Jean-Francois Lyotard. *The Other's Rights* in *"On Human Rights,* The Oxford Amnesty Lectures, 1993, 1994", Shute & Hurley, eds. Basic Books, NY, at p 136.

[26] Stanley J A. Grenz. "*The Social God and the Relational Self*". Westminster John Knox Press, Louisville & London (2001), see in particular pages 133 et seq for Grenz's comments on Foucault's centre-less universe called"heterotopia" and "the chaotic self".

[27] Jacques Maritain. *"The Person and the Common Good" Notre Dame, IN: University of Notre Dame Press, 1985,* at pp. 12–13

[28] Emmanuel Mounier. "*Personalism*", first published in French 1950, English transl. Published in the States 1952, and London 1962.

[29] Karol Wojtyla, "*Thomistic Personalism*", English transl. From Polish, by Theresa Sandok, in" Person and Community": Selected Essays, Vol. 4 of Catholic Thought from Lublin, edited by Andrew N. Woznicki (New York: Peter Lang, 1993): 165–75. After he became Pope, Karol Wojtyla continued to invoke personalistic arguments, for example, in his Address to the International Theological Commission, December 5, 1983 in *Human Rights in the Teaching of the Church, from John XXIII to John Paul II, ed.* George Filibeck (Vatican City: Libreria Editrice Vaticana, 1994), 40 and in his encyclical letters *Laborem Exercens,* 15; and *Ut Unum Sint,* 28, *Letter to Families,* 14.

the metaphysical realism of Aristotle and Thomas Aquinas with the sensitivity to human experience of Max Scheler.[30]

Nevertheless, considered in its broadest sense as a philosophy which treats personality as a supreme value and the key in the search for self-knowledge and as a measure of reality, personalism in fact has a history which goes back to ancient times and its roots can be found in many cultures and parts of the world, including India, South East Asia, China and Japan. It spread to America where Martin Luther King Jr. translated into social action the personalism developed by people like Borden Parker Bowne and the African American John Bowen at Boston University. Martin Luther King Jr. regarded personalism as his basic philosophical position.[31]

3.9 What Form of Personalism Is Adopted Here? The Basic "PRP" Principles and Framework

The personalist relational framework presented here, and the realist anthropology on which it is based, may be elucidated by way of **eight overlapping propositions**, of which the first (*the principle of a shared humanity*) is ontologically prior to and underpins the rest and of which the last is the **Personalist Principle** which is a *practical* expression of the underlying philosophy.

1. **Despite human singularity and genetic diversity, human beings as members of the human race share a common humanity that is verified or attested to in a multitude of ways, including the empirical sciences, and accordingly because they are all beings of the same natural kind there is no rational basis for treating any human being as *intrinsically* different from another**.

In line with this principle of a shared humanity, the Universal Declaration on the Human Genome and Human Rights, adopted by UNESCO in 1997 and endorsed by the General Assembly of the UN the next year, proclaims in Article 1: "The human genome underlies the fundamental *unity* of all members of the human family as well as the recognition of their inherent dignity and fundamental freedoms." Article 2 goes out of its way to say that the dignity that "everyone" has makes it imperative not to *reduce* "*individuals*" to their genetic characteristics but requires respect for their uniqueness and diversity. It emphasizes that the recognition of the genetic diversity of humanity must not give rise to *any interpretation of a social or political nature* which could call into question "*the inherent dignity and....the equal and inalienable rights of all members of the human family*".

[30] See Thomas D. Williams, 2, *Who is my Neighbor? Personalism and the Foundations of Human Rights* (Catholic University of America Press, Washington, DC)(2005)

[31] See Rufus Burrows, "*Personalism, a Critical Introduction" St Louis, MO: The Chalice Press,* (1999).

2. **A human being possesses a rational nature which is what objectively and radically distinguishes a "person" from a non-person and therefore every human being *as such* is a person and must be treated accordingly.**[32]

Indeed it is worth noting that, quite apart from the fact that Universal Declaration of Human Rights, 1948 ("**UDHR**") refers to "everyone" and "all members of the human family", the terms "human person" and "human being" are justifiably used interchangeably in the UDBHR and other human rights instruments,some of which are recited in the UDBHR. Its Preamble refers to "the dignity of the human person" without differentiation from "the dignity of all human beings." Indeed, Article 10 of the UDBHR speaks of "the fundamental equality of **all** *human beings* in dignity and rights". I understand this to refer to the intrinsic equality in dignity and rights possessed by all human beings *as such.*

It follows that inasmuch as human rights are rights which human beings possess simply in virtue of their shared humanity, then it would be arbitrary and illogical to deny to babies (to take just one example) such fundamental human rights as the right to life. Indeed Article 6(1) of the International Covenant on Civil and Political Rights (the "**ICCPR"**) declares that "*all human beings* have an inherent right to life".

Thus, a baby is no less human and is entitled to no less love and protection than a fully grown adult able to reason and fend for himself or herself. Indeed the more vulnerable a human being is, the greater is the need for protection. I believe that an ideology that ignores, discriminates against or otherwise repudiates the rights of human beings especially those who are most in need of protection by categorizing them as non-persons and thus separating them from those deemed to be persons is thoroughly unjust and undermines the very basis on which the universality of human rights is founded.

3. **The uniqueness and centrality of the human person that must be accorded to all human beings in terms of equal intrinsic worth and dignity flows from that which radically distinguishes a person from a non-person**.

Only a person can simultaneously be a subject and an object. A person is not just a thing or a "what" but is a "who" (cf Paul Ricouer's "hermeneutics of the self" in which he distinguishes between what he calls "*idem*- identity" where the focus is on

[32]This is consistent with the famous and long-standing definition of "a person"by Boethius (ca.480–524.) Boethius defined a person as "an individual substance [subject] of a rational nature" ("*Persona est. rationalis naturae individua substantia*"). Aquinas reformulated it as "*individuo subsistens in rationali natura*": see Laura Palazzani, *Introduction to the Philosophy of Biolaw,* English Trans. by Victoria Bailes, Edizioni Studium (2009), Rome, at page 31 et seq, where Palazzani explains that by thus applying a concept of individual substance to a human being. "it becomes clear that the functions which he exercises and the acts which he undertakes do not exist in themselves, but exists only as functions and acts "of" a substantial human individual, which is their singular and permanent reference point, their real ontological condition. "In line with Aquinas' definition, Karol Woytyla in his 1961 paper (ibid., *footnote 29*), defined a person to mean "*a subsistent subject of existence and action*".

the "what" and "*ipse*-identity" where the focus is on the "who")[33]: Martin Buber speaks of the "I-Thou" and the "I-It" ways of dealing with reality and posits the "I-Thou" way as the ideal for the human person's dealing with all reality[34] whereas other personalists would say that the I-Thou way is the only appropriate way of dealing with persons and the "I-It" way with mere things. In any event it is the *possession* of a rational nature that makes the radical difference between a person and a thing, and not the actual *exercise* or the ability to exercise any particular capability that flows from that nature at any particular moment or stage of life of a living being. In other words: "It is not the *expression* of rationality that makes us human but it is belonging to a kind that is capable of rationality that makes us human".[35]

4. **Human beings possess an "interiority" and "subjectivity" that is irreducibly rooted in their very nature as human beings with all that flows therefrom, whether actualized or only existing potentially, such as rational self-consciousness, free will, conscience, moral agency, autonomy and self-determination.**[36]

It is in this context, without falling into any mind-body dualism or destroying the unity of the human subject, that one can speak of the intellectual and spiritual nature of the human person, of human intuition, insight and creativity, of the human "psyche", of human beings as "causes of their own actions" and of certain distinctively human capabilities whether actualized or existing potentially, including the capacity for self-transcendence and authenticity.

5. **At the same time, precisely because they are both subjects as well as objects, human persons can affect and be affected not only by "internal" as well as "external" realities and events, including cultural and environmental, but also by their own and others' dispositions, choices and actions, thereby engaging or bringing into salience moral/ethical and other distinctively human dimensions and concerns.**

These include what claims one can in justice make upon and what co-relative or other duties are owed by or to others as individuals or groups or the community as a whole or the rest of the humanity and the lifeworld. As stated in Article 29(1) of the UDHR "*everyone has duties to the community in which alone the free and full development of his personality is possible*". It is in this context that we can intelligibly speak of such things as responsibility in freedom, of civic friendship and of human solidarity as well as of stewardship of the earth and its resources.

[33] Paul Ricouer, "*Oneself as Another*", ibid. at pp. 147–148.

[34] Martin Buber, "*I-and-Thou*" English ed. translated from the German *Ich und Du* (2nd Ed., 1923) by Ronald Gregor Smith. Edinburgh: T & T Clark, 1987.

[35] Daniel Sulmasy, *Perspectives in Human Dignity – A Conversation* eds. Malpas & Lickiss, Springer 2007, Chap. 2, at p. 16). See also Laura Palazzani, "*Introduction to the Philosophy of Biolaw*", ibid. at p. 33 et seq.

[36] See Karol Wojtyla, ibid. at p. 178.

6. **Human persons possess, as a deeply ingrained and constitutive part of their embodied, inter-subjective, affective and relational nature, not simply a capacity for social relations that is generally acknowledged to be part of human sociality but a disposition towards inter-personal communion.**

At least four aspects may be highlighted here. In the *first* place, a profound difference exists between mere sociality and a disposition towards inter-personal communion. As pointed out by Aristotle in his thesis that man is by nature a political animal[37] there are aspects of man's social nature which are shared by some animal species but not, *inter alia*, the capacity for *logos* or speech that forms an important aspect of human communicative action. *Secondly*, inter-personal communion paradoxically requires a capacity for freedom of choice or self-determination in that the deepest inter-personal communion involves total mutual self-giving in freedom and in love. This goes beyond the language of rights to that of unconditional gift. *Thirdly*, the human person is a "being-for-others" and all that I have said about the capacity of the relational self to see in the self a figure of the other applies here. *Fourthly*, all this fundamentally distinguishes inter-personal communion from individualism on the one hand and collectivism on the other.

7. **It is in the capacity for and disposition towards inter-personal communion, and in the practice of virtues which puts love and compassion and self-giving at the heart of ethics, that the human person finds his or her true self and becomes a relational locus of human flourishing *for* and *with* others as individuals and in community of which "the family is a natural fundamental group unit"** (cf Article 23 of the ICCPR).

This proposition brings *virtue-ethics* into the PRP framework, integrating it with an ethic of benevolence and care and authentic human flourishing in its all various dimensions, including the personal, the familial and the communal. In this context, the common good is to be understood as the sum of those conditions which allow human persons as relational beings full and ready access to their own integral human development as individuals and in community.

I should mention in passing that although the words "*benevolence*" and "*beneficence*" are sometimes used interchangeably, I use the term "benevolence" to include both subjective well-wishing and feelings of goodwill towards as well acts and deeds directed at benefiting others ("beneficence"). Ethicists distinguish between "obligatory" beneficence and "ideal" beneficence somewhat similar to the way in which "commandments" may be distinguishable, though not always, from "counsels of perfection".

In the context of human rights and duties:-

(i) The notion of beneficence and care is not necessarily inconsistent with *rights-based* norms. The law is often called upon to deal with rights and duties arising

[37] See Aristotle, (*Pol*, 1,2, 1253a), *Politics*, trans. E. Barker (Oxford University Press, Oxford), 1948.

in situations of dependence and vulnerability, especially in education and healthcare including bio-medicine. A duty of beneficence and care may, as a matter of social justice and social welfare, generate or co-relate with rights of the child, the elderly, the poor, the sick, the disabled and others most in need of care and protection; the law may even impose a duty of beneficence and care on humans even where there is no mutuality between subject and object e.g. the prohibition against cruelty to animals and laws protecting the environment.

(ii) Moreover, where *conflicts* of rights and/or duties actual or potential arise in situations of vulnerability and relationships of dependency, the resolution of the conflict between the parties affected (e.g. by acting *in favour* of the more vulnerable party) may be dictated or facilitated by considerations of justice which do *not* exclude those of beneficence and care. It is only by such and other relevant considerations that one right will not arbitrarily be allowed to be trumped by another, especially where there is asymmetry and no equality of bargaining power.

(iii) Further, the integration of *virtue-ethics* with the ethic of care and authentic human flourishing resonates with the Confucian Relational Self (*infra*) and, in varying degrees, with values from different religions and traditions mentioned below. It also underlines the importance of a holistic approach to human rights and duties and of *right relations*. To exclude considerations of right relations from justice and human rights and divorce the ethic of care and authentic human flourishing from virtue-based ethics (virtues being *habits,* and not mere abstract principles, of right thinking and right action) would be to impoverish each of the concepts employed and lead to inauthenticity, self-contradiction and fragmentation.

8. ***The Personalist Principle*:- No human being must ever be used as a mere means to an end. *All* human beings by reason of their nature must be respected as *persons* of equal *intrinsic* worth and dignity *and* must also be treated with benevolence and care**.

This principle includes but goes beyond the Kantian imperative of according respect to and never using human beings as mere means to an end. It extends to treating all human beings as persons and with benevolence and care[38] (especially those who are most vulnerable and in need of protection and who may be in no position to reciprocate).

Love and responsibility, compassion and benevolence and the ethic of care are at the axiological core of most cultures and religions: the Judeo-Christian "*agape*", the Christian "*caritas*", the Confucian "*ren*" (仁), the Daoist "*ci*"(慈), the Buddhist and Hindu "*karuna*" and "*ahimsa*", the Islamic "*rahmah*" (although I am far from suggesting that there are no differences in meaning between these key concepts).

---

[38] Compare this with the formulation of the Personalist Principle by Domènec Melé in "*Integrating Personalism into Virtue-Based Business Ethics: The Personalist and the Common Good Principles*", *Journal of Business Ethics (2009) 88:227–214,* Springer.

The principles of *alterity* and good neighbourliness are reflected in the Good Samaritan parable in Luke 10:25–37 and that of *reciprocity* is encapsulated in "the Golden Rule" in its various formulations, both positive as in Mathew 7:12 and negative as in Confucius' *Doctrine of the Mean* (中庸 Ch. XIII. 3) but with Mencius declaring that the Confucian *zhong shu* (忠恕) way of reciprocity is "the shortest route to benevolence" and that it is not just a negative injunction (*Mencius,* Bk VII, Pt. I, Ch. IV.3).

3.10 The "Confucian Relational Self": Personalistic & Naturalistic Elements

Especially in societies in which Confucianist ideas and attitudes still play a cultural role, an understanding of the "Confucian Relational Self" is important not only to the clinical practice of healthcare and bio-medicine (including in particularly the care of the elderly) but generally. The deeply relational nature of Confucian ethics is reflected, amongst other things, in the Chinese term for ethics "*lun-li*" (倫理) which means the principles of relationships. Thus insofar as Confucianist philosophy as well as the PRP are both imbued with relationality, there is present in both a shared key personalist element (among others, *infra*).

It is true that of the five Confucian role relationships or *wu-lun* (五倫) (traditionally expressed in terms of ruler-subject, father-son, elder brother-younger brother, husband-and-wife and friend- and- friend) four are not equal and only the fifth is equal or dyadic. However, the Confucian Relational Self includes but goes far beyond the five role relationships.

A person's relationships embrace all that is affected by the cultivation and practice of the four Confucian principal virtues, namely those of humanitarian-benevolence (*ren*) (仁), appropriateness (*yi*) (義), propriety (*li*) (禮) and wisdom (*zhi*) (智), "*ren*" being the inner aspect of "*li*" (sometimes translated as "ritual propriety" but which means more than mere external observance of "rites"). "*Ren*" (仁) is the key source and condition of other virtues. Indeed it is the virtue or quality that makes one a human being. "*Ren zhe ren ye*" (仁者人也) in the *Doctrine of the Mean* (Ch.XX.0.5) may be translated as "Benevolence is man" or as "To be *ren* is to be a human being".

Consistent with the Confucian doctrine of "rectification of names" (正名*zhengming*), which is based on the principle that language should be in accordance with the truth of things (Analects Bk XIII, Ch.III.3, 5) the *junzi* (君子) is a person who in observing the outer virtue of "*li*" (禮) or ritual propriety must conform to and manifest the inner virtue of *ren* without which mere external rituals become empty and meaningless. In order to be and to merit the name of *junzi*, therefore, a human being must embody existentially *in his person* the quality of *ren* and *in his actions* the quality of "*yi*" (義) meaning what is right and fitting.

At the heart of Confucius' thinking is the idea that there is a natural capacity or basis for goodness in human beings. Confucius presupposes that there is *"dao-de"* (道德) under Heaven or a way of ethics that leads to virtue ("*de*") (德), the *de* in human life being derived from Heaven's *"dao"* (道). Confucius speaks of a heavenly mandate to restore the "*dao*" of Heaven by the cultivation of the self ("*shiu ji*") (修己) and it is by such a process that "*ren*" and all that which characterizes a person of excellence and virtue ("*junzi*") (君子) can be achieved.[39]

In the Confucian *Doctrine of the Mean* (Ch.XXII) we find a famous passage on authenticity ("c*heng*" 誠), translated by James Legge as "the most complete sincerity", which begins with the words: "It is only he who is possessed of the most complete sincerity that can exist under heaven ("*tian xia zhi cheng*" 天下至誠) who can give its full development to his own nature ("*xing*" 性), and, by reason of that ability, "he can do the same to the nature of other men" and then "he can give their full development to the natures of animals and things" and then "he can assist the transforming and nourishing the powers of Heaven and Earth" and then "he may with Heaven and Earth form a ternion." ("唯天下至誠,為能盡其性。能盡其性,則能盡人之性;能盡人之性,則能盡物之性;能盡物之性,則可以贊天地之化育;可以贊天地之化育,則可以與天地參矣。").

In Confucianism, therefore, the cultivation (*"shiu ji")* (修己) of the authentic *"junzi"* (君子) or person of virtue and excellence has not only a personal dimension but also a much larger and indeed even a cosmic significance. "Ternion" here effectively means a trinity of Man, Heaven and Earth. Confucius puts the full integral development of human personality or character at the centre of his ethical concerns. His concept of human relationships *inter-se* is always in terms of relations between concrete human beings.[40] He speaks of human nature and of self-cultivation in terms which pre-suppose that there is an individual substance or ontology of the self (or, more accurately, an ontology of the self-cultivating person). A human being must first exist before his or her capacities can be actualized or fully realized.

In the context of the expression "*tian xia zhi cheng*" 天下至誠, the word "*cheng*" (誠) does not simply mean "honesty" or "complete sincerity" but has been appropriately interpreted by Jiyuan Yu to mean "self-completion" in the sense of the highest manifestation of human excellence (*ren*).[41] In order to bring out more explicitly the notions of authenticity and integral human development in the passage I have

[39] See Jiyuan Yu, *Confucius' Relational Self and Aristotle's Political Animal*, History of Philosophy Quarterly, Vol. 22, Number 4, October 2005.

[40] See Qingjie James Wang, "*Genealogical Self and a Confucian Way of Self-Making*", International Philosophical Quarterly Vo. 42, No. 1 Issue 165 (March 2002), especially at pp. 100–102: "Relationships are important to a Confucian, but the persons who make the relationships possible cannot simply be reduced or forfeited within the relations. Therefore, a Confucian not only thinks that a human self is relational or *inter*-personal but, more importantly that the self is an inter-*personal* being. The emphasis on the personal nature of human social and communal relations, I believe, will help us to understand better the historical, hierarchical, and bodily characteristics of the Confucian 'relational self'"(ibid. at p 102).

[41] Jiyuan Yu. "*The Ethics of Confucius and Aristotle: Mirrors of Virtue.*" *(New York and London: Routledge, 2007),* xii, at p 177.

referred to above (Chapter XXII of *The Doctrine of the Mean))* I would respectfully suggest that "*cheng*" in its context be translated as *authentic* self-completion.

In my view, the concept of "*cheng*", in its context, can serve at least as a functional equivalent of *eudaimonia*. Confucius takes a holistic approach to the making of an authentic "*junzi*" by combining in the "*junzi*" all the cardinal Confucian virtues the realization of which is necessary for full integral development or human flourishing. **In short, important aspects of the key elements mentioned in Proposition 7 above and which form part of the personalistic approach are present in varying degrees in Confucianist thinking.**[42]

In my view, there are both personalistic as well as naturalistic elements in Confucianist thinking which can contribute to a natural law theory that is based on what characterizes and befits us all as relational beings with a shared humanity - in other words, on the "*renxing*"(人性) which is part of our human nature (and which is what distinguishes us from mere things and non-persons) and through the cultivation and authentic completion of which the "ternion" or union of three between Man, Heaven and Earth is fully achieved (*supra*).[43]

I am here using the terms "human being" and "human person" interchangeably for reasons already given in the discussion of the personalist relational framework, and for the additional reason that in Confucianism there is, as far as I am aware, no separate notion of a "human person" as distinguished from a "human being". This is not surprising. The recognition of human dignity and human rights in the "West" was historically also not based on any separationist theory between human beings and human persons. On the contrary, it was based on the affirmation that all human

[42] As regards problems of incommensurability that may need to be addressed or explored, see Alasdair MacIntyre, "*Incommensurability, Truth, and the Conversation Between Confucians and Aristotelians About Virtues*" in Eliot Deutsch, ed., *Culture and Modernity* (Honolulu: University of Hawaii Press, 1991) pp. 105, 106, 112. For an argument against MacIntyre, see David Hall and Roger Ames, *Thinking from the Han* (Albany; State University of New York Press, 1998) pp. xii-xv. See Sor-Hoon Tan, "*Cultural Crossings Against Ethnocentric Currents: Towards a Confucian Ethics of Communicative Virtues* "in the International Philosophical Quarterly (December, 2005). See Vincent Shen "*Creativity as Synthesis of Contrasting Wisdoms: An Interpretation of Chinese Philosophy in Taiwan since 1949*" Philosophy East and West: A Quarterly of Comparative Philosophy 43 (1993) 43: at pp. 178–287.

[43] The *Book of Odes* speaks of Heaven producing the teeming masses and that "*where there is a thing there is a norm*" 有物有則 (cited by Mencius at Bk. 6, Pt. I, Ch. VI. 8). According to Mencius, Confucius himself affirms the principle, adding the word 必 or "must" for emphasis, saying 故有物,必有則 "where there is a thing, there *must* be a norm" (Mencius at Bk VI,Pt. I, Ch.VI.8). It is clearly implicit in Confucian ethics that *where there is a human being, there must be a norm.* Confucius himself has in effect taught what that norm consists of - authentic self-completion of the person of virtue and excellence, the *junzi,* in which what is achieved is the unity of human, heaven and earth through obedience to Heaven's Will and the realization of the cardinal virtues, primarily *ren*. I have elsewhere suggested that, in line with the Confucian doctrine of "rectification of names", the notion of natural law should *not* be literally translated into Chinese as *ziranfa* 自然法 but should be translated by reference to the Confucian concept of *xing* 性 (nature) or *renxing* 人性 (human nature but here meaning the rational and humanitarian or best part of human nature, *ren*). The translations I have suggested for "natural law" are either "*renxing ziranfa*" 人性自然法 or better still *renxing gongtongfa* 人性共同法 which means a norm, springing from co-humanity, which is common to all human beings by reason of that which characterizes and befits us all as fellow human beings. See Denis Chang, ibid. at page 257.

beings share the same nature and are intrinsically different from mere things and non-persons and not intrinsically different from one another and must therefore all be treated as persons.[44]

3.11 Relevance to Bioethics & Human Rights

Much of biomedicine is concerned with rights and duties in the contexts of the beginning and end of human life and other settings in which human beings are at their most vulnerable and in need of respect, benevolence and relational support and care; bioethics of course also includes within its concerns such ethical issues as unethical human experimentation and inhumane treatment of animals in scientific and medical research, and the use and abuse of technology.

Thus compassion and a personalist ethic of relational care are accordingly profoundly relevant to healthcare in general and biomedicine in particular; and what are often referred to as the four principles of biomedical ethics - **autonomy**, **beneficience**, **non-maleficence** and **justice**[45] can in varying degrees be engaged or are directly or indirectly affected thereby. A shift to the relational self can affect, for example, how physicians and care-givers approach the issues of informed consent, truth-telling and shared healthcare decision-making in different cultural settings, with different competing models being applied or proposed such as "paternalistic, informative, interpretative and deliberative".[46]

It is too early to say what precise impact, if any, such a shift will have in all the varied circumstances of so many places and cultures. In all this one has to take into account such crucial factors as what the law says and the courts' attitudes especially in places where the rule of law is well developed. For example, it is now just over two decades since the landmark Judgment of *Re C (adult: refusal of treatment)* [1994] 1 All ER 819 in England which held that a competent patient's rights to refuse treatment must prevail over the clinical views of what would be in the patient's "best interest".[47] Would it make any difference if a similar problem had presented itself today with all the members of the family except the patient fully

---

[44] For an insightful and succinct sketch and critique of various philosophies or ethical positions which conflict with the PRP presented here and which introduce separation theories putting human beings into different categories see Laura Palazzani's *Introduction to the Philosophy of Biolaw, ibid.*, at pages 13–48.

[45] Thomas J. Beauchamp and James Childress, *Principles of Biomedical Ethics*, Fourth Edition. Oxford. 1994

[46] See Joseph Tham and Maria Catherine Letendre, "Healthcare Decision Making: Cross-cultural Analysis of the Shift from the Autonomous to the Relational Self," *The New Bioethics* 20.2 (2014), 174–185.

[47] See David Gurnham in Special 20th Anniversary issue of Medical Law International: "*Best interests in an age of human rights*" (2013) Medical Law International 13(1), 3–5. See also Jonathan Herring, "*Forging a relational approach: Best Interests or human rights?*" Medical Law International 2013 13:32 available at http://mli.sagepub.com/content/13/1/32

supporting the doctors' views? Regardless of the family background and relationships, would the courts still say that the patient's autonomy should trump everything else, including his or her own best interest? If not, why not?

The notion of "**relational autonomy**" in feminist writings e.g. those of Jennifer Nedelsky[48] carries certain tensions and potential conflicts with such concepts as that of self-determination which need to be addressed.[49] The notion of "relational human dignity" needs to be explored in terms of the different interpretations of dignity, including "**intrinsic dignity**" meaning the worth that people have simply because they are human (as used, for example, by Kant), "**attributed dignity**" meaning dignity conferred by others (Hobbes' use of the term) and "**inflorescent dignity**" meaning dignity derived from a virtue which is congruent with intrinsic dignity (Aristotle's use of the term).[50]

Insofar as I am able to discern, Confucius' use of the term" *junzi*" (君子) incorporates a notion of dignity that rests on complete authenticity, is fully in accord with intrinsic dignity that comes from the possession of *renxing* and the natural capacity for goodness and is also a dignity that is *derived* from cultivation of virtues that are *congruent* with intrinsic dignity. There is at the same time an absolute refusal in Confucius' ethics to add by *attribution* any undeserved or false dignity to a "small person"(*xiaoren)* (小人) who is the opposite of a *junzi*. Thus for Confucius, intrinsic, attributed and inflorescent dignity (*supra*) converge and are embodied in the person of the *junzi.*

3.12 Concluding Remarks: Towards a New Ecology, Hermeneutics and Praxis of Human Rights?

Insofar as the personalist framework needs to be "fleshed out" or "filled in" in accordance with the PRP principles it retains a heuristic dimension, enabling the further determination and specification to be made where necessary by way of a process which involves the derivation from very general first order principles of practical reason (which can be as general as "good is to be done and evil is to be avoided") to more concrete second order principles and the solution of co-ordination problems via the method of *"determinatio"* mentioned earlier.[51]

The relatively young discipline of "biolaw" always seems to lag behind the rapid developments in biomedicine and the life sciences. Nevertheless, that there is increasing interest in the relational self is borne out in many ways and reflected in

---

[48] Jennifer Nedelsky, "*Law's Relations*", *ibid.,* pp. 38, 45, 54, 59, 65, 118 et seq

[49] See John Christmas, "*Relational Autonomy, Liberal Individualism and the Social Constitution of Selves*" in Philosophical Studies 117: 143–164, 2004 for a critique of "relational autonomy" (including proceduralist and non-proceduralist notions).

[50] Daniel Sulmacy, "*Perspectives on Human Dignity*", ibid., at p. 10

[51] See John Finnis in *Aquinas*. (New York: Oxford University Press, 1998) at pp. 267–274.

the growing literature on the subject. It is not restricted to biomedicine and bioethics.

Indeed there have been and are continuing attempts to generate new rights, such as collective rights and environmental rights, using relationships as the foundation.[52] There are also attempts to use the relational approach by governments, at least professedly, to reduce confrontation and foster a more harmonious society.

In Singapore, for example, we see the development of what is there called "**relational constitutionalism**" in order to advance a communitarian policy and also to manage religious disputes within a multi-religious contexts by using non-judicial methods rather than law-based and rights-based approaches.[53]

It is outside the scope of this paper to do a full critique of the Singapore model or of the *hexie shehui* (和諧社會) or "harmonious society" model on which the so-called *hexiequan* (和諧權) or "harmony rights" advocated by authorities in Mainland China are professedly based.[54]

I wish, however, to make the following ten bullet-points as my concluding remarks:

(i) The **PRP** presented here is more than just a *relational* approach to human rights; it is a *personalist* relational philosophy. Relationality comes into it because human beings are by nature relational. In short there is not just the **R** that is in the middle of **the two P'**s but also the **two P's** themselves.

(ii) It follows, therefore, that under **the PRP framework** the human person remains at the centre of human rights concerns as both subject and object. Without this the universality of the norms could easily be undermined and the norms themselves short-changed into putative "rights" which can be made or unmade at will by the state, thereby facilitating abuse of power and suppression of legitimate dissent in the name of harmonious relations. The power of rights would then always be subordinated to the rights of power.

---

[52] See, for example, Richard Hiskes, *The Relational Foundation of Emergent Human Rights: From Thomas Hobbes to the Human Right to Water* (2010) APSA 2010, APSA 2010 Annual Meeting Paper, available at SSRN: http://ssm.com. See also Pamela J. Lomelino, "*Individuals and Relational Beings: Expanding the Universal Human Rights Model*", Social Philosophy Today 23 (2009): 87–102. See Ruth Zafran. "*Children's Rights as Relational Rights: The Case of Relocation*", Journal of Gender, Social Policy & the Law [Vol. 18:2, 163 et seq], 2010.,

[53] Li–Ann Thio. *"Relational Constitutionalism and the Management of Religious Disputes: The Singapore "Secularism with a Soul" Model.* Oxford Journal of Law and Religion (2012) 1(2) 446–469.

[54] Xinhua News, "CCP Central Committee Resolution on the Construction of a Socialist Harmonious Society"18 October2006. http://news/xinhuanet.com/politics/2006-10/18/content_5218639.htm. The term *hexiequan* ("harmony rights") was reportedly first used by Xu Xianming of the China University of Politics and Law at an international conference in 2006 in a paper entitled "*Hexiequan: Di sidai renquan" ("Harmony Rights": The Fourth Generation of Human Rights)* which generated much satirical comment and adverse criticism from netizens, human rights lawyers and others: http://211.167.236.236/china/newzt/2006magazine/2006020064 24160801htm and see Eva Pils: *The Dislocation of the Chinese Human Rights Movement* in "*A Sword and a Shield"* eds Stacy Mosher and Patrick Poon, published in 2009 by China Human Rights Lawyers Concern Group Lawyers, pp. 141–149.

(iii) This is not to say that the **"R"** in between the two P's is not important. It actually has a triple significance, first in terms of **relationality**, second in terms of **rights** and third in terms of the **Confucian *"ren"***.
(iv) Notwithstanding the philosophical underpinnings, the **PP or Personalist Principle** is a *practical* expression of the personalist relational approach. It boils down to saying that all human beings must not only be respected in their intrinsic worth and dignity as persons but also be loved.
(v) Thus the **PP** is a practical proposition which can be accepted by religious and non-religious people alike even if they are not entirely in agreement regarding the precise philosophical justification of the principle.
(vi) There is really nothing mysterious or esoteric about the philosophical justification offered here. The starting point is a realist anthropological principle that we are all human relational beings because of a shared common nature.
(vii) The common nature we speak of is the "X" that makes us all fellow human beings and at the same time distinguishes us from mere things and non-persons. We should all therefore be treated as persons who have basic rights and fundamental freedoms and dignity by virtue of being human.
(viii) A truly "relational" state should give concrete expression to and uphold all those basic rights, freedoms and human dignity which are intrinsic to our nature of relational human beings. The fact that many people believe that human beings are created by a loving, merciful and relational God should be an added reason for recognizing the sacredness and intrinsic worth and dignity of human beings.
(ix) An awareness of our relationality should help us to value civic friendship and human solidarity and mitigate unbridled individualism on the one hand and fragmentation of the self on the other. Our shared human nature should at the same time help us to understand and learn from one another and to have cultural sensitivity and cross-cultural mediation in the working out and implementation of human rights and freedoms without short-changing basic global values and norms.
(x) An understanding of rights and freedoms in relational terms in a personalist framework should therefore help in our on-going search for a new ecology, hermeneutics and praxis of human rights which will uphold our fundamental rights and freedoms, not allow one right to be wrongly and unfairly trumped by another, and at the same time lead to a truly harmonious and just society that includes within its vision human flourishing *and* protection and care of the most vulnerable.

Chapter 4
Convergence of Human Rights and Duties: Towards a Global Bioethics

Alberto Garcia, John Lunstroth, Dominique J. Monlezun, and Claudia R. Sotomayor

Abstract Global bioethics is an emerging concept. In 2005 the UNESCO Universal Declaration on Bioethics and Human Rights was passed by the acclamation of 193 states. In spite of that, some critics argue that ethical relativism is so deeply engrained it prevents the emergence of substantive universal norms, permitting only procedural approaches to shared norms. We question that conclusion. An examination of the notions of rights, duties and dignity in the major religious traditions suggests that there may be paths, through those concepts, to substantive normative convergence. If rights and duties are seen as a unitary thing then their ideological functions will not play such a prominent role in divisiveness among the traditions, but the unified concept(s) could encourage convergence towards norms acceptable to all traditions.

Keywords Global bioethics • Cultural diversity • Religious pluralism • Human rights

---

A. Garcia (✉) • C.R. Sotomayor
UNESCO Chair in Bioethics and Human Rights, Rome, Italy
e-mail: agg@arcol.org; csotomayor@unescobiochair.org

J. Lunstroth
Health Law & Policy Institute, University of Houston Law Center, Houston, TX, USA
e-mail: lunstroth@gmail.com

D.J. Monlezun
Tulane School of Medicine, New Orleans, LA, USA

Ateneo Pontificio Regina Apostolorum, Rome, Italy
e-mail: dmonlezu@unescobiochair.org

J. Tham et al. (eds.), *Religious Perspectives on Bioethics and Human Rights*,
Advancing Global Bioethics 6, DOI 10.1007/978-3-319-58431-7_4

4.1 Introduction

Bioethics emerged as an interdisciplinary academic field in the latter half of the twentieth century in response to the ethical dilemmas surrounding the concept of the person that were spurred by technological progress in the health sciences. Most developed countries today allow a widening influence of bioethics on public policy and international relations, as national bioethics committees range from the Japanese Ad Hoc Committee on Brain Death and Organ Transplantation to the Mexican National Bioethics Committee (Beauchamp and Childress 2001).

These national entities are joined on the international stage by such bioethics bodies as the UNESCO and its Universal Declaration of Bioethics and Human Rights, the World Health Organization (WHO), non-governmental organizations (NGOs) such as the Council for International Organizations of Medical Sciences (CIOMS) and the World Medical Association (WMA), and other academic and normative institutions across the globe. The project of global bioethics emerged in conjunction with the spread of scientific medicine after World War II. Early on NGOs such as the WMA and the CIOMS published norms on the doctor/patient relationship and then the regulation of scientific research in foreign jurisdictions, especially considering human experimentation undertaken by Northern and Western states in Southern and Eastern states. After the end of the Cold War globalization took off rapidly. The conditions for it in the life-sciences began about 1980, when Reagan and Thatcher promoted the value of capitalism in their respective legal systems. When the Cold War ended the international legal order was ripe for instrumentalization by the life-sciences oligarchy, the global pharmaceutical, agriculture, chemical and other life-sciences transnational corporations. The Western life-sciences as ideology and practice are now ubiquitous over the globe, but the normative systems that constrain and inform it in the West, bioethics, have not followed the life-sciences into all the jurisdictions in which the globalizing powers are trying to establish them (for the purposes of markets for drugs and devices, for sources of humans for experimentation, and for resources). A global discussion about regulation of the life-sciences is greatly needed.

Within our current era characterized by pluralism, globalization and diversity, the question as to whether or not there a global bioethics that can span different civilizations, traditions and religions becomes of utmost importance if we are to secure some sort of shared normative order and adequately regulate medical and technological advancements within our shared global society. In our current era of globalization, a pressing question that must be addressed is whether there is, or is not, a global bioethics. Contemporary societies are characterized by plurality and diversity, challenging aspirations of ethical consensus. Given this situation, it may appear that any substantive resolution of ethical dilemmas through a common global bioethics framework may be destined to fail.

In our search for foundations of a global ethics, we sometimes use the word *universal* synonymously with *global*. The word universal is confusing inasmuch as it both refers to an Aristotelian notion of the universal, and to an Enlightenment notion. (Lunstroth 2015). The Enlightenment notion, with roots in medieval Augustinian theology, refers to a law-like principle that applies to a defined territory for all time. For example, the laws of physics are said to be universal in this way. We call this strict or legal universalism. In contrast, Aristotle, who coined the term/concept, used it to refer to a whole, and associated it with identity, species, parts and other related concepts. E.g., the characteristics of a species are universals. Western liberalism assumes about the human species that its main components are individuals, each with free will, rights, duties and dignity, and that these individuals live in a world best described in the framework of a system of strict universals defined and explored by the hard sciences. As a foundational matter we reject strict universalism for living things, such as species. When we refer to the universal, we are referring to an Aristotelian universal. At the same time we recognize another of Aristotle's fundamental propositions, that there are no parts without first there being a whole. Given this metaphysical context, we seek to relate the particulars of individual human beings as seen by their religions or tradition to species norms or universals. We use a system of logic that is neither inductive (in a Humean sense) nor deductive, but proceeds through a direct recognition of the universal in the repeated particular. (Aristotle 1984, 166; *Apo* 100a15-b5).

One way to explore the possibility of a relatively universal system of norms is through the notion of religion. Religion is a vague word that best works as a reference to the "monotheistic" or Abrahamic traditions, Judaism, Christianity and Islam. If the notion is used to refer also to Hinduism, Buddhism, and Confucianism/Taoism, words that refer more to collections of ways to live, then we can say nearly 90% of the world's population identifies with at least one religion (USCIA 2010). If we consider these ways of life as consisting of well-articulated substantive systems of belief and values then we can query whether they have similarities in the way they approach regulating the life-sciences.

After Rawls we think of such problems as questions of justice, and we understand that there are general procedural and substantive ways of analyzing justice problems. Is there a universal system of justice that orders the relationship between the life-sciences and the larger civic order within which it exists? Rawls' "overlapping consensus" would perhaps be the most well-known path to an answer, focusing on commensurabilities in higher order ethical structures such as manifest in systems of justice.

In Part II we distinguish our approach from that of Rawls. Rawls began his analysis of political agreement, or overlapping consensus, assuming a liberal, constitutional, pluralist democracy. We do not, rather we look into the religions and traditions themselves as they are a primary reason a political association would be characterized as pluralistic.

In Part III below we briefly describe three approaches to the problem. Engelhardt suggests there is no possibility of such a universalism. MacIntyre suggests that as a historical matter systems of justice can merge, perhaps in the way Buddhism was incorporated into both Hinduism and Confucianism, but his short-term solution is a kind of Rawlsian over-lapping consensus approach. Durant proposes another Rawlsian approach. We then briefly turn to the more substantive Aristotelian theories of John Finnis and Martha Nussbaum. They approach the problem differently that the Rawlsians. Instead of beginning with individuals and trying to reason to universal norms, they begin at the species level. They each argue, but differently, that an examination of the human species can lead at least to the articulation of substantive universal values (which in turn can be used as sources of legal norms). It is their focus on the species level theory of the person that is important to our argument.

In Part IV, we briefly describe the various approaches taken by the major religions towards the concepts of dignity, rights and duties. We think these three values are good places to begin since they have been identified as universal norms, but they are weak institutionally and practically because they leave ambiguities that permit the utilization of the concepts for particular, not universal, ends. That means that the existing normative systems, such as the UNESCO Universal Declaration on Bioethics and Human Rights, can be fruitfully critiqued.

In Part V we explore the possibility of converging norms using a method developed by John Lunstroth. (Lunstroth 2013). He argues that Enlightenment thought is based on a reductionist approach to knowledge that results in a fragmented way of understanding political, legal and ethical concepts, all of which share a unified or central meaning. If dignity, rights and duties are seen as a unitary thing then their ideological functions will not play such a prominent role in divisiveness among the traditions, but the unified concept could encourage convergence towards norms acceptable to all traditions.

4.2 Rawls' Overlapping Concept

Rawls developed his notion of "overlapping consensus" (OC) in conjunction with or as a part of his more general theory of political justice. (Rawls 1971, 1987). OC is a way to describe how political agreement can be reached in a constitutional, liberal and pluralist society, assuming the absence of shared meanings. His stature in political philosophy is such that we must both orient ourselves to his thought to place ourselves properly in the history of ideas, and we must either distinguish our ideas from his or acknowledge we are undertaking a Rawlsian project. Rawls himself must do the same, as the political problem of seeking commensurability of values and meaning in a pluralist political association is hardly new. (Rawls 1987, 2). We distinguish ourselves from Rawls in the following way.

Rawls, in both his Theory of Justice and his notion of OC frames, or limits, his argument by assuming a constitutional, democratic and pluralist state. With regard to the OC we argue this assumption does all the heavy lifting. Democracy itself is a political solution to the problem of pluralism, and one that has been deeply criticized at least from Plato onwards. Having assumed a democracy peopled with diverse and ethically incommensurable groups, he then describes the democratic process as though it is an explanation of that very democratic process. We are not sure Rawls is really saying anything new or even interesting.

We see ourselves as approaching the problem, of pluralism in the political association, differently inasmuch as we do not assume a democracy or a republic. When

Rawls wrote democracy seemed to have won the global war of values, but that victory now seems pyrrhic. Fukuyama famously argued that the victory of democracy and Western liberal political values signaled the end of [a Hegelian kind] of history. (Fukuyama 1989). But now it is clear the rupture of the West's identification of capitalism and democracy teaches that capitalism, the dominant ideology of the Western liberalism, does not require or imply democracy in the least. Capitalism, an economic theory, works within socialist and authoritarian regimes (e.g., China and Russia) as well. We are focusing on meaning structures within the major religions or traditions, as they play a major role in the pluralism, without regard to particular types of political associations.

Like Rawls we think that the theory of the human being plays a central role. (Rawls 1987, 7) But where Rawls assumes as his starting point a political individual in a liberal state, we explore each religion for concepts associated with its own concept of the human that bear similarity to a unified concept of rights/duties/dignity. We recognize that the individual concepts of rights, duties and dignity arise from and within the Western liberal tradition, but we submit that by unifying them they are disconnected from their political origins, and their unified meaning, which we allow to exist without further analytic description, describes something in human nature itself. If this is true, then we should find similar meaning structures within each religion or tradition, and then we can seek convergence using this unified concept. If this concept does not work, then we can use the process to probe further into the various religions and traditions for concepts that do work.

4.3 The Critique of Global Bioethics

Critics of moral relativism or emotivism, such as Tristram Englehardt, argue that modern societies are in the "ruins of attempts at global bioethics." (Englehardt 2006) He argues that differences regarding the "foundational character of morality itself" prevent the resolution of what are irresolvable ethical controversies. Explaining his position he writes: "Individuals need not possess starkly different moral views in order to have different moralities" (Engelhardt 2000, 37). Referring to individuals who adhere to different moral traditions yet who disagree on the foundational basis of such convictions, despite being in agreement on certain issues, Engelhardt doubts that any process of mutually understanding one another's moral systems will assist in the resolution of our deepest bioethical disagreements. He argues that: "Moral strangers need not be morally opaque to each other. They may be mutually fully acquainted with each other's position, while in disagreement so as not to be able to resolve controversies" (Engelhardt 2000, 37) because "the resolution of controversies depends on the acceptance of one particular ranking or ordering of moral values or moral principles over other possible ranking or orderings" (Engelhardt 2000, 37). Engelhardt advances a straight-forward Rawlsian argument that justice is best sought through procedural mechanisms.

According to Engelhardt, consensus documents on universal values produced by international institutions such as the UNESCO's Universal Declaration of Bioethics and Human Rights are illusionary and simply self-congratulatory, because people from different traditions are unable to arrive at a consensus on the foundation of morality. All we have is two "moral strangers" locked in conflict as a result of their incompatible moral values and modes of reasoning. Consensus statements simply reflect superficial points of agreement, or similarity, that cannot do the hard philosophical work of moral resolution.

Engelhardt's solution is to appeal to a purely procedural framework of justice, rather than a comprehensive global morality, to serve our 'post-secular' ethical-political needs. His would abandon the quest for consensus altogether and enact a *modus vivendi* approach of coping with controversial bioethical issues founded upon a principle of permission (Engelhardt 2000).

Alasdair MacIntyre, one of today's most senior critics of relativism, describes four historically and philosophically distinct ethical systems in the west, the Aristotelian, the Augustinian, the Scottish Enlightenment blend of them, and liberalism. (MacIntyre 1988). These are "socially embodied traditions of rational inquiry," which produce divergent forms of practical rationality, i.e., ethics. MacIntyre argues that in the long run different traditions, through historical processes, accommodate each other, perhaps in the way Buddhism was assimilated into the Hindu traditions and the Confucian/Taoist traditions over historical periods of time. In the short term, when one tradition faces another though, he argues to what, in our opinion, looks like the Rawlsian "overlapping consensus" approach.

Chris Durante develops another variation of the Rawlsian approach. He argues that "the similarity and compatibility of concepts must not be conflated with identicality, and consensus must not be conflated with unanimity. By allowing and encouraging distinct perspectives to justify similar concepts in their own unique ways, pragmatic perspectivism acknowledges that there will be interpretive differences from the outset, yet does not see this as a threat to the possibility of consensus envisioned as an on-going and multi-tiered processes of forging agreements, discovering compatibilities despite differences of opinion and enjoining in a reciprocal endeavor to mutually understand one another's perspectives" (Durante 2009, 2015).

The philosophical argument seems impossible to resolve on a substantive level, except by ceding to one of the comprehensive systems described by MacIntyre. Thus the Rawlsian procedural arguments have tremendous power. Since human needs are at some level common, each tradition will overlap to some degree with the others, and in those areas we can reach agreements at least about how to solve some mutual problems without resorting to first principles (which would lead to discord).

We think, however, that if we focus on the commonalities of the human species, we can, if not discover the basis for universal norms, at least expand the areas of convergence or agreement. Both John Finnis and Martha Nussbaum have advanced similar arguments, and both are associated with Aristotelian system of justice. (Finnis 1980; Nussbaum 2006). Finnis, arguing from a positivist, Thomistic or natural law perspective, looks at the human species and identifies a short list of requisites for human flourishing that then become the basis, through reason (thus "positivist"), for his theory of natural law. Nussbaum, hewing more closely to Aristotle, seeks those characteristics of the human species that are required for flourishing without interposing reason, and produces her own list. She then links her theory of justice with human rights discourse. Their lists are similar.

We approach the problem with an empirical examination of the religious traditions through the lens of the contemporary international normative concepts of *dignity*, *right* and *duty*. In a way we seek to add unitive content to those concepts. We seek to bridge the distance from religious traditions to the core human characteristics through those concepts. We seek to discern those concepts in all of the religious traditions, which finding, if accepted within the traditions, would open the area of convergence of norms to the entire species, ideally. We find ourselves aligned most closely with the Aristotelian tradition, like Finnis and Nussbaum, because it is the most basic, the most empirical approach to defining the species and its basic norms.

We begin with the method of unifying the concepts of dignity, rights and duties. The first step occurs after we recognize intuitively that rights and duties are two sides of the same coin, are parts of a unified concept. We recognize then that while we do not necessarily have a word for the unified concept, its existence teaches that we can combine legal concepts while retaining coherence. If we generalize the process of unifying related concepts we quickly come to understand we are rebuilding a whole of some kind. With this realization we link to Aristotle's thought, at the center of which is a complex philosophical set of ideas linking wholes to living things, identity, form, and/or species. The main whole that suggests itself as the whole that is being rebuilt is the human person, the particularization of organic species. This in turn leads us to the speculation that it is in the vision of the human being in each tradition that we can find the commonalities we seek. This may at first seem obvious, but if one starts with notions such as the human as being a rights-holder, one is not led to consider the being as the "political animal" philosophized by Aristotle, rather one's attention is drawn to theories of rights and conflicts between rights-holding individuals and rights-holding communities, and other conflicts among analytic, reductionist concepts related to rights. In the following section we explore the notions of dignity, rights and duties in the religions as preparation for some tentative conclusions about convergence of norms in the final section.

4.4 Human Rights and Duties from the Perspective of the Religious Traditions

Hints for ways to attain substantive convergence can be gleaned from more detailed analysis of the respective ethical traditions supporting it. First, the eastern traditions will be addressed, and then the western.

4.4.1 Buddhism

Buddhism does not follow the western principles of individualism and autonomy because its views are focused on a cooperative scheme that leads to compassion (Huxley 1999). It postulates duty as a result of Dharma, which is may be loosely translated as "natural law." Buddhism maintains that within this worldly realm of existence there exists a natural order to all forms of living from which a moral order can be derived for human relations with both one another and nature. The five moral precepts that Buddhism argues are universally applicable are: (1) Avoid killing or causing harm to other sentient beings; (2) Avoiding theft; (3) Avoid Sexual impropriety (4) Avoid lying or misleading others; (5) Avoid intoxicants. Within the Buddhist paradigm moral psychology plays an integral and is intimately connected to its deontological framework. One who upholds such precepts in the pursuit of awakening (nibbana/nirvana) will come to embody (for lack of a better term) karuna, or compassion. Hence, the ultimately moral mode of being in the world is to perpetually act with sympathetic consciousness of others' distress which will lead to the motivation to alleviate their suffering.

Despite the absence of an articulated concept of 'dignity' within the Buddhist tradition, there is indeed an appeal to some form of commonality shared by all persons in the form of anatta, or 'no-self' and the correlative ethical injunction to see all living beings as interrelated and fundamentally sharing in an emptiness of their nature. Unlike the pessimistic renderings of emptiness held by some post-modernists, within Buddhism the recognition of our ultimate emptiness leads one to a mode of behaving selflessly toward others.

For some, the egalitarian aspect of Human Rights conflicts with dharma's allocation of different duties to different people (Ihara 1995), but for Damien Keown, arguing from the Theravada tradition of Buddhist thought, current formulations of human rights complement moral values of classical Buddhism, by describing what is due under Dharma (Keown et al. 1998). Even though the Buddhist 'Five Commandments detail duties for the victimizer, such duties must first hold that the potential victim has rights that should not be infringed on by the victimizer (Huxley 1999). The importance given by Buddhists to interdependence and compassion entails care for those who need special protection and respect due to their conditions that make them vulnerable (Hongladarom 2014).

Moreover, in the Mahayana tradition of Buddhism there is a concept that more closely resembles the Western notion of human dignity. This concept is "buddha-nature," which may be described as the potential buddhahood, or abilitiy to become a buddha, inherent within each human life. Buddha-nature distinguishes humans from non-humans and serves to invigorate an ethical impulse in each individual who attain awareness of this. Hence, despite the lack of a common foundational paradigm, both Christianity and Buddhism share a deep concern for the duties and obligations humans have to another and toward the overall safeguarding of well-being. The Buddhist conceptions of duties associated with Dharma overlap with those a number of western traditions, including those of the Abrahamic religious traditions with their conceptions of natural law and divinely mandated duties and obligations. For instance, protection of and assistance to persons in need as well as altering the conditions that give rise to injustice are foundational elements of the ethical systems of all three of the Abrahamic faiths as well as numerous strains of western legal and ethico-political thought. In this way, all these traditions can make common appeals to the existence of social duties to aide those in need and protect persons from harms.

4.4.2 Confucianism

In a similar way, Confucianism sees personhood in the context of a network of human connections among individuals; one becomes a person as a result of the relationship with others. In other words, the way to be acknowledged as a person is by learning how to stand in dutiful relation to others (Bockover 2010). Ren (仁) places autonomy and individuality after the interests of society (Huaiyu 2012). Responsibility, especially in a social context, is a key factor to live a good life (Bockover 2010).

The concept of human rights in early Confucian societies is not clear, perhaps because they relied on rites rather than laws to govern human relationships. This ritual-government system determined what was due to and from each person (Sim 2013). These ideas have evolved, and despite the absence of a well-defined policy of human rights in modern China there are numerous ideas related to human rights embedded within Confucianism. For example Confucians have said that we should benevolently care about the well-being of all-under-heaven, and that this should be harmonized with other responsibilities (Angle 2012) The vision of Confucian morality is naturalist, in that Confucian morality maintains that human nature is characterized by a 'natural goodness." Some have argued that such a belief can provide a foundation for a universal and naturalistic approach to human rights for China to pragmatically implement in line with its own traditional morality.

4.4.3 Hinduism

For Hinduism, the concept of human rights is rather foreign. The Hindu conception of dharma is key to keeping society together because when dharma is followed, the person is in conformity with the Truth (Dharma 2007; Desai 2014). There is a division of social order in four classes that according to Rig Veda were created from the body of the primeval person, and then due to the invasion of European countries and the mixing of races, these classes where determined by skin color (Desai 2014). The differentiation into classes was accented by guna theory in which the acknowledgment of differences among people is based in the idea that people are composed by three strands of qualities or gunas: Lightness, Energy, and Heaviness.

These qualities express themselves differently in each person, therefore, the different ratios of gunas create unique individuals. This uniqueness comes with a particular code of conduct or dharma that guides each person. Nowadays, the caste division and the concept of personhood is complex because a person's identity depends on other factors such as class, caste, sex, age, and occupation. Also, every individual is born with five debts: debt to God, debt to sages, debt to ancestors, debt to humanity, and debt to nature. These debts create responsibilities and duties that provide moral and ethical guidelines.

4.4.4 Judaism

From a Jewish perspective, there is a distinction between modern [western] rights-centered societies and Judaism's duty (or mitzvah)-centered society (Crane 2007). This focus is evidenced in the word mitzvah used when a child has their bat or bar mitzvah, signifying their entrance into Jewish society as adults ready to assume the obligations within the community (Walzer 2006).

This tradition is thus similar to eastern society's belief systems with their duty focus, and the major monotheism religions of Islam and Christianity with their founding of human rights and duties in the value of the person made in the image of God, supported by their respective sacred texts. Crane classifies Jewish arguments about human rights into three broad categories: temporal arguments that appeal to historical events, innate arguments that detail the aspects of Judaic tradition compelling concern for human rights, and philosophical arguments that articulate reasons inspiring concern for human rights.

Judaism focuses on both rights and duties lest it miss the "essentially religious character" of this tradition, to "imitate the Divine" with reverence for the rights of all people "'created in the image of God' (Genesis 1:27)." The evolution therefore of this tradition's formulation of the person's unique rights tightly bound to duties, and its foundational role in the more rights-based Christian system that developed from it, potentially position it as a bridge from the eastern to the western belief systems.

4.4.5 Christianity

For Christianity, the protection of the vulnerable and the most needy is a fundamental aspect of its' philosophy. For some scholars, this need is found in the ethic of agapé—a testament to the immeasurable love of God—that moves a person to give comfort and support to those in distress (Tzitzis 2014). Early Christian teachings expanded on that concept through the teachings and life of Jesus Christ, drawing from the Jewish roots in this religion. The influence of Greek and Roman ethical-legal systems were incorporated into Western Christianity's ethical-legal teachings that served to create the foundations upon which much of the Western secular ethical and legal traditions drew upon to formulate many of their key concepts. These concepts were later used to codify formulations of human dignity, equality, liberty and democracy underlying modern views of human rights in the western world (Witte and Alexander 2010).

Within the wide spectrum of the Protestant Christian churches, Methodist theologian J. Robert Nelson highlights how Calvinism superseded Lutheranism "as [a] stimulus and tutor to human rights," arguing this denomination cultivated the development of democratic government within a covenant paradigm (Nelson 1982). In the twentieth century, Thomistic personalist and Catholic philosopher Jacques Maritain was involved in the drafting of the 1948 United Nations' Universal Declaration of Human Rights. Citing this declaration, the Catholic Church's Compendium of the Social Doctrine of the Church provides a comprehensive elaboration of its argument that rights and duties flow from the dignity of the person made in the image and likeness of God. This position asserts just societies are only able to be realized by protecting every persons' dignity as society's purpose (Pontifical Council for Justice and Peace 2004).

4.4.6 Islam

Islamic doctrines center on the belief that whatever God wills is just; therefore, to create a just society, every individual must align their conduct with God's will. The Muslims' sacred text, the Qur'an, views humanity as a single community of individuals that have a shared nature capable of recognizing moral good and possessing an internal scale to differentiate right and wrong (Sachedina 2009).

Islam has a more defined framework of rights with resultant duties than both Judaism and Christianity. In Muslim states, human rights can only be guaranteed within the context of the Qur'an and Shari'ah law because these instruments define religious responsibilities that create balance in the communities recognizing their authority (Pohl 2010). This pivotal belief led Muslim states to create their own declaration of human rights as an alternative to the UDHR, the Cairo Declaration on Human Rights in Islam (1990). This document asserts the Shari'ah law, rather than the UN appeal to a common human dignity or any other authoritative source or concept, is the sole source of human rights for the Islamic people. Their conception of human rights with resultant duties is thus more explicit like the western formulation.

But unlike both western and eastern belief systems, the Islamic rights and duties framework is self-contained entirely within their own beliefs and laws, leaving uncertainty how this framework claims normative guidance on ethical conduct in global bioethics to non-Muslims. The later Arab Charter on Human Rights (1994) more closely approximates a global bioethics that invokes the western conception of human dignity with subsequent rights and resultant duties and directly affirms the UN Declaration of Human Rights.

In this Sect. 4.4 we only touched on arguments alluding to the unity of rights and duties, the first step of our larger and much more complex argument. Coming to an understanding of how a religion envisions the human species is perhaps a fool's errand. First, we recognize that since the notion of religion is not universal, the question itself is inarticulate. It is better to ask about the theory of the human species in each tradition. We then encounter the problem that there are numerous deep divisions within each tradition that result in sub-traditions that are of the same status as traditions. If we add to this the problem of the transcendent, often referred to in English as God, then we are in extremely ambiguous territory. Two self-identified *religions*, Christianity and Islam, claim to be universal for all mankind. Our argument depends on looking at the person, or the theory of the person, at the center of each tradition, in a sense dislocating them from their relationship to the divine (since we are looking for answers to problems common to all humans, to the human species). Moreover, our inquiry assumes there is only one human species, but perhaps there are varieties of humans, as there are varieties within traditions, and there is no one kind within the human species, except as regards their form. The foregoing are all strong arguments a Ralwsian procedural solution is the only possible way we can speculate about *substantive* convergence if we are going to respect the unique identities of the traditions.

4.5 Multiculturalism: Towards a Global Bioethics

We now return to the difficulty of establishing a global bioethics due to apparently incommensurable religious and cultural moral traditions and value systems. One approach is to see the dignity of the person as the foundation on which human rights are based, whether a human community is seen as person-centered in the West or person-network-focused in the East. This approach, adopted in the International Bill of Human Rights, allows for both individual and collective views on dignity, grounded in the basic rights and freedoms that confers value to the person either primarily or as consequence of duty to them safeguarding their rights.

This conception as discussed above is supported within Islam, Judaism, and Christianity, as human dignity is based on the belief that we were all created in the image of God. Islam additionally qualifies in the Qur'anic vision of dignity that this human quality is manifested particularly as an expression of God's favor and grace (Kamali 2002). In the light of Confucian thought, an individual qualifies as fully human and thus possessing dignity when he or she takes into account respect for others through optimal social relations (Koehn and Leung 2008). In Buddhism, the Dalai Lama articulates a duty-based political conception of dignity related to the western formulation of dignity: "the aspiration for democracy and respect for fundamental human rights relies on the responsibility that rests with those who do enjoy freedom, and human rights." (2014). Hinduism presents dharma comparable to the Confucian or Buddhist relational or distributive dignity across the persons in the human network of a larger whole, but arising from dharma's foundational belief of divine law prevailing on every level of existence.

When the Eastern traditions are examined for concepts that are similar to "rights", "duties" and "dignity", various linguistic and substantive equivalences suggest themselves. However, what remains obscure is the extent to which the worldviews within which those concepts are given meaning permit the conclusion that the concepts are commensurable. Rawls/Englehardt argue they cannot be, while MacIntyre recognizes that in historical processes those meanings can become commensurate. If we approach the issue historically, per MacIntyre, which histories do we investigate? We begin with the decidedly western concepts of dignity, rights and duties. The meanings of these concepts rest first in the Enlightenment, as positivist philosophical forces disassembled Aristotelian political/human wholes. Another important layer of meanings is suggested at the end of World War II, in the formation of the United Nations; and yet another, perhaps the most important, dates from the late 1970s, when from deep in the heart of the Cold War the human rights Conventions came into force and human rights discourse began to assume dominance in international moral discourse. (Moyn 2010). In general, we can associate the current notions of dignity, rights and duties with Enlightenment scientism in the law and political theory.

To answer the historist question we would look to compare the meanings of the relevant terms from the mid-nineteenth century, the era during which Enlightenment scientism began to take root in India and China. It is clear that in the periods we described above, that China and India have recognized the concepts of dignity, right and duties, as such, since the end of WW2, and especially since the 1970s. Once the terms were recognized as political entities, then a kind of literature could arise in which the new concepts are compared to traditional concepts. The problem with this is that the older terms have at least two millennia of meanings, often defined with great philosophical sophistication, and within a variety of distinct sub-traditions. If historicist processes have been adequate to graft "dignity", "rights" and "duties" as Enlightenment concepts onto the eastern traditions, then it will have happened in the last 40 or so years, and the western meanings will become just another layer on the ancient meanings. There is an argument that the reciprocating historicist process pointed to by MacIntyre, in which the two once incommensurable traditions mutually influence one another, will not be complete until the strict, legalist, sense of the universal found in the west is supplanted by the Aristotelian notion in which the universal is related to identity and wholes, something also characteristic of the east. (Lunstroth 2015). Following this trail leads us inexorably to the conclusion it is in the vision of the human person, the species individual whole, that the various perspectives converge.

Ultimately, establishing a truly global bioethics will require the settlement of complex linguistic transformations in which the relationship between concepts of reality are sorted out. There are both general and foundational questions such as: Is the Dao the same as God the Father? Are Jesus and Buddha the same kind of figures, do they share the same essence? Is the living teacher of Sufism, Hinduism, Buddhism, Taoism and many other traditions of the same essence and function as Jesus Christ or Mohammad? And there are more specific questions that focus on the sources and nature of political, ethical and legal norms: What is the common good?

If a person can flourish in one political entity, are there political entities in which they would not flourish? In what terms can norms that lead to flourishing best be expressed? Is political association natural, or the result of man's reason? Does man have an essence that includes claims on the political association? Is the political association more important than the individual, or vice versa? And there are yet more specific normative inquiries, the kinds this paper seeks to explore: By what authority is technology to be limited, if it is? What special normative concerns do the life-sciences give rise to? What are the legitimate sources of norms with which to govern or regulate the life-sciences?

UNESCO's Universal Declaration on Bioethics and Human Rights is a comprehensive framework of norms governing the life sciences that purports to ground its authority and legitimacy in human rights and dignity. After the exploration of the various religions though, it is obvious the mere reference to human rights and dignity is not by itself a sufficient reason to accept the norms as they are written. That the states adopted them by consensus is also not sufficient reason. Both the reference to human rights and dignity and the consensus acclamation, may be necessary, but for substantive norms that the plural and diverse states can all adopt, a deeper layer of convergence between the political/ethical/legal communities must be sought.

We looked through the lenses of the major traditions to explore whether the concepts of dignity, rights and duties could be focal points of convergence, despite their origins in Enlightenment positivist legal theory. When we started from the intuition that rights and duties are two sides of the same coin, we found we could make conceptual progress not by trying to define the resulting unity, but from the recognition we could join related legal/political concepts together to make larger unities. After joining the concepts of rights, duties and dignity into a unified concept, we were led to conclude that the individual organic person, the species representative, is the central case of both religions and our target concepts. But the individual organic whole is not the Enlightenment individual, rather closer to the "political animal," an entity whose identity is inseparable from larger groups. Moreover, it is this organic individual that we can examine as the species norm. This individual is not the Rawlsian liberal individual, a deeply limited individual. Nor is it like the morally fixed individuals of Engelhardt, nor like the negotiators of the various iterations of the overlapping consensus. Finnis' positive reasoning individual, is closer, but Finnis cannot abandon the strict legalist universalism that concludes there are some positive laws that should apply to everyone. It appears that the neo-Aristotelian approach of Nussbaum and Macintyre, as representatives of the west, that best provide tools with which to seek convergence. MacIntyre opens the conceptual space by recognizing that the processes of history can certainly lead to convergence; and Nussbaum focuses on the key characteristics of the species, giving us a universal (whole) picture of the person which can then be the subject of universal (whole) norms that lead to flourishing but which are not necessarily the same for everyone.

Recognizing that rights and duties seem to be two sides to the same coin has several beneficial outcomes. It leads to identification of points of convergence, or unity; it informs the positive expression and the ideological content of the norms; it offers a thorough or integral vision of the whole debate on human rights and duties that could improve praxis and the reason for the existence of the life-science norms themselves; and it opens the door to the reconceptualizing of the concept of dignity. The strengthening of the identity of rights and duties strengthens the spirit of solidarity and dignity while protecting diversity and pluralism in a healthy way. This kind of understanding leads to an integral and solidary humanism.

References

Angle, S.C. 2012. *Contemporary confucian political philosophy: Toward progressive confucianism*. Cambridge: Polity.
Aristotle. 1984. In *The complete works of Aristotle*, ed. Jonathan Barnes, vol. 1, 166. Princeton: Princeton University Press. (*APo* 100a15-b5).
Bockover, M.I. 2010. Confucianism and ethics in the Western philosophical tradition: Foundational Concepts. *Philosophy Compass* 5 (4): 307–316.
Beauchamp, T.L., and J.F. Childress. 2001. *Principles of biomedical ethics*. New York: Oxford University Press.
Crane, J.K. 2007. Why rights? Why me? *Journal of Religious Ethics* 35 (4): 559–589.
Dalai Lama. 2014. *Messages*. http://www.dalailama.com/messages/world-peace/human-rights-democracy-and-freedom. Accessed 12 Dec 2014.
Desai, P. 2014. Between tradition and modernity: Bioethics, human vulnerability and social change. In *Religious perspectives on human vulnerability in bioethics (Chapter 8)*, ed. J. Tham, A. Garcia, and G. Miranda. Dordrecht: Springer.
Dharma. 2007. *Hinduism Today* 29 (2): 15.
Durante, C. 2009. Bioethics in a pluralistic society: Bioethical methodology in Lieu of moral diversity. *Medicine, Healthcare, and Philosophy* 12 (1): 35–47.
———. 2015. Dialogue despite diversity: Sharing norms when our moralities differ. *Studia Bioetica* 8 (1): 7–17.
Engelhardt Jr, H.T. 2006. *Global bioethics: The collapse of consensus*. Salem: M&M Scrivener Press.
Engelhardt, H.T. 2000. *The foundations of Christian bioethics*. Lisse: M&M Scrivener Press.
Finnis, J. 1980. *Natural law and natural rights*. Oxford: Oxford University Press.
Fukuyama, F. (1989). The end of history?. The National Interest. Summer.
Hongladarom, S. 2014. Buddhist perspective on four vulnerable groups: Children, women, the elderly and disabled. In *Religious perspectives on human vulnerability in bioethics (Chapter 11)*, ed. J. Tham, A. Garcia, and G. Miranda. Dordrecht: Springer.
Huaiyu, W. 2012. Ren and gantong: Openness of heart and the root of Confucianism. *Philosophy East & West* 62: 4.
Huxley, A. 1999. Buddhism and human rights. *Bulletin School of Oriental and African Studies University of London* 62 (1): 166.
Ihara, C. 1995. Why are there no rights in Buddhism, a reply to Damian Keown. In *Buddhism and human rights Buddhism and human rights*, ed. D. Keown, D. Prebish, and C. Husted. Richmond/Surrey: Curzon.
Kamali, M.H. 2002. *The dignity of man: An Islamic perspective*. Cambridge: Islamic Texts Society.
Keown, D., C. Prebish, and W.R. Husted. 1998. *Buddhism and human rights*. Richmond/Surrey: Curzon.
Koehn, D.A., and A.L. Leung. 2008. Dignity in Western versus Chinese cultures: Theoretical overview and practical illustrations. *Business and Society Review* 113 (4): 477–504.
Lunstroth, J. 2013. *Renewing legal theory: History and the unity of legal things 2013*. http://papers.ssrn.com/sol3/papers.cfm?abstract_id=2225910.

———. 2015. *History, universalism and religion: West and East*. Bioethics, Multiculturalism and Religion Blog entry at https://unescobiochair.wordpress.com/2015/01/29/history-universalism-and-religion-west-and-east/.
Moyn, S. 2010. *The last Utopia: Human rights in history*. Cambridge, MA: Belknap Press of Harvard University Press.
Nelson, J.R. 1982. Human rights in creation and redemption: A protestant view. In *Human rights in religious traditions*, ed. A. Swindler. New York: The Pilgrim Press.
Nussbaum, M. 2006. *Frontiers of justice: Disability, nationality, species membership*. Cambridge, MA: Belknap Press.
Pohl, F. 2010. *Modern Muslim societies*. Tarrytown: Marshall Cavendish.
Rawls, J.A. 1971. *Theory of justice*. Cambridge, MA: Harvard University Press.
———. 1987. The idea of an overlapping consensus. *Oxford Journal of Legal Studies* 7 (1): 1–25.
Sachedina, A.A. 2009. *Islam and the challenge of human rights*. Oxford: Oxford University Press.
Sim, M. 2013. Confucian values and human rights. *Review of Metaphysics* 67 (1): 3–27.
Tzitzis, S. 2014. The ethical and legal aspects of vulnerability in the Christian perspective. In *Religious perspectives on human vulnerability in bioethics (Chapter 6)*, ed. J. Tham, A. Garcia, and G. Miranda. Dordrecht: Springer.
United States Central Intelligence Agency. 2010. *World Factbook*. https://www.cia.gov/library/publications/the-world-factbook/geos/xx.html. Accessed 12 Feb 2015.
Walzer, M. 2006. *Law, politics, and morality in Judaism*. Princeton: Princeton University Press.
Witte, J., and F.S. Alexander. 2010. *Christianity and human rights: An introduction*. Cambridge: Cambridge University Press.

Part II
Asian Religions: Buddhism

Chapter 5
On Human Rights and Freedom in Bioethics: A Philosophical Inquiry in Light of Buddhism

Ellen Y. Zhang

5.1 Introduction

The concept of human rights, with its unique cultural matrix of socio-political and intellectual developments in the Enlightenment of the West, has been a highly disputed one in contemporary ethical discourse. The United Nations' *Universal Declaration of Human Rights* (hereafter UDHR, 1948) and its subsequent human rights conventions aim to make "the rights of every individual" a legally binding agreement that can go beyond cultural boundaries and religious or ideological differences. The *Universal Declaration on Bioethics and Human Rights* (hereafter UDBHR, 2005) follows the same direction. For instance, in Article 3:1, it is said, "Human dignity, human rights and fundamental freedoms are to be fully respected." In Article 3:2, it is said, "The interests and welfare of the individual should have priority over the sole interest of science or society." Here, we have three key words: dignity, rights, and freedoms, all of which point to a fundamental idea that each individual, as a free agent or a self-determined person, should be protected via recognition of his/her dignity and rights. In other words, the respect of human dignity and the protection of human rights define the *minimum* of what is necessary in order to safeguard the freedom of individual agency and freedom of self-determination. If we say that in politics, the concept of human rights sets limits to more powerful collectives and institutions such as state, society, and religion, the idea of human rights in bioethics sets limits to scientific research and experimentation, as well as various technological developments in medicine (e.g. stem-cell research and the use of various forms of genetic technology).

It is not suggesting here that Buddhism is a coherent and monolithic tradition, but the discussion focused in the paper is on some common Buddhist theories concerning relevant issues.

E.Y. Zhang (✉)
Religion and Philosophy Department, Centre for Applied Ethics, Hong Kong Baptist University, Kowloon Tong, Hong Kong
e-mail: eyzhang@hkbu.edu.hk

J. Tham et al. (eds.), *Religious Perspectives on Bioethics and Human Rights*,
Advancing Global Bioethics 6, DOI 10.1007/978-3-319-58431-7_5

Concurrently, the concept of rights intends to set up an egalitarian model in society to replace a hereditary one accepted by various cultural traditions in the past. Yet the tricky part in contemporary politico-philosophical discussions is what constitutes "rights" or "human rights" since both ethicists and legalists employ the same term yet very often use it with different connotations. Can the concept of rights competently deal with the complexity of bioethical issues we are facing today? How can rights approach manage a non-natural right such as a right generated by a promise or legal agreement, say, a medical insurance plan? How can rights approach manage an extended content of a right such as a right to healthcare when the definition of a duty bearer is not clear? Should human rights be the new *lingua franca* of bioethics for public health and human well-being? Do human responsibilities and human rights supersede each other or complement each other? Would too much emphasis on rights compromise what is perceived as "good"?

In *Human Rights as Politics and Idolatry*, Michael Ignatieff speaks of human rights as a means not only to protect individuals but also to affirm what he calls "moral individualism" (Ignatieff 2001: 66). Since the notion of "individuals" here refers to every person regardless of his/her race, color, sex, religion, birth, etc. these human rights are viewed as valid for everyone equally and universally. The UDBHR intends to use the general concept of human rights "to underline the importance of biodiversity and its conservation as a common concern of humankind" (Article 2:h) with its language of expansiveness and inclusivity. Since the intention here is to use a general principle to cover potential diversities in bioethical controversies across nations and cultures, this principle must be easily accepted and applicable. The question under the debate is how one can justify the claim to universal validity of human dignity and rights indicated in the UDHR as a global ethics in a post-modern age whereby a consensus on anything transcendent and universal seems difficult if not impossible across different cultures, religions, and ideologies. In this paper, I shall use Buddhism as an example to explicate what kind of human rights Buddhism would accept and what kind of human rights Buddhism may find problematic.

5.2 Human Dignity and Human Rights

Human dignity and human rights are usually mentioned side by side. The concept of human dignity seems less controversial at the first glance. Yet the problem is that it is very difficult to justify one particular understanding of human dignity in the contemporary pluralistic world through a rational formulation without defining the term. In the Western tradition, the ontological basis of human dignity in the sense that each person is "unique and unrepeatable" is argued either philosophically or theologically.[1] The idea of human dignity also comes from the idea of "natural

---

[1]The notion of human dignity is derived from the concept of human rights. The earliest direct precursor to human rights could be found in the notions of "natural right" developed by classical Greek philosophers, such as Aristotle, and further developed by Thomas Aquinas in his *Summa Theologica*.

right" and the belief of "universal moral law" rooted in the "justice of God" in Judeo-Christian tradition. Nevertheless, the concept of human dignity, particularly the notion of "intrinsic dignity" as we often suggest today, is a product of the historical evolution of modern thought.

No doubt, rights-talk is not historically Buddhist, yet Buddhism would accept the modern notion of "dignity" as a general principle, since the Buddhist idea (in Māhayāna in particular) that all sentient beings possess Buddha-nature provides a basis for the respect of the individual's inherent dignity. But at the same time, Buddhists may see both human dignity and human rights having an "anthropocentric implication" (i.e. humans vs. non-humans) that might be problematic in some cases. In his essay "Buddhism and the Idea of Human Rights: Resonances and Dissonances," Perry Schmidt-Leukel has observed that "in Buddhism human beings do not occupy an absolutely privileged position but are seen against the doctrine of rebirth as being continuous with all 'sentient beings,' that is, with all forms of existence in which rebirth can take place" (Schmidt-Leukel 2006: 39).[2] This explains why many Buddhist scholars insist on supplementing the concept of "animal rights" whenever they are engaged in rights talk. However, a non-anthropocentric position may compromise the absolute rights of human beings. For example, should we use animals for medical experimentations? Obviously, the practice of medical experimentations on animals is in conflict with the Buddhist doctrine of not doing any harm to animals.

Another problem facing Buddhism is the notion of a "self-embedded individualism" entailed in the very concept of human rights. One of the central tenets of Buddhism is that there is no self ontologically. That is to say, there is no substantial or fixed self that underlies a person's experience, and thus an individual is nothing but a sequence of causally linked psychological and physical events and processes. If Buddhism denies the essential nature of individual or self, then the idea of an essential/unalienable nature of individual dignity and rights would be questionable unless the Buddhist takes the issue from a broader perspective.

Damien Keown, one of the leading scholars of Buddhist studies, contends that for Buddhists "human beings live in relationship with one another is not a moral argument about how they ought to behave" since classical Buddhism is largely devoid of a systematic philosophy of human rights, or any form of normative ethics perceived in the West (Keown 2005: 30).[3] Although Buddhism is an intellectually dynamic tradition, says, Keown, it is "lightweight" in moral and political philosophy in a modern sense.[4] For Keown, normative ethics is prescriptive telling people

---

[2] See Perry Schmidt-Leukel, "Buddhism and the Idea of Human Rights: Resonances and Dissonances." *Buddhist-Christian Studies*, Vol. 26, 2006, p. 39.

[3] Keown insists that there is no normative ethics in Buddhism because it lacks theories about the justification of moral norms that philosophers in the West are normally do. This point is also noticed by the response paper by Soraj Hongladarom.

[4] See Damien Keown, "Are There 'Human Right' in Buddhism?" *Journal of Buddhist Ethics*, Vol. 2 1995 3–27. Also, et al. (eds). *Buddhism and Human Rights*. Richmond: Curzon Press. 2000.

how things ought to be, and it is always questionable whether "ethical theories" in the West — deontology, consequentialism, or virtue ethics — are appropriate lens through which to approach non-Western ethical thought like Buddhism or to approach non-Western ethical concept like human rights.[5] Nevertheless, it does not mean that we cannot talk about Buddhist moral teachings and their theoretical implications to the rights issue in a normative way, as long as we acknowledge the limitation of such approach. Hence Keown asserts that there are some elements in the Buddhist tradition that can be looked at from a vantage point of the modern idea of rights. For example, the right to life can be understood from the Buddhist precept not to kill, and that the right to private property can be seen from the precept not to steal (Keown 1995: 31–33). In addition, Keown argues that the Buddhist concept of duties and virtues of a king (Dharma) anticipates the modern notion of human rights in its "embryonic form" in that duties imply certain rights (Keown 1998: 22).

It is true that ethical discussions, including moral precepts in Buddhism, are often conducted in practical terms (i.e. concerning the application of precepts) rather than in a pure theoretical manner. Yet Buddhist-inspired moral teachings have elements that can be employed and extended when we bring Buddhism into the conversation with contemporary ethical discourse. For example, although the language of rights is absent in Buddhism, it seems to me that certain components in Buddhism are synchronistic with what is called "negative rights" from its broader perspective. Wesley Hohfeld (1879–1918), the American legal theorist calls this kind of rights as "privileges" or "liberty rights." According to Hohfeld, *A* has a privilege to *x if and only if A* has no duty not to *x*.[6] For instance, a person's right to life and property exists independently of someone's actions. Concerning bio-medical ethics, it has been widely accepted as a general moral principle requiring that doctors perform or refrain from performing particular actions which will harm the patient. In his article "Human Rights and Compassion: Towards a Unified Moral Framework," Buddhist philosopher Jay L. Garfield makes an argument that "rights" are asserted when they are violated or threatened, and thus they are fundamentally protective and negative in character (Garfield 1998:1–14).[7] In view of protecting human life and freedom, Buddhists would have no problem accepting the concept of human rights. In other words, human rights are necessary because they reflect certain moral standards of how humans should be treated, and how a violation of such standards should be condemned.

[5] What makes the issue more complicated is question who represents Buddhist ethics. Is it the Theravāda tradition, the Mahāyāna tradition, or the folk tradition of a particular kind? As a matter of the fact, the nature as well as the scope of Buddhist ethics is a topic of inquiry that is increasingly garnering the critical attention of contemporary Buddhist scholars. Due to the scope of the paper, this issue will not be explored as the major question under discussion can be shared by various traditions in Buddhism.

[6] Stanford Encyclopedia of Philosophy: http://plato.stanford.edu/entries/rights/ (cited as 08-22/13)

[7] See Jay L. Garfield, "Human Rights and Compassion: Towards a Unified Moral Framework." *Journal of Buddhist Ethics* (Online), Oct 1995, pp., 1–14. Also see Keown and et al. (eds). *Buddhism and Human Rights*. Richmond: Curzon Press. 2000.

When talking about the Buddhist concept of dharma, Keown attempts to suggest that rights and duties are mutually interdependent. From legal and moral perspectives today, a duty-based or duty-dependent right is sometimes called "positive right" or "claim right." A claim right is a right which entails responsibilities, duties, or obligations on another person as a duty bearer for the right-holder. That is to say, *A* has a claim that *Bx if and only if B* has a duty to *A* to *x*. In political and moral philosophy, a distinction between negative and positive rights is often employed by some normative theorists, especially those with a libertarian bent.[8] The right-holder of a negative right focuses on permission and non-interference whereas the right-holder of a positive right is entitled to provision of some good or service: A right against assault and harm is a classic example of a negative right, and a right to welfare assistance or Medicaid systems is viewed as a positive right. The language of rights, particularly the language of claim rights, suggests a person's "entitlement" that needs to be treated justly which, in turn, implies a corresponsive obligation by someone else in order to make that entitlement actualized. Along this line of thinking, the UN's Declaration embraces both negative and positive rights.

I concur with Keown that in the Buddhist tradition duty and right are mutually dependent. This argument is also consistent with the Buddhist notion of interconnectedness of everything both ontologically and ethically. However, it should be noted that if we examine what constitutes rights closely, we will see that even though some rights presume duties and obligations, it does not mean all duties and obligations can be translated back into rights. This is particularly true from a modern (Western) liberal point of view. On this point, Craig Ihara has made a good point, saying that "while it is true that from every right a corresponding duty can be deduced, the converse does not hold, that is, one cannot deduce from every duty the claim to a corresponding right (Ihara 1998: 45). I am quite intrigued by Ihara's points of view when he claims that it is important to draw a line between cooperative activities and the kind of moral property which constitutes a right. The debate on human rights, Ihara argues, would be better served if it could be shown that "rights talk" in Buddhism is a "skillful means" *(upāya)* towards the elimination of suffering rather than something that is fixed and essential as unalienable rights, or functions as a universally shared framework for addressing all social problems, including bioethical problems. To put it differently, the Buddhist doctrine of interconnectedness is responsibility-oriented rather than individual-, right-based. Accordingly, the UN statement about the interests and welfare of the individual vis-à-vis the sole interest of science or society (Article 3:2) makes more sense if one sees the article as a useful means to respond to the ethical questions that arise in life science and biotechnology. Historically speaking, from the very beginning cases in terms of human research/experimentation such as Nuremberg Trials and US vs. Brandt are meant to address the question of how to protect a human life from the atrocities committed by physicians and scientists in the name of the interest of the

---

[8] Libertarians in the US tend to avoid using human rights in a positive way since they think that rights-talk has become more socially and economically oriented in past decades, which would infringe on individual liberty.

state, or the purported interests of medical and scientific progress. From the perspective of Buddhism, this is not simply an issue of human rights, but an issue concerning a physician's responsibility to protect the life of each individual patient in clinical practice because of the interconnectedness of all sentient beings. Yet on the flip side, does society have a duty that goes beyond individual interests to explore the fundamental importance of a population's health and well-being? It seems that Buddhism would reject a universally shared principle on this issue.[9]

Here, we run into a long-standing debate between rights and duties/responsibilities. Buddhism, like most other Asian traditions, tends to focus on duties rather than rights. Duty is connected to the idea of compassion. In other words, instead of speaking of the rights of the right-holder, Buddhism prefers to talk about the duty-giver whose "good" action is not merely a result of a legal and compulsory requirement but a "voluntary" ("volitional" in a Buddhist term) action. The word "compassion" (*karunā*) in Buddhism is usually understood as "active sympathy" or a "willingness to bear the pain and sorrow of others." In Māhayāna Buddhism, compassion, along with enlightened wisdom (*prajña*), is the key moral character to be cultivated on the bodhisattva (i.e. Buddha-in-making) path. Chinese Buddhism translates the Sanskrit word *karunā* as *bei* (悲) which means "sympathy", "empathy", or "pity." This word is also connected to another word, "loving kindness" (Pali, *mettā;* Chinese, *ci* 慈), being understood in English as "compassion." The ethics of compassion indicates that everyone in the world is interrelated. Unlike the Confucian tradition in which the notion of loving kindness (*ren* 仁) is characterized by familial distinctions (i.e. a graded love or care), compassion in Buddhism emphasizes a shared human experience, particularly the experience of human vulnerability. The Buddhist monastic order (*sangha*) as a social institution has a long tradition of treating and taking care of the sick regardless of his/her sex, religion, and social class.

Since Buddhism speaks of a shared human experience, the issue that may bother Buddhists regarding the language of rights is the concept of individualism, or to be more exactly, the atomic notion of individualism (in Charles Taylor's term) embedded in the very idea of human rights. Although people talk about collective rights, that is, the rights of a particular group or community (such as children's rights, women's rights and gay rights), the idea of human rights, whether positive or negative, is based on free-standing individuals and individual autonomy. When speaking of rights against the Buddhist doctrine of compassion, Garfield makes an important distinction between liberalism in which the spirit of human rights is formulated vis-à-vis compassion as the guiding principle of Buddhism. Central to liberalism,

---

[9]For instance, the Jataka tale of Captain Goodheart in the Buddhist tradition is one example of taking a person's life (i.e., a violation of the precept by conducting killing) for the sake of saving lives of other people. In the story the Buddha-to-be has been born as the captain of a merchant ship. When Goodheart discovers that one of a thousand merchants on his ship plans to kill all of the others and steal their wealth, he kills the merchant, thus preventing the death of all other people on the ship. Even though the story shows justification of killing in an extraordinary situation in the Buddhist tradition, it does not offer a direct answer to many moral dilemmas in contemporary bioethical debates, such as human experimentation and euthanasia.

Garfield states, is "the protection of the private," and central to that protection is "the protection of individuals from obligations to undertake any particular attitudes or visions of the good life" (Garfield 1998:1–14). Quite obviously, Garfield interprets "negative rights" in a more "negative" manner by suggesting that right is a means to avoid obligations one has for others. He then further points out that "to begin from compassion is to begin by taking the good of others as one's own motive for action" (Garfield 1998:1–14). Garfield's critique of the individual-oriented approach to rights supports his argument for fellowship implied in the Buddhist ethics of compassion. For Garfield and many other Buddhist scholars, compassion or obligation to other fellow men/women should be the primary moral language, while the concept of rights functions as a protective mechanism to safeguard human life and freedom.[10] It seems to me that Garfield's argument for compassion is quite similar to that made by communitarians in the West such as Alasdair MacIntyre, Charles Taylor, and Michael J. Sandel. For them, the drawback of rights-talk lies in not only its overemphasis on preferences and choices of someone who is "antecedently individuated", but also in its potential undermining of one of the fundamental issues in moral philosophy. That is, "what is right" (a pun here) has replaced "what is good" which provides a strong foundation for good society and the flourishing of human beings.[11]

Buddhism implies similar arguments. For Buddhists, the language of rights indicates the primacy of a self-embedded individualism that is antithetical to Buddhist moral teachings. Ihara, for instance, contends that "...invoking rights has the inevitable effect of emphasizing individuals and their status, thereby strengthening the illusion of self. While Buddhism has a holistic view of life, the rights perspective is essentially atomistic" (Ihara 1998: 51). To respond to this problem, an online symposium in 1995 entitled "Buddhism and Human Rights" sponsored by the *Journal of Buddhist Ethics* issued "Declaration of Interdependence" as a supplemental document to UN's Declaration of Human Rights, in which one reads,

> Those who have the good fortune to have a "rare and precious human rebirth," with all its potential for awareness, sensitivity, and freedom, have a duty to not abuse the rights of others to partake of the possibilities of moral and spiritual flourishing offered by human existence. Such flourishing is only possible when certain conditions relating to physical existence and social freedom are maintained. Human beings, furthermore, have an obligation to treat other forms of life with the respect commensurate to their natures (Harvey 2000: 121).

[10] Garfield argues that liberal moral theory may be properly conceived as the social face of Buddhist moral theory which is grounded in compassion, and hence there is no conflict in the position of. Dalai Lama when he advocates the cultivation of compassion as the most basic moral task while at the same time advocating recognition of human rights. Garfield, "Human Rights and Compassion: Towards a Unified Moral Framework," pp., 1–14.

[11] Critics of rights-talk like also contends that "Our rights talk, in its absoluteness promotes unrealistic expectations, heightens social conflict, and inhibits dialogue that might lead toward consensus, accommodation, or at least the discovery of common ground. In its silence concerning responsibilities, it seems to condone acceptance of the benefits of living in a democratic social welfare state, without accepting the corresponding personal and civic obligations" See Mary Ann Glendon, *Rights Talk: The Impoverishment of Political Discourse*, New York: Free Press, 1991, p.14.

The citation shows two distinctive moral frameworks maintained by Buddhists: (1) it puts rights–if the language of rights has to be employed–into the assumption of interconnectedness; and (2) it adds the rights of other life forms, that is, non-human forms into the category of rights. The former stipulates an intrinsic relation between rights and duties while the latter focuses on an eco-centric position emphasized by Buddhism. From the Buddhist doctrine of (inter)dependent-origination, duty for oneself and duty for others do not necessarily contradict each other, as the Buddhist scripture puts it, “Protecting oneself, one protects others; protecting others, one protects oneself” (*Samyutta-Nikaya* 47, 19).[12] The point here is not to say that there is absolutely no conflict (or moral dilemma) between protecting oneself and protecting others; instead it attempts to emphasize social responsibilities albeit the value of individualism.

From another perspective, I do not think the doctrine of (inter)dependent-origination can discount the importance of the idea of individual rights; instead, it can be used to articulate the importance of respecting each individual. In the Chinese tradition, this idea is particularly expressed through what is known as the “negative golden rule,” i.e. not imposing on others what you yourself do not like. In the Confucian teaching we have a well-known saying that “One should not treat others in ways that one would not like to be treated” (己所不欲,勿施於人 *Analects* 5, 11). The same idea can be found in Buddhism as well: “For a state that is not pleasant or delightful to me must be so to him also; and a state that is not pleasing or delightful to me, how could I inflict that upon another?” (*Samyutta-Nikaya*). I do not think that liberals in the West would have any problem with the statement here. Peter Harvey, for instance, defends that Buddhists would accept the basic idea of rights although the radical idea of self is at odd with the Buddhist concept of no-self. In his book *An Introduction to Buddhist Ethics*, Harvey admits the fact that “Buddhists are sometimes unhappy using the language of ‘rights’ as they may associate it with people ‘demanding their rights in an aggressive, self-centered way, and may question whether talk of ‘inalienable rights’ implies some unchanging, essential Self that ‘has’ these, which is out of accord with Buddhism’ teaching on the nature of selfhood” (Harvey 2000: 119). Yet this does not lead to the conclusion that Buddhism would reject the concept of human rights, particularly the rights “of other people” categorically. What Harvey seems to emphasize is that the critique of atomic individualism should not deny other moral implications suggested by human rights. To be more exactly, Buddhism would fully accept the negative rights and welcome certain aspects of positive rights with qualifications.

Probably, most people would agree that in a well-functioning community or society, individual rights and social responsibilities are well attended to rather than one negating the other. But very often the concept of human rights is emphasized more often because of the existence of all sorts of violation of human dignity, rights,

[12] Also see Harvey 2000, p. 33.

and freedom in the world, including in healthcare systems. Take the healthcare situation in China, for example, it is a common practice for hospitals to forge an informed consent in order to get the blood sample from a patient or a particular ethnic group in the name of life science and social good. Most doctors I have interviewed in recent years would defend such kind of practice, believing that they did so out of social responsibility and the common good. Thus in China we need to fight for more individual rights; while in a society like the US where unrestrained greed and self-interest have pushed individualism too far, we need to talk more about care, compassion, interconnectedness, and the common good.

5.3 Human Freedom

How do we interpret the notions of "freedom" of individual agency and freedom of self-determination implied in the UDHR? According to liberalism, the good society is viewed as "a collection of self-interested individuals, free to choose their own life projects, bound together by *agreement* to respect the rights of others in the pursuit of these projects" (Theobald and Dinkelman 1995:14).[13] As such, freedom to choose is based on recognition of each individual's self-interest; society is built on mutual consensus.

To follow this contractarian line of thinking, the notions of individual agency and the freedom of self-determination in bioethics are usually linked with the principle of autonomy, informed consent, right to choose, etc. The word "autonomy" comes from the Greek *autos-nomos* meaning "self-rule" or "self-determination". The UDBHR clearly articulates the freedom of individual agency in terms of self-determination. Today self-determination becomes a central principle in the medical arena, which has been gradually moving away from a paternalistic approach towards a more individualistic, client-centered approach. The patient, as an independent entity, plays a more active role in his/her own health decisions.

Of course, such modern concept of freedom may not exist in Buddhism. Freedom as absence of coercion is not emphasized by Buddhism either. Nevertheless, the idea of choice and consent in medicine can be found in the Buddhist tradition. For example, according to early Buddhist monastic codes, the patient's personal choice is respected. That is to say, the intention of the patient is given a serious consideration in the decision-making process.[14] Freedom of self-determination is equally important for Buddhism in the contemporary situations such as euthanasia and organ transplantation. However, if the patient lacks knowledge concerning what is

---

[13] For detailed argument on the issue, see Paul Theobald and Todd Dinkelman's essay "The Parameters of the Liberal-Communitarian Debate," *Peabody Journal of Education,* Vol. 70, No. 4, 1995. pp. 5–18.

[14] See Paul D. Numrich, "The Buddhist Tradition: Religious Beliefs and Healthcare Decisions, "Religious Traditions and Healthcare Decisions" Handbook Series, the Park Ridge Center for the Study of Health, Faith, and Ethics, 2001, p. 4.

occurring, whether due to extreme physical pain or mental disruption, he or she will not considered be morally responsible for making medical decisions. As for truth-telling vis-à-vis confidentiality in medical practice, the Buddhist notion of "right speech" requires wisdom on the part of a physician to know what kind of medical information should be disclosed to the patient and his/her family members.

That being said, we should not expect a radical notion of freedom in Buddhism. Despite that most Buddhist scholars and Buddhist followers claim that Buddhism is a religion of freedom, we know they are talking about different kind of freedom, a freedom best labeled as "spiritual freedom" rather than freedom of choice in a modern socio-political sense. Very often, freedom in Buddhism pertains to an intrapersonal rather than an interpersonal *relationship. In the case of freedom with reference to* interpersonal *relationship,* a social relationship is considered "free" if all parties in that relationship can exercise their equal and reciprocal rights without coercive interference by others. In the case of freedom in Buddhism, *it* focuses more on releasing oneself from the bonds of *samsāra* caused by desires, or at best, aims at the possibility of existential transformation of one's mind so that he/she is capable of being engaged with his/her living ambience in a spontaneous way so as to de-limit boarders, boundaries, and limitations of all kinds. Personal wisdom, instead of personal rights therefore, is the main theme of Buddhist discourse on freedom.

So the question of freedom-from-cum-freedom-to in Buddhism is closely associated with its attempt to be free or liberated from dis-ease (*dukkha*) derived from the emotive attachment that leads to an individual's existential anxiety in coping with impermanence and changes. Attachment sometimes refers to *alāya*, a particular form of consciousness that "tends to get solidified into concepts of incorruptible and ultimately real objects every time it occurs." This tendency is also applied to occasions of sense experience (Kalupahana 1992: 191). *Alāya* consciousness functions in two ways: (1) internally it appears as the constituents of a self; and (2) externally it becomes the consciousness of the object as "the other." Vasubandhu, the Buddhist philosopher of the School of Consciousness-Only or Yogācāra (*weishi* 唯識宗) speaks of freedom attained by an *arhat* (*aluohan* 阿羅漢) in terms of dissipation of *alāya*, i.e., the mental and emotional attachment. According to Vasubandhu, all ideas have mind (*mano*) as a pre-condition, and the mind as a special faculty is different from other faculties (eye, ear, nose, tongue, and body) in that it tends to substantiate and conceptualize things/objects it has experienced, which eventually leads to attachment, not only to a metaphysical object but also to a metaphysical self. Non-attachment, in this sense, means a freedom from a metaphysical essence, and more importantly, from a metaphysical self that perceives mind as independent and incorruptible. As one can tell, the Buddhist notion of human freedom is not grounded "free choice" *per se*; rather, it is a kind of "spiritual freedom."

One of the major critiques of Buddhism is connected to the Buddhist notion of karma which is viewed very often as a form of "determinism" that denies a freedom of choice. For Buddhists, however, karma refers to "action and reaction" which includes three kinds of action, that is, the physical, the mental, and the verbal. Buddhists use the term karma specifically referring to volition or choice, that is, the intention or motivation behind a mental formation and action. This intention can also be understood the "act of will" in that an individual person is responsible for his/her actions and the consequences of those actions. According to Buddhism, it is the volitional will behind the action that determines the karmic consequences. Volition, in turn, is shaped and reshaped by acts of attention, which influence perceptions and determine the views from those perceptions. Keown rightly points out that in Buddhism individuals have free will and their destiny is "the function of their choice" known as karma.[15] Because one can attend to the results of one's intentions, there is an internal feedback loop allowing one to learn and control. Because attention can ask questions, it can monitor that feedback to determine how best to put it to use. From this perspective, I think Buddhism cares more on the *content* of the choice than *a procedural act* that shows one has the right to choose. This point can be best illustrated by using the example of informed consent dealing with risks in medical ethics. One of the problems of informed consent today is that it becomes a procedural act that sometime is used as a means to protect doctors instead of patients due to the asymmetrical relationship between physicians and patients. It follows that Buddhists may prefer the paternalistic model instead of the model of patient autonomy in certain cases which allows the intervention of doctors that best promotes the health and well-being of their patients.

Accordingly, "free choice" raises the question as to how far the choice which one seems to exercise in his/her conduct and actions is actually a free choice or only a "causal necessity" in the sense that what is conceived as "free will" or "choice" is nothing but a mere matter of habit, or of likes and dislikes engendered by heredity and environment, over which one has little control.[16] Therefore, volition as contrasted to natural causality points to logical or extensional causality because it is involved in a rational process through which logical inference may occur.[17] But if causality is volition, it could be much more complicated than a mechanical relationship in forms of natural causality represented by uniformities and regularities, for the required and necessary conditions are also "conditioned," either immediate or

---

[15] Damien Keown, "Buddhism and Medical Ethics: Principles and Practice," p. 42. http://www.buddhismuskunde.uni-hamburg.de/fileadmin/pdf/digitale_texte/Bd7-K03Keown.pdf. The same argument is seen in Keown's book, *Buddhism and Bioethics*. New York: St Martin Press. 1995. In fact, Keown sees Buddhist ethics as a form of virtue ethics in which character and action combine with one another. On Keown's account, virtues motivate or cause a person to *choose* to enact virtuous courses of action.

[16] For instance, the Stoic metaphor of a rolling cart that one either willingly follows or which drags one unwillingly along. Scholars like Karl H. Potter contends that karma in terms of predetermination is "habit" that is similar to the pyschologistic analysis of the role of habits in human existence. As he puts it, "Habits, necessary to success, constitute a source of bondage. As one becomes more and more successful through the development of these habitual responses, he/she tends to become less and less capable of adjusting to fresh and unusual contingencies." See Potter, *Presuppositions of India's Philosophies*. New Delhi: Motilal Banarsidass Publisher, p. 12

[17] In the Western philosophical tradition, the concept of will "is usually connected to rationality as one of two complementary activities of the mind: the faculty of choice and decision, whereas the reason is that of deliberation and argument. Thus a rational act would be an exercise of the will performed after due deliberation." But in Buddhism, the concept of will includes a psycho-intuitive account of one's mind as well.

far-reaching, by the specific relationship between the agent and his/her consciousness/will. As a choice-model of ethical conduct, karma indicates a prescriptive as well as a normative dimension. That is to say, "A ought to do x in order to achieves y," or "X is the right thing to do." Therefore, when a person understands that karma is based on volition, he/she will see enormous responsibilities and has to become conscious of the intentions that precede his/her actions. Thus, Buddhists insist that taking personal responsibilities is crucial for moral life.

But the question of free choice remains. If someone is conditioned, or dependent-arising, how can he/she be totally free (for a hope-for result), or be extricated from causal chains of determination? A "logical determinist" would question how choices can be free, given that what one does in the future is already determined or conditioned somehow in the present. This skeptical view implies that conditionality and freedom are mutually exclusive. But for Buddhists, the doctrine of interconnectedness shows that the conditionality is always a process of infinite conditioning and being infinitely conditioned, as causality itself is devoid of self-nature, and the same thing applies to freedom as well. The present as such is never a "clean slate" since it has partially shaped by influences from the past and the immediate results of present actions. Therefore, the implications of karma involve the notion that predestination and free will exist simultaneously.[18]

The compatibility of causality and volition suggests that freedom for Buddhism does not mean being absolutely free from anything whatsoever; instead, the choice is free because it is conditioned. To be more specific, Buddhism accepts "freedom of choice" in the sense that a person can think, reflect upon things, emotions, etc., and act upon according to his/her judgment, yet all these are done within a cluster of "lived" (not mechanical) conditions, as operating according to a set of fixed, knowable laws. Meanwhile, the Buddhist doctrine of centrality (the middle way) in reference to non-attachment also aims at avoiding the two extreme views of freedom and fatalism. Thus the Buddhists accept the notion of self-determination yet put more weights on self-responsibilities instead of rights.

5.4 Conclusion

This paper focuses the attention on some key theoretical issues concerning human rights and freedom in bioethics in light of Buddhism. How should the concept of human rights be translated to a non-Western religion such as Buddhism and to the local level such as in Chinese society? How can we compromise between rights and responsibilities, or individualism and collectivism? All there are complicated questions. Very often, we hear scholars claiming that human responsibilities and human

[18] Here one may argue that "influences from the past" cannot logically identified with "causality," as it does not "determine" the will, which remains free, but only strengthens or weakens it, facilitating or easing its operation in a certain direction. Because of the scope of this presentation, I have to skip this argument in details.

rights should not supersede but complement each other. But from political and judicial perspective, this is quite a vague statement as it does not offer a clear picture of what constitutes "responsibilities" and what constitutes "rights." Liberals, libertarians, and communitarians keep fighting because of their different definitions regarding the parameters of responsibilities and rights both morally and legally. For the Buddhist the gap can be even bigger since Buddhism does not have the rights-based conception of freedom. One of the crucial differences lies in the fact that Buddhism and Buddhist philosophy did not emerge either as a social philosophy, or as a social religion (in comparison to Christianity). In fact, Buddhism is quite individualistic (in a different sense though), aiming at individual emancipation and enlightenment via attaining a personal moral and spiritual transformation.

In sum, both rights-talk and duties-talk are important in ethical and bioethical discourse, yet neither should be confined to an ideological cage. Differently put, when the society tilts toward one side, the other must be shored up. In addition, the concept of human rights is better served as a protective mechanism and thus using the language of rights without qualification to grapple with every moral issue "is analogous to treating every sickness with the same medication... It is crude and ineffective" (Benatar 2006: 19).

References

Benatar, D. 2006. Bioethics and health and human rights: A critical view. *Journal of Med Ethics* 32 (1): 17–20.

Garfield, Jay L. 1998. Human rights and compassion: Towards a unified moral framework. In *Buddhism and human rights*. Richmond: Curzon Press.

Glendon, Mary Ann. 1991. *Rights talk: The impoverishment of political discourse*. New York: Free Press.

Harvey, Peter. 2000. *An introduction of Buddhist ethics*. Cambridge: Cambridge University Press.

Ignatieff, Michael. 2001. *Human rights as politics and idolatry*. Oxford: Oxford University Press.

Ihara, Craig. 1998. Why there are no rights in Buddhism: A reply to Damien Keown. In *Buddhism and human rights*. Richmond: Curzon Press.

Kalupahana, David J. 1992. *A history of Buddhist philosophy: Continuities and discontinuities*. Honolulu: University of Hawaii Press.

Keown, Damien. 1995. *Buddhism and bioethics*. New York: St Martin Press.

———. 2005. *Buddhist ethics: A very short introduction*. Oxford: Oxford University Press.

Keown, D., C. Prebish, and W. Husted, eds. 1998. *Buddhism and human rights*. Richmond: Curzon Press.

Keown, Damien, et al., eds. 2000. *Buddhism and human rights*. Richmond: Curzon Press.

Numrich, Paul D. 2001. *The Buddhist tradition: Religious beliefs and healthcare decisions*, Religious traditions and healthcare decisions. Handbook Series, the Park Ridge Center for the Study of Health, Faith, and Ethics.

Schmidt-Leukel, Perry. 2006. Buddhism and the idea of human rights: Resonances and dissonances. *Buddhist-Christian Studies* 26: 33–49.

Theobald, Paul, and Todd Dinkelman. 1995. The parameters of the liberal-communitarian debate. *Peabody Journal of Education* 70 (4): 5–18.

Chapter 6
A Buddhist Response to Ellen Zhang's "On Human Rights and Freedom in Biomedical Ethics"

Soraj Hongladarom

Zhang's paper is an insightful inquiry on what Buddhism has to say on human rights and freedom. She cites numerous literature, both from modern social and political philosophy and from traditional Buddhist canons, to support the view that Buddhism is at least not inimical to the ideas behind human rights and human freedom, and in many cases strongly support them. In this response I will focus on three topics: Firstly, I will touch upon the issue, developed by Damien Keown, whether there is such a thing as a Buddhist ethics at all. This has quite a lot to do with Zhang's discussion in the paper. Then I'll focus on Zhang's treatment of human rights and human freedom according to Buddhism, respectively.

In *Buddhist Ethics: A Very Short Introduction*,[1] Keown argues that there is actually no "ethics" in Buddhism. By this he means that there is no normative ethics, the kind of theorizing about the justification of moral norms that philosophers in the West are accustomed to. There are a large number of "moral teachings" in Buddhism, and Zhang cites several of them in her paper, but there is, according to Keown, very little in Buddhist literature in ethical deliberation or ethical theory. Compared to the writings of Plato and Aristotle, Buddhist literature has almost nothing to offer which could be regarded as ethical theorization. The closest thing to ethics properly speaking is sila, which is usually translated as "morality," but in fact refers more to self discipline. As to the philosophical reasoning behind such tenets of self discipline, Keown sees that Buddhism has nothing to offer, which raises a curious question as to why that is the case.[2]

The answer, for Keown, is twofold. On the one hand Buddhism grew up among a number of absolute monarchies. The totalitarian lands ruled by emperors or kings,

[1] Damien Keown, *Buddhist Ethics: A Very Short Introduction* (Oxford University Press, 2005), pp. 27–29.

[2] Keown, *Buddhist Ethics*, pp. 27–29.

S. Hongladarom (✉)
Department of Philosophy, Faculty of Arts, Chulalongkorn University, Bangkok, Thailand
e-mail: hsoraj@chula.ac.th

J. Tham et al. (eds.), *Religious Perspectives on Bioethics and Human Rights*,
Advancing Global Bioethics 6, DOI 10.1007/978-3-319-58431-7_6

which comprised the political environment for early Buddhism, left little room if any for the kind of development of independent thought which is necessary for ethical theorization. According to Keown, "In such a context, in which power resides with kings and emperors rather than with citizens, the disciplines of politics and ethics are largely redundant."[3] On the other hand, the renunciation movement fostered by Buddhism made it difficult for its followers to be actively engaged in the political life of the regimes they found themselves in. If the goal in becoming a member of the Order is to renounce the world, then it does not look coherent for these members to be engaged in a kind of theory making that purports to justify this or that particular theory in ethics or social and political philosophy. The upshot of all this, according to Keown, is that when Buddhism becomes transplanted in the West, scholars and practitioners in Buddhism found that there was a need to discuss Buddhist *ethics*, in the sense of an ethics that is commonly known and discussed in the philosophical literature in the West. For Keown, this is the origin on the interest in Buddhist ethics as a branch of philosophical deliberation and an academic discipline.[4]

One wonders, however, that Keown's two reasons for Buddhism's apparent lack of interest in ethical theory are all there is to it. Is there anything within the content of the teaching of Buddhism at all that could explain this apparent lack of interest? The political environment of sixth and fifth century B.C.E., which was roughly the period when the Buddha started teaching and found the religion, does not seem a necessary condition as to why there is such a lack, because it seems adventitious. The second reason, that of Buddhism's renunciation nature, appears to be closer to the core teaching, but other religions also promoted renunciation such as Jainism, but Jainism had a much more active theory of ethics that Buddhism did.[5] Hence, Keown's two reasons do not seem to be the end of the matter. There has to be a deeper reason.

It is this deeper reason that links my discussion here of Keown's view with Zhang's view presented in her paper. Zhang argues that Buddhism has a view which is rather friendly to the view of the liberal theory in western political philosophy, where the idea of human rights is justified and respected. I agree with her completely. I think the following is key to Zhang's argument:

> I do not think the doctrine of (inter)dependent-origination can discount the importance of the idea of individual rights; instead, it can be used to articulate the importance of respecting each individuals, particularly the idea of "negative golden rule," i.e., not imposing on others what you yourself do not like. In the Confucian teaching we have a well-known saying that "One should not treat others in ways that one would not like to be treated" (己所不欲,勿施於人 *Analects* 5, 11). The same idea can be found in Buddhism as well: "For a state that is not pleasant or delightful to me must be so to him also; and a state that is not pleasing or delightful to me, how could I inflict that upon another?" *(Samyutta-Nikaya).*

That is, one argues from the statement in the *Samyutta-Nikaya* that is quoted by Zhang to the conclusion that one then has rights that should be respected. Respecting

---

[3] Keown, *Buddhist Ethics,* p. 29.

[4] Keown, *Buddhist Ethics,* p. 30.

[5] For example, there is a direct link in Jainism between the teaching of *anekanta,* the view that no view has a monopoly on absolute truth with the moral doctrine of *ahimsa.*

individuals and respecting their rights basically amount to the same thing. However, as Keown has argued, there is no theory of ethics in Buddhism, so the statement in the *Samyutta-Nikaya*, namely "For a state that is not pleasant or delightful to me must be so to him also; and a state that is not pleasing or delightful to me, how could I inflict that upon another?," is taken to function as a premise leading to the conclusion that one ought to respect others' rights. Is this a kind of Buddhist political or legal theory? It would be so if there is a systematic theorization that explains how the premise and the conclusion here are linked up with each other. How is it the case that the realization that we share the same feelings as others leads to the conclusion that we ought to respect their rights? Here Buddhism, as Keown says, is rather silent.

One can of course speculate. We might think that by seeing ourselves in others, the interests that we take to be ours in fact are shared by others. We assume a broader perspective which is not merely limited to our own narrow view of ourselves or our egos alone. And as rights are manifestations of the respect of the inviolability of human beings, we understand this inviolability is due to the interconnectedness that we feel we share with our fellow human beings (and indeed with other sentient beings, as Zhang says in her paper). We feel that our bodies and our condition as a human being should not be interfered or taken advantage of, because if it is allowed that our condition (our bodies, our properties, and so on) are able to be violated freely we would not be on an equal footing with those who do the violating, and that would contradict both the violator's and our own condition as human beings. Thus connectedness among human beings lead to respect of dignity and rights. Is this sketch of a theory something remotely Buddhist? I don't see why not. It is different from the standard liberal theory of rights because the latter does not emphasize interconnectedness among people at all, but the autonomy and subjective nature of individuals. But if either emphasizing interconnectedness or autonomy lead to the same conception of human rights equally well, then it does not matter which one among the interconnectedness theory of the autonomy theory is the correct one. If it succeeds in bringing about the results equally, then they are equally good. The principle, then, is justified through its efficaciousness—how well the principle brings about desired consequences. Thus, if two theories are equally efficiacious, then they are equally justified.

I think this is the real underlying basis of the Buddhist's reluctance to theorize about ethics. The main goal of becoming a Buddhist is to release oneself from the bonds of samsara. This is done through full realization of the empty nature of all phenomena and subsequent mental and physical disciplines designed to train the mind to get rid of its habit of seeing things as thingy or as separate, individual, substantive *things*. This, of course, includes persons and the self too. The ultimate emphasis is on oneself. You are responsible for your release from samsara alone; even the Buddha himself cannot automatically bring people to the side of nirvana. Each one must make the effort to get there by themselves; the Buddha can only show the way. Thus, when the main goal is to arrive at the shore of nirvana, to engage in theory making or in justificatory projects that explain how it is that an action which is considered a good action is indeed good would seem rather pointless. Perhaps this is the underlying reason why there is so little theoretical work on ethics in the whole of the voluminous Buddhist literature. Trying to justify the moral norms—saying why what is considered to be good is indeed good—would seem to the Buddhist to be similar to those who are being stricken by an arrow to inquire about the look of the shooter, what kind of wood the arrow is made of, and so on; it just does not make sense. The purpose of right action *(sammā kammanta)* is that by doing it one gets closer to the Goal; one does not spend time arguing and debating why the right action is indeed right, whether it is right because it promotes universal happiness or because it accords with deontological logic. Doing that would seem to be even unbuddhist.

But we have to be careful in pointing out by doing so, that is by regarding the task of justifying moral norms to be akin to asking what kind of wood the arrow is made of, we do not thereby abandoning all theorization altogether. Again, if theory making, arguing, debating, etc. can lead us on the path moving toward the Goal, then so much the better. This is the Buddhist attitude toward ethical theory. The value of the theory is not that it helps us move closer to the truth, but the theory can only have any positive value if it leads us toward the goal, toward nirvana. However, since it might take eons eventually to arrive at nirvana, any action that would help us edge even a little closer toward the Goal in this lifetime would be valuable. Perhaps this obvious teleological viewpoint is so obvious that Buddhist scholars do not see that it is important to stress it every time. That is to say, any possible ethical theory would have to refer to the role of action in leading toward the Goal—how much, how effective, or whether it does lead there at all. It is so obvious that scholars and philosophers don't see any need to argue for it or make up a theory about it. The sheer fact of the matter that the action does contribute to the move toward the Goal is enough. There is then no need for ethical theory; what is left is a rather empirical investigation of whether such and such action does contribute to getting closer to the Goal or not.

If theory making can have its positive aspect in Buddhism, then a move that links up Buddhist teaching with modern liberal theory would also be positive. Zhang is certainly right when she maintains the rights talk within the context of the Buddhist teaching. Even though Buddhism does not advocate any particular ethical theory, this does not mean that one cannot make any claim about the Buddhist perspective on any matter, such as human rights and freedom. Even though Buddhism does not claim to advocate any theory justifying human rights, one can well talk about human rights in Buddhism and how Buddhism supports the notion of human rights without incurring a contradiction. This is because Buddhism does not say "No theory is possible," but instead it says "If by doing theory you can eventually arrive at the Goal, then by all means do it!" Thus, as respect for human rights could be seen as emerging from seeing the interconnectedness among individuals, and as seeing interconnectedness among phenomena is an important step toward realizing Liberation, the Buddhist certainly has nothing against rights talks at all. On the contrary, they will certainly support and promote it. Interconnectedness of people is indeed one aspect of interconnectedness of things in general. It is the complete knowledge that things, including people, are interconnected, that eventually lead one to Realization.

Another topic that Zhang discusses in her paper concerns freedom. Buddhism is a religion that is concerned very much with freedom; it could be said that the whole reason for being of Buddhism is that it exists so that people can arrive at absolute freedom, that is, freedom from suffering, freedom from having to wander around for eons in samsara. However, this kind of freedom is not what is talked about in discourses about human rights and social justice. The kind of freedom there, of course, is political or civic freedom and, perhaps to be lesser extent, freedom from poverty or lack of well-being. This, as we have learned from Keown, is not emphasized much in Buddhism. Buddhism tries to accommodate itself in as many type of social and political arrangements as possible. I remember there is a story where the Buddha advises his followers to leave when the local king becomes too oppressive, but on the whole the Buddha tries to accommodate his Order within the laws of whatever land he and his followers find themselves in. If the land there restricts some degree of personal freedom, then the Buddha would advise his followers to abide by the rule if it is not too much to bear. This shows that Buddhism does not have a full fledged theory of social and civic freedom. However, as is the case for human rights, this does not entail that Buddhism is against the idea of personal or civic freedom. This kind of freedom is part of the environment within which the Buddhist practitioner finds either conducive or inconducive to the practice of the Teaching. If the restriction is done for the purpose of maintaining security and peace, then perhaps the Buddhist would find that rather conducive, but again if the restriction is too much, then there is a motivation for the Buddhist to leave.

Zhang is right again when she separates these two kinds of freedom and maintains that for Buddhism "spiritual freedom" is given much more attention. However, this does not mean at all that Buddhism would have nothing to say at all in terms of criticizing the practices of some regimes when those practices curtail personal freedom intolerably and without justification. A regime that restricts the freedom of its citizen too much beyond the need to maintain security broadly construed deserves censure also from Buddhism because by doing so they violate the principle of interconnectedness and fundamental equality of everyone which logical arises from the interconnectivity. We are all equal in this sense because in the web of interconnectivity, our own individual, egoistic point of view is only one among many and deserves no special privilege at all when compared with the points of view of countless others in the web. Again, Zhang's quote from the *Samyutta-Nikāya* is apt: For a state that is not pleasant or delightful to me must be so to him also; and a state that is not pleasing or delightful to me, how could I inflict that upon another?"

6.1 Conclusion: Relevance to Biomedical Ethics

During the Hong Kong workshop, a question was raised during the presentation of this paper about the relevance of this theoretical discussion on the more concrete problem in biomedical ethics, so I would like to spend the remaining space allotted for this paper for this discussion. Basically my argument is that we can certainly base the broadly liberal system of values concerning rights and freedom on Buddhist teachings due to pragmatic grounds, and Buddhist is pretty much a pragmatic religion from the beginning. This may or may not be the same as Zhang's own view, but it's certainly my own view. So in order to see the relevance let us look at a concrete example. One of the most intractable bioethical problems about rights concern the rights of competing individuals. The well known example is the problem of abortion where the right of the unborn is pitted again that of the mother. However, in this paper we shall look at a relatively easier problem. It is commonly accepted that patients have rights; after all, patients are human beings, and all human beings have rights. However, often the rights of the patient are ignored because the doctor may think that in order for an effective treatment of the patient to go ahead, the rights of the patient can be ignored. Suppose the doctor sincerely believes that they know about the patient's best interest better than the patient herself, so the doctor continues to prescribe a treatment or an intervention overriding the patient's consent. However, Article 6 of the Universal Declaration on Bioethics and Human Rights says: "Any preventive, diagnostic and therapeutic medical intervention is only to be carried out with the prior, free and informed consent of the person concerned, based on adequate information." This clearly states that the doctor who continues to perform intervention without the consent of the patient is violating the latter's rights.

What would Buddhism say in such a case? The doctor's argument is that she is doing her job as a doctor and the patient's best interest lies in the latter's being cured of the disease and if the only way of achieving that is overlook or override some of the patient's rights, then so be it. Perhaps the patient is refusing the treatment but in the best judgment of the doctor this would jeopardize the patient's own best interest. The justification for Article 6 is that each and every human being has rights, and one of the key rights concerns the integrity of the body. Thus even if it is, according to the best judgment of the doctor, it is in the patient's own interest that the doctor go ahead with the intervention, the doctor would be violating the right of the patient if she did so. In this Buddhism would first counsel that there be an open talk between the patient and the doctor where no information is withheld. If the patient would like others such as her close relatives to join in the discussion then that has to be allowed to. This is also in accordance with Article 6. In any case, sooner or later the theoretical point of whether an individual human being has rights which are not violable has to come in, since this point underpins the whole intent of Article 6. As Buddhism has no objection whatsoever to the idea that each human being has a system of rights which are internationally accepted as we have seen, then here is where Buddhism can make a fundamental contribution to bioethics and to practical considerations. One might wonder why there is no differences between the Buddhist pronouncements and the internationally accepted standard as seen in the UNESCO Declaration, the answer is that Buddhism, at the level of pure teaching, has no pronouncements either for or against the Declaration, but in order for the global community to be able to live together peacefully and ethically, following the Declaration is better than not following it. This is also because the process leading up to the promulgation of the Declaration is a correct one. And this is an important point.

Chapter 7
A Response to Ellen Zhang's "On Human Rights and Freedom in Biomedical Ethics: A Philosophical Inquiry in Light of Buddhism"

Colleen M. Gallagher

Applying religious teachings to legal concepts and determinations is always a challenge. Professor Zhang has given us a means to consider Buddhism's teaching related to human dignity, rights and freedom as stated in the Declaration of Human Rights and the Universal Declaration on Bioethics and Human Rights. She has pointed out that the concept of "human rights" is not directly addressed by Buddhism but is not incompatible with Buddhist tradition. Zhang approaches this by discussing the Declaration of Human Rights (1948) which discussed "the rights of every individual" and how these are protected in legal form. She correctly points out that dignity, rights and freedoms are often based in the idea of self-determination.

The challenge of addressing the distinction of self-determination and a tradition that teaches that human beings do not occupy a privileged position can be daunting. However, Zhang takes on the challenge and provides insight into ways of expanding on Buddhist teaching in ways that are not always evident to those from other traditions.

Self-determination seems most often to be approached from the perspective of the individual and the concerns of that individual in a legal format according to Zhang. While this assumption is not found in most religious traditions it is in western legal traditions. Her discussion of philosophical terms is clear as she explains distinctions among dignity, freedom and rights. Zhang argues ways in which the Buddhist ethic of compassion could serve as a supplement to the concept of human rights. Hughes states that an obligation is to ensure that citizens do not fall into poverty as this begins a cycle in which other social ills follow. This he likens this to a Buddhist approach to human rights and health care access (Hughes 2007).

C.M. Gallagher (✉)
Section of Integrated Ethics in Cancer Care, Department of Critical Care and Respiratory Care, University of Texas MD Anderson Cancer Center, Houston, TX, USA
e-mail: cmgallagher@mdanderson.org

J. Tham et al. (eds.), *Religious Perspectives on Bioethics and Human Rights*, Advancing Global Bioethics 6, DOI 10.1007/978-3-319-58431-7_7

One of the first challenges Zhang points out is that the concept of human rights and dignity might be seen as giving humans privilege in comparison to non-humans. This itself would be different than Buddhist teaching.

While teachings may be quite different, Christian traditions teach that the individual lives in society and has duties toward others. Self-determination also must take into account the effects to others. Duties and rights are connected but not without distinction of each. Zhang points out that Keown discusses Buddhist teaching stating that duties and rights are mutually dependent. Zhang's discussion of the negative and positive rights is essential to understanding the distinction and the interplay among the two.

In Christian traditions the concept of social justice is more linked to human rights, while human dignity is more closely aligned with individual self-determination. This is not so different than what Zhang discusses regarding negative rights. A society may determine that it is a human right to have healthcare provided while at the same time not require a society to provide or pay for the same. The same may not remain constant when considering the role of the healthcare provider who takes on a duty through their profession. In other traditions the interplay of duties and rights are linked to the principle of justice.

Zhang discussed human freedom and the idea of self-determination and states that Buddhism does not have a direct teaching in relation to the modern concept of freedom. Her description of Buddhist teachings on culpability and "right speech" are examples of how some ancient teachings can be applied in modernity without disruption.

I would have liked to see a stronger treatment of biomedical ethics in the philosophical inquiry. Several of the current biomedical questions can be discussed in light of Buddhism and the discussion of human rights that Zhang provides. The discussion of self-determination and human dignity can be linked to the concept of "the self" as done by Hongladarom in his work on privacy and genetic information. He considers providing genetic information as a convenient designation of self rather than as a property defining the human person. He links this to the Doctrine of Non-Self. Similarly he discusses privacy in light of bioinformatics and respect for individuals (Hongladarom 2009).

Zhang briefly mentions euthanasia and organ donation but does not go into detail. In many Christian traditions the question of personal freedom, rights of the individual to self and other, and the duty of individual providers come into conflict in these particular issues. These are both discussed by Masao Fuji using the Fourfold Holy Truths and the Noble Eightfold Path. In the discussion it is stated that euthanasia is unacceptable because the person in incapable of judging for him or herself. He also used the concept of compassion as in it the person is to respect his own life as well as the life of others (Fuji 1991). Organ donation itself is often linked to questions of what is commonly called "brain death". Keown and others have discussed this and come to the conclusion that the definition of death is the primary question. Meyer provides a systematized approach to the discussion and concludes that the cerebral definition of death is the most reasonable and most conforms to the general Buddhist doctrine (Meyer 2005).

Zhang gives a good discussion of balancing determinism and freedom as she considers the Buddhist concept of karma. In Christianity it is taught that a person is to be virtuous which requires volition of the individual. It is also taught that God is all-knowing but gives free will to humans. Ratanakul has written about the struggle for Buddhist precepts as western bioethics has entered into Thailand. The approach used was the consideration of biomedical questions in light of Buddhist precepts that emphasize the motive of an action more than its consequence. Examples given are veracity and non-injury to life. Veracity is considered a duty. Non-injury to life is used to address questions of euthanasia. In addition, the link between the principle of justice and ideal of compassion is made. Using this Ratanakul is able to discuss social justice or what the Declaration on Bioethics and Human Rights would consider human rights (Ratanakul 1998).

Essential to any discussion of biomedical ethics and human rights is an understanding of how an individual or a community defines health. "According to Buddhism, to be active and healthy, one needs to live a spiritual life" (Hewaparthirane 2001, p. 6). Sorajjakool and Naewbood remind of us this as well as stating that "Disease, on the other hand, is the result of ignorance leading to craving desire, impurity, indulgence that leads to disharmony at the physical, emotional, and spiritual levels" (Sorajjakool and Naewbood 2010).

Among her most intriguing comments, Zhang uses what she calls the "negative golden rule." She quotes Samyutta-Nikaya "For a state that is not pleasant or delightful to me must be so to him also; and a state that is not pleasing or delightful to me, how could I inflict that upon another?" This manner of consideration of violation of what is called by others a human right is one that is likely understood and easily accepted by most religious, ethical and legal scholars.

Zhang asserts that compassion, explained as active sympathy or willingness to bear the pain and sorrow of others, is a duty. If this is a duty that all can share it can bring us to a common understanding of ethics (behavior) that also would be unwilling to inflict pain or sorrow. Is it possible that we might commonly agree that this alone would bring about the full affirmation of human rights, dignity and freedom?

References

Fuji, Masao. 1991. Buddhism and bioethics. In *Theological developments in bioethics: 1988 1990*, Bioethics Yearbook, vol. 1, 61–68. Dordrecht: Kluwer.

Hewaparthirane, D. 2001. Buddhism, healing and wellbeing. *Wisdom* 9 (1): 6–8.

Hongladarom, S. 2009. Privacy, the individual and genetic information: A Buddhist perspective. *Bioethics* 23: 403–412. doi:10.1111/j.1467-8519.2009.01716.x.

Hughes, J. 2007. Buddhist bioethics. In *Principles of health care ethics*, ed. R.E. Ashcroft, A. Dawson, H. Draper, and J.R. McMillan, 2nd ed. Chichester: Wiley. doi:10.1002/9780470510544.ch17.

Meyer, J. 2005. Buddhism and death: The brain-centered criteria. *Journal of Buddhist Ethics* 12: 1–24. doi: 1076-9005.

Ratanakul, P. 1998. Bioethics in Thailand: The struggle for Buddhist solutions. *The Journal of Medicine and Philosophy* 13: 301–312.

Sorajjakool, S., and S. Nawwbood. 2010. Buddhism. In *World religions for healthcare professionals*, ed. S. Sorajjakool, M. Carr, and J. Nam. New York: Taylor & Francis.

Part III
Asian Religions: Confucianism

Chapter 8
Universal Declaration on Bioethics and Human Rights: A Confucian Critique

Jonathan Chan

Abstract The paper discusses the moral position of Universal Declaration on Bioethics and Human Rights which takes human rights, and its related moral precepts, to be the fundamental ethical framework in dealing with ethical issues raised by medicine, life sciences and associated technologies as applied to human beings. The paper begins by identifying the fundamental principles as well as some other derivative and specifying principles of the ethical framework in question. It then moves to discuss some general problems with adopting the ethical framework of human rights by focusing on the rationality of the notion of human rights. The paper then discusses the moral position of the Declaration from a Confucian perspective.

8.1 Introduction

In the foreword to *Universal Declaration on Bioethics and Human Rights (UDBHR)*, which was adopted by the General Conference of UNESCO in October 2005, the then Director-General of UNESCO, Koichiro Matsuura, gave the following remark on the Declaration

> In dealing with ethical issues raised by medicine, life sciences and associated technologies as applied to human beings, the Declaration, as reflected in its title, anchors the principles it endorses in the rules that govern respect for human dignity, human rights and fundamental freedoms. By enshrining bioethics in international human rights and by ensuring respect for the life of human beings, the Declaration recognizes the interrelation between ethics and human rights in the specific field of bioethics. (Matsuura 2005)

The remark makes two points. First, the Declaration takes human rights to be the ethical framework of dealing with ethical issues raised by medicine, life sciences

---

UNESCO, *Universal Declaration of Bioethics and Human Rights* (2005). Available online at http://portal.unesco.org/en/ev.php-URL_ID=31058&URL_DO=DO_TOPIC&URL_SECTION=201.html

J. Chan (✉)
Religion and Philosophy Department and Centre for Applied Ethics, Hong Kong Baptist University, Hong Kong, China
e-mail: klchan@hkbu.edu.hk

J. Tham et al. (eds.), *Religious Perspectives on Bioethics and Human Rights*, Advancing Global Bioethics 6, DOI 10.1007/978-3-319-58431-7_8

and associated technologies as applied to human beings. Second, in adopting such an ethical framework, the Declaration recognizes a certain theoretical or conceptual connection between ethics and human rights in the field of bioethics.

The first point finds its explicit expression in the following Articles: Articles 2, 3, 5, 6, 7, 9, 10, 11, 12, 14, and 22. Article 2 states the aims of the Declaration. According to the article, one major aim of the Declaration is to provide a universal framework of principles and procedures to guide states in the formulation of their legislation, policies or other instruments in the field of bioethics. The principles affirmed by the framework are stated throughout Articles 3–17. These principles are to a very large extent re-affirmation of the morality of human rights and the extension of the morality to the field of bioethics, which indicates that the Declaration takes the bioethical issues, to a great extent, to be human rights issues.

In what follows, the paper will discuss the moral position of the Declaration which, as we have seen, takes human rights, and its related moral precepts, to be the fundamental ethical framework in dealing with ethical issues raised by medicine, life sciences and associated technologies as applied to human beings. The paper will begin by identifying the fundamental principles as well as some other derivative and specifying principles of the ethical framework in question. The paper then moves to discuss some problems with adopting the ethical framework of human rights. The discussion will focus on the rationality of the notion of human rights. The paper then will discuss the moral position of the Declaration from a Confucian perspective.

8.2 The Ethical Framework of UDBHR

Let us first take a look at some of the principles which are affirmed by the Declaration, particularly those affirming or invoking the moral authority of human rights. The fundamental ones are affirmed in Article 3 under the title of "Human dignity and human rights".

Article 3 (1) Human dignity, human rights and fundamental freedoms are to be fully respected.
(2) The interests and welfare of the individual should have priority over the sole interest of science or society

The above two principles of human dignity and human rights are what I call the framework principles, meaning that they serve as the foundational principles of the ethical framework which the Declaration adopts. The two principles are the most abstract and general ones of the framework. They do not tell us what specific actions are morally permissible and what not. The rest of the principles can be either regarded as the derivatives of the framework principles or the specifications of how the principles in question are to be understood in the field of bioethics. Articles 10 and 11, with the title "Equality, justice and equity" and "Non-discrimination and non-stigmatization" respectively, are instances of those derivative principles.

Article 10 The fundamental equality of all human beings in dignity and rights is to be respected so that they are treated justly and equitably.

Article 11 No individual or group should be discriminated against or stigmatized on any grounds, in violation of human dignity, human rights and fundamental freedoms.

These two derivative principles add no new moral content to the two framework principles. They are simply logical consequences of the principles in question. Some other specific principles which the Declaration endorses, by contrast, are not merely logical consequences but further specifications of the principles in question. Articles 5, 6 and 7, with the titles "Autonomy and individual responsibility", "Consent" and "Persons without the capacity to consent" respectively, are examples of those specifying principles. These principles focus on the autonomous aspect of human individuals and require this aspect of human individuals be respected. Article 5 states the general principle of respect for autonomy, whereas Articles 6 and 7 state how the principle is to be understood and implemented in the field of bioethics. Another article worth noting is Article 14. The clause (2) of the article asserts by implication that "the enjoyment of the highest attainable standard of health is one of the fundamental rights of every human being without distinction of race, religion, political belief". As the right to "the enjoyment of the highest attainable standard of health" is not included in the Universal Declaration of Human Rights of 10 December 1948 (UDHR), the right in question is at most an extension of the list of human rights affirmed by the UDHR.[1] Other significant specifying principles can be found in Articles 4, 8, 9, 12, 15, 16 and 17, which help either specify the framework principles or how the principles in question are to be understood and implemented in the field of bioethics.

8.3 Human Rights and Personhood

As shown in the above discussion, the Declaration holds the moral position which takes human rights, and its related moral precepts, to constitute the fundamental ethical framework in dealing with ethical issues raised by medicine, life sciences and associated technologies as applied to human beings. In what follows, I shall discuss the rationality of the moral position of the Declaration. The discussion will focus on some general problems concerning the moral position first. Then, I shall move on to discuss some specific problems concerning the moral position from a Confucian perspective.

[1]The right in question, however, is affirmed by the International Covenant on Economic, Social and Cultural Rights (ICESCR). Article 12 of ICESCR states: "The States parties to the present Covenant recognize the right of everyone to the enjoyment of the highest attainable standard of physical and mental health." United Nations, *International Covenant on Economic, Social and Cultural Rights* (1966). Available online at: http://www2.ohchr.org/english/law/cescr.htm

Since the moral position of the Declaration presupposes the moral authority of human rights, to assess the rationality of the moral position of the Declaration requires us to assess the rationality of human rights. To assess the rationality of human rights, in turn, requires us to consider the following questions: Does the notion of human rights have a clear sense? What is the moral basis for human rights? Are they universal? Obviously, these questions are the ones which need to be answered if human rights are to have the rationality which they are supposed to have.

Does the notion of human rights have a clear sense? The answer seems to be obvious: human rights, by definition, are rights that we have simply in virtue of being human. That this is the meaning or intension which the notion of human rights has is uncontroversial. However, is the meaning in question clear, or clear enough? In his important book, James Griffin argues that the notion of human rights is an incomplete "historical notion", which acquired its present sense only at the end of Enlightenment. Although the notion, according to Griffin, has undergone some development since the end of Enlightenment, it never reaches its perfect form. In Griffin's view, one of the problems with the notion of human rights is that it lacks a determinate sense. "The term was left with so few criteria for determining when it is used correctly, and when incorrectly, that we often have only a tenuous, and sometimes a plainly inadequate, grasp on what is an issue." (Griffin 2008, p. 2) Without an adequate set of criteria for the use, i.e., without a determinate sense, of the notion of human rights, we are unable to settle debates over human rights issues in a rational and fruitful way. We cannot tell, say, whether parents have a human right to decide the number and spacing of their children or whether a woman has a human right to determine what happens in and to her body or whether we have a human right to health. It needs more explanation if the notion is to have any moral force. (Griffin 2008, p. 14).

Griffin proposes to remedy the incompleteness of the notion by working on "the idea that human rights are protections of our human status and that the human status in question is our rational or, more specifically, normative agency." (Griffin 2008, p. 2) Human rights, according to Griffin, can be understood as protections of our normative agency. And the idea that we are normative agents can be explained by referring to the following picture of who we are

> We human beings have a conception of ourselves and of our past and future… We form pictures of what a good life would be…And we value our status as human beings especially highly, often more highly than even our happiness. This status centres on our being agents – deliberating, assessing, choosing, and acting to make what we see as a good life for ourselves. (Griffin, 2008, p.32)

From the above, it is clear that for Griffin, the notion of normative agency is not very different from the notion of personhood. To be a normative agent is to be a person. To protect our normative agency is to protect our personhood. Griffin argues that our personhood or agency depends on three things: (1) our being autonomous; (2) our having minimum provision of resources and capabilities and (3) our having some basic liberties. (Griffin 2008, p. 33) To protect our personhood, then, is to ensure these three human conditions not being violated.

By specifying human rights as protections of our personhood, Griffin's account of human rights seems to be able to provide some useful criteria for governing the use of the notion of human rights. The notion of personhood, for instance, can help generate most of the conventional list of human rights as well as explain their moral force. By using the three criteria provided by the notion in question, we are, at least, able to tell what is at issue in a human rights dispute.

8.4 Human Rights and Personhood

In what follows, I shall discuss the moral position of the Declaration with reference to Griffin's account of human rights.[2] Griffin's account of human rights does help clarify some moral principles which the Declaration affirms. By taking human rights to be protections of personhood, the meaning of Articles 3, 10 and 11 become clearer. Also, Articles 8, 9, 12, 15 and 16 can be given a clearer interpretation based on the above understanding of human rights. We may take, say, Article 16 to be saying that the impact of life sciences on future generations should be given due regard so that their personhood would not be compromised. Article 5 and 6 which put so much emphasis on individual autonomy can be explained in terms of Griffin's account as well.

However, there are some other articles which seem to be unable to get support from Griffin's account. For instance, Article 5 states

> …For persons who are not capable of exercising autonomy, special measures are to be taken to protect their rights and interests.

The notion of personhood is understood in terms of a person's status as an autonomous being, in the sense that he or she is capable of exercising autonomy. If an individual lacks such a capability, he or she cannot be called an "autonomous" being and therefore lacks personhood. In that case, there is no question of protecting that individual's human rights, since the individual would have no human rights at all, according to Griffin's account of human rights. Article 7 with its intention to protect the rights of "persons without the capacity to consent" encounters similar difficulty too. Another difficulty is to explain the right to "the enjoyment of the highest attainable standard of health" which Article 14 asserts by implication. Although health is important to our personhood, to maintain our personhood does not require "the enjoyment of the highest attainable standard of health". Many of us do not enjoy "the highest attainable standard of health", and their personhood is left intact.

8.5 A Confucian Critique of UDBHR

In the above, I have discussed some general problems with the moral position of the Declaration. In what follows, I shall discuss the moral position in question from a Confucian perspective. I shall first sketch the general position of Confucianism with

---

[2] That the present paper focuses on Griffin's account of human rights does not mean that there is no other account of human rights worth our attention. But in my view, Griffin's account is the clearest and best capturing the idea of human rights as advocated by the human rights tradition among others. For a critical review of other accounts, see Griffin 2008, pp. 20–28.

regard to human rights. I shall begin with the following claims, which characterizes the Confucian general position on human rights:

C1 Individual or human rights can never be the ground or the foundation of morality.[3]

C2 The notion of individual or human rights requires a social structure which affirms some sort of sharp distinction between individuals and gives primacy to it.

C3 It is exactly such a kind of sharp distinction between individuals that is absent in the Confucian society whose social structure is designed to cultivate the virtue of *ren* in every member of the society.

C1 says that it is impossible to ground morality on individual rights. Some explanation with regard to the claim is needed. C1 is not saying that it is impossible to construct a logically consistent theory of moral obligations on the basis of individual rights. C1 is obviously false if it says so. What C1 says is that given the Confucian understanding of morality, which is the only right kind of morality, it is impossible to ground such a morality on individual rights. C2 and C3 are supposed to provide justification for that being the case. Let us consider them in turn.

The truth of C2 depends on our analysis of the notion of human rights. But whatever analysis of the notion we come up with, the following must be included in the analysis: To assign a certain scheme of individual rights to an individual is to define a sphere for that individual which other people are not allowed to enter or intervene without her permission.[4] The individual is supposed to have complete control over any matter which falls within the sphere or can do anything she deems appropriate in that sphere. The sphere, so to speak, separates the individual from others. To see this, we only need to focus on some of the functions of rights: rights are concerned with the distribution of power and protections of the individual's autonomous status. Those with rights have enforceable claims, and need not rely on the good will of others. (Donnelly 1999, p. 61) To emphasize on the distribution of power and protections of the autonomous status of the individual is to emphasize a sharp distinction or boundary between people. The notion of individual rights, therefore, implies a sharp distinction of some sort between individuals of society. Thus, one is supposed to have complete control over, say, what religion one should believe, if the scheme of rights consists of the right to religious freedom. In the same vein, she is supposed to have complete control over what character she should develop, for instance, she may choose to be a hedonist, a playboy, an egoist or a morally decent person, if the right to liberty is included in the scheme. The distinction between individuals can also be explained in terms of the breakdown of the unity among the individuals: the weaker the unity among individuals the sharper the distinction between them. The concept of unity here is mainly an ethical one. What unites people is their upholding of a single and substantive normative order. The normative order is substantive in the sense that it prescribes a certain way of living. The notion of individual rights is at odd with the aforementioned concept of unity.

---

[3] I take individual rights and human rights to be the same thing.

[4] Here, we refer to the negative rights.

We can have different views concerning the nature of the distinction in question. Some critics of the notion of individual rights even go so far by arguing that the distinction which the notion of individual rights implies is not only social but also metaphysical. For these critics, the notion of individual rights presupposes a certain view about human selves. Charles Taylor, for instance, argued that the notion of individual rights presupposes "a [certain] view about human nature and the human condition which (among other things) makes a doctrine of the primacy of rights plausible."[5] Taylor called the view "atomism", which holds the metaphysical thesis that human beings are self-sufficient. What this means is that humans can in principle live a flourishing life, i.e., developing their full human capacities such as rationality, moral agency and autonomy, without society. This view implies that no metaphysical tie between an individual and society is necessary for the individual to live a flourishing life. Individuals may be biologically connected with someone else but they are metaphysically distinct or disconnected.[6] Henry Rosemont held a similar view when he wrote: "My own scepticism is not directed toward the moral or political theory in which rights have a role but toward the foundational view of human being as free, autonomous individuals on which all such theories more or less rest."[7] On Rosemont's view, all rights-based theories, whether moral or political, rest more or less on a conception of the human self which takes human beings to be free and autonomous individuals.

I am sympathetic to the idea that the notion of rights requires a certain conception of the human self. However, I will not discuss the idea here. What I want to argue is a more limited thesis that the notion of individual or human rights defines a social sphere for an individual, which separates the individual from others and draws a sharp distinction or boundary between the individual and others. The distinction need not be metaphysical. Its existence is due to adopting a certain social or political practice, i.e., adopting the regime of individual rights.

Now let us turn to C3. C3 amounts to saying that the distinction among individuals affirmed by the scheme of individual rights is at odds with the social structure required by Confucian ethics. To see the truth of C3, we need to know about the moral concern of Confucian ethics. For the Confucian, distribution of power and protections of the autonomous status of a person can never be a central issue of our moral concern. What we need to concern about are virtues and harmony. To emphasize virtues and harmony, however, is to emphasize a certain sort of interdependence of people. In a society with such moral concerns, the interests and welfare of the individual do not have priority over the interest of society, given the interests of the Confucian society are to develop virtues for the members of the society and maintain the harmony of society. Nor does individual autonomy have normative priority over other moral considerations.

[5] See Charles Taylor, "Atomism," *Philosophy and The Human Sciences: Philosophical Papers 2* (New York: Cambridge University Press, 1985), p. 189.

[6] Ibid., p. 191.

[7] Henry Rosemont, "Human rights: a Bill of Worries," *Confucianism and human rights*, eds. Wm. Theodore de Bary and Tu Weiming (New York: Columbia University Press, 1998), pp. 54–66.

That the cultivation of virtues is the most important moral concern of Confucian ethics can be seen from some passages of *The Analects*. Consider the following.

> The exemplary person devotes his efforts to the fundamental, for once the fundamental is established, the Way will grow therefrom. Filial piety and fraternal respect – are they not the fundamental of a person? (*The Analects* 1:2)

For the Confucian, family is the basic unit of society. It embodies the most important human relations. Only by living in family could an individual lead a flourishing life. It is because of the Confucian's emphasis on the importance of family that the Confucian places high priority to familial virtues such as filial piety and fraternal respect, which Confucius took to be the fundamental of a person. They are fundamental in the sense that without them, one cannot be fully human. To realise one's full humanity, one needs to develop them in oneself. The two virtues are important not only within family but also outside family. This is because the two virtues are also of utmost importance for building a harmonious society. Thus, Confucius said,

> A young man, when at home, should be filial, and when out in the world should be respectful to his elders. He should be earnest and truthful. He should overflow with love, and cultivate the friendship of the good. (*The Analects* 1:6)

For the Confucian, one should extend one's moral concern to people outside family. One must care about not only one's parents but also other senior members of society; not only senior members but also members of other age groups. Society is, thus, seen by the Confucian as an "extended family". That can explain why Tzu-hsia, a disciple of Confucius, had the following response when Ssu-ma Niu said that he had no brothers while others had

> I have heard it said: life and death are a matter of Destiny; wealth and honour depend on Heaven. The gentleman is reverent and does nothing amiss, is respectful towards others and observant of the rites, and all within the Four Seas are his brothers. What need is there for the gentleman to worry about not having any brothers? (*The Analects* 12: 5)

For the Confucian, all members of society can be seen as one's brothers. But this suggests that the Confucian society is somewhat like an extended family. (Let us call this "family-based society".) Without this image of society, i.e., the image of society as an extended family, the idea that all members of society are one's brothers would not have any sense. One important feature of the family-based society is that no sharp boundary can be drawn among individuals; nor does a clear cut line exist between the group and the individual. This is due to the special social structure of the family-based society, which is determined by the individuals' web-like social networks. (Fei 1992, p. 63) This social network is a network of human relations, in which some are important and some less important, including the relations of rulers and subjects, fathers and sons, husbands and wives, older and younger brothers, friends, seniors and juniors, the close and the remote. Within such a social network, we can see the path which runs from the self to the family, from the family to the state, and the state to the whole world (all under heaven). In a society which operates on these web-like social networks, the most important ethical principle is the principle expressed by the Confucian dictum "Discipline oneself and return to rituals."[8] For the Confucian, rituals are more than just a set of ceremonial rules. They provide standards of excellence for assessing all kinds of activities in human life. In such a society, individual or human rights have no place in moral and social life at all.

8.6 Conclusion

That the Confucian takes the virtue of *ren* to have moral priority over the individual's interests or welfare or autonomy has significant implications for the acceptability of the Declaration from the Confucian standpoint. It is evident that from the Confucian point of view, Article 3 is unacceptable. The article has a clause that "[t]he interests and welfare of the individual should have priority over the sole interest of science or society." It is exactly this clause that the Confucian finds problematic. As we have seen, the Confucian takes the cultivation of the virtue of *ren* in people to be the ultimate goal of society. The goal in question thereby is an important interest of a Confucian society. Along this line of thought, for the Confucian, it is never true to say that "[t]he interests and welfare of the individual should have priority over the sole interest of science or society." Articles 5, 6 and 7 are unlikely to be accepted by the Confucian as well. For these articles give personal autonomy a kind of top moral priority, which, as we have seen, is contrary to the ethical orientation of the Confucian ethical framework. To say this does not mean that personal autonomy has no place at all in the Confucian moral framework. The point is that the value of personal autonomy within the Confucian ethical framework does not have the high priority which the Declaration accords to it. Along this line of reasoning, Article 12 would not be accepted by the Confucian either. It is because the Confucian takes the Confucian values to be representing an aspect of a certain culture, giving them higher priority than anything else.

I would like to close the discussion by making some remarks concerning the central ideas of the paper. Firstly, the paper argues that the Confucian society is a family-based society, i.e., like an extended family, in which no sharp boundary can

[8] Consider the following passages from *The Analects*

> Yan Yuan asked about *ren* or humaneness. Confucius said, "Discipline yourself and return to ritual is what constitutes *ren*. If for a single day people could discipline themselves and return to ritual, all under heaven would return to *ren*. The practice of *ren* depends on oneself alone, and not on others."
>
> Yen Yuan said, "I should like you to list the items."
>
> Confucius said, "Do not look in a way that is contrary to ritual propriety, do not listen to what is contrary to ritual propriety, do not speak in a way that is contrary to ritual propriety, and do not move in a way that is contrary to ritual propriety." (*The Analects* 12:1)

The above quotation shows how Confucius sees the importance of ritual for building a virtuous society. For Confucius, rites are more than just a set of ceremonial rules. They provide standards of excellence for assessing all kinds of activities in human life.

be drawn among individuals; nor does a clear cut line exist between the group and the individual. This might give us the impression that in the Confucian ethical framework, the individual disappears, completely subsumed in the family and society, and has no say or identity. This, however, is a misunderstanding. No sharp boundary does not mean no identity or individuality. For the Confucian, a person's identity or individuality is constituted by his or her place in the network of social relations that the person has, e.g., being a child of x and y, a brother or sister of z and so on. Nor does this imply that a person has no say on his or her personal matters. It is true that Confucianism does not accord high priority to personal autonomy as human rights do. However, it does not follow that personal autonomy has no place in the Confucian ethical framework at all. The individual of course can have his or her say on many personal matters, provided that his or her choice would not endanger the moral order of society.

Secondly, the paper argues that the scheme of human rights affirms the existence of the sphere of autonomy for an individual, which other people are not allowed to enter or intervene without his or her permission and that the Confucian ethical framework denies the existence of such a sphere. In other words, the paper argues that some sort of incompatibility between human rights and Confucian moral system exists. This does not mean to deny that there are points of convergence or meeting ground between the Human rights principles and the Confucian thought or ethics. But the point is: even if there are points of convergence or meeting ground between the Human rights principles and the Confucian thought or ethics, it does not follow that the central claims C1, C2 and C3 of my paper are untenable. For instance, both the Confucian principle of *ren* and the human rights norms affirm the wrongness of killing innocent people. But this does not imply that Confucianism gives or has to give personal autonomy a high priority over the interests of the society to develop the virtues of the members and maintain the harmony of society.

Thirdly, it is obvious that the incompatibility thesis aforementioned depends on how the notion of human rights is understood. The paper agrees to the idea that human rights are protections of the individual's autonomous status or personhood and takes the latter to be representing the core meaning of the notion of human rights. This understanding of the notion of human rights has a strong historical ground. And it is this historical ground which informs us how the notion has been used and thereby constitutes the basic meaning of the notion. (Griffin 2008, pp. 30–37) Any definition of the notion lacking this historical root will result in changing the meaning of the notion. To define "human rights" in terms of moral obligation is a case in point. Obviously, the logical relation between moral obligations and human rights is asymmetrical. To make them equivalent via definition is to change the meaning of the notion of human rights. This is the strategy that some compatibilist use to argue for the compatibility between human rights and Confucian moral thinking, re-defining human rights as moral obligations to individuals (not to deprive them of certain things or withhold the things from them). This strategy of defending the compatibility view consists of two reasoning errors. First, the strategy can succeed only by making the compatibility view trivial. This is so because we can make any incompatible pair of concepts, x and y, become compatible by changing the meaning of x or y. Second, the strategy commits the fallacy of irrelevance by changing the subject. It is because to give a new meaning to the notion of human rights in this context is to change the subject.

Chapter 9
Developing Confucian Virtue-Based Rights: A Response to Jonathan Chan's Confucian Critique of the Universal Declaration on Bioethics and Human Rights

Ruiping Fan and Wenqing Zhao

Dr. Jonathan Chan has presented an excellent critique of the Universal Declaration on Bioethics and Human Rights (UDBHR) from the Confucian perspective. He has pinned down one of the major disagreements between the ethical framework proposed in UDBHR and the core beliefs of Confucianism: should the concept of human rights be seen as the fundamental ground of morality? As Jonathan Chan has made clear in his critique, "the moral position of the Declaration which, as we have seen, takes human rights, and its related moral precepts, to be the fundamental ethical framework in dealing with ethical issues raised by medicine, life sciences and associated technologies as applied to human beings." In contrast, Confucianism sees the concept of virtue as the ground of morality. Indeed, Confucianism is essentially a virtue-based and family-oriented form of life and ethical theory. It appreciates the cultivation of virtue, which is unachievable without solid, healthy family relationships, as the highest mandate of good governance. This of course extends to considerations of bioethics that is largely framed by the language of individual rights as made explicit in Articles 3–17 of the UDBHR.

Is Confucianism compatible with human rights? To answer this question, it is necessary to distinguish a thin concept from a thick conception. The "thin" and "thick" distinction was populated by Clifford Geertz (1973) and Gilbert Ryle (1968) in discussions of culture ethnology. Martha Nussbaum (1988) applies this distinction to cross-cultural ethical studies, using it to show that we can describe something in at least two ways: "Thin" descriptions have little theoretical content and thus are often widely shared, even between members of different traditions, whereas "think" descriptions are detailed accounts that are framed in terms of more distinctive

R. Fan (✉)
Department of Public Policy, City University of Hong Kong, Kowloon Tong, Hong Kong
e-mail: safan@cityu.edu.hk

W. Zhao
Center for Comparative Philosophy, Duke University, Durham, NC, USA
e-mail: zhaowenqing711@gmail.com

J. Tham et al. (eds.), *Religious Perspectives on Bioethics and Human Rights*,
Advancing Global Bioethics 6, DOI 10.1007/978-3-319-58431-7_9

concepts and commitments, which are often unique to particular traditions (292).As Baruch Broody suggests, a thin concept of rights simply indicates correlatives of obligations between individuals: "X has a right to Y against Z if and only if (just in case) Z has an obligation (not necessarily an overriding obligation) to X not to deprive X of Y or not to withhold Y from X." (p. 22) Such a thin understanding of human rights is content-less because it requires no substantive assumptions of moral good, nor any particular understanding of the nature of human persons or agents. It gives us a clean slate to draw more comprehensive accounts of what social atmosphere should be encouraged for human flourishing.

A liberal understanding of human rights, along with Confucian and some other traditional views, in a sense have a thick conception of human rights. It is heavily dependent on the liberal individualist notion of human agents (contractors) first taken as free and equal citizens in order to consider their important interests. The liberal conception of human rights is first and foremost an equal entitlement to liberty. The major issue is thus not whether Confucianism is compatible with any concept of human rights. Confucian scholars can certainly draw on the thin concept of rights to develop a thick Confucian conception of rights. Chan might have made a false dichotomy here. The real issue is rather whether Confucianism is compatible with the liberal individualist conception of human rights (Fan 2010, p. 57).

Confucianism cannot accept the absolutist principlism and individualism that characterize the liberal version of human rights (Fan 2010, p. 57). For Confucians, as Joseph Chan has put it, "rights as entitlements may be necessary as a fallback apparatus to protect legitimate self-interests when the virtues fail to obtain or people's personal relationships break down." (p. 230) Adding to this point, rights are not necessary in an ideal Confucian society where virtues prevail. In cases of virtue failure, individuals could bring their rightful interests to the attention of others under the name of "rights" (Fan 2010, p. 58).

In particular, a proper Confucian conception of human rights can be derived from the Confucian conception of virtues. Let us take elder care as an example. Filial piety (*xiao* 孝) is a cardinal Confucian virtue that is substantialized in the parent-children relationship. A filial child, daughter and son alike, must undertake the obligation of taking care of one's parents, especially in the case of debility and sickness. This makes taking care of one's parents, not only financially but also emotionally, an obligation for exercising the virtue of filial piety. Accordingly, the entitlement of the elderly parents to receive such care can be set down as their right. Having the right to elder care protects and to an extent encourages the practice of filial piety. To substantialize it by law sends a clear message to the society of the importance of taking care of one's parents. Confucianism would not object and in fact welcome such right as one of the fundamental rights of human.

This leads to the last remark of my response to Jonathan Chan's essay. In the end of his article, Jonathan Chan argues that Confucianism will necessarily reject Article 3 of the UDBHR for it states that human dignity, human rights and fundamental freedoms are to be fully respected and at the same time puts the priority of the interests and welfare of the individual over the sole interest of science or society (p. 9). Jonathan Chan writes,"It is exactly this clause that the Confucian finds problematic.

As we have seen, the Confucian takes the cultivation of the virtue of *ren* in people to be the ultimate goal of society. The goal in question thereby is an important interest of a Confucian society" (pp. 9–10). He has had the same objection to Article 12. However, following the idea of virtue-based Confucian rights, the installation of some Confucian human rights contributes to the ideal picture of Confucian society. In fact, we will argue in line with Joseph Chan that the recognition of a set of basic human rights can protect individual welfare when virtues fail to obtain or people's personal relationships break down. John Rawls, in our opinion, has come up with a reasonable, minimalistic list of such basic rights for international practices: "Among the human rights are the right to life (to the means of subsistence and security); to liberty (to freedom from slavery, serfdom, and forced occupation, and to a sufficient measure of liberty of conscience to ensure freedom of religion and thought); and to formal equality as expressed by the rules of natural justice (that is, that similar cases be treated similarly)" (p. 65).

Jonathan Chan also thinks "Articles 5, 6 and 7 are unlikely to be accepted by the Confucian as well. For the articles give personal autonomy a kind of top moral priority, which, as we have seen, is contrary to the ethical orientation of the Confucian ethical framework." (p. 9) However, we think whether Confucianism would accept this clause depends on the interpretation of the idea "autonomy". Article 5 says, "The autonomy of persons to make decisions, while taking responsibility for those decisions and respecting the autonomy of others, is to be respected." If the idea of autonomy here is understood as solely individual directed, Confucianism would necessarily reject such imposition of excessive individualistic value. But Confucianism would be very much compatible with a family-oriented notion of autonomy, in the sense that family is taken as the basic unit of society to make health related decisions for family members, and of course take full responsibility for those decisions.

To conclude, unlike Jonathan Chan, we believe that Confucianism is not incompatible with human rights in general. It is only incompatible with the liberal understanding of human rights which often imposes excessive individualistic values on other cultural traditions. Confucian rights, which are virtue-based and family-oriented, can also serve an important role in achieving an ideal Confucian society. In facing the UDBHR, we should be careful and make clear that we are rejecting its underlying liberal individualistic values. We are, however, not rejecting human rights all together. In particular, we are not rejecting the instrumental use of human rights as a common legal language to protect culture-specific values.

References

Fan, Ruiping. 2010. *Reconstructionist confucianism: Rethinking morality after the west*. New York: Springer.

Geertz, Clifford. 1973. Thick description: Toward an interpretive theory of culture. In *The interpretation of cultures: Selected essays*, 3–30. New York: Basic Books.

Nussbaum, Martha. 1988. Non-relative Virtues: An Aristotelian Approach. *Midwest studies in Philosophy* 13 (1): 32–53.
Ryle Gilbert. 1968. *The thinking of thoughts: What is 'Le Penseur' doing?*. University Lectures, The University of Saskatchewan.

Chapter 10
Response to Jonathan Chan, *Universal Declaration on Bioethics and Human Rights*: A Confucian Critique

Alex Yeung

Prof. Jonathan Chan's paper, "*Universal Declaration on Bioethics and Human Rights*: A Confucian critique," expresses substantial reservations that the Declaration can be acceptable from a Confucian standpoint. The focus of the Confucian moral system is placed on the concept of *rén,* or human-ness, rather than on individual autonomy.[1] The following remarks seek to be placed within a positive dialogue between Christian and Confucian ethics in the search for a universal ethic and bioethic.[2] I do not wish to simply repeat here a presentation of the Christian ethic appealing to public reason[3]; instead my perspective will be taken more from within the specifically Catholic Christian vision in relation to what I understand may be implied in a Confucian vision of the human person and their role in society.

Prof. Chan sets up his Confucian critique of the idea of individual rights, taking as a foil James Griffin's notion of human rights as protections of our status as human beings, or more specifically our rational and normative agency.[4] In turn, protecting the normative agency of human beings is protecting personhood, which depends –

[1] "In such a [Confucian] society, the interests and welfare of the individual do not have priority over the interest of society, given the interest of society is to turn the individual to be a person of *ren*. Nor does individual autonomy have the normative priority over other moral considerations which the Confucian takes to be essential to cultivating the individual to become a person of *ren*." (J. Chan, "*Universal Declaration on Bioethics and Human Rights*: A Confucian critique", pp.119–123.

[2] The search for overlapping consensus as a basis for a universal ethic is at the root of John Rawls' idea of a stable liberal society. In such an overlapping consensus, citizens support the same basic laws even if for different reasons, religious, political or otherwise.

[3] For this I refer to Prof. Laura Palazzini's paper given at this conference.

[4] Cf. J. Griffin, *On Human Rights*, Oxford University Press, Oxford 2008, 2 cited in J. Chan, "*Universal Declaration on Bioethics*", pp. 119–123.

A. Yeung (✉)
School of Philosophy, Ateneo Pontificio Regina Apostolorum, Rome, Italy
e-mail: ayeung@legionaries.org

J. Tham et al. (eds.), *Religious Perspectives on Bioethics and Human Rights*,
Advancing Global Bioethics 6, DOI 10.1007/978-3-319-58431-7_10

on Griffin's account – on our being autonomous, our having a minimum provision of resources and capabilities, and our having some basic freedoms.[5]

First of all, I readily concur with Prof. Chan's analysis of the founding of the notion of "human right" on the notion of personhood, and his conclusion that the reduction of the understanding of personhood to "autonomous being" would be both insufficient and inconsistent. It is important to note here that the use of the term "person" in contemporary ethical discourse is not uniform and can be ambiguous because of its multi-valency. The Catholic tradition does not automatically equate the notions of "personhood" and "autonomy" (freedom and the capacity to exercise it physiologically and effectively), though autonomy is certainly a manifestation of personhood. In this regard, many a Catholic ethical scholar will point out that many contemporary currents of Western ethical thought, which uproot of the talk of "human rights" from the notion of human and personal dignity and the nature and end of the human person, can only lead eventually to abuse of the term "right".

The critique of the overly individualist approach to the relationship between individual and society expressed by certain advocates of human rights is a second point of consensus between the Confucian and the Catholic moral approach.[6] Here, the Catholic position is very much at ease with a position that emphasizes not rights-claims, but the search for societal harmony, under the notion of "common good;" or perhaps better put, the common good of society is part and parcel of the personal good, not only because intersubjectivity is a fundamental dimension of the human person, but because personal human happiness is achieved only through the love and service of others.

To appreciate the Confucian position on the individual and social relations, it is necessary to enrich the concept of *rén* with other basic Confucian notions – among others – such as *yì* (moral rectitude or moral obligation), *lǐ* (dutiful ritual), and *shù* (self-reflection, seeing the self in others). The concept of *rén*, human-heartedness, is based on the recognition of the other person as a fellow human being. In the Confucian tradition, the norm of reciprocity (*shù*) is expressed in the "Golden Rule": "What you do not desire for yourself, do not do to others" (*Analects* 15.24). Although as it stands, the Golden Rule may be interpreted as enlightened benevolence, not wishing to provoke others to perhaps harm us in the future, if we link the concept to *yì* (moral rectitude) and *rén*, and not *lì* (self-benefit), we should rather see a sense of real benevolence based on the perception of the other's dignity – as a person, and as the kind of person he or she is.

This human-hearted benevolence is found in the Jewish tradition,[7] and is repeated by Jesus in its positive formulation: "Do unto others what you would have them do unto you" (*Matthew* 7:12; *Luke* 6:31). The Christian tradition will go further: "Love one another *as I have loved you*" (*John* 13:34), says Jesus Christ. The concept of

---

[5] Cf. *Ibid.*, 33, cited in J. Chan, "*Universal Declaration on Bioethics*", pp. 119–123.

[6] The Jesuit priest, Matteo Ricci (1552–1610), who made an in-depth study of the ancient classical Confucian texts, concluded that there existed a profound ethical overlap – except for the one case of polygamy – and that classical Confucianism was not contrary to the Christian faith.

[7] For example, in *Tobit* 4:15.

sacrificial charity, in which one can give one's life for the sake of another, is not wholly absent in the Confucian tradition, but is explicitly commanded in the Christian, and particularly after the example of Christ who laid down his life for sinners to redeem them.

It is interesting to note that human-heartedness, or I would say person-orientedness, is directed in both traditions only towards other human beings. The notion of *rén* thus points to a natural intuition that personal dignity is connected to discerning individuals of *human* nature. For example, neither Confucius nor Christ commanded their disciples to lay down their lives for non-human animals, whale, horse, dog, or otherwise; in fact, this would be un-ethical. Why? Because animals are not persons. But could we not as a society grant personal dignity to animals? No, because personal dignity is grounded on nature. We have in this regard *Analects* 10.17: "When the stables were burnt down, on returning from court Confucius said, 'Was anyone hurt?' He did not ask about the horses."[8] (This does *not* mean of course that human beings can abuse animals, for in discerning the capacity for sensitivity in animals in differing degrees, the unnecessary causing of pain in animals is harmful of *human* dignity, who sees in animal sensitivity, a participation in his own sensitivity.[9])

Fundamentally, in the Christian tradition, personal dignity is based on the *nature* of man, and this nature comes from being created as "image and likeness" of God (cf. *Gen* 1:27). To the Christian mind, the *imago Dei* is such that God can open a dialogue of truth and love with man; that God can assume a full human nature without setting aside his divine nature (cf. the Incarnation of the Son of God in Jesus); and that men and women can be adopted as *children of God*, through a participation in Jesus' divine Sonship. It is such a concept of human nature from which the Christian tradition derives the concepts of personal dignity and derivatively "human rights."

Going beyond Prof. Chan's paper, and perhaps even beyond a standard view of Confucianism, it would be interesting to consider whether Confucianism, in which social relations take family relations as their model, and which are manifested in the ritualized relationships (*lǐ*), could be fundamentally open to this primordial relationship between God and man, and therefore establish human rights and duties on a transcendent basis. Confucius, perhaps, was somewhat agnostic about a personal God, though implicitly he founded his moral system on a transcendent basis, since the system of social relationships expresses the decree of Heaven (*Tiānmìng*).[10] I wonder what he may have thought about St Paul's affirmation that all human

---

[8]Also cf. *Analects* 18:6: "One cannot herd with birds and beasts. If I am not to be a man among other men, then what am I to be?"

[9]Cf. *Catechism of the Catholic Church*, 2418: "It is contrary to human dignity to cause animals to suffer or die needlessly. It is likewise unworthy to spend money on them that should as a priority go to the relief of human misery. One can love animals; one should not direct to them the affection due only to persons."

[10]Cf. International Theological Commission, *In Search of a Universal Ethic: A New Look at the Natural Law*, 2009, 15.

fatherhood comes from the Divine Fatherhood (cf. *Eph* 3:14–15), or St Peter's affirmation that the king participates in God's authority (cf. *1 Pet* 2:13).

On the other hand, the deep sense of social harmony as is present in the Confucian tradition, I believe, can also spur currents of Christian philosophy to recover other lines of thought concerning the dignity of the human person based on the concept of relationality, or even of external honor. These lines of thought have been present in the Christian rational tradition, though perhaps underdeveloped in the neo-Scholastic tradition.[11]

For example, St Thomas Aquinas, who agrees that the *ontological* definition of person is "an individual of rational nature",[12] also considered whether the notion of person was itself based primordially on the conferral of dignity, in other words, whether *being a subject distinguished by dignity* was the basis of personhood. Such a concept, present in diverse Christian authors of the High Middle Ages,[13] sees the personhood of the Trinitarian Persons as founded not so much upon their nature, but rather on their dignity as Father, Son and Holy Spirit. Such a notion of personhood is, I would venture to affirm, is found in Confucian society, where the notion of person and the duties owed to him or her, is due to their dignity recognized in society: for example, as king, as father, as older brother, etc.

Such a way of seeing things may seem to preclude the possibility of *universal* human rights, because individuals are found in a variety of societal relationships in which they must act according to pre-established ways. But what happens if we were to admit into the network of relationships that other "familial" relationship, the relationship of creature to Creator-Father, referred to a moment ago. I would presume to say that we would in most cases be able to save the existing network of societal relationships with their corresponding ritualized relationships. But in a communal perception and respect for the Creator-creature relationship, we would be able derive a number of proper duties and corresponding rights: such as duty to respect one's free adhesion to God (he right to religious freedom) and the other rights that are incumbent on our being able to make such a free and adult decision (right to life, nutrition, education, culture).

This "relational dignity" can, in a second moment, lead to a theoretical reflection and the founding of all dignity on *ontological* personhood.[14] Such a moment of theoretical resolution would be necessary to stabilize the source of personhood especially in those cases when the external perception of dignity is made difficult due to particular circumstances – which are often the cases of which bioethics deals – or when conflicts arise between societal responsibilities and one's personal relationship with God. In this regard, the Catholic rational tradition, as expressed in

[11] Contemporary Christian personalism is perhaps a recovery of this relational line of thought.

[12] Cf. *Summa theologiae,* I, 29, 1; *Quaest. disp. de potentia* IX, 1.

[13] Cf. Thomas Aquinas, *Summa theologiae*, I, 29, 1 and 3; Albert the Great, *Summa theologiae*, Tractatus 10, 44, 2; Bonaventure, *In Sent.* I, dist. 25, 1; Alexander of Hales, *Summa fratris Alexandri*, I, n. 387, 9.

[14] In other words, that the person's rational nature and immediate finality in knowing and loving God is the original dignity conferred by the Creator.

St Thomas, and taken up again by Jacques Maritain, seeks to show that each individual person is related to the entire community as a part is related to the whole.[15] In *Integral Humanism*, Maritain states it this way: "Man is not only a person, i.e., spiritually subsistent, he is also individual, an individuated fragment of a species. And this is why he is a member of society as a *part* of it, and has need of the constraints of social life in order to be led to his very life as person and in order to be sustained in this life."[16] Even so, human individuals are a part of society not according to their entire self: "Man is not ordained to the body politic according to all that he is and has… But all that man is, and can, and has, must be referred to God."[17]

In conclusion, the Confucian focus on the importance of relationships, does not, as Prof. Chan rightly concludes, mean that personal autonomy has no place in the Confucian moral framework. We could also suggest that neither does it eliminate the question of universal human *nature,* upon which human rights are ultimately founded – at least according to the Christian rational tradition. In fact, we could suggest that a human person manifests their nature fully precisely in the *correct* relationships they have with other persons and with the cosmos in general,[18] expressible through the societal rituals that have been transmitted from time immemorial. Achieving a spontaneity of *rén* through a lifetime of the effort to live the rituals would express the *ideal* of human nature, yet also imply the *foundational natural capacity* shared by all people to achieve such an ideal, as well as the fundamental right of all to live according to that capacity.

---

[15] Cf. *Summa theologiae*, II-II, 64, 2; I-II, 96, 4; II-II, 61, 1; II-II, 65, 1.

[16] J. Maritain, *Integral Humanism: Temporal and Spiritual Problems of a New Christendom*, University of Notre Dame Press 1973, 135.

[17] *Summa theologiae*, I-II, 21, 4 ad 3.

[18] Cf. J. A. Adler, «Descriptive and normative principle (li) in Confucian moral metaphysics : is/ought from the Chinese perspective», *Zygon* 16/3 (1981), 285–293, 290.

Part IV
Asian Religions: Daoism

Chapter 11
Daoism and the Universal Declaration on Human Rights and Bioethics

Bede Benjamin Bidlack

Abstract Daoism does not find anything objectionable in the Universal Declaration of Human Rights and Bioethics, but the rationale for the rights are quite different with the result that some of the articles will need elaboration. This argument attempts to demonstrate two conclusions: (1) All people are manifestations of the Dao and therefore have rights. *Ziran*, a person's inviolable place in the Dao, is the basis for a Daoist discussion of human rights. (2) The Daoist body, as a cosmic body, brings together the rights of the individual with the well-being of the community and cosmos. For this reason, individual rights must be understood as being conjoined with individual duties, especially in the realm of health and medicine.

11.1 Introduction

In his 1948 introduction to *Human Rights: Comments and Interpretations*, Jacques Maritain wrote that the philosophers of various religious traditions who contributed to the UNESCO Universal Declaration of Human Rights could agree on the idea of human rights in practice, but differed in their first principles, or truth claims, that supported their assertion that all people have rights. "'Yes,' they said, 'we agree about the rights but on condition that no one asks us why'" (Maritain 1948, i). While that approach initially served, Maritain did assert that truth claims matter because the practical implementation of those rights will differ so long as the rationales behind the rights remain disparate (Maritain 1948, iii).

I am grateful to the organizers of this volume and the preceding meetings in Jerusalem (2009) and Rome (2011), where different religious positions can have a discussion and perhaps move closer to a unified rationale for human rights, in general, and human rights in bioethics in particular.

Rights talk is not historically Daoist. Daoists can, however, identify theology in their tradition supportive of human rights. Global discussions of human rights are divided not only across theory and practice, as Maritain points out, but also across

B.B. Bidlack (✉)
Department of Theology, Saint Anselm College, Manchester, NH, USA
e-mail: BBidlack@Anselm.Edu

J. Tham et al. (eds.), *Religious Perspectives on Bioethics and Human Rights*,
Advancing Global Bioethics 6, DOI 10.1007/978-3-319-58431-7_11

the place of rights with regard to the relationship between the individual and the community.[1] Daoism may provide resources that help draw together discussions of human rights that are divided on the issue of individual autonomy with regards to the responsibilities of the individual to the community.[2]

Before beginning the exploration, it serves to remember that—like every tradition represented here—there is no such thing as a homogenous Daoist religion, but only Daoisms.[3] The tradition is particularly rich in its diversity due to its lack of a central authoritative body or a central collection of texts held as equally valid or sacred to all branches of Daoism. Schools of Daoism have risen, flourished, and fallen. Today the two extent schools of Daoism are a lay religion, Celestial Master Daoism, and a monastic form, Complete Perfection Daoism, whose primary pursuit has historically been religious fulfillment by means of assiduously practicing the Daoist method of meditation called internal alchemy (*neidan*). Although Celestial Master and Complete Perfection Daoism are the two schools, each of these traditions has many sects and sub-sects. This presentation does not pretend to represent all of them nor does it pretend to address all of the concerns of these schools and sects. The point is one of diction. Just as one uses the singular "hair" to refer to all the hairs of a person's head, so one must understand a plurality within the use of the singular "Daoism."

This paper's thesis is that Daoism can provide balance between rights of individuals and considerations of the community, as well as support an insistence on individual duties along with any discussion of individual rights. The period most supportive of this thesis is modern Daoism—that is, Daoism since the Song Dynasty (960–1279)—because since the Song Dynasty, the starting place for Daoist practice is the body. Understood differently than that of modern, western medicine, the body is at once the very means of autonomous religious fulfillment and at the same time, a center of cosmic harmony with Ultimate Reality, the Dao.[4]

---

[1] See summary of Jerusalem and Rome http://www.unescobiochair.org/index.php?option=com_content&view=article&id=70%3Aconclusions&catid=50%3Adocs&Itemid=103&lang=en, accessed July 16, 2013 and *Studia Bioethica* vol. 4, no. 2 (2011) available at www.uprait.org/sb/index.php/bioethica/issue/view/vulnerabilità, accessed July 16, 2013.

[2] As an American who is greatly concerned about rights violations of his country with the illegal holding of terrorist suspects in Guantanamo, I write this with some humility. These violations turned to bioethical concerns with the force-feeding of prisoners. In addition, rights talk in the U.S. has been fragmented, especially by the abuse of the word "rights." The word extends to critical issues, such as the rights of the unborn, to the commercial, such as the "right" to fee free banking. The upshot is that the term is abused and leaves citizens with a very opaque understanding of what rights are, see Glendon 1991, x-xi. Lastly, the American context is generally unsupportive of a Daoist worldview and symbol system. One need only pay attention to the commercial use of the *taiji tu*—the familiar black and white illustration depicting the interaction of yin-yang, or the multitudinous books entitled "The Tao of…" that are more about the "…" and much less about anything recognizable as historical or contemporary Daoism, see Grasmuck 2004.

[3] Much like what Prakash Desai pointed out in Rome 2011 with respect to Hinduism, see Desai 2011, 21–22.

[4] Beginning a discussion of human rights with anthropology is a notion shared by some Christians. Anthropology precisely in relation to Ultimate Reality is definitive for human rights, but goes

11.2 Universal Rights

Daoists can agree to human rights, but for reasons that differ from the origins and assumptions of rights as they are understood in the West. Rights today are "legally protected entitlements of individuals in society" (Ching 1998, 68). The historian and scholar of comparative philosophy, Julia Ching, colorfully describes the origins of rights with procreative imagery:

> [Rights'] mother is liberal moral and political philosophy —the French Enlightenment and liberal English thinking, among other things; its father is international law, while its midwife is revolution: first the Revolution of American Independence and then the French Republican Revolution of the late eighteenth century. (Ching 1998, 68)

The revolution in the modern West was a break from the medieval understanding that God bestowed rights on the Christian (Catholic) Church and on kings, who bestowed them on their lords. Most people, the serfs, had only duties to those who held the rights protected by laws. This is to say, as Ching points out, that most people did not have rights. With the break from God that resulted from the revolution in America and the Secularization in Europe, came the assertion that all people had rights and that these rights were upheld by the law (Ching 1998, 68–69).

While it might seem like God was left behind in rights talk, when time races to the post-War period of the twentieth century and the drafting of the Universal Declaration of Human Rights, God and the notion of natural law—that is, the belief in the universal application of divine law—was alive and well. However, it divided those who accepted natural law theory and those who rejected it (Maritain 1948, v). At the dawn of the twenty-first century, the events of September 11, 2001 again call attention to the importance of the question of natural law and the place of religion in global politics. Religion must play a role in discussions of human rights because commitments to normative claims about Ultimate Reality are relevant, powerful, and will affect the degree to which people honor declarations on human rights and bioethics. That such declarations come from an international body will not convince many people of consensus or progress. Thus investigations into the intersection of human rights and Ultimate Reality are as urgent as ever. For years, now, scholars of Daoism have noted striking differences between Abrahamic and Daoist visions of Ultimate Reality: God and the Dao respectively.

Consider Christianity for instance. Since the Church Fathers,[5] God has been equated with Being of the Greek philosophers. All things have the basis of their being, or substance, from this one source of being. The belief of creation *ex nihilo* is that God created the world out of nothing, and without God, nothing would exist. God created beings or substances, and as creator, remains transcendent, though still active in creation. God, understood in the Greek sense, is eternal, timeless, unchang-

beyond the boundaries of human reason alone, see Lee 2005. Thus, different conceptions of Ultimate Reality will result in differences in anthropology and therefore human rights.

[5] Church Fathers are bishops and theologians of the first through the sixth centuries whose writings are not sacred, but highly revered and authoritative.

ing, and by definition cannot be reduced or equated with a changing universe. This early understanding of God has shaped Christian thinking and was the foundation from which sprang the many philosophical movements since the Middle Ages.

The Dao is quite different. The Dao, "the Way," is eternal, but not in the sense of eternity being the lack of change. The Dao is ever-changing within Itself and is the source of all things. Things emanate from the Dao, have their moment, then return to the Dao, all the while never being separate from the Dao but only flowing with it to a greater or lesser degree (see for example *Daode jing* 25 and 42.). Poem 42 of the foundational *Daode jing* has:

The Dao generates the One
The One generates the Two
The Two generates the Three
The Three generates the ten thousand things (everything).

As early as the Celestial Master *Xiang'er Commentary* (ca. 200 CE), the Dao is closely associated with the One (Chen 2008, 1258). The Two are two modes of the single continuum of the Dao known as yin and yang. Beings experience these modes through qi—variously translated as "breath," "pneuma," or "material energy" of the universe. The Three is the interaction of qi as yin-yang from which all particular things come to be. All things are composed of qi and have their origin grounded in, but never separate from, the mysterious Dao.[6] Everything is rooted in the Dao, in Ultimate Reality. The Daoist world, therefore, is primarily a monistic one, which is entirely the Dao.[7]

However, immediately following the classical, pre-Han period of this Daoist worldview,[8] gods appear, but even these are manifestations of the Dao, not powerful competing gods, like one might find on Mount Olympus. The complexity of Daoist theology is not only monistic, but also polytheistic, panentheistic, panhenic ("Nature" as the force behind reality), animistic, and somatic (Komjathy 2011, 76–80).

To express the idea that everything has a proper place in the Dao, Daoist thought uses the term *ziran*, translated as "naturalness" or "spontaneity." In her discussion of rights, Ching describes *ziran* as freedom, but this is a qualified freedom. *Ziran* is the freedom gained from remaining in harmony with the flow of the Dao. People, however, have a tendency to wander from the Dao and fall into disharmony. Disharmony with the Dao leads to suffering of all types: spiritual, psychological, financial, ethical, and physical. This theme of straying from the Dao is taken from more ancient medical literature, such as the *Yellow Thearch's Inner Classic* (*Huangdi neijing*). At birth, people are in perfect harmony with the Dao and only wander from the Dao as they age. The search for harmony with the Dao after falling

[6] The enigmatic descriptions of the Dao in the *Daode jing* (e.g. Poem 1) render It a concept that can only be intuited, but not grasped or understood. This is the foundation for medieval mystical philosophy, see Kohn 2005.

[7] For an ontological comparison of Dao and Being see Li 1999, 11–33.

[8] The classical period spans roughly from the writing of the *Daode jing* around the fourth century BCE to the beginning of the Celestial Master School in the second century CE.

into disharmony is constant in the Daoist tradition all the way through the modern period and to the present.[9]

At this point, Daoists can agree with the ontological conclusion of the first conference on Human Rights and Bioethics in Jerusalem: all people have rights by virtue of their origins in Ultimate Reality. Furthermore, their natural state (*ziran*) is a state of harmony with the Dao; disharmony is unnatural. The Daoist project is to return to the natural, perfect state of *ziran*.[10]

Ziran is the basis for any discussion of human rights in Daoism. Every person has an inviolable place in the Dao. Every person should be regarded as a potentially perfected person whose foundation for being is the Dao. To violate people's harmonious existence in the Dao is to violate the flow of the Dao and to cause disharmony. Disharmony is analogous to conventional notions of evil and is antithetical to individual or communal harmony. Harmony, therefore, is analogous to conventional notions of the good. The turn from this understanding of human rights in general to human rights with regard to bioethics is an obvious one for Daoists, since the initial place for establishing harmony is one's body.

11.2.1 Rights & Duties

The tendency to drift from the Dao is something Daoists since the Song Dynasty have sought to reverse by attending to their bodies.[11] For this reason, modern and contemporary Daoism is a somatic theology, that is: "theology and mystical experience [that] locates the sacred *in and as* the body" (Komjathy 2011, 77–78). The human body is a microcosmic flow of the Dao that resonates with the entire cosmos.[12] Furthermore, the body should be understood as the whole person in the process of living in the Dao and not reduced to the flesh and bone of western medicine (see for example, Ames 1993; Bidlack 2012). In the authenticated Daoist (or "immortal," *xian*), the flow of the energies of the body perfectly harmonizes with the flow of the Dao and the cosmos.

---

[9] For example, using *Yijing* trigrams, Li Daochun (fl.1288–1306), the author of *Collection of Central Harmony* (*Zhonghe ji* DZ 249), holds the view that people at birth are initially harmonious with the Dao, only to gradually have their qi fall into dissipation and corruption. He does so in the context of internal alchemy, a meditation practice aimed at reversing this process through mentally guiding and refining qi through the body.

[10] A widespread practice is pursuing this harmony through the practice of internal alchemy. While texts of internal alchemy make reference to *ziran*, usually other anthropological terms—such as inner nature (*xing*) and destiny (*ming*) or essence (*jing*), qi, and spirit (*shen*)—dominate.

[11] While the body is the beginning of Daoist practice since the Song, the organization of space beginning with the body, then extending to the household, and the kingdom and cosmos is far more ancient, see Lewis 2006.

[12] *Ganying* 感應, or resonance and response, is the idea that Daoists seek to sense the rhythms of the cosmos and to flow with them, and the cosmos responds in kind.

This cosmic view of the body can be found as early as the Latter Han (25–220 CE) in the *The Most High Lord Lao's Book of the Center* (*Taishang laojun zhongjing* DZ 1168), where the body is visualized with a complete with interior landscape.[13] While mentally gazing inward, the Daoist adept sees such features as the sun and moon, stars, clouds, mountains, lakes, buildings, and other human artifacts (Schipper 1993, 105–106; Schipper 2004, 93).[14] Seeing the body as the cosmos reappears throughout the centuries as evidenced by graphic body maps like those found in materials that crossover from medical texts into Daoist mystical texts, such as the thirteenth century *Book of Debating* (*Nanjing* DZ 1024) by Li Jiong (fl. 1269), or the *Diagram of Inner Passageways* (*Neijing tu*) which can be found in most clinics of Chinese medicine today.[15]

The somatic theology and the cosmic body of Daoists are supported by the much older correspondence system of Zou Yan (ca. 305–240 BCE) along with foundational medical texts, such as the *Yellow Thearch's Inner Classic*.[16] Also known as correlation theory, correspondence sees movements of the cosmos as reflected in, and applicable to, other aspects of life: from medicine to ethics and to military arts (Graham 1986). In the *Yellow Thearch's Inner Classic*, the yin-yang dyad is expanded into a system of Five Phases (*wuxing*): wood, fire, earth, metal, water. In medical texts these corresponded to Five Orbs (*wuzang*), energetic concentrations within the body that participate in its proper functioning. The Five Orbs are associated with, but not equivalent to, five organs: liver, heart, spleen, lungs, kidneys (Porkert 1974). From here, the system gets expanded even further to include directions, colors, and seasons, rendering an understanding of the body as intimately tied to the physical and temporal universe (see Table 11.1).

The fifth century Buddhist *Sutra of Tapusa and Bhallika* adds a moral element to this when it links each phase to the five precepts of Buddhism—do not kill, get intoxicated, lie, engage in licentious behavior, or steal. This text additionally matches the prohibitions with Confucian virtues: benevolence, wisdom, faithfulness, propriety, and righteousness. Celestial Master texts, such as the *Precepts of the Hightest Lord Lao* (*Taishang Laojun jiejing* DZ 784) of the late fifth century matches correspondences and Buddhist precepts—and by extension Confucian virtues (Kohn 2004, 31; Table 11.1). The body that is functioning in harmony with the Dao

---

[13] According to Livia Kohn, there are three fundamental views of the body according to Daoism: the cosmic body, the bureaucratic body, and the divine body. Recently, Louis Komjathy subdivides these categories in to seven: the cosmological, the naturalistic, the bureaucratic, the theological, the ascetic, and the alchemical, and the mystical. Practically speaking, most Daoist visions of the body are combinations of these however one categorizes their aspects. For simplicity's sake, I am only writing on the cosmic body since it is exemplary for my argument. See Kohn 1991 and Komjathy 2011, 71.

[14] The meditation practice of looking inward is called, *guan* 觀 or *neiguan* 内觀 "inner observation," is inspired by Buddhist *vipasyana* meditation, see Kohn 1989.

[15] For rich descriptions of this body as cosmos diagram, see Bidlack 2015, Komjathy 2008 and 2009.

[16] Zou Yan did not invent Chinese correspondence theory, but he did systematize yin-yang and Five Phases cosmology, see Graham 1986.

Table 11.1 Five Phases correlation of the body, cosmos, and ethics

yin/yang	Phase	Direction	Color	Season	Orb 1 (Yin)	Orb 2 (Yang)	Precept	Virtue
Lesser yang	Wood	East	Green	Spring	Liver	Gall bladder	Killing	Benevolence
Greater yang	Fire	South	Red	Summer	Heart	Sm. intestine	Intoxication	Wisdom
Yin/yang	Earth	Center	Yellow		Spleen	Stomach	Lying	Faithfulness
Lesser yin	Metal	West	White	Fall	Lungs	Large intestine	Licentiousness	Propriety
Greater yin	Water	North	Black	Winter	Kidney	Bladder	Stealing	Righteousness

See *Precepts of Highest Lord Lao (Taishang Laojun jiejing* DZ 784)

is a moral body that resonates outward to affect the Daoist's physical and moral universe.

From this, a second conclusion follows: the Daoist body brings together the individual, the community, and the cosmos. On the one hand, the community has no right to interfere with the bodily functioning of the individual, since the person's body is an event of the Dao and since interfering with the body is interfering with the whole person and not an isolated body part. On the other hand, the individual has a duty to the community and cosmos to strive for a body that resonates with the Dao so as to be a source and center of harmony. The ideal, Daoist sage, in fact, becomes a source of blessing for the entire community. The harmony the sage enjoys radiates outward to affect the lives of those around him or her. To the extent that each member of a Daoist community finds harmony with the Dao, a general harmony arises within the community as a social body and even contributes to the well being of each person within it. Thus, there is a reciprocal relationship between the community and its members.

The individual has a duty to maintain and enhance bodily health. Health in Chinese medicine is harmonizing the energetic and spiritual elements of the body within the individual—and by extension with the Dao. Daoists combine this medical view with the moral life reflected in Buddhism and Confucianism. Thus bodily health will result in ethical behavior, and ethical behavior enhances and supports bodily health. By working towards bodily health, Daoists benefit not only themselves, but also their households and communities. In this way, the somatic theology of Daoism offers a unifying vision of individual and community, though different from similar formulations of other cultures and religions.

The somatic theology of Daoism underscores the connection between bodily, psychological, and spiritual health with the entire cosmos. As a Daoist approaches perfection, he or she becomes a blessing, as they harmonize Heaven and Earth.[17] Conversely, degenerate people not only harm themselves, but also their immediate and distant environments. For example, intoxication will not only affect one's kidneys, but also one's virtue of wisdom, as well as those aspects of the cosmos associated with the phase water, the direction north, and the season of winter (see Table 11.1).

Thus Daoists can agree with rights talk focused on protecting the individual, but only with the balanced understanding that the individual has a duty of self-care due to the cosmic consequences.[18]

---

[17] An early expression of this is the fourth century *The Essential Precepts of Master Redpine* (*Chisongzi zhongjie jing* DZ 185), see Kohn 2004, 14.

[18] By way of example, Daoist Zhuang Qingxin asserts that each person must strive for self-perfection, to know the Dao, in order to understand that Heaven and humans are one. This, he concludes, is the Daoist ethical response to the environmental crisis, see Meyer 2001, 232.

11.3 Conclusion: Expand the Conversation

The above argument attempts to demonstrate two conclusions: (1) All people are manifestations of the Dao and therefore have rights. *Ziran*, a person's inviolable place in the Dao, is the basis for a Daoist discussion of human rights. (2) The Daoist body, as a cosmic body, brings together the rights of the individual with the well-being of the community and cosmos. For this reason, individual rights must be understood as being conjoined with individual duties, especially in the realm of health and medicine.

A glance at three continuous themes that run through the Chinese worldview and into Daoist theology support these conclusions. Those themes are:

1. the central place of the body
2. the cosmic view of the body as supported by the correspondence system of yin-yang and Five Phases cosmology
3. the moral element of correspondences introduced by Celestial Master Daoism

Thus the Daoist focus on body cultivation to address moral issues is not solely out of self-interest, but is a way of addressing the moral needs of the cosmos. The body is that portion of the cosmos most under the adept's control and responsibility.

These observations serve as a starting point for a discussion of human rights and bioethics.[19] This starting point, though, is a call to expand the conversation in two directions: (1) to expand the conversation to consider Chinese medicine, and (2) to expand the notion of rights to the non-human.

First, the brief Universal Declaration of Human Rights and Bioethics cites "science" thirty-seven times—or some derivative of the term often paired with "technology." Do not readers assume that "science and technology" means modern, western science and technology? Since this is a document drafted by an international body and addressed to the whole world, one can assume that "science and technology" means modern, western science. The assumption is that the western scientific method is beyond nations and cultures and can therefore be agreed upon by all peoples (see Article 1).[20] But western medicine is not the only model for healing, and western medical studies have confirmed this, especially in regard to mind-body healing (Astin et al. 2003; Wang et al. 2004).

Efficacy of Chinese medicine is built upon the integral worldview of Chinese and Daoist cosmology. In contrast, the western medical view of health sees the body of the sick patient as sealed off from the outside world with the skin serving as a border. The physician is an unrelated actor administering foreign medicines to repair a broken mechanism in the body. This description of western medicine is a caricature. Indeed, the preamble to the Universal Declaration of Human Rights recognizes the

---

[19] To consider whether the basis for a Daoist bioethics should be *ziran* or *de* "virtue" see Chan 2004.

[20] The western scientific method is the testing of hypotheses through deduction and replication. Chinese medicine relies on induction and cannot easily be replicated across groups due to its appreciation of individual differences among similar cases.

importance of other factors beyond science and technology that influence health. At the same time, it is not without a good deal of truth. While such a modern view has produced wonders in the art of healing acute illnesses and postponing death, many people East and West, have availed themselves of both methods of healing, often pursuing eastern and western therapies concurrently.

Nonetheless, an isolated individual is not the Daoist view of the body, cosmos, and healing. Therefore, addressing specific bioethical situations for universal application is not on the Daoist map. For instance, must an artificial respirator be provided for people who will not be able to breathe on their own? Maybe. Daoist communities may or may not opt for extraordinary measures of life preservation in deference to allowing the person to die, as tragic as that may be. Daoists and practitioners of Chinese medicine focus much more on immediate instances and not on universal claims. The immediate circumstances of one person facing euthanasia will be different from another person facing euthanasia, and the repercussions for the decision for life or death will also be different. Instead, case-by-case judgments are the norm.

Introducing other forms of science and technology into the conversation is not at odds with the Universal Declaration of Human Rights and Bioethics. In fact, Article 17 allows these into the discussion. However, as globalization makes alternative forms of medicine more readily available and as more and more studies support their efficacy, Article 17 may need elaboration.

In addition to expanding the discussion beyond western notions of science and technology, a second expansion of the discussion of rights to include the non-human is needed for Daoist reflection on rights and bioethics. The basis for human rights in Daoism, *ziran*, is not exclusive to humans. *Ziran* is the self-so-ness of all reality. Therefore, beings, by virtue of their existence, have a right to exist. Beyond that, the rights they have will be different from human rights. "Trees have tree rights, insects have insect rights, rivers have river rights, mountains have mountain rights" (Berry 1999, 5). Article 2.h states: "The aims of this Declaration are…to underline the importance of biodiversity and its conservation as a common concern of humankind," but the nature of this concern must be relational, not simply a human concern over the utility of the non-human. The cosmic body of Daoism explicitly demonstrates this intimacy and relationship between the human and the non-human. Taking this seriously will inevitably result in bioethical concerns when the good of the human appears to conflict with the good of the non-human realm. Biomedical waste, for instance: Does a therapy, or the experimental pursuit of a therapy, justify the resulting biomedical waste? Daoists would want to reflect upon the human right to pollute a river or an ocean for the sake of immediate human health. Does Article 4's consideration of minimizing harm extend to the non-human? It is not that Daoists eschew the use of technology or the manipulation of nature. On the contrary, inventiveness is part of being human.[21] But the use of technology must be preceded by

[21] The many agrarian images from Daoist materials, such as the *Daode jing* to the *Nejing tu*, are evidence against any notions that Daoists should not use technology. On the point that inventiveness is part of the human place in the Dao, part of human *ziran*, I argue a bit more strongly for a Daoist view of medical intervention than Jonathan Chan, see Chan 2004.

moral reflection. If humankind overreaches its harmony with the non-human, suffering and illness will surely follow. Such considerations are not evident in the contemporary intoxication with science and technology.

In summary, Daoism does not find anything objectionable in the Universal Declaration of Human Rights and Bioethics, but the rationale for the rights are quite different with the result that some of the articles will need elaboration.

Acknowledgement I would like to thank the organizers of this volume for including Daoism. Daoism has long been overshadowed by its brothers and sisters of other religions in international conversations. This Chinese tradition—both ancient and contemporary—has contributions to make to discussions of Ultimate Reality, the human condition, and ethics.

References

Ames, Roger T. 1993. The meaning of body in classical Chinese philosophy. In *Self as body in Asian theory and practice, SUNY series, the body in culture, history, and religion*, ed. Thomas P. Kasulis, Roger T. Ames, and Wimal Dissanayake, 157–177. Albany: State University of New York Press.

Astin, J.A., S.L. Shapiro, D.M. Eisenberg, and K.L. Forys. 2003. Mind-body medicine: State of the science, implications for practice. *The Journal of the American Board of Family Practice* 16 (2): 131–147.

Berry, Thomas. 1999. *The great work: Our way into the future*. New York: Bell Tower.

Bidlack, Bede Benjamin. 2012. Divine lives: Christ, community, and divine embodiment. *Studies in Interreligious Dialogue* 22 (2): 134–146.

———. 2015. In good company: The body and divinization in Pierre Teilhard de Chardin, SJ and Daoist Xiao Yingsou, East Asian comparative literature and culture. Leiden/Boston: Brill.

Chan, Jonathan. 2004. Daoism and bioethics: *Daode jing*'s doctrine of naturalness and the principle of non-action. In *Religious perspectives in bioethics*, ed. Mark Cherry, 221–231. London/New York: Taylor & Francis.

Chen, Yaoting. 2008. Zhengyi. In *Encyclopedia of Taoism*, ed. Fabrizio Pregadio, vol. 2, 1258–1260. London/New York: Routledge.

Ching, Julia. 1998. Human rights: A valid Chinese concept? In *Confucianism and human rights*, ed. William Theodore De Bary and Tu Weiming, 67–82. New York: Columbia University Press.

Desai, Prakash. 2011. Between tradition and modernity: Bioethics, vulnerabilities, and social change. *Studia Bioethica* 4 (2): 21–32.

Glendon, Mary Ann. 1991. *Rights talk: The impoverishment of political discourse*. New York/Toronto: Free Press/Collier Macmillan/Maxwell Macmillan.

Graham, A.C. 1986. *Yin-Yang and the nature of correlative thinking*. Singapore: The Institute of East Asian Philosophies, National University of Singapore.

Grasmuck, Oliver. 2004. *Geschichte und Aktualitat der Daoismuserezepion im deutschspachingen Raum*. Munster: LIT Verlag Munster.

Kohn, Livia. 1989. *Taoist meditation and longevity techniques*. Ann Arbor: Center for Chinese Studies, The University of Michigan.

———. 1991. Taoist visions of the body. *Journal of Chinese Philosophy* 18: 227–252.

———. 2004. *Cosmos and community: The ethical dimension of Daoism*. Cambridge, MA: Three Pines Press.

Komjathy, Louis. 2008. Mapping the Daoist body (1): The Neijing tu and the Daoist internal landscape. *Journal of Daoist Studies* 1: 67–92.

———. 2009. Mapping the Daoist body (2): The Neijing tu and the Daoist internal landscape. *Journal of Daoist Studies* 2: 64–108.

———. 2011. The Daoist mystical body. In *Perceiving the divine through the human body: Mystical sensuality*, ed. Thomas Cattoi and June McDaniel, 67–103. New York: Palgrave Macmillan.

Lee, Kevin P. 2005. Deeper longings: The relevance of Christian theology for contemporary rights theories. *Ave Maria Law Review* 3 (1): 289–302.

Lewis, Mark Edward. 2006. *The construction of space in early China*. Albany: State University of New York Press.

Li, Chenyang. 1999. *The Tao encounters the west: Explorations in comparative philosophy, SUNY series in Chinese philosophy and culture*. Albany: State University of New York Press.

Maritain, Jacques. 1948. Introduction. In *Human rights: Comments and interpretations*, i–ix. Paris: United Nations Educational, Scientific and Cultural Organization.

Meyer, Jeffrey F. 2001. Salvation in the garden: Daoism and ecology. In *Daoism and ecology ways within a cosmic landscape*, ed. N.J. Girardot, James Miller, and Xiaogan Liu, 219–236. Cambridge, MA: Center for the Study of World Religions, Harvard Divinity School. Distributed by Harvard University Press.

Porkert, Manfred. 1974. *The theoretical foundation of Chinese medicine*. Cambridge, MA: MIT Press.

Schipper, Kristofer. 1993. *The Taoist body*. Berkeley: University of California Press.

———. 2004. Taishan Laojun Zhongjing. In *The Taoist Canon: A historical companion to the Daozang*, ed. Kristopher Schipper and Franciscus Verellen, vol. 1, 92–94. Chicago/London: The University of Chicago Press.

Wang, Chenchen, Jean Paul Collett, and Joseph Lau. 2004. The effect of Tai Chi on health outcomes in patients with chronic conditions: A systematic review. *Archives of Internal Medicine* 164 (5): 493–501.

Chapter 12
Daoism and Human Rights: Integrating the Incommensurable

David A. Palmer

Abstract There is practically no explicit discourse on human rights in the Daoist tradition or in contemporary Daoist scholarship and practice. This article begins by discussing the ontological incommensurability between Daoist notions of inner spontaneity and self-transcendence, and the external frameworks of the state, agonistic legal systems, and contractual rights and obligations between self-interested individuals that underpin human rights regimes. And yet, while Daoism and human rights may be incommensurable, they are compatible. In an imaginary Daoist utopia, a legal regime of human rights would be unnecessary, as all people would attain a spontaneous harmony in which no person would infringe on another. But since, in the reality of the world of common people and rulers, most people are unable to control their will to power over others, human rights are thus necessary as a basic protection for each individual against the interference of others and of the state. A Daoist, then, might see human rights as a desirable foundation, that must be coupled with the supreme value of self-cultivation to embody Dao, ultimately transcending the very need for human obligations and rights.

I'm neither a theologian nor a philosopher, nor am I a scholar of human rights; as an anthropologist I'm interested in the "native point of view" – what might real, living Daoists themselves say and do about human rights? Over two decades of interacting with Daoists in China, I have hardly ever heard human rights mentioned in their conversations with me or among themselves; nor am I aware of a single article or publication by a Chinese Daoist practitioner on the topic of human rights.

The absence of an explicit Daoist discourse on human rights does not, however, indicate the absence of conceptual elements in Daoist thought that can be correlated with human rights, as shown by Bede Bidlack in his contribution to this volume.[1] The discourse on human rights emerged from the European enlightenment out of a

---

[1] So far, the literature directly addressing the relationship between Daoism and human rights seems to be limited to two articles: "Preserving one's Nature: Primitivist Daoism and Human Rights" by the American-based Jung H. Lee, *Journal of Chinese philosophy* 34:4 (2007), 597–612; and "Daoist thought and concepts of human rights" (*Daojiao sixiang yu renquan guannian*) by the Chinese scholar Guo Wu, in the Hong Kong Daoist magazine *Hongdao* no. 2, 2001.

D.A. Palmer (✉)
Department of Sociology, The University of Hong Kong, Pokfulam, Hong Kong
e-mail: palmer19@hku.hk

J. Tham et al. (eds.), *Religious Perspectives on Bioethics and Human Rights*, Advancing Global Bioethics 6, DOI 10.1007/978-3-319-58431-7_12

culture matrix inflected by Christianity and Greek philosophy; through the spread of Western civilization and institutions, it has now become part of the global normative order. Most other cultural and religious traditions have, during this process, been drawn into this discourse and forced to rethink and sometimes reform their teachings and practices in consequence.

Daoism is a latecomer to this conversation. In order to understand the reason for this, a discourse on Daoism and human rights needs to consider the location of the Daoist tradition in an embodied, social context. The focus of Daoist practice is the body – the transformation of the individual body through techniques of "life cultivation" (*yangsheng*), meditation and inner alchemy; and the coordinated activity of bodies through communal rituals. At a basic level both types of practice share the common aim of promoting human flourishing through health, security, prosperity and harmony, to which individual practices of the body add the ultimate aim of spiritual transcendence. At either level, Daoism is primarily a trove of technical knowledge, based on a common cosmology. Daoist "discourse" is primarily a means to practical, embodied or mystical ends rather than conceptual debate. Thus, Daoist religious specialists have traditionally been trained in technical and embodied knowledge rather than intellectual discourse, working among the people, in local communities. Daoist philosophical discourse or so-called "philosophical Daoism" has primarily been the work of people located within discursive communities outside the living Daoist tradition – historically within the primarily Confucian social elite or, in modern times, within academic departments that operate according to the disembodied discursive practices of Western philosophy. A genuine conversation between Daoism and human rights, however, requires not only an engagement between different forms of discourse, but also between different ways of being in the world.

Perhaps such a conversation could begin with the words of my main Daoist informant and teacher over the past decade, whom I will call Master Wen, in deference to his pursuit of anonymity. A deeply devoted and highly accomplished practitioner, he also has a high level of intellectual sophistication and is the most knowledgeable Daoist I have met during my years of research. Master Wen was previously the deputy director of the Daoist Association of a famous sacred mountain; but, weary of monastic politics, he returned to secular life and now lives an anonymous life as an obscure urban hermit. One day as we sat in a teahouse, he began a rant about the "slave mentality" of Chinese people that, in his view, the Chinese state has nurtured over 2500 years. When I mentioned to him that Daoism has been criticized for doing nothing to restrain this authoritarian culture, Wen himself mentioned human rights, emphatically stating that "Daoism absolutely upholds human rights because it is opposed to asking the individual to sacrifice himself for others, for the collectivity." He praised the philosopher Yang Zhu (440-360 BC) who famously said that he would not pluck a hair from his body to benefit others, and Zhuangzi's teaching that we should model ourselves on the useless old tree. For Master Wen, notions of service to others are used as pretexts to sacrifice individual rights and freedoms for the benefit of political power, in the name of the collective. "You take a few people who have sacrificed themselves, you make them into heroes, you say it is very good to sacrifice yourself, and then you ask everyone to sacrifice themselves for the political authority. Even if you offer yourself up in sacrifice, you are setting yourself up as an example, and saying that either you are morally superior to others, or that others should sacrifice themselves too. … You will expect others to follow you and obey you in return. That's what so many saints and sages have done. They act so selfless, but then they want you to worship them. And then those who don't sacrifice themselves, are labeled as evil; they will be oppressed and killed."[2]

While Wen's discourse is inflected by his lived experience in socialist China, in which notions of sacrifice and "serving the people" have been deployed in the service of political authoritarianism, it is consistent with both his explications of Daoist spiritual cultivation and with a streak of libertarianism that can be traced back to the *Zhuangzi*. Master Wen's discourse was actually not about "rights", but a scathing critique of the notion of "duty". And yet, he was equally critical of Western appropriations of Daoism in the service of individual freedom: "Daoist cultivation doesn't mean that you can just be who you want – there is a work of self-transformation, to reach your true self *(zhenwo)* which is at one with all beings in the cosmos (*tiandiwanwu*). You can't just take non-action (*wuwei*) and say it means that you make no effort and can do whatever you want. *Wuwei* refers to non-interference, to not imposing your self on others – but you still need to make an effort on your self."

Wen's discourse on spiritual cultivation stresses self-transcendence, beginning with "quiescence" (*jing*), letting go of the turbulence of mental and bodily desires, leading to alignment with one's "true self" or "heart-nature" (*xinxing*) that is at one with the cosmos. He repeatedly emphasizes that morality is fundamental to this process – but morality is not a "duty" to others, nor is it a set of norms derived from an abstract principle – rather, it is a spontaneous expression of authentic being. True morality is thus an expression of *ziran* or natural spontaneity. Immoral and selfish behavior consists in the will to power of an individual who tries to impose himself and his desires on others, in violation of his authentic spontaneity that is in line with the organic harmony of all beings.

Under a condition of *ziran*, both rights and duties, understood as part of a binding social contract, are thus unnecessary. Under *ziran*, people will find a natural harmony; they will not interfere with or harm each other. A "duty" to do anything beyond *ziran*, or the "right" to do anything other than cultivate *ziran*, would be contrary to cosmic harmony. When all are in spontaneity, all are in harmony; there is no need for contractual rights and duties; there is no need for a state. A discourse on human rights would thus seem to be irrelevant.

The Daoist vision, however, is a utopian one. Daoist spontaneity has never been realized in a true polity (or is imagined to have existed only in a primitivist golden age); *ziran* can only be attained through a regimen of self-cultivation that is only accessible to a small number of people. And, as Master Wen concluded after he reflected on his disappointment at the low level of spiritual cultivation of most

[2] Interview recording, Chengdu, 20 June 2013.

Daoist monks in China, it can only be so – since the principle of spontaneity also militates against making strenuous effort to implement this utopian ideal and practice among a whole population. Human rights, on the other hand, address the reality of morally imperfect states and individuals – what *external* laws and ethical principles can restrict the actions of rulers and individuals who do *not* spontaneously restrict their will to power over others? Given that most people and states are *not ziran*, and tend to impose their will on others, an external, legal framework is required to define and enforce mutual rights and obligations, and the rights of individuals in relation to the state.

From this perspective, the project of human rights may well be entirely incommensurable with Daoism, since it presupposes accepting a social reality that Daoist cultivation precisely strives to transcend. In practice, Daoist practitioners strive to attain *ziran* and *wuwei* in a social context in which most people around them do not engage in Daoist cultivation, are not spontaneously moral, and constantly try to impose their will on others. Through practicing *wuwei*, although living among other people, Daoist practitioners avoid entanglements in the mutual conflicts and negotiations among people, and try to exert a positive influence on others, again in a spontaneous manner, without imposing their ideas and practices. Human rights regimes, on the other hand, are not only theoretical constructs; they are social practices and institutions that have, historically, come into being only through protracted struggles between people and states through social movements and revolutions; and that are given flesh and substance through negotiations and struggles in the streets, in the media and in the courtrooms over the application of general principles in specific cases. Virtually every stage of human rights as social practice involves contests between different parties organizing themselves to impose their demands – a far cry from Daoist spontaneity and non-interference! The *practice* of human rights appears to be as alien to Daoist cultivation as its theory.

We cannot, however, draw the conclusion that Daoism is necessarily opposed to, or indifferent to human rights. Daoism is not a monopolistic ideology that rejects any system of thought and practice that cannot be logically derived from its own first principles. On the contrary, human rights can be incorporated into Daoism, following the logic of what I would call "polyontological complementarity" – the pragmatic integration of incommensurable ontologies. To illustrate this dynamic, let us consider how Daoism has integrated other systems of thought, using the example of Confucianism as well as Buddhism. In chapter 38 of the *Daodejing*, we read:

When Dao is lost, we have Virtue (*de*)
When Virtue is lost, we have benevolence (*ren*)
When benevolence is lost, we have righteousness (*yi*)
When righteousness is lost, we have ritual propriety (*li*).

This passage is one of the most polemically anti-Confucian of the *Daodejing*. And yet, as a community of practice, Daoism has gladly incorporated Confucianism into its own system. This does not necessarily reflect a random eclecticism or syncretism, as is often assumed. Rather, Daoism has constructed a systemic hierarchy.

For example, in the passage quoted above, the highest and most preferable state is described as being in Dao. But not all people have reached that state, and so the next best thing for them is Virtue. But not all people have Virtue, so the next best thing is (Confucian) benevolence, righteousness and ritual propriety. In this structure, Daoist concepts and practices are considered to be the superior ones, but Confucian morality and propriety are taken to be inferior but necessary foundations for the Daoist spiritual path. For example, according to Wang Chongyang (1113-1170), the founder of the order of Complete Perfection, wrote in his *Instructions on the Gold Pass and Jade Lock* that Buddhist precepts and compassion, and Confucian filial piety and loyalty, are essential prerequisites for advanced Daoist cultivation:

> Perfected Chongyang instructed, "First, you must observe the precepts and develop clarity, stillness, forbearance, compassion, genuineness, and goodness. You must abstain from the ten evils, practice expedient means, and strive to save all sentient beings. You must also be loyal to the ruler and king, and be filial and reverent to parents and teachers. This is the method of cultivation. *Then and only then* can you practice the exercises of [Daoist] perfection (*zhengong*).[3]

The Daoist integration of Daoism, Confucianism and Buddhism (which has a radically different ontology from the former two teachings) in what is often called the "Union of the Three Teachings" (*sanjiao heyi*) does not paper over the philosophical and practical differences between the three, but places them in a complementary hierarchy. In this structure, the independence of the three teachings is recognized and preserved. All three are understood to be different but compatible on a pragmatic level.

Following the same logic, it is possible to consider a complementary integration between the "two teachings" of Daoism and human rights. On the one hand, as I have argued in this paper, Daoism and human rights come from radically different historical and cultural genealogies, and are incommensurable on an ontological level. It may be impossible to derive one from the other, as argued by Chia in his contribution to this volume. On the other hand, one can argue that Daoism is *compatible* with human rights and, as demonstrated by Lee[4] and by Bidlack, one can *correlate* aspects of Daoist teachings and practices with aspects of human rights discourse. A genuine Daoist practicing *wuwei* and spontaneity would spontaneously respect the human rights of others. And, as claimed by American Daoist practitioners I have interviewed,[5] it can be argued that human rights and freedoms provide a better foundation for Daoist cultivation than Confucian patriarchy. Thus, while essentially distinct, Daoism and human rights are complementary, and are potentially mutually reinforcing. Indeed, it could be argued that without Daoist spirituality, the philosophical "baggage" of the discourse and practice of human rights – strong

---

[3] Quoted in Louis Komjathy, *Cultivating Perfection: Mysticism and Self-Transformation in Early Quanzhen Daoism*. Leiden: Brill, 2007, p. 151.

[4] Lee, "Preserving one's Nature", *op. cit.*

[5] See David A. Palmer and Elijah Siegler, *Dream Trippers: Global Daoism and the Predicament of Modern Spirituality*. Chicago: University of Chicago Press, 2017

commitments to competitive self-interest, radical autonomy and disengaged freedom[6] – risks placing too much emphasis on what is little more than the unfettered desires and willful imposition of the individual ego. On the other hand, without human rights, it can be argued that Daoist spontaneity and non-interference are too easily co-opted by forms of authoritarian and patriarchal oppression that are antithetical to Daoist cultivation.

From a Daoist perspective, such a combination should be a hierarchical one, in which human rights would provide a lower-level social foundation, while Daoist cultivation is a path to higher-level spiritual progress. Since, in the reality of the world of common people and rulers, most people are unable to control their desires and their will to power over others, human rights are thus necessary as a basic protection for each individual against the interference of others and of the state. But unlike for many in the West and elsewhere who see human rights and freedoms as the supreme value and the end goal of history, a Daoist might see human rights as simply a desirable foundation, that must be coupled with the supreme value of union with Dao, ultimately transcending the very need for human obligations and rights.

[6] Lee, "Preserving one's Nature", 599.

Chapter 13
Daoism, Human Rights, and Bioethics

Roland Chia

Abstract In his engaging paper entitled, 'Daoism and the Universal Declaration on Human Rights and Bioethics', Bede Bidlack attempts to show that although 'rights talks is not historically Daoist', Daoist philosophy could contribute meaningfully to human rights discourse and address certain deficiencies in the Western account. In this paper, I argue that Daoist metaphysics, especially its concept of the impersonal *Dao*, is unable to provide a sufficiently robust basis for morality. In similar vein, central Daoist concepts like *ziran* and *wu-wei* do not offer the moral framework for thinking about human rights. In addition, Daoist anthropology and its aversion to rules and conventions also substantially limit its contribution to the modern human rights discourse.

In his engaging paper entitled, 'Daoism and the Universal Declaration on Human Rights and Bioethics', Bede Bidlack attempts to show that although 'rights talk is not historically Daoist', Daoist philosophy not only could contribute meaningfully to human rights discourse, but that it could also address certain deficiencies endemic in the Western account. For example, Bidlack suggests that 'Daoism may provide resources that help draw together discussions of human rights that are divided on the issue of individual autonomy and the responsibilities of the individual to the community' (p. 1). Daoism can also sharpen the focus on the importance of establishing a proper and balanced relationship between individual rights and duties (p. 2). Bidlack also emphasises the comprehensive vision of Daoism that checks the anthropocentric predilections of Western discourses on human rights. We are reminded that significant concepts that could be commandeered to shape a Daoist vision of human rights like *ziran* apply to all of reality, not just to humans and human sociality (p. 11). The holism of Daoism insists that reflections on human rights must never be bracketed away from legitimate and sometimes pressing concerns about the non-human animals and the natural environment. These are undoubtedly important issues and concerns for any public discourse on human rights, and they have profound ramifications to a plethora of bioethical questions and issues.

R. Chia (✉)
Trinity Theological College, Singapore, Singapore
e-mail: roland@ttc.edu.sg

J. Tham et al. (eds.), *Religious Perspectives on Bioethics and Human Rights*,
Advancing Global Bioethics 6, DOI 10.1007/978-3-319-58431-7_13

Several questions came to mind as I studied Bidlack's learned and nuanced essay. They have to do with what I perceive to be serious philosophical difficulties associated with the Daoist system that appear to obfuscate a coherent vision of human rights. These questions therefore articulate my own perplexities and uncertainties about whether the Daoist system could indeed support a robust account of human rights for bioethics.

13.1 Dao and Morality

I begin with Daoism's most basic concept, the Dao, and examine its relation to morality or ethics. This line of enquiry is established on the view that before human rights could be said to belong to the domains of political and legal theories, it is fundamentally and irreducibly an issue of morality. In addition, the moral vision within which human rights discourse must be located is beholden to a particular ontology, or more precisely, a specific anthropology. Put differently, human rights are determined by a line of moral reasoning that is grounded on a certain understanding of the inviolable dignity of the human being. As Thomas Nagel explains: 'The existence of moral rights does not depend on their political recognition or enforcement but rather on the moral question whether there is a decisive justification for including these forms of inviolability in the status of every member of the moral community' (Nagel 2002). Thus, if Daoist anthropology is inextricably bound to the Dao – as it invariably must be – the first and perhaps most basic question is whether this concept of ultimate reality could provide the requisite moral compass to think substantially about human rights.

To probe this question, we must have a clear grasp of this important metaphysical concept. According to Roger Ames, 'The constant *dao* is the Daoist epithet for the sum total of reality. It can be described as the ultimate metaphysical reality, the absolute, the unconditioned, the undifferentiated and holistic, the uncreated, the all-pervading, the ineffable' (Ames 1994). Bidlack agrees with this definition. Although the Daoist account of reality may be properly described as panentheistic, panhenic and somatic, it is fundamentally a monistic one. This means that the different descriptions and permutations of nature or reality are simply 'perspectival' in that they are dependent on one's angle of vision and point of departure. In the same way, the animistic and even polytheistic character of certain versions of Daoism does not contradict its basic monism because ghosts and gods, as I understand it, are simply different epiphanies of the Dao.

More crucially – and here we come to the crux of the matter – the Dao as ultimate reality is an amorphous and amoral force. Liu Xiaogan explains that although in some ways the Dao may be said to be similar to God, the significant difference is that it 'has nothing to do with will, feelings, and purpose' (Liu 2001). As another author succinctly puts it, the Dao simply 'abides in all things' (Jochim 1986). Consequently, Daoism postulates no intelligent design, no purpose, and no teleological goal. The Dao is to human beings what the law of gravity is to physical objects. And despite the many personifications of the Dao in the celebrated *Tao te Ching*, the fact remains that the Dao is an impersonal and cold force. To be sure, Daoism has a profound sense that 'everything has its proper place in the Dao', as Bidlack points out. But can the Daoist idea of nature and its conceptual cognates like 'naturalness' and 'spontaneity' be interpreted in moral terms or even provide the conceptual tools for constructing a moral framework? The Daoist understanding of nature, when viewed within its strictly monistic metaphysics, is unable to provide the resources for discerning any intrinsic moral principle. Strictly speaking, such a metaphysic would make the idea of morality or moral order quite impossible.

Since according to the monist vision, the Dao encompasses every aspect of reality, the many and sometimes cataclysmic changes in nature, as well as the magnificent and mysterious inter-play of polar opposites (including moral opposites), are in fact ultimately synthesised (or, to use a different metaphor, symphonised) in the Dao. In the final analysis, they are not really opposites, contradictions and paradoxes. They only appear to be the case because of our noetic inadequacies. But if our understanding of nature is incomplete, perspectival and even skewed, as the Daoist sages constantly remind us, which aspects of nature should we adopt after which to model our lives and our society? According to Liu, in speaking about human relationships 'what Laozi seeks is a situation where interpersonal relationships are marked by unadorned simplicity, naturalness and peacefulness' (Liu 2001). Again, on the basis of Daoist monism, why these qualities are preferred over others is far from obvious. Put more sharply, why should these qualities be privileged when nature includes opposite realities like complexity and conflict (Kohn 2004)?[1]

13.2 Ziran and Wu-Wei

In his paper, Bidlack maintains that in Daoist thought *ziran* – interpreted as 'naturalness' or 'spontaneity' – is crucial to understanding 'the idea that everything has a place in the Dao'. Bidlack argues that *ziran* can be understood as freedom, although he is careful to add that it is 'qualified freedom' because it is a freedom that must

[1] The evolution of Daoist ethics shows that the shape that it eventually took is in part influenced by other traditions, especially the Buddhist. The early Celestial Priests gleaned from the *Tao te Ching* a set of moral precepts that would later be given normative status. In the fourth century, a text attributed to the defied Laozi contains 180 precepts that included prohibitions against theft, adultery, killing and intoxication. Scholars believe that these precepts were in part inspired by the rules of the Buddhist community. For example, Livia Kohn concurs with Benjamin Penny that 'the appearance in China of Buddhist precepts inspired Daoists to write precepts of their own' (Kohn 2004). The *Great Precepts of Self-Observation*, dated at the sixth century and based on revelations granted by the medium Yang Xi in the 360s, contains 300 precepts. Perhaps the gradual shaping of an ethical framework (the emergence of norms and conventions?) by borrowing eclectically from other religious and moral traditions may be said to be necessary recourse because the concept of the Dao itself offers very little clear possibilities for ethics.

conform to or be in harmony with the flow of the Dao. In Daoism, Bidlack asserts, '*ziran* is the basis for any discussion of human rights' (p. 5). The interpretation of *ziran* as 'naturalness' is well supported by scholars of Daoism and Chinese philosophy. Here, *ziran* is understood as primordial and pristine natural 'reality'. In his commentary on the *Tao te Ching* 25, Wang Bi proposes this naturalistic understanding of *ziran*: 'Tao [dao] does not oppose *Tzu-jan* [*ziran*] and therefore attains its nature. To follow Nature as its standard is to model after the square while within the square and the circle while within the circle, and not to oppose Nature in any way' (Commentary 1979).

According to this interpretation, since the Dao holds together the natural and human worlds, there is 'continuity between Heaven and humanity'. Through the use of suggestive figurative language such as 'uncarved wood', 'still water' and 'mirror', early Daoists hope to show that human beings realise the good by imitating or reflecting the patterns and processes of nature (Lee 2000). Thus, in Daoist philosophy, the sage (*shengren*) and persons of authenticity (*zhenren*) are models of the productive harmony (*he*) inherent in nature because they practice *ziran*. A related account sees *ziran* as 'unconditioned spontaneity' or as 'what-is-so-of-itself'.[2] But, as Bidlack has pointed out, 'unconditioned spontaneity' does not suggest absolute freedom from all encumbrances. However, it does refer to freedom from conventions. As Cheng explains, 'One important aspect of *tzu-jan* [*ziran*] is that the movement of things must come from the internal life of things and never results from engineering or conditioning by external power' (Cheng 2008).

This brings us to the related concept *wu-wei*, which Bidlack does not discuss in his paper. Like *ziran*, the Daoist concept of *wu-wei* is integral to the Daoist notion of harmony. According to R. Kirkland, *wei* refers to 'human action intending to achieve results', especially those thought to be 'superior to what would result if nature were simply allowed to take its own course' (Kirkland 2001). Since *wu* negates this, *wu-wei*, according to Liu, means 'not to engage in human action intending to achieve results superior to those that would naturally occur' (Liu 2001). In his book, *A Daoist Theory of Chinese Thought* Chad Hansen presents a slightly different perspective that helps to enlarge our understanding of *wu-wei*. According to him, there are two meanings of *wei*. The first meaning of *wei* is to 'act', that is, to bring about certain socially specific goals. The second and more profound meaning of the word is to 'deem', to judge and to evaluate. According to Hansen, Daoism rejects all forms of 'deeming' or judging that are governed by certain conventions and norms. Thus, according to this interpretation, *wu-wei* (passivity) should not be contrasted with *you-wei* (activity). Rather *wu-wei* is to act without being in any way restricted or conditioned by convention, that is, by received norms and values (Hansen 1992). Daoist scholars are careful to stress that the *ziran-wuwei* ethic does not totally eliminate the need for norms and principles. According to these scholars, what the *Tao de Ching* urges is simply that spontaneity must be given paramount

---

[2]This understanding is derived from the literal combination of *zi*, which refers to 'self' and *ran* which means 'so'. *Ziran* is therefore 'self-as-it-is-so'.

importance (Lai 2007). Norms and principles, where they apply to any situation, must always play a secondary role.[3]

Two questions present themselves. The first is whether *ziran* can serve as a sufficiently robust moral basis for human relationality. The naturalistic interpretation of *ziran* advocates an almost unreflective surrender to the Dao, which can be variously interpreted as ultimate reality or nature. We recall Wang Bi's account: 'Nature as standard is to model after the square while within the square … and not to oppose Nature in anyway'. If this is in fact what *ziran* means, can we still speak of spontaneity in a meaningful way? And even if we allow for this idea, how much spontaneity should be encouraged? What happens when there is a conflict? Should there not be norms and conventions to guide human behaviour and social intercourse by restricting certain spontaneous actions, especially those with negative repercussions and consequences? The second issue with the *ziran-wuwei* ethic recalls the question that I raised above concerning the nature of nature. Put differently, how should nature be interpreted? What aspects of life are 'natural' and 'artificial'? Needless to say, in bioethics these are important and pressing issues.

13.3 Human Rights and Bioethics

In this final section, I take up two important topics that have both direct and indirect bearing on human rights and bioethics. The first is Daoist anthropology, specifically the question concerning how human beings are related to one another and to the cosmos. There is much in the Daoist vision that postulates the individual as part of the complex network of other human individuals, the non-human animals and the environment that should be commended. *Ziran*, as Bidlack puts it, refers to – among other things – a person's inviolable place in the Dao, which in turn encompasses everything. Bidlack ably shows how the concept of the Daoist body brings out this profound relationship between the individual, the community and the cosmos. Not only does this perspective check the stark individualism that very often undergirds modern discourse on human rights, it also urges us to rethink important 'dogmas' of modern bioethics such as autonomy.

However, the non-dualism of the Daoist perspective raises a number of important issues for modern bioethics. Bidlack alludes to one such issue when he discusses the 'rights' of non-human animals and the natural world, quoting Thomas Berry (p. 11). Bidlack is right to say that this concern for other creatures and the environment is in concert with Article 2 of the Declaration of Human Rights and Bioethics. But as he perceptively saw, this very emphasis will raise some thorny issues in bioethics especially 'when the good of the human appears to conflict with the good of the non-

[3]There is a possible 'political reading' of the *Tao te Ching* according to which *ziran* signifies a refusal to submit to the oppressive totalitarian control of the state that takes a form of civil disobedience. Based on this interpretation and depending on the context, *ziran* may arguably be said to support human rights. I owe this point to Professor Ellen Zhang.

human realm' (p. 11). This is an important issue not just in relation to biomedical waste, but also in relation to the use of animals for experiments that could translate into therapeutic applications that would save many human lives. Again, this is essentially a problem associated with Daoist metaphysics, which, strictly speaking makes no allowance for any kind of hierarchy in the natural order. The concept of *ziran* when applied consistently to the natural order would indeed result in the notion that trees, insects, rivers and mountains have rights. But if the rights of nature are to be strictly respected, it follows that its destruction by humans in any way cannot be countenanced.

We turn, albeit very briefly, to the second issue: the role of rules and conventions. As we have already seen above, the Daoist approach has an aversion to rules and conventions. This is brought out historically by early Daoism's critique of Mohism and Confucianism, especially for developing their moral philosophies on the basis of rules and rites (*li*). Eschewing such approaches as crude, Daoism purports to offer a more refined and sophisticated understanding of morality by directing one's response to the particular and the concrete, and to a sense of responsibility established on one's rootedness to the natural patterns of the cosmos. In this way, Daoist moral theory serves as a critique to much of Western moral philosophy since the Enlightenment inspired by Immanuel Kant, with its focus on principles, rules and laws. In addition, Daoist moral theory appears to advocate an 'other-centred' rather than a 'self-centred' approach.[4]

However, this approach which places spontaneity above principles and rules poses a problem for modern human rights practice as well as for modern bioethics, both of which must inevitably be governed by principles, protocols and the rule of law. In any ethical society, rules provide the basis for the evaluation not only of the conduct of individuals but also the practises, procedures and policies of complex institutions. In bioethics, rules provide the basis for evaluating the practises and conduct of physicians as well as institutions like hospitals and governmental research outfits. In many ways, principles and rules provide the clearest articulation of normativity in both religious and philosophical ethics. Rules do this insofar as they prescribe, permit and prohibit conduct. In addition, because of the 'timeless' character of rules, they are able to provide stability, consistency and continuity in social practice. As Richard Miller has pointed out, rules serve as a prospective, contemporaneous and retrospective guide (Miller 2005). They provide guidance in directing future and current behaviour, even as they serve as the basis for the assessment and evaluation of past conduct.

A sophisticated conception of rules would postulate that rules are linked to and therefore receive their rationale and form from higher-order principles. As such, as Miller again helpfully clarifies, 'Rules state what a person or group should, should not, or may do. Although they regulate behaviour, they do not *establish* that one

[4]This is seen particularly in the way in which some Daoists have even eschewed the famous Golden Rule, namely, 'Do unto others what you would have them to do unto you'. They prefer what Yong Huang has called the Copper Rule, which states: 'Do unto others what they would have us do unto them' (Yong 2005). The Copper Rule is allegedly established on the notion of *ziran*.

should, should not, or may not do something' (Miller 2005). Put differently, while rules guide human behaviour the latter is established on more fundamental principles like justice, equality, and dignity. That is why rules themselves must be justified through moral reasoning based on these principles. In addition, because rules are directive and prescriptive of actions, they can be revised when the situation changes so long as these revisions are consistent with the general principles that give them their rationale. The fact remains that many activities such as just war are rule-governed in that they must adhere to established ground rules and rules of assessment. These activities must be conducted in keeping with the regulations that are put in place (often by international bodies) to justify certain actions as well as to constrain others in order to prevent these activities from degenerating into amorality or immorality. Insofar as human rights practices and bioethics may be generally categorised in this way, rules and the principles and values that inspire them must continue to play a significant role.

References

Ames, Roger T. 1994. *The Art of rulership: A study of ancient Chinese political thought*. Albany: State University of New York Press.

Chung-ying, Cheng. 2008. On environmental ethics of the Tao and the Ch'i. *Environmental Ethics* 8: 351–370.

Commentary on the Lao Tzu by Wang Pi. 1979. *Monograph 6 of the society for Asian and comparative philosophy*. Trans. Arianc Rump. Honolulu: University Press of Hawaii.

Hansen, Chad. 1992. *A Daoist theory of Chinese thought*. Oxford: Oxford University Press.

Huang, Yong. 2005. A copper rule versus the golden rule: A Daoist-Confucian proposal for global ethics. *Philosophy East & West* 55 (3): 394–425.

Jochim, C. 1986. *Chinese religions*. Englewood Cliffs: Prentice-Hall.

Kirkland, R. 2001. Responsible non-Action in a natural world: Perspectives from the Neiye, Zhuangzi and Dao de Jing. In *Daoism and ecology: Ways within a cosmic landscape*, ed. N.J. Girardot et al., 293–304. Cambridge: Harvard.

Kohn, Livia. 2004. *Cosmos and community: The ethical dimension of Daoism*. Cambridge: Three Pines Press.

Lai, Karyn. 2007. Ziran and wuwei in the Daodejing: An ethical assessment. *Dao* 6: 325–337.

Lee, Jung H. 2000. Finely aware and richly responsible: The Daoist imperative. *Journal of the American Academy of Religion* 68 (3): 511–536.

Liu, Xiaogan. 2001. Non-action and the environment today: A conceptual and applied study of Laozi's philosophy. In *Daoism and ecology: Ways within a cosmic landscape*, ed. N.J. Girardot et al., 315–339. Cambridge: Harvard.

Miller, Richard. 2005. Rules. In *The Oxford handbook of theological ethics*, ed. Gilbert Meilaender and William Werpehowski, 220–236. Oxford: Oxford University Press.

Nagel, Thomas. 2002. Personal rights and the public square. In *Concealment and exposure and other essays*, 31–53. Oxford: Oxford University Press.

Part V
Asian Religions: Hinduism

Chapter 14
Duties and Rights in Hinduism: Before and After India's Independence

Prakash N. Desai

The language of rights is alien to the Indian culture. Often thought of as synonymous, India and Hinduism are not. Although there slightly over 80% of the people of India are *Hindus*, remaining over half Muslims and the rest comprise of Christians, *Sikhs*, *Jains*, Buddhists etc. Even this, the 80% are not homogenous. Over a quarter of these are so called tribal and the untouchables, not quite within the fold of mainstream Hinduism. Even of the remaining a sizable number are designated "other backward castes", a label derived from their socioeconomic status, and practice a heterodox religion.

As Hajime Nakamura, a Buddhist and Hindu scholar says, "we don't usually speak of rights in our tradition," referring to all of the Eastern religions, (Cited in Rouner 1988). On the other hand the religious texts are replete with the concepts of duty, often translated as dharma same as religion. Rights imply entitlements, duties are obligations. Dharma, (or for a short translation, religion) has its origin in the oldest religious texts, the *Vedas*, regarded as revelation, and are also known as *shrutis*, that which was heard (by the ancient sages). As such the corpus of what we now call Hindu religious literature spans several millennia starting in about the middle of the 2nd millennium BCE and continues to be refined and redacted. Following the heard texts are the remembered texts, the *Smritis*, or the Law books, principle and best known among them is the *Manusmriti*, (as remembered by Manu, a famous scholar and sage), and many others named after the principal writer or redactor of a particular text. This text is an elaboration on the nature of the social order, and among other things the four classes of people, the four stages of life, and the duties of each according to class, age, gender and status or relationship. There was an explicit hierarchy ordained among the four classes, the *Brahmins*, *Kshtriyas*, *Vaishyas* and *Sudras* in that order. Later Hindu works are the *puranas*, or histories, devoted to a particular mythological story or a Hindu deity. There are over a hundred

P.N. Desai (✉)
UICMC, University of Illinois at Chicago, Chicago, IL, USA
e-mail: PDesai@psych.uic.edu

J. Tham et al. (eds.), *Religious Perspectives on Bioethics and Human Rights*,
Advancing Global Bioethics 6, DOI 10.1007/978-3-319-58431-7_14

such texts. The two epics, *Ramayana* and the *Mahabharata* are also important religious text in classical as well as popular forms of Hinduism.

The *Brahmins* established centers of learning, ashrams, where young acolytes sent away to the ashrams by their families learnt at the feet of their gurus. The tradition of Guru-disciple relationship had another important developmental implication for Hinduism. Many sects and quasi-religious cults were founded by various Gurus and became popular at least regionally in their name. Some Gurus came to be regarded as saints, or more correctly *sants*, a word derived from the Sanskrit '*sat*' meaning true or truth, and thus pious, religious, venerated etc. Their teachings became a path to religious enlightenment. Whereas the former *brahminical* tradition of *Vedas*, *Upanishads*, and the *dharmashastras* provide a larger framework for religious conduct and social boundaries, the essential popular Hinduism is a tradition populated by various *sants* and local deities, worshipped by people with unfettered joy, each one to his or her fancy. In the medieval era a number of Saint-poets emerged all over India establishing a different trend at assimilation, integration, and syntheses of the various religions and different cults, at once eliminating many differences in worship practices, the path of *bhakti* (derived from the Sanskrit word *bhaj*, meaning to worship, more accurately to participate in, to be part of) enabling a personal connection to god for each person, and democratizing the practices by eradicating caste distinctions. The path of *bhakti* was articulated first in a much older text of the *Bhagvadgita*, often referred to simply as *Gita*, a much celebrated dialogue between a protagonist of the epic *Mahabharata* and his mentor Lord Krishna. This text was popularized during the independence movement, especially by Mahatma Gandhi who embraced its theory of duty, or Karma that is *Gita's* famous dictum that one has a right to one's duties or actions, not to the fruits of the action. *Gita* advocated that death in the performance of one's duties than someone else's which is perilous. Thus we find that popular Hinduism is polyphonic, that it speaks in many voices, and is a manifestation of diversity of all manner that is Hindu India. Speaking of diversity, Ashis Nandy (2013) says, and without any exaggeration, "Hinduism in all its diversity—its innumerable castes (some figures go as high as 70,000), tens of thousands of village god and goddesses, hundreds of sects, thousands of vernacular religious epics and *jatipuranas,* family priests, and personal and familial".

14.1 Dharma

The Sanskrit word dharma, often translated as religion, is also translated as duty or obligation. From the Sanskrit verb dhr, which means to hold, or sustain, *dharma* is that which holds a person and a society together. It is the principle that lends coherence to the personal and the social world. It derives from an older *vedic* concept of rta, meaning order, as in that of seasons *Dharma* is the cosmic and moral order of the universe. It is also related to a later word, Sat meaning truth. The ancient texts of the *Vedas* and the *Smritis* are the two principle sources of *dharma*.

A third source of *dharma*, was good conduct, or rather the conduct of good men. This is an important development as it appears that conduct of good men, or largely the prevailing tradition trumps the Law-givers. In clarifying the issue Robert Lingat, a French scholar cautions that "One must take care to avoid confusing this "ideal custom" with what we call custom, that is to say practices confirmed by immemorial usage, custom followed by everyone, habitual practices of a group, perhaps arising from convention. Custom pure and simple is indeed a source of law, but is not a source of *dharma*", (Lingat 1973).

Robert Lingat goes on to illustrate this principle by showing that "the author of the code of *Manu* was hostile to marriages between the *dvija* (the upper classes) and a *Sudra* (the lowest class), to the act of meat-eating, to *niyoga* (the custom of childless – usually son-less couple, having a younger brother of the husband or a good Brahman impregnate a woman), to second marriages of a widow, but he was confronted by custom too deeply rooted for prohibitions to be efficacious. All he could do was to try to discredit them and to limit their practice and their importance, (op cit page 182). Thus tradition trumps law. The foregoing is an important discussion about custom as we shall see later, in modern India the enactment of a new constitution for independent India trumps all customs by the laws enshrined in the new constitution, inspired by Western liberal values.

The fourth and the final source of dharma was 'that which was pleasing to the self.' This did not mean that everybody could do what they pleased and 'anything goes' but had to be according to ones conscience, and generally regarded as appropriate to ones age, gender and class. The four sources of dharma did not carry equal weight and in fact it meant that four were important in a descending order, that is the final arbiters of dharma were the *Vedas*, and when *Vedas* were silent on an issue, the later *smriti* (remembered) texts, the law books held sway, after which came custom or conduct of good men and finally absent all the three a person had to act according to his or her conscience.

This is a development that is perhaps related to the dispersal of population from the plains bounded by the rivers Indus and Ganges, originally occupied by the Indo-Europeans and later the area bounded by the rivers Ganges and Yamuna recognized as the land of the *Aryas*. As the population expanded and grew, it moved farther east and south, away from the center, and thus a necessity for new schools of scholarship, that is ashrams of renowned teachers. As the tradition was essentially oral, written script having developed well after the fifth century BCE, the lore handed down as remembered by a particular scholar differed ever so slightly from the earlier. Thus the number of recognized law books grew into dozens. Another factor that also gave importance to custom was the interaction of the big tradition, which is that of the Indo-Europeans, with the little traditions, which is that of the local inhabitants where the Indo-Europeans moved in, especially the south and East of India. P.V. Kane (1968–1977), a renowned scholar whose work on the law books attests to this. This process of interpenetration of the great (*brahminical*) tradition with myriad smaller local tradition gave *Hinduism* its essential diversity. Thus developed a polytheistic tradition, both the gods of the *Shrutis* and *Smritis* and those worshipped by pre-*aryan* local inhabitants emerged from a multiple of interpenetrating traditions. In all this the Guru-disciple relationship remained a very crucial path to learning and interpretation of the various texts. Although not bounded by an *Ashram* established by a particular Guru, the tradition of this relationship plays an important role to this day. It was also the path for a young student to find a compass to steer his (the disciples were almost exclusively male) life. The proliferation of religious literature continues thru our present time, enriched in different parts of the country and at different times by a Guru who obtains a cult status, acquired through a process of assimilation of small and somewhat bigger aspects of other world religions, beginning with *Buddhism* and *Jainism* and continuing thru the *Abrahamic* religions, and even from religion that grew out of this process of assimilation, *Sikhism*. In the end Hinduism grew into three major paths, with three deities presiding, *Shiva*, *Vishnu* and the (female) *Shakti*, and proliferation of each of the three.

14.2 Differentiation of Duties

Like rights, the concept of equality is also alien to Hindu tradition. From the very moment of creation, according to the *Rig-Veda* human beings were not crated equal. *Purushasukta* Hymn visualizes a simple giant, the first created cosmic man. *Purushu* (the person) is the one who performs the sacrificial ritual that connects him to the creator (Doniger 1981). *Purusha* is a differentiated entity which arises from an undifferentiated uncertain and indefinable matrix, *Brahman*, (Campbell 1969). In the hymn *Purusha* falls apart in the act of creation, is broken down into parts which become the elements, his breath the wind, his eyes the sun, etc. He becomes the foundation of the social order, from his mouth come the priests (those who enunciate the laws), *Brahmins*, from his arms come warriors, the *Kshtriyas*, from his thighs come the commoner, the *Vaishya*, (agriculturalists) and his feet, the *Sudra*, the manual workers, the toilers. Thus a hierarchy between the various classes is given from the very act of creation. The classes were unequal from the beginning and therefore, their duties were also different.

There were duties common to all and incumbent on human beings alike. First among these was to speak the truth, followed by non-violence toward sentient beings, the two duties that Mahatma Gandhi later made his guiding and abiding life principles. True to geographic dispersal of population and rise of multiple schools of scholarship, the oral tradition had differing lists of duties common to all as the number of *smritis* (remembered) works multiplied. Here also there must have been accommodation to local custom. For example, one work has "avoiding back-biting jealousy, pride, egoism, unbelief, crookedness, self-praise, abuse of others, deceit, covetousness, delusion, anger and envy is the dharma of all life-stages (Kane 2.1.6). Kane further adds that "In the midst of countless rules of outward conduct there is insistence on the necessity to satisfy the inner man (*antara-purusa*) or conscience. This returns us to the fourth source of *dharma*, that which is appropriate to the self.

The four classes, or *Varnas* originally meaning color, that is the color of the skin, supposedly distinguish the invading/immigrating Indo-Europeans who were white and the original inhabitants of India who were dark. The light-skinned ones are the *Brahmins*, the priest scholars and teachers, the *Kshtriyas*, the rulers, soldiers and the protectors, the *Vaishyas* who were agriculturalists and traders, and the dark skinned ones are the *Sudras* who did manual work. The untouchables, a much later designation, was reserved for those who did the most menial work and became polluted by coming in touch with human waste, dead bodies and dead animals, etc.

Bhagavad Gita, (*Gita* hereafter) a later religious text, one to achieve a truly all India status and remain a living guide over the last two millennia, extolled the virtue which is holding fast to duty assigned to one's caste when it declared that death is preferable in doing one's duty than following someone else's, as that is perilous (Miller-Stroller, 3.35). Here the *Gita* invokes the *Guna* theory, the notion that although all the *Gunas* or strands (*satva*, *rajas*, and *tamas,* i.e., goodness, passion and darkness or sloth resp.) are present in all beings some are dominant in one as opposed to another. In the case of different classes (*Varnas*) goodness strand, which promotes contemplation, reflection, study, etc) is dominant in the *Brahmins*, passion as the name suggests promotes aggression, dominant in the warrior class (*Kshtriyas*), *Vaishyas* have mixed dominance and *Sudras*, the toilers have sloth dominance. With time, the classes became biological and hence hereditary from being simply occupational. And hence the duties incumbent on a particular class also become given and permanent.

Age was an important variable that assigned special duties. Elders received respect, deference and obedience as well as veneration. Small differences in age called for differences in status, and in turn entailed upon the elder the obligation to care for and protect the young. This authority and dependence became closely tied to each other, although an aged father became dependant on his son. Gender also regulated status in that women were subservient to men. It is said that a woman is dependant on the father as a child, on her husband as a wife and on her son when she gets old. In practice though, a mother commands respect of her children even when they become adults. As in the case of classes, so also for age and gender, hierarchy was the order of the relationships, (Dumont 1980). Surabhi Sheth (1987) correctly points out that hierarchy is the opposite of equality, but, she adds, the system allowed for a harmony of motives and a sense of balance prevailed and that the rules and codes were always contextualized, which then permitted discretion, mobility and transitions.

As one can easily see rights which in some ways presuppose equality is not a concept that Hindus focused upon from early on. The idea that "all men are created equal" is certainly a Western product, resulting from the interaction of the early Middle Eastern religions with Greek thought and culture and much later socio-political, economic, philosophical and religious developments during the periods of Reformation and especially the Renaissance. Twentieth century American dominance, experience of the holocaust, and communism became later imperatives that focused on Human Rights.

Rights can be constructed imaginatively, that is not by text or tradition in the Hindu tradition, but by looking at duties from the other end, that is if a son has a duty to his father and teacher to obey them, then the father and the teacher have a right to expect obedience from the son. If a King or a ruler – from the *Kshatriya* (warrior) class has a duty to protect those over whom he rules, the populace has a right to expect protection. But this is logical thinking, certainly something that attains in practice regularly, but is not part of the religious tradition and its discourse. But here too, there is no notion that duties or rights are common to all humans or those duties and rights are reciprocal processes presuming equality. As we have seen it is difficult to draw a clear demarcation between what is religion and what is custom or tradition. Thus although rights do not find a distinct category addressed by religious laws or literature, in practice or by tradition they are found stressed in variable contexts. A man exercises his rights over his wife and his progeny, a guru over his disciples, a landlord over those to whom he farms out his land, a master over his servants and so forth. It might be useful to indicate here that it is custom then that lends Hindu relationships their authoritarian character and hence to the culture.

14.3 Rights and Conflicts

India's independence from the British in 1947 ushered in a new era, not just in the obvious fashion, but especially in the area of human rights. The idea of human rights has been incorporated in the Indian Constitution drafted after independence in 1947. The slow march to independence and a century of struggle to attain independence from the British Raj culminating in the leadership of Mahatma Gandhi did usher in an era of liberation of the down trodden from centuries of discrimination. Gandhi embarked on the culturally difficult path of eliminating untouchability and "kicked up a storm" among the conservative Hindus and religious leadership. His mass movement encouraged women to join the fight which also was opening new doors but approved with less apparent conflict. Jawaharlal Nehru, the chosen political heir to Gandhi was a flaming liberal and as he gradually assumed Gandhi's mantle he began to steer the elite thinking more in the direction of Western liberalism. But even as a champion of the new constitution Jawaharlal Nehru bemoaned the fact that the constitution enumerated rights for citizens but no duties, "All of us now talk of and demand rights and privileges, but the teaching of the old dharma was about duties and obligations. Rights follow duties discharged" (Nehru, J. (1959), cited in Kane, op.cit, Vol V p 1664). Here was an example of the reverse of what happened at the beginning, namely the law triumphed over tradition.

A constitution needed and to be drafted to embrace the infinite variety of people, religions, sects, regions and so on. India was not only a multi-religious society but also multilingual, multiethnic and many different demands on the polity from these diverse people. New statutes had to be drafted, debated and adopted, no easy task, made slightly easier by the heady wine of independence. Foremost among the imperatives was to unshackle the populace from a caste ridden, hierarchical and highly stratified society with a gaping divide between the rich and the poor, the urban and the rural, the upper castes and the untouchables, not to speak about religions. Having championed against the prospect of an undivided India between mostly Hindu India and a mostly Muslim Pakistan, even after the cause was lost, Indian leaders felt compelled, duty bound to accommodate all of the minorities and especially the Muslims and the untouchables (although they did not demand a separate state, the untouchable leaders, particularly, B. R. Ambedkar advocated for a separate electorate at one time).

When it came to choosing an intellectual to head the drafting a new constitution Nehru, as the Prime-Minister of India, chose for the job, Bhimrao Ramji Ambedkar, an untouchable himself, but educated at Columbia in economics and Anthropology and in Law in London, and a leader of the untouchables. (Ambedkar converted to Buddhism as that religion for him was a way of liberating himself from the humiliation of being an untouchable), The resulting document was fashioned after the American Constitution with its notion of human rights as the point of reference, with special reparatory reservations in educational institutions, as well as jobs for the former untouchables. The institution of untouchability was formally abolished. But in practice this was easier said then done. Former untouchables continue to struggle to this day for their rights and continue to be victims of harassment, cruelty, flogging, blinding, and just plain murder in retaliation by the upper castes for their assertion of their rights, especially in rural areas. Riots have broken out in city streets against "quotas" as the people call reservations for those dubbed the lowest castes in the Hindu hierarchy (termed scheduled castes in the constitution as they are listed in a special schedule, along with the tribal populations referred to as scheduled tribes).

The situation with women's rights is a little less virulent but far more pervasive as it is a story of every household, albeit that in most urban areas and in many parts of India, women have achieved a far greater public space than in the past both through education and employment. But domestic abuse occurs on a massive scale as is rape. The more recent incident of gang rape and eventual murder (she died as a result of massive internal injuries) of a young woman (who has been given the name *Nirbhaya*, (the one without fear) in the capital city of New Delhi has created a national uproar all over the country and has forced the hands of politicians to enact a new law to prosecute the crime of rape. The discrimination against women is best told by the adverse gender rations in India. In contrast to most of the Western world there are fewer women to men in India, which is an indication of their neglect as infants and children both in forms of nutrition and health care, as well as female feticide, infanticide (Miller 1981) and poor access to peri-natal care for mothers, and their female off-spring.

The revolution that occurred in political thinking in independent India with adult franchise and the place of human rights and secular laws has far outpaced a similar cultural revolution. Perhaps the last religious revolution in India was in the times of Buddha who led an anti-brahminical movement, promising people of all classes to an equal access to God and equality before the deities.

A more recent and a pernicious development has been the revival of caste (these are further divisions of the classes into smaller groups, called *Jatis*, a word of common origin with the Latin genera, with strict rules about marriage and sharing of cooked foods), *panchayats*, old institutional arrangements in which a group of elders (panch-meaning five) who act as a court adjudicated disputes between members of the caste. Some *panchayats* have taken a strong stance against marriages of young man and women with partners of their own choice who may belong to other castes or religion. Starting with sanctions against the whole family should such an arrangement go through, sometimes culminating in murders to preserve the prestige of the caste and the affected family, the *panchayats* (and the affected family) seek to enforce the tradition of their caste.

Another area of conflict emerged when the Indian parliament enacted the so called Hindu Code Bill, especially its provision for daughters to inherit their ancestral property. The prevailing Hindu traditional inheritance laws until then, accepted under the British, only the sons inherited their parents' ancestral property. The change in the new constitution for daughters to have equal rights was a major departure from tradition and although there was a great deal of consternation the Bill was finally enacted. Today there is little discussion of this provision in the law. In spite of claims to having ushered in a secular era and equality in the eyes of the law for all people, the legislature, in order to assure that Muslims felt at home in India after partition into India and Pakistan, enacted different civil codes for the conduct of their traditional practices like allowing polygamous marriage for Muslims and for tax laws affecting Hindu family arrangements. This has been a major cause of strife, sometimes explicit and at others not, especially since the emergence of a political party that champions the Hindu tradition. The slogan of the party is to uphold "*Hindutva*", the essence of being a Hindu and a call to and expectation of other religious groups who are in minority to adopt this sense of "*hinduness*" This is what is being labeled as identity politics.

Questions of cultural and political identity are at the heart of the rise of Hindu fundamentalist sentiment and a political party, and civil unrest between the two communities more seriously so in the last 25 years but an issue ever since the demand for a separate state for Muslims arose in India. And with her later partition communal tensions became virulent. Mahatma Gandhi's assassination was a manifestation of this strife. As might be expected Christian Churches have also been targets of violence on account of their conversion practices.

14.4 Health Care and Human Rights

When it comes to medical ethics, India had its more than 2000 years old medical tradition, the Ayurvedic medicine. Its earliest text, written and compiled over centuries and by multiple authors, finally attributed to *Carak*, a legendary physician and another text attributed to *Sushruta*, a court physician to a Buddhist king. The contribution of Buddhist monks, physicians and scholars first and later by Jain monks and physician is monumental. It is important to emphasize that the development of medical science grew in tandem with religious philosophies, especially in the area of body construction (Desai 1989). The early texts have a clear expectation of ethical practice, respecting patient's privacy, the role of the family, injunctions against extra-professional relationship with a patient or a relative, of not doing harm, physical or economic, and rules about birth control, abortion, and care of the dying patient. Without modern technology, some questions had just not risen or had been anticipated in ingenious ways with standards of care.

In modern India, within the area of health care the real ethical problem is that of access to health care for the poor and especially in the rural and tribal areas and hence the principle of justice, a fair distribution of resources is an empty dream. A fragmented, and either commercialized or bureaucratic system of health care, neither easily accessible nor affordable, is the issue and has defied decades of attempts at solution. Modern medicine, that is western or called Allopathy or cosmopolitan medicine has pushed to the periphery traditional Ayurvedic as well as the Yunai (from Ionian, developed and patronized mainly by the Muslims) Although soon after Independence India embarked on providing community based health care through primary Health Care Centers in rural areas with Satellite clinics further into the hinterland which made a dramatic difference in especially the provision of a maternal and children's health care, it is far from adequate. In fact mortality which stood at 180 per 1000 live births in the 1950s has dropped to 47.2 in a 2013 according to the WHO and UNESCO statistics (Index Mundi 2013). Similarly there has been a marked drop in maternal mortality, and death and birth rates. Population growth has also abated through aggressive family planning campaigns of health education and free contraceptive services but remains an area that needs more work. Abortions were legalized in India in 1972 without much public opposition save the Christian church and press.

The care of female children is still problematic. Infanticide of female children was practiced in India at one time, especially in the North and Northwest regions and only an occasional occurrence is reported more recently. When prenatal gender diagnosis became available through amniocentesis and other technologies a national outcry arose against female feticide. Subsequently, in 1984 all preconception and prenatal diagnostic testing was banned in India, although an underground network offering such services continues to operate. The gender ratio in India, not surprisingly, is adverse for women. For the country as a whole it stands at 940 females per 1000, with a wide variation between regions of India. In the northern state of *Haryana* the ration of females to males stands at 877:1000, whereas for the Southern state of *Kerala* the ratio is 1084:1000. The statistics for *Kerala* are likely the result of a number of historical, cultural, religious, socio-economic and political dimensions of the state (Indian Guide 2012). In short, the practice of infanticide and feticide along with poor care of female children, have led to these adverse gender ratios, (Singh 2010).

The relatively more recent introduction of assisted reproductive technology has been a boon to infertile couples, and especially to women for whom infertility is a stigma. In vivo and in vitro fertilization, as well as surrogacy are easily available. India's poverty and low health care costs compared to those in the West make it ripe ground for Western couples seeking ova donors and surrogate mothers. For a while this was a free-for-all market place which engendered a variety of ethical human rights questions as well as legal and economic problems. A bill was introduced in 2008 to regulate this market and still under deliberation, attempting to protect donor and surrogate mothers as well as eager Indian and Western couples (Rajesh and Desai 2012).

As I said earlier some issues have been dealt with in culture specific ways, especially as the principle of autonomy is concerned. A hierarchical and patriarchal society holds that elders, especially male elders though not exclusively, know best. Neither the law or any traditional imperative demands that a patient himself or herself be informed and give his or her consent voluntarily. Even the texts ask that unfavorable or especially dire prognosis be withheld, sometimes not only from the patient but also from the family. Injectables can be given and are given against a patient's will when it comes to the care of the mentally ill. Even oral medications are disguised mixed with food or by giving an acceptable name. But nobody is worked up about violation of patients' rights. This has one major adverse development in the area of pharmaceutical research. Western pharmaceuticals have had access to a pharmacologically naïve population in many drugs and hence a ~~a~~ very desirable population to induct in research studies. Not only the illiteracy but also the silence of both tradition and the law in the area of informed consent has often led to gross unethical practices although there is developing a greater vigilance in the press and the leaders about the issue.

When it comes to the care of a dying patient with no hope of recovery, traditional that is Ayurvedic injunctions are as modern as in today's Western practices to withdraw treatment and then nutrition gradually when futility of treatment is determined (Desai 2014).

Neither the publicly funded health care system nor the parallel private health care services that mainly cater to the upper and middle class~~;~~ in both urban and semi-urban areas fill the woeful gaps in health care. The paradox is that in the metropolitan areas state of the art hospitals cater to those who can afford them and large swaths of India go without any respectable delivery of health care. Given the large differences between ~~in~~ health care costs in the West (and the rich from the Middle East) and in India, these medical centers have become a haven for medical tourism. Emigration of physicians and nurses to the West has not helped improve the health care network in India. Cultivation of mobile health care has been taken over by non-governmental voluntary agencies as like in the West, it is difficult to get health care professionals to settle in the rural areas of the country.

14.5 Conclusion

Hindus have from the inception of the tradition focused on duties rather than rights. A highly hierarchical social order is not hospitable to Human rights but the constitution that the people adopted after India's independence in 1947 visualizes equality, universal adult franchise and a set of Human rights that have attempted to neutralize centuries of discrimination against certain population and also, to equalize the status of women. Heath care and Human rights are still developing notions in India and continue to call for attention. Conflicts between traditional practices and changing expectations of a young nation are rife with conflicts. Social and political reformers will have to pay close attention to these areas of concern.

Bibliography

Campbell, Joseph, ed. 1969. *The philosophies of India*, 77. Princeton: Princeton University Press.

Desai, Prakash. 1989. *Health and medicine in the hindu tradition*. New York: Crossroad.

———. 2014. *Bioethics, in south Asia, in encyclopedia of bioethics*, 4th ed, ed. Bruce Jennings. McMillan Reference USA 214. Farmington Hills, MI P2990–2998.

Dumont, Louis. 1980. *Homo Hierarchicus*. Chicago: University of Chicago Press.

Index Mundi. 2013. *Health indicators*. http://www.indexmundi.com/facts/topics/health. Accessed 6 Aug.

Kane, Pandurang Vaman. 1968–1977. *History of Dharmasastra*, vol 5. Poona: Bhandankar Oriental Research Institute.

Lingat, Robert. 1973. *The classical law of India*. Trans. J. Duncan and M. Derrett. Berkeley/Los Angeles: University of California Press.

Miller, Barbara D. 1981. *The endangered sex: Neglect of female children in rural north India*. Ithaca: Cornell University Press.

Miller-Stroller, Barbara. 1986. *The Bhagwaral-Gita*. New York: Bantamn Press.

Nandy, Ashis. 2013. *Regimes of narcissism, regimes of despair*, 27. New Delhi: Oxford University Press.

Rajesh K., and Pranav N. Desai. 2012. *Risk frames and representation in the assisted reproductive technologies (Regulation) Bill 2008*. Indian: Science and Technology, 214–219. New Delhi: National Institute of Science, Technology and Development Studies.

Rouner, LeRoy, ed. 1988. *Human rights and world religions*, 1. Indiana: University of Notre Dame Press.

Sheth, Surabhi. 1987. Equality and in equality in the hindu scriptures. In *Equality in the religious traditions of Asia*, ed. R. Siriwerdena. India: Palgrave MacMillan.

Singh, J.P. 2010. Socio-cultural aspects of the high masculinity ratio in India. *Journal of Asian and African Studies* 45 (6): 628–644.

The Rig Veda: An Anthology. 1981. Trans. Wendy Doniger (O'Flaherty). Harmondsworth: Penguin Classics.

Chapter 15
UNESCO on Cultural Diversity, Bioethics and Hinduism: A Response Essay (2013)

John Lunstroth

Participants in the Third International Conference on Bioethics, Multiculturalism and Religion (2013) were asked to discuss the relationship between "universal human rights and cultural diversity in the life sciences" based on Article 12 of the UNESCO Declaration on Bioethics and Human Rights from the perspective of a particular religion. Professor Prakash Desai presented the main paper from the Hindu perspective, and in this essay I respond to his paper.

> Article 12 – Respect for cultural diversity and pluralism
>
> The importance of cultural diversity and pluralism should be given due regard. However, such considerations are not to be invoked to infringe upon human dignity, human rights and fundamental freedoms, nor upon the principles set out in this Declaration, nor to limit their scope.

The much discussed problem with cultural diversity is that local norms can conflict with international human rights norms.[1] In this Article UNESCO identified local norms as "cultural diversity and pluralism" and the international human rights, or universal, norms as "human dignity, human rights and fundamental freedoms." What UNESCO failed to grapple with is that those local norms, cultural diversity and pluralism, are not only protected by international human rights, a significant part of the human rights political theory is addressed to permitting and resolving the problems of pluralism.[2] The Article indicates local norms should be "given due regard", but clearly subordinates them to the universal norms.[3]

---

[1] See e.g., PHILIP ALSTON & RYAN GOODMAN, International Human Rights (Oxford University Press. 2012), pp. 531–684.

[2] See e.g., International Covenant on Civil and Political Rights, Art. 1.

[3] See John Lunstroth, CULTURAL DIVERSITY IN UNESCO BIOETHICS – **SAME VOLUME**

J. Lunstroth (✉)
Health Law & Policy Institute, University of Houston Law Center, Houston, TX, USA
e-mail: lunstroth@gmail.com

J. Tham et al. (eds.), *Religious Perspectives on Bioethics and Human Rights*,
Advancing Global Bioethics 6, DOI 10.1007/978-3-319-58431-7_15

In this essay I use Immanuel Wallerstein's perspectives about European universalism to comment on science and bioethics, and the functioning of Article 12 in India.[4] He argues that science is a western universalist strategy used to extend colonialist impulses. Consistent with his notions, described in more detail below, I first describe science as a philosophical undertaking, as Enlightenment metaphysics that has become a dominant global ideology. I then argue bioethics is philosophically dependent on the metaphysics of science. In the final section I use Wallerstein's point of view about science in comments on the application of Article 12 to the political situation in India given the inherent nature of the life sciences and the philosophical scope of bioethics.

15.1 Western Science, Scientific Institutions and Economic Interests in India

Western or positivist science is a set of beliefs, or a metaphysics, about nature that can function as an ideology. An ideology is a way in which "meaning serves to establish and sustain relations of domination.[5] The ideology of positivist science includes a materialist and physicalist ontology, and the related conclusion (via Darwin) that all living things are machines. Prior to the European Enlightenment the west was communitarian, and just as in India, only the powerful had rights.[6] By the seventeenth century the individual emerged as the central actor in political theory. This developed in political theory into the ideology of individualism and the rights holder; and in science the individual became the basic mechanical unit of living things. Casting individuals as machines stripped them of moral significance. However, it was not until the late nineteenth century that scientific medicine and the related technologies, such as pharmaceutical drugs, found significant social authority through the bacterial theory of disease and development of the laboratory sciences and biostatistics (1870–1920).[7] That authority reached its apotheosis in the decades following WW2.

---

[4] IMMANUEL WALLERSTEIN, European Universalism: The Rhetoric of Power (The New Press. 2006).

[5] SUSAN MARKS, The Riddle of All Constitutions: International Law, Democracy, and the Critique of Ideology (Oxford University Press. 2000), p. 10

[6] See generally, ALASDAIR MACINTYRE, After Virtue: A Study in Moral Theory (University of Notre Dame Press 3rd ed. 1981/2007); BRIAN TIERNEY, The Idea of Natural Rights: Studies on Natural Rights, Natural Law, and Church Law: 1150–1625 (John Witte Jr. ed., William P. Eerdmans Publishing Company. 1997).

[7] See generally, PAUL STARR, The Social Transformation of American Medicine (Basic Books. 1982); J. ROSSER MATTHEWS, Quantification and the Quest for Medical Certainty (Princeton University Press. 1995); HARRY M. MARKS, The Progress of Experiment: Science and Therapeutic Reform in the United States, 1900–1990 (Charles Rosenberg ed., Cambridge University Press. 1997).

Beginning in about 1980, as neoliberal economic theory began to be implemented in the US and UK, the pharmaceutical companies began to gather strength as various regulatory schemes that had controlled it were dismantled. When the Cold War came to an end in 1989, the world itself saw radical changes to the international community that resulted in the flourishing of globalization, and at the forefront of globalization were the pharmaceutical companies, never more powerful. Their influence extended into UN organs such as the WHO and the GATT/WTO, and they deeply influenced the development of laws in the various large state markets such as the US and the EU.[8]

To grow economically the pharmaceutical sector needs two things: (1) human bodies on which to experiment; and (2) populations that have been medicalized, taught that the proper response to getting sick is to take pills made by pharmaceutical companies. India has always been one of its primary targets. It has an immense population that is not medicalized which is good for finding relatively chemically "clean" human to experiment on; and it has an immense potential market.

15.2 Bioethics, Human Rights and India

Bioethics emerged in the west in the 1960s as philosophers and lawyers began to question the medical profession and other medical scientists in their acts towards experimental subjects and their patients.[9] There had been earlier references to core ideas such as consent, in case law dating from the late nineteenth century, and then again in the doctor trials at Nuremberg after WW2; however none of those references or doctrines would flourish until after the 1960s, and for all practical purposes it was not until the 1980s that the discussion took off,[10] and not until the 1990s when it began to assume its current popularity. It may seem like bioethics is some kind of long-established branch of ethics, but it is not.[11]

Bioethics is a child of science. It represents a socio-political response to the immense power medical scientists began to use on human beings (and animals) in the 1950s and 60s. Thomas Beauchamp and James Childress, both philosophers, are credited with creating the first coherent bioethical framework, contained roughly within the parameters of three principles: consent, beneficence and justice.[12]

---

[8] See e.g., TARIQ SADAT, ROSLYN RUSSELL & MARK STEWART, Shifting paths of pharmaceutical innovation: Implications for the global pharmaceutical industry, International Journal of Knowledge, Innovation and Entrepreneurship, Volume 2 No. 1, 2014, pp. 6–31.

[9] DAVID J. ROTHMAN, Strangers at the Bedside: A History of How Law and Bioethics Transformed Medical Decision Making (Basic Books. 1991).

[10] RUTH R. FADEN & TOM L. BEAUCHAMP, A History of Informed Consent (Oxford University Press. 1986).

[11] Arras, John, "Theory and Bioethics", The Stanford Encyclopedia of Philosophy (Winter 2016 Edition), Edward N. Zalta (ed.), URL = <https://plato.stanford.edu/archives/win2016/entries/theory-bioethics/>.

[12] TOM L. BEAUCHAMP & JAMES F. CHILDRESS, Principles of Biomedical Ethics (Oxford University Press 1 ed. 1979).

Unfortunately, both Beauchamp and Childress are naturalist philosophers, believing in the limitations science has imposed on nature. In other words, their philosophical framework contains a deep and unpleasant commitment to the idea nature and all living things are physical machines.

The development of human rights, as a political/legal/moral movement, occurred just beneath the development of bioethics, prior to bioethics temporally and theoretically.[13] Human rights, those legal/moral things we talk about now, are similar to but not the same as the natural rights spoken of so frequently in the late 18th, and virtually ignored from about 1800 to the end of WW2.[14] The main difference is that human rights are said to originate in human dignity. That formulation was adopted by the international community in an effort to remove human rights, as the objects of legally binding treaties, from natural law talk and religio-political commitments.[15]

Bioethics, because of its commitment to naturalism (the physical machine theory of life), is fundamentally at odds with political order, with human rights, and with any vision of life that recognizes life itself and the capacity for free will.[16] Machines cannot make decisions.

15.3 Scientific Universalism, Bioethics and India

Wallerstein argues that colonialism is a form of western universalism used to exploit the non-western world. In time, as colonialism lost status it was superseded by orientalism as an ideology with which the west exploited the non-west. The universalist ideology of orientalism was in turn superseded by the universalism of science.

Science, and its dependent ethical system bioethics, are universalist systems of values and practices that are intervening and influencing values and practices in India. Article 12 says that India should simply accept the imposition of such values and practices (as principles in the Declaration). This means in practice that since India is a patchwork of hundreds of communities and does not speak with one voice, then all critique of science comes from a minority or diverse community and under Article 12 should be squelched, as critique per se seeks to "infringe" and "limit [the] scope" of science and bioethics. Article 12 then, replicates the attitude of colonialism.

---

[13] SAMUEL MOYN, The Last Utopia: Human Rights in History (Belknap Press of Harvard University Press. 2010).

[14] See e.g., JEREMY WALDRON, The Decline of Natural Right, in The Cambridge History of Nineteenth Century Philosophy (Allen Wood & Songsuk Susan Hahn eds., 2009).

[15] JOHANNES MORSINK, The Universal Declaration of Human Rights: Origins, Drafting, and Intent (University of Pennsylvania Press. 2000).

[16] Lunstroth, John, The Unity Thesis: How Positivism Distorts Constitutional Arguments (August 13, 2012). U of Houston Law Center No. 2012-W-2. Available at SSRN: https://ssrn.com/abstract=2128639 or http://dx.doi.org/10.2139/ssrn.2128639.

The failure to clearly understand what it was trying to achieve causes Article 12 to be incoherent. The incoherence is particularly acute when it comes to India.

Such repression would be in direct violation of rights granted by the international human rights regime, and by the Indian Constitution of 1950. Moreover, teachings permeate the Subcontinent that consciousness is central to all life, contrary to the machine theory of life. The idea that local discourse can be suppressed because it seeks to limit the excesses of science clearly has imperialist and colonialist values.

UNESCO certainly did not set out to draft a norm establishing the dominance of science over all critique, but it has done so. In the process it privileges the transnational drug and chemical companies, and the values of western medicine. In essence, then, the Declaration supports the worst effects of globalization, at the same time it purports to be promulgating norms that protect local communities from them. In the next iteration of UNESCO bioethical norms, UNESCO should not invoke universal principles, rather it should seek to bolster its attempts to promulgate quasi-legal norms with specific human rights norms, such as, for example, Articles 7 and 27 of the International Covenant on Civil and Political Rights.

As I understand the task, we are to view the conflict in the life sciences between the local and the universal through the lens of Hinduism. How might, or do, the values of Hinduism provide guidance, or an ethics, in resolving conflicts that arise when science seeks to change or intervene in nature, or does things that degrade human dignity?

Dr. Desai, in his contribution to this series, admirably describes the situation in India with regard to rights and bioethics. Following him I treat Hinduism not as a religion, rather as a westernized reference to the way of life on the Indian subcontinent. The idea of a religion per se is foreign to India, yet it has accepted that language as a constitutional or political matter both in response to Islam, and to western scientific constructs of what religion means. In a sense all of the constructs of the task are western scientific ideas that self-claim universal status. I supplement Dr. Desai's paper by highlighting the colonialist overtones of the western universalisms that seem to dominate some parts of the UNESCO Declaration.

Chapter 16
Hinduism and Human Rights

Martha Tarasco

16.1 Hinduism and Human Rights: Basic Statement

Hinduism is not a religion with a single vision but a sum of philosophical theories or a unified system of beliefs and ideas (Pargament 2001; Park 2002). It is a phenomenon that represents a broad spectrum of beliefs and practices, in which on one hand you can find a type of pantheism and polytheism, and on the other, very profound, abstract, metaphysical ideas. There is not only *one Hindu* perspective (Hick 2004).

One of the difficulties we encounter in religious studies is the system of beliefs in different religions (Reckwitz 2002). In the Catholic system, the Magisterium has competence in the area of moral issues (Gula 1989). In this way there is always an official doctrinal interpretation in the discussion of any particular problem. Even if there could be local or individual controversies, Magisterium states cleasrly the "what" and the "why"S of moral and faith issues (Perry 2000). That does not happen in other religions (Calkins 2000). The lack of an exclusive directive to understand the first principles of social changes means that different answers are possible for the same problem. This incoherence, which may seem illogical, is acceptable in these systems of religious beliefs (Armstrong 2010; McGrath and McGrath 2011).

But on the contrary, if we examine them according to the philosophical system of logic, two or more contradictory statements cannot be true at the same time. That is, everything depends on the position adopted, because the range of possibilities is wide open (Riegel 1973). I think that this is one of the difficulties from a Hindu perspective, because there are no teachings to resolve the different interpretations. From the point of view of Human Rights, Hinduism will also take on a relativist interpretation (Brems 1997; Donnelly 2013; Ignatieff and Gutmann 2003).

I will try to demonstrate that certain elements of Hinduism are incompatible with a singular view of Human Rights because of its inner structure and beliefs. This is

M. Tarasco (✉)
School of Bioethics, University of Anahuac, Mexico City, Mexico
e-mail: mtarasco@anahuac.mx

J. Tham et al. (eds.), *Religious Perspectives on Bioethics and Human Rights*,
Advancing Global Bioethics 6, DOI 10.1007/978-3-319-58431-7_16

so especially because according to Karma and the Old Vedic point of view, such as Dharma and Samsara, violation of Human Rights will not be perceived as a problem (Benhabib 2002; Brems 2001).

To do so, I will use the Logical Method establishing a major premise (Smith 2000)[1] based on the Universal Declaration on Human Rights, and then contrast it with the concept of Samsara and Dharma as foundation for the minor premise.

16.2 Conflicts of Human Rights Claims and Accepted Religious Practices in This Tradition

One of the most difficult areas to reconcile Hinduism with Human Rights is the reincarnation theory, called Samsara (Ryan 1999; Milner 1993). It is important to note that all religious beliefs, if they are really personal beliefs, have implications with daily practices. That is, religious beliefs convert themselves in actions that can be evaluated by a third party observer, without analyzing the "inner forum" or "mental states" of the believer (Mansour 2009; Kroll and Sheehan 1989).

The basic principle of Human Rights is the idea that all human beings "belong" to it, and "participate" in it. As the Declaration states, "ethical issues… should be examined with the respect to the dignity of the human person and universal respect for, and observance of, human rights and fundamental freedom" (Kunz 1949).

All these terms: "universal", "fundamental" etc. imply in some instances the need and recognition of duty, which in a Kantian sense is unconditional and without exceptions (Kant 2009; Dávila 2006). Following the document, we can find, without doubt, evidence of that interpretation: "1. Human dignity, human rights and fundamental freedoms are to be fully respected" (Kunz 1949). It is important to point out the term "fully" means there cannot be circumstances where they should not be completely followed. There should not be exceptions, for example, to differentiate females from males in religious rituals because they belong to different classes. It is important to point out that in Hinduism, their reason is not based on religious reasons but because they are considered different classes of human beings. The best example for this is the caste system (Stevenson 1954; Sagar 1975; Mencher 1974).

With this example the major premise of the argument established in the form of syllogism could be:

If you accept a Human Right it has to be applied in all circumstances.

[1] "Few persons care to study logic, because everybody conceives himself to be proficient enough in the art of reasoning already. But I observe that this satisfaction is limited to one's own ratiocination, and does not extend to that of other men". In: Peirce, C. S. (1877). The fixation of belief. *1877.*

16.3 Samsara and Human Rights: Exceptions of the Rule?

16.3.1 The Concept of Samsara in the Syllogism

"As the embodied soul continuously passes, in this body, from boyhood to youth to old age, the soul similarly passes into another body at death. A sober person is not bewildered by such a change". This text of Bhagavad Gita illustrates the basic idea of metempsychosis, i.e., the real human being interchanges space and time with other "bodies" (Raza 2012; Ashrafi 2015). Of course the note is very brief, so to have an interpretation of it, the master **Srila Prabhupada comments:**

> Since every living entity is an individual soul, each is changing his body every moment, manifesting sometimes as a child, sometimes as a youth, and sometimes as an old man. Yet the same spirit soul is there and does not undergo any change. This individual soul finally changes the body at death and transmigrates to another body; and since it is sure to have another body in the next birth—either material or spiritual—there was no cause for lamentation by Arjuna on account of death, neither for Bhishma nor for Drona, for whom he was so much concerned. Rather, he should rejoice for their changing bodies from old to new ones, thereby rejuvenating their energy. Such changes of body account for varieties of enjoyment or suffering, according to one's work in life. So Bhishma and Drona, being noble souls, were surely going to have spiritual bodies in the next life, or at least life in heavenly bodies for superior enjoyment of material existence. So, in either case, there was no cause of lamentation (Gosvāmī 1995).

It is possible to extract from this passage the key to the second or minor premise in traditional logic. Transmigration of the soul has a moral value, the value of perfection, in the sense that you must transmigrate to improve. The degree of suffering or enjoyment of our past lives appears to become a justification of suffering, a sort of necessity for this change into something better (Dāsī 2000). If one needs to suffer passively those consequences in order to improve, the need to defend basic Human Rights becomes unclear, or else it would depend on the new moral status of the person with the transmigrated soul (Whitman 2007). That is, if the new transmigrated soul needs to suffer in the new life in order to become a better being; this soul does not need to appeal to Human Rights, because the passive or active suffering is lived as a good. This is so especially if the moral status of the person with the transmigrated soul needs to improve (Gächter 1998). It is counter intuitive that anyone would passively accept their condition of life, even in the worst circumstances, without trying to change their destiny, only so that in the future their souls could have a better corporeal existence.

After explanations of these elements, the syllogistic form of the argument could be as follows:

Major Premise: If you accept a Human Right it has to be applied in all circumstances.
Minor Premise: Dharma cannot accept Human Rights in all circumstances, because it contradicts the basic principle of Karma and Samsara.
Conclusion: In some cases the Dharma cannot accept Human Rights.

Nevertheless there is another aspect about Dharma, which is that it does not imply an absolute lack of action and that one must act with compassion in every situation. Even so, in Hinduism all souls are considered equal, but to be consistent with the notion of maintaining the universal order, the individual must follow their own Dharma and that implies to some extent the negation of Human Rights (Pavenkov 2014).

Another possible option is to distinguish the concept of "Human Right". For example, theologian Raimundo Panikkar (Panikkar 1987, 1999), argues that the Hindu notion of *dharma* requires: (1) that Human Rights be not only the rights of individuals or even humans, but of every living being (2) that Human Rights involve duties and relate us to the whole cosmos, and (3) that Human Rights are not absolute, but are relative to each culture (Donnelly 2007). So for the serious believers of Hinduism, disequilibrium in the universe occurs when one interferes with personal Dharma. For this reason, there are difficulties in prosecuting violations of Human Rights (Dandekar 1962).

16.3.2 Samsara and Consent

Another way to show the difficulties in the discourse of Human Rights and Hinduism is the problem of consent. The principle of consent appears in articles 6 and 7 of the Declaration. It was developed later in the International Bioethics Committee of UNESCO and published in a 2009 report:

> Initially drafted in a very simple fashion, the crucial principle was subject to profound discussion during the entire process of elaboration of the Declaration, especially during the intergovernmental meetings of experts, resulting in two full articles in the declaration devoted to the principle of consent… Considerable lack of clarity exists when it comes to the question of how the principle of consent can or should be applied in practice and in various contexts of application (ten Have and Jean 2009).

This is a problem with Hinduism and with other religions (Sharma 1977). In medical decisions, it is well known and clear for most people that a patient must be consulted about the treatment and interventions. But how much information should be given? Should the family be consulted? How can consent in the case of children be dealt with? It is not too clear. That is, while the principle is "clear", adjustments must be made when applied to particular cases to avoid the extreme positions of unlimited autonomy or paternalism.

Because of this, the UNESCO Report explains wisely that:

> A principle cannot simply be affirmed without examining the conditions of its implementation and the consequences of its application… the content of the information; the conditions of obtaining consent; the manner of expressing consent; specific difficulties in the application of the principle of consent (International Bioethics Committee 2010).

Anyway, I think that even if we accept that the principle requires adjustment to particular situations, clear difficulties appear in any other cultural or religious view.

The same happens with the tenets of Hinduism. The original dilemma shown above appears again (Flood 1996; Sharma 1977).

The Report clearly points out the conditions for a real consent. But in the Hindu tradition, the circumstances of application show again the difficulty to adjust the principle (Enoch et al. 2005). We can see this in an example of a Public Health case. Some diseases require interventions to control or at least, contain their propagation. Implementation of public health measures should be made. Since attention to health is a Human Right, problems with Hindu tradition may appear, as the Samsara allows for situations that are clearly unhealthy and contrary to human rights (Wendler and Miller 2004). There is a famous Temple in which the rats are object of veneration. The temple is named Kami Mata:

> The legend says that Karni Mata, a mystic matriarch from the 14th century, was an incarnation of Durga, the goddess of power and victory. At some point during her life, the child of one of her clansmen died. She attempted to bring the child back to life, only to be told by Yama, the god of death, that he had already been reincarnated. Karni Mata made a deal with Yama: From that moment forward, all of her people would be reborn as rats until they could be born back into the clan. So in the Temple full of rats, shoes are not permitted, tourists and worshippers hope to have rats run across their feet as a sign of good luck. Eating food or drinking water previously touched by a rat is considered to be a supreme blessing.

As a result of this belief, people are not informed when coming to the temple, exposing themselves to health risks when they get in contact with the rats and their food. Since they are not informed, they cannot exercise consent to visit the temple or not.

This poses the problem of zoonosis. Rats are capable of transmitting diseases that are harmful to humans, such as the Rat-bite fever (Vimala et al. 2014; Madhubashini et al. 2013). The Temple in Deshnoke however believed and has reported that no disease relating to rats (kabas) have occurred to date, even though they have lived within the confines of the temple for centuries. As a tourist destination and in an era of international travel with possible health risk, Public Health education and disease monitoring are necessary preventive measures (World Health Organization 2007). If there is evidence of disease transmission by the rats (kabas), it will be necessary to eliminate the rats, control their propagation and reduce human risk. Non-violence toward sentient beings in India associated with the Jain philosophy[2] is not apparently a factor here regarding the reverence towards the kabas. One would also need to consider the right of the parents to prevent children from harmful exposures. Since children are not old enough to give consent, they should be protected especially (Archard 2014).

[2] In Jain doctrine absolutely everything (physical and spiritual) have always existed. Living and without life energies constitutes universe. Souls exist separated from bodies, and souls are eternal. If a soul ends with its karmas it achieves the nirvana state. Part of it is not interfering with the rest of the universe. Bhattacharyya, Narendra Nath. "Jain philosophy: historical outline." (Bhattacharyya 1999).

16.4 Conclusions

The Hindu believer should recognize that there are religious beliefs and practices in their tradition that are incompatible with Human Rights.

Maybe it would be better to accept the differences, and consistently affirm that Human Rights are sometimes incompatible with specific religious creeds, and that it is difficult for the believer to choose between fidelity to one's tradition and safeguarding human rights. This is especially true for social, political or economical leaders if they have to decide for an entire population.

Human rights presuppose a social order to accommodate these rights, and rights in a Hindu society are associated with duties towards others and society with heterogeneous groups. Duty-based Dharma can expand its duties and privileges towards groups such as the untouchables and women in view of their proven abilities to achieve and contribute in India and abroad, through the evolution brought about by Gandhi and Nehru in the last century. Rights founded on duty would preserve certain positive traditions of dharma in Hindu society with law of rights and privileges for disadvantaged and vulnerable groups. This would balance rights and privileges with obligations, heeding Nehru's thought of "Rights follow duties discharged".

I agree with Dr. Gomez that in some cases of religious dilemmas, it is preferable to recognize expression and freedom of beliefs and convictions as a Human Right as well (Álvarez 2006). At the same time, believers should be informed of the consequences of religious rites and rituals so that they could choose not to engage in certain religious actions or medical procedures. For example, fasting for religious purposes can be dangerous for some clinical conditions such as diabetes. Persons with those conditions should be informed of those risks. In the same way, the practice of sharing food and water with rats can be dangerous for health, and believers should be informed of the risks.

Human Rights can sometimes create real conflicts among different goods, such as religious beliefs, and there may not be rational options to resolve these conflicts.

In those cases where Human Rights conflicts with religious practices, the exercise of conscientious objection is the best way to preserve both positions, i.e., the dignity of the religious practice and the need to preserve and respect Human Rights in a liberal society.

Bibliography

Álvarez, J.G. 2006. La religión, la bioética y los derechos humanos: una nota argumentativa sobre su relación y pertinencia. *Medicina y ética: Revista internacional de bioética, deontología y ética médica* 17 (2): 123–132.

Archard, D. 2014. *Children: Rights and childhood.* Taylor & Francis Group: Routledge.

Armstrong, K. 2010. *The case for God.* New York: Random House Digital, Inc.

Ashrafi, S. J. Professor Jane Malcolm ANG1005: The poetics of car culture 8 December, 2015 The car as the propeller of re-incarnation in 'On the Road' (376–377) and 'Crash' (101–102).

Benhabib, S. 2002. *The claims of culture: Equality and diversity in the global era*. Princeton: Princeton University Press.

Bhattacharyya, Narendra Nath. 1999. "Jain philosophy: Historical outline."

Brems, E. 1997. Enemies or allies? Feminism and cultural relativism as dissident voices in human rights discourse. *Human Rights Quarterly* 19 (1): 136–164.

———. 2001. *Human rights: Universality and diversity*. Vol. 66. The Hague/London: Martinus Nijhoff Publishers.

Calkins, M.S. 2000. Recovering religion's prophetic voice for business ethics. *Journal of Business Ethics* 23 (4): 339–352.

Dandekar, R.N. 1962. Man in hindu thought—A broad outline—. *Annals of the Bhandarkar Oriental Research Institute* 43 (1/4): 1–57.

Dāsī, M.D. 2000. Srila Prabhupada is Coming. *My personal memoriesof his divine grace AC Bhaktivedanta Swami Prabhupada*. Mayapur: Bhaktivedanta Book Trust.

Dávila, V.A. 2006. Ética y filosofía del derecho en Kant y su influencia en la declaración universal de los Derechos Humanos. *A DE CIENCIAS JURIDICAS* 110: 199.

Donnelly, J. 2007. The relative universality of human rights. *Human Rights Quarterly* 29 (2): 281–306.

———. 2013. *Universal human rights in theory and practice*. Ithaca: Cornell University Press.

Enoch, S., H. Shaaban, and K.W. Dunn. 2005. Informed consent should be obtained from patients to use products (skin substitutes) and dressings containing biological material. *Journal of Medical Ethics* 31 (1): 2–6.

Flood, G.D. 1996. *An introduction to Hinduism*. New York: Cambridge University Press.

Gächter, O. 1998. Evil and suffering in Hinduism. *Anthropos* 93 (4-6): 393–403.

Gosvāmī, S.D. 1995. *Srila Prabhupada-lilamrta*. Los Angeles: The Bhaktivedanta Book Trust.

Gula, R.M. 1989. *Reason informed by faith: Foundations of Catholic morality*. New York: Paulist Press.

Hick, J. 2004. *An interpretation of religion: Human responses to the transcendent*. New Haven: Yale University Press.

Ignatieff, M., and A. Gutmann. 2003. *Human rights as politics and idolatry*. Princeton: Princeton University Press.

International Bioethics Committee. 2010. *Report of the International bioethics committee of UNESCO (IBC) on social responsibility and health*. Vol. 2. Paris: UNESCO.

Kant, I. 2009. *Crítica de la razón pura*. Ediciones Colihue SRL.

Kroll, J., and W. Sheehan. 1989. Religious beliefs and practices among. *The American Journal of Psychiatry* 146 (1): 67–72.

Kunz, J.L. 1949. The United Nations declaration of human rights. *The American Journal of International Law* 43 (2): 316–323.

Madhubashini, M., S. George, and S. Chandrasekaran. 2013. *Streptobacillus moniliformis* endocarditis: Case report and review of literature. *Indian Heart Journal* 65 (4): 442–446. http://doi.org/10.1016/j.ihj.2013.06.019.

Mansour, N. 2009. Science teachers' beliefs and practices: Issues, implications and research agenda. *International Journal of Environmental and Science Education* 4 (1): 25–48.

McGrath, A., and J.C. McGrath. 2011. *The Dawkins delusion?: Atheist fundamentalism and the denial of the divine*. Downers Grove: InterVarsity Press.

Mencher, J.P. 1974. The caste system upside down, or the not-so-mysterious East. *Current Anthropology* 15 (4): 469–493.

Milner, M. 1993. Hindu eschatology and the Indian caste system: An example of structural reversal. *The Journal of Asian Studies* 52 (02): 298–319.

Panikkar, R. 1987. The Jordan, the Tiber, and the Ganges: Three kairological moments of Christic self-consciousness. In *The myth of Christian uniqueness: Toward a pluralistic theology of religions*, ed. J. Hick and P.F. Knitter, 89–116. Maryknoll: Orbis.

———. 1999. *The intrareligious dialogue*. New York: Paulist Press.

Pargament, K.I. 2001. *The psychology of religion and coping: Theory, research, practice*. New York/London: Guilford Press.
Park, C. 2002. *Sacred worlds: An introduction to geography and religion*. London: Routledge.
Pavenkov, O.V. 2014. Christian ethic of love and Hindu ethic of dharma: Comparative analysis. *Studia Humanitatis* 3 (9): 9–18.
Perry, M.J. 2000. Catholics, the magisterium, and moral controversy: An argument for independent judgement (with particular reference to Catholic law schools). *University of Dayton Law Review* 26: 293.
Raza, M. 2012. *In search of oneness: The Bhagvad Gita and the Quran through sufi eyes*. London: Penguin.
Reckwitz, A. 2002. Toward a theory of social practices a development in culturalist theorizing. *European journal of social theory* 5 (2): 243–263.
Riegel, K.F. 1973. Dialectic operations: The final period of cognitive development. *Human Development* 16 (5): 346–370.
Ryan, M.P. 1999. Samsa and Samsara: Suffering, death, and rebirth in "The Metamorphosis". *German Quarterly* 72 (2): 133–152.
Sagar, S.L. 1975. *Hindu culture and caste system in India*. Delhi: Uppal Book Store.
Sharma, A. 1977. Al-Biruni on the Hindu notion of Samsara. *Islamic Culture* 51: 165–169.
Smith, R. 2000. Aristotle's logic.
Stevenson, H.N. 1954. Status evaluation in the Hindu caste system. *The Journal of the Royal Anthropological Institute of Great Britain and Ireland* 84 (1/2): 45–65.
ten Have, H., and M. Jean (eds.). 2009. *The UNESCO universal declaration on bioethics and human rights: Background, principles and application*. Paris: UNESCO.
Vimala, G., A.M. Rani, and V.R. Gopal. 2014. Leptospirosis in Vellore: A clinical and serological study. *International Journal of Microbiology* 2014 (2014): 643940. doi:10.1155/2014/643940. Epub 2014 Jun 23.
Wendler, D., and F.G. Miller. 2004. Deception in the pursuit of science. *Archives of Internal Medicine* 164 (6): 597–600.
Whitman, S.M. 2007. Pain and suffering as viewed by the Hindu religion. *The Journal of Pain* 8 (8): 607–613.
World Health Organization. 2007. *Cancer control: Knowledge into action: WHO guide for effective programmes*. Vol. 2. Geneva: World Health Organization.

Part VI
Monotheistic Religions: Christianity & Catholicism

Chapter 17
The Christian-Catholic Religious Perspective: Human Rights, Cultural Pluralism and Bioethics

Laura Palazzani

17.1 Christian-Catholic Religion and the Human Rights Doctrine: Divergences and Convergences

Where human rights and fundamental rights are concerned, those rights are equal for each human being regardless of his condition, by reason of his humanity and human nature. And for the very reason that they are fundamental they are inalienable and cannot be disposed of: anyone can claim them towards other individuals and assert them in the face of political power.[1] This is the minimum meaning of the doctrine of human rights. The elaboration of the list of the rights that all humans have, has a long history and a slow evolution.

17.1.1 Initial Opposition

If the relationship between the Catholic Church and the doctrine of human rights is analysed, we first see an initial opposition to human rights, in particular with reference to the 1789 declarations. Many are the possible explanations of this opposition[2]: the main explanation may be connected to the use of human rights as an

[1] For a general picture of the history of human rights see Cronin K. (1992) *Rights and Christian Ethics*. Cambridge, Cambridge University Press.

[2] Pio VI, *Quod Aliquantum*, 1791; Gregorio XVI, *Mirari vos*, 1832; Pio IX, *Quanta cura*, 1864; Leone XIII, *Immortale Dei*, 1885, *Libertas*, 1888, *Rerum novarum*, 1891. See Wackenheim C. (1979) *The Theological Meaning of the Rights of Man*, in *The Church and the Rights of Man*, New York, The Seabury Press, p. 52.

L. Palazzani (✉)
National Bioethics Committee of Italy, Rome, Italy

Department of Law, LUMSA, Rome, Italy
e-mail: palazzani@lumsa.it

J. Tham et al. (eds.), *Religious Perspectives on Bioethics and Human Rights*,
Advancing Global Bioethics 6, DOI 10.1007/978-3-319-58431-7_17

instrument to affirm individualistic freedom and liberal political and social claims, recalling the doctrinal belief that man may be saved only obeying the natural divine law established by God. The use of freedom without any reference to God cannot save man; in the Christian perspective, a 'real/authentic' freedom consists in living in conformity with the eternal law. The reasons for the initial opposition can be traced back to the interpretation of human rights as one of the ways in which the appeal for liberalization/liberalism and secularization was expressed in the modern age, where secularization was taken to be an anti-clerical negation of God and Christ by means of the explicit exclusion of a religious and theistic foundation of such rights. The core of the tension may be identified in the conflict between secularism/secularization and revealed religion, between reason and faith, rather than between temporalism and anti-clericalism. If man is autonomous and has rights which he may know through rationality, revelation becomes no more necessary. Faith may enlighten what man can reach by himself. The tension between human rational rights and Christian divine law. Religion cannot be reduced to private life; it should be expressed publicly, finding harmony between religion and politics.[3]

17.1.2 Adhesion and Recognition

The initial conflict, suspicion, hostility of the Christian Catholic Church, however, becomes an explicit adhesion to and recognition of human rights, as well as their defence and promotion in practice.[4] This happened after World War II, with the Second Vatican Council. In spite of this historical delay in the recognition of human rights by the Catholic Church, today the Church uses the language of human rights to express a number of values and fundamental rights in the context of cultural, religious, and ethical pluralism, of the diversity of religious standpoints among believers, and of the conflict between believers and non-believers.[5]

The convergence is to be found between the human rights doctrine and the Christian-Catholic one, in the recognition of the *dignity of every human being* as a fundamental value. In this line of thought, the Church acknowledges that human dignity is the minimum shareable ethics in a universal sense, a fundamental value that is knowable by human reason and therefore, on principle, by all men.[6] This

[3] Lewis V.B., *Democracy and Catholic Social Teaching: Continuity, Development, and Challenge*, "Studia Gilsoniana", 2014, 3, pp. 167–190.

[4] See Etchegaray R. (1991) *Du rejet à l'engagement*, in *Culture chrétienne et droits de l'homme. Christianity and Human Rights,* Bruxelles-Louvain-la-Neuve, Bruylant Academia, pages 3–15.

[5] For the historical evolution and the doctrinal position of the Church on the topic see Pontifical Commission Iustitia et Pax, *The Church and Human Rights*, Vatican City, 1st Edition 1975, 2nd Edition 2011.

[6] Driven by the crimes against humanity perpetrated by the totalitarian regimes, coming to a head during the World War II, most of the liberal democratic countries considered it impossible to shirk the moral duty to give national and international protection to man also with regard to any form of power. The rights defined as human received a successive positivization – in the context of the

value, recognized as being fundamental, has to be translated into positive law as the only way to guarantee the minimum core of ethics, identified in the principle of equality.

The doctrine of human rights introduces a jusnaturalist foundation of rights. A jusnaturalist foundation means, in opposition to legal positivism which reduces law to positive law issued by the legislator, the recognition of a dualism of the law (positive and natural) and the moral superiority of natural law with respect to positive law. It also means that the dignity of every human being is a value, before and above state legislation.[7]

The Christian Church affirms that the doctrine of human rights, in this sense (the recognition of the dignity of every human being) is not 'modern' (specifically created by the Enlightenment), but goes back to the roots of the Judaic and Christian sources. It may be considered a 'modern version' of the natural law doctrine.[8]

17.1.3 Tensions

There is a divergence in the *foundation* of human rights. The Catholic Church founds man's rights in the viewpoint of St. Thomas's classical doctrine of natural law, which thematized a synthesis between the ancient vision of natural law (Aristotle) and the claims of Christianity. This interpretation diverges from the interpretation rooted in modern jusnaturalism, which considers natural rights as rational rights (jusrationalism) in an individualistic framework.

With respect to laical juridical reason, Christian thought offers a religious and theological foundation and justification to human dignity[9]: Christianity thematizes a strong justification of the obligatoriness of the respect for man. Christian thought maintains that man has a dignity because he is the "image and likeness" of God; he is a person, with strong original value since he was created by God, wanted by God and loved by God through the reconciliation of Christ; his life is sacred insofar as given and offered by God as a gift, and hence cannot be disposed of at his free will. In this sense, 'dignity' means 'intrinsic dignity', which requires a strong protection and respect.

---

universal declarations and the national constitutions – which transformed them into positive law with protection at institutional level (super-national and national), also by means of judicial protection. It is thanks to these rights that the existence of conditions of life that respect human dignity is guaranteed.

[7] This concept is the horizon of thought in Giovanni Paolo II, *Evangelium vitae*, 1995.

[8] Kolakowski L. (1990) *Modernity on Endless Trial,* Chicago, The University of Chicago Press, p. 214.

[9] Kasper W. (1990) *The Theological Foundation of Human Rights*, in "The Jurist", 50, pp. 153–154; S. Moyn (2015) *Christian Human Rights*, University of Pennsylvania Press; Witte J., Alexander F.S. *Christianity and Human Rights: an Introduction*, Cambridge, Cambridge University Press.

The Christian faith integrates rationality in a metaphysical and transcendental dimension. It does not dictate contents from which to deduce a code of rules to be applied to ethical action, but rather opens and activates reason to sense, showing reason the way to grasp the ultimate meaning of things. Christianity therefore strengthens and further founds human dignity, a value that man, thanks to his reason, is nonetheless able to grasp, know, and understand. The Christian religion recognizes the value of human rationality, both because "in the beginning was the Word" according to John 1:1, and also because all that exists can be understood by man. Hence the knowledge and the search for an understanding of the world is something good since it brings us closer to God.

In this sense, Christianity offers a strong ethics for the foundation of human rights. If law – in particular human rights – is limited to defending the coexistence of men through justice in a merely horizontal sense, Christianity adds a vertical and transcendental sense because of its eschatological faith in the providential design of God. One's neighbour is not only recognized as an individual belonging to society – the other as another, but as brother, the other as being "next to"; therefore a Christian is called upon not only to respect and protect him, but also to love him as himself, as the way to salvation, in the hope of salvation.

Human rights defend human dignity through justice, rooted in the principle of equality in symmetry and reciprocity: justice makes us understand that the other is the bearer of an "objective" value that demands to be recognized, according to symmetry, a right which is claimed, must be claimable by anyone else in the same situation, and by reciprocity, the right of an individual must correspond to the duty of another individual to respect it. Christian thought teaches us something that goes beyond justice, symmetry and reciprocity: the other must be recognized regardless of whether his own right is recognized, i.e. even in a condition of non-symmetry and non-reciprocity. Christianity demands love and charity.

It is the Christian thought that teaches us to enter into the sphere of charity, compassion, and mercy as a philanthropic, gratuitous and giving welcome, which even manages to forgive the wrongdoing in the name of love, demanding and claiming nothing in return. Rights are limited to an ethical minimum that impedes the use of arbitrary force against man and his dignity. It is the "minimum" necessary ethics, the ethics of measure and limit, which leaves to the "maximum" moral, expressed by Christian thought, the personal search "beyond" the measure, the active and continuous commitment of the individual in view of the complete and concrete realization of the respect of human dignity and responsibility towards others.

A Christian believes in Creation, where God creates the world with knowledge, intelligence, and intentionality: man is a creature with the gift of reason – a reason that is not absolute like God's but qualitatively distinct – and hence has the capacity to know and critically understand the sense of nature, the intelligibility of nature. Christianity does not demand a blind and irrational adhesion to morality, but has faith in reason as an openness to the truth. Christian thought is not dogmatic or irrational, but rational in its own principle. The complementarity in Christianity between faith and reason in the interpretation of reality and law, the recognition of the common root in the *logos*, results in social ethics being founded in natural law:

the appeal to human rights and man's dignity, in short, is valid for believers and non-believers insofar as it is based on natural truth.

The Christian way is the naturalist and rational legitimation of law, given the close connection between philosophy of law and Christian philosophy of law or philosophical theology of law, as regards the way of understanding and interpreting natural law/natural rights. Insofar as defending human nature, the law has philosophical and theological importance: it is the instrument of social order, but it is also the way to salvation. The law has theological importance not just because of its content – although it contains divine precepts or divine law – but because the law, is an instrument for salvation.[10]

There are two risks for a Christian today. On one hand, there is the risk of appealing to the Christian faith as a convenient alternative way to the long, hard effort of philosophy in reasoning regarding the existence of truth: a faith that escapes rationality becomes irrational faith *credo quia absurdum*, "vertical, singular, illogical," merely consolatory faith. On the other hand, the risk of limiting oneself to reason alone and forgetting the announcement of the Word, leaving the Christian message unheard and irrelevant.

The task of a Christian in today's complex pluralist society is to make himself heard, to carry out a dialogue with non-believers and different believers, to rationally find the common truth together again, but also not to give up the specificity of his faith, not to stop at a generic Christian inspiration of ethical action, and not to forget the divine precepts. Christianity must avoid the temptation of privatizing faith and moving publicly at the level of reason alone, but must also socially witness values and the Christian announcement.

These are the main points of tension between the Christian Church and the doctrine of human rights: it is a complex topic, which is object of discussion inside and outside the Church.

17.2 Maritain and the Rights of Man

Among the most prominent Catholic philosophers who have dealt with human rights is Jacques Maritain.[11] He is the first Catholic to have formulated a theory of human rights in the context of a philosophical thought inspired by the vision of St.

---

[10] In this sense the Protestant path led to the "Christocratic sublimation of law", to the separation between theology of law and philosophy of law, the taking root of law in one single faith (without the mediation of reason). Because of sin the relationship with God is considered corrupt and it is thought that man can save himself from the corruption of his sinful nature not by means of reason or his works but only through faith and grace. In this sense worldly law is not condemned in itself but for itself: even though it is recognised as the instrument of social order, it is considered irrelevant for salvation. The law has as theological valence in the contents and precepts of God as a way for charity and grace.

[11] Maritain J (1942) *Les droits de l'homme et la lois naturelle*, New York, Editions de la Maison Francaise, *Allocution à la première séance pléniere de la deuxième session de la Conférence*

Thomas and applied to modern political life, directly taking part in the proclamation and affirmation of the universal declaration of human rights. In his main work, *The rights of man and natural law*, the author outlines the central elements of his philosophical perspective which form the basis of his conception of human rights: finalism as theory of nature, cognitivism as theory of knowledge, universalism as ethical theory and jusnaturalism as theory of law.

In this sense, it is very important to deepen the analysis of Maritain's work. Maritain made a strong effort to argue, publicly, regarding human rights in a natural and rational perspective which could be accepted and shared by believers and non-believers, without forgetting his faith and outlining the relevance of it in the theoretical foundation.

Taking up classical realism once again – Aristotelian, Thomistic and Neo-Scholastic -, this perspective is placed in the horizon of a creationist finalism that recognizes an order in nature that mirrors the divine sapiential plan in the world: nature is composed of bodies, vegetable, animal, and human, that are intended for an end written in their nature through inclinations. All creatures are ruled by eternal law: inanimate bodies take part in it through physical need, animals through instinct, and finally man, as a being with reason, participates in the divine sapiential plan by means of his intellect and is therefore able on principle to grasp the truth in nature through progressive acquisition. This is a cognitivist vision. Natural law is "part" of eternal law, that part that is "imprinted" in man's reason: it is thus quantitatively inferior, but qualitatively identical.

Reason on a practical level stems from the observation of man's natural tendencies: the conservation of being, and hence the conservation of life and physical integrity in common with all living beings; reproduction, in common with animals; the knowledge of the truth and living in society, characteristic of the rational being. Reason translates and interprets inclinations, formulates the rules of conduct that establish and make the achievement of aims binding: good is what is in agreement with the ends of nature; evil is what is dissimilar to the ends of nature.[12]

The first absolutely general principle is the principle of finality, on the basis of which everybody acts for an end and the end coincides with good; good is what everything is inclined or tends towards, and evil what distances itself and deviates from the end. While good is the first concept of practical reason, deontological judgements or precepts are specific rules that reason deduces from the first principle, applying it to human nature and its activity: respect life or do not kill others or

générale de l'Unesco, Mexico, 6 November 1947, in *Droits des peoples, droits de l'homme*, edited by the Institut International Jacques Maritain (1984), Paris, Le Centurion; United Nations General Assembly, 183rd session. "Resolution 217 (1948). *Universal Declaration of Human Rights"* (A/RES/183/217). 10 December 1948. Available online: http:/ /www.un.org/en/documents/udhr. Id. (1951), *Man and the State*, Chicago, University of Chicago Press.

[12] Reason, formulating natural law, transforms the description of the natural inclination into an obligation (setting down action in conformity with the end): the inclination is an empirical tendency, the law is a norm. One therefore passes from the empirical order of the inclinations to the rational and normative order of the precepts. In this sense one goes from being to having to be, starting from being as essence or end.

yourself; protect procreation in the family; search for the knowledge of truth or promotion of knowledge and avoidance of mistakes; associate with others, being open to solidarity and interpersonal relationality, avoid individualistic refusal to collaborate.[13]

In this philosophical stance, the concept of person understood as the uni-totality of body and spiritual soul in a hylemorphic sense emerges: the person is defined as an "individual substance of rational nature", a subsistent that exists for itself, soul as substantial form of the body. A person tends to open up to others: sociality is a structural need of human nature. It is a vision that has Christian roots behind it: the spirituality of personhood goes back to the metaphysical and transcendent dimension, and in final analysis to God's creation.

It is the vision of a non-reductionist anthropology, an ontological anthropology, philosophical and at the same time theological, that lays the foundation of the absolute and intrinsic dignity of the human person, of every human person. Maritain recognizes that this vision is not the "monopoly of Christian philosophy": it is common to all the philosophies recognizing the existence of an Absolute in the order of the universe as "supertemporal value of the human soul". In this sense according to Maritain, even those who are not Christian or Catholic or who have no religious beliefs at all, regardless of the founding justification of human dignity, can recognize values and rights and collaborate in their realization.

In his opinion, the rights of man must be defended, at the temporal level, without preferences for the single religious groups; the good of the person and the common socio-political good may be recognized irrespective of religious belonging. Human rights constitute the "horizontal movement" of natural law, which in the Christian perspective has a "vertical dimension" too. As the expression of natural law, human rights refer to human nature, considered one and the same in all men.

In his address at the first plenary sitting of the second session of the General UNESCO Conference of November 1947, less than 1 year before the Universal Declaration in December 1948, while highlighting the pluralism of the trends of thought and spiritual traditions, and the difficulty of finding common elements among these, Maritain explicitly announces the principle according to which, if a "theoretical assent" at speculative level is not possible, a "practical agreement" is. It is not possible to recognize the same concept of the world, of knowledge or of man, but it is possible to agree on elements and convictions that guide the action of all men, so as to guarantee the coexistence of everyone and social peace.

Maritain differentiates the "what" and the "why" of human rights. The strength of human rights is the possible agreement on the "what", even if there is a dispute on the "why".[14]

Maritain is convinced that his Christian and philosophical justification of the rights of man is firmly based on truth, but that does not stop him from agreeing on

[13] For Maritain natural law and natural rights are closely correlated: natural law expresses the tendencies of human nature at a moral level; they found law, that is, the possibility to be claimed and demanded (natural law).

[14] Maritain J., *The Man and the State*, cit., page 22.

the practical convictions with those who are certain that their way of justifying them – totally different in the theoretical dynamics – is equally the only one to be founded on truth. Even if the justifications between Christians and non-Christians are different or incompatible, it is possible to find a common dialogue.

The core of his thought may be found in his speech at UNESCO: "Since the aim of UNESCO is a practical aim, agreement among its members can be spontaneously achieved, not on common speculative notions, but on common practical notions, not on the affirmation of the same conception of the world, man, and knowledge, but on the affirmation of the same set of convictions concerning action. This is doubtless very little, it is the last refuge of intellectual agreement among men. It is, however, enough to undertake a great work; and it would mean a great deal to become aware of this body of common practical convictions.[15]

Different cultural, spiritual and philosophical or ideological contexts do not allow any agreement on the rights of man at a theoretical level in the order of justifications and interpretations, but only a common conviction at a practical level of action.[16] The objective of human rights is not that of expressing a common theoretical consensus, but only a practical consensus for immediate operational ends to a limited extent.

And yet Maritain himself is aware of the limitations, alongside the relevance of human rights: the material agreement on man's rights is not sufficient. A common scale of values is indispensable for hierarchy, interpretation, and application in the case of conflict. The same rights can be interpreted, hierarchized and applied differently in various cultural contexts.

In this sense, it needs to be underlined that the perspective of Maritain on human rights is nowadays object of debate, above (but not only) in bioethics, where the strong pluralistic pressure both in theory and in practice emerges in front of the new possibilities to intervene on human life.

17.3 The "New Catholic Look" at Human Rights in Cultural and Moral Pluralism

Within the context of the Catholic Church the line of thought of the relationship between religion and human rights was further elaborated in the documents[17] of the Pontifical Commission 'Iustitia ed Pax', and in particular in the document *The Church and the rights of man* 1975, reprinted in 2011.[18] The document stresses the need to strictly correlate rights and duties – "to speak of rights is like enouncing

[15] *Ibid.*, pages 77–78.

[16] *Autour de la novelle déclaration universelle des droits de l'homme*, Editions du Sagittaire, cit., pp. 14–15.

[17] These documents do not coincide with the official position of the Church but constitute a significant contribution to its internal reflection.

[18] Quoted in note 7.

duties" – and on the widening of rights and duties from the individual to the community, both as far as concerns civil and political rights and economic, social and cultural ones.

In the international theological Commission two texts with particular reference to human rights were drafted. *Dignity and rights of the human person* (1983) stresses the need to clearly define man's rights and to establish their juridical formulation, with a view to a common interpretation of the rights of man, at least in political and social terms. In the document *In search of a universal ethic: a new look at the natural law* (2009) the urgent need to reinterpret natural law, natural right and human rights in the context of religious and philosophical pluralism, secularization and the recent historical-social transformations, particularly with regard to techno-scientific development, are addressed.

The 'new look' at the 'natural law' refers to the thematization of a number of elements.

An openness is outlined to establish a dialogue with non-believers or with those of other religions without giving up one's own religious roots: such a standpoint is supported on the basis of a historical reference, 'natural law' which existed in pre-Christian times, and a present day reference, given the necessity to find shared rational criteria in an ethically fragmented society. This is an arduous pathway that the Christian is called upon to undertake, without forgetting faith but perhaps finding a source of further motivation in it. A philosophical pathway that is made necessary for a rigorous rational foundation of 'natural law' that might allow a fitting orientation of moral action and legislation.

The Commission underlines that the reference to the 'natural law' refers to two possible ethical approaches: the deductive approach and the critical-dialectic approach. The deductive approach proposes a derivation of the 'law' from 'nature': this presupposes an evident, complete and definitive a priori knowledge of the 'given' truth from which to consequentially deduce norms a posteriori, to be organized in a code that regulates all possible conduct. It is this course that presents a number of critical points, in reference to the difficulty of proposing one truth in a pluralistic, complex, dynamic society: such proposal is accused of a dogmatic, unilateral, static and uncritical imposition which does not take into consideration the concreteness of situations and the new emerging historical demands. The critical-dialectic approach permits a rethinking and a reinterpretation of the classical vision of 'natural law',[19] highlighting the 'knowability' of the truth which is never fully acquirable and definitively expressible by human reason, recognizing by reason the capacity of 'interpretation' and prudent and gradual 'discernment' of true from false, to be carried out in the single situations. The 'new look' at 'natural law' is considered indispensable for the internal needs of the Church and the external demands of public, international and interreligious debate.

The Catholic Church has become aware of the relevance for human beings to seek common rules for living together in a just and peaceful society: in this sense,

[19] Expressed to the objection of 'naturalistic prejudice' that deduces the having to be from the being, deducing a normative code from the essence.

the intention to share with the religions and philosophies of the present time the resources of the concept of natural law is becoming clear. Natural law consists in the foundation of a universal minimum ethics which is rooted in our common human nature, which can be observed by everyone. It is the moral law inscribed in each human being. This natural law is not static in its expression. It does not consist of a list of definitive, complete and immutable precepts. It is a source of inspiration which may give rise to different interpretations, but which may ensure a framework for an objective foundation for a universal ethics.

According to the Catholic faith, Christ revealed the fullness of what is human by realizing it in his person. But this revelation expresses elements already present and acceptable in the rational thought of the wisdom traditions of humanity. The concept of natural law is a philosophical concept that allows a dialogue that, always respecting the different religious perspectives, appeals to what is universal in every human being. This truth is consistent both on a religious and philosophical level, both at the theoretical level of concepts and the practical level of experience. All rational persons may understand the requirements of life in society.

Societal life regards a whole spectrum of relations, from the family to international relations, passing through civic, economic and political life. In order to be universal, the norms of behaviour in society should have their source in the human person, in his needs, in his inclinations. These norms, based on the observation of reality, are then elaborated by reflection and translated into law: in this sense they can be interiorized by all. After World War II, the *Universal Declaration of Human Rights* is a very important expression of the fact that the source of inalienable human rights is grounded in the dignity of every human person.

The reference to human rights as natural rights is a relevant contribution to the search for a universal ethics, rooted in a rationally justifiable basis. In this sense, it is the possible source for religious and philosophical dialogue. Each tradition and religion may undertake an analogous work, beginning from their own sources, in order to search a common recognition of universal moral norms based on a rational approach to reality. This effort is necessary and urgent.

Beyond the differences of religious convictions and the diversity of cultural presuppositions, the goal is the one of expressing the fundamental values of our common humanity, in order to work together for understanding, mutual recognition and peaceful cooperation.

17.4 The Christian-Catholic Perspective on Bioethics and Human Rights: Sharing of Principles and Limits with Respect to Specific Recent Issues

The dynamic discussion on human rights is clearly present in the expression "generations". Each generation represents specific historical and social issues, which need to be expressed through the evolution and transformation of human rights.

The first generation is the one of civil and political rights; the second of economic, social and cultural rights; the third of rights to peace, communication, the environment; the fourth of the rights of women, minors, the disabled and the new rights of bioethics, arising in relation to scientific and technological progress. The list of human rights cannot be complete and definitive since the historical and social transformations highlight new needs to guarantee their protection even in the face of emerging powers, represented by techno-science. The most recent generation of fundamental rights appears in the man-biotechnologies relationship, expressed in the UNESCO *Universal Declaration on Bioethics and Human Rights*.

At the moral level, the Christian-Catholic stance shares the general principles outlined in the Declaration: in particular with respect to human dignity, the preeminence of man with respect to scientific and technological progress; the respect for the principle of autonomy combined with responsibility; the informed consent in clinical trials; the protection of the vulnerable; the principles of equality, justice, equity, non-discrimination and stigmatization; the principles of social responsibility and international cooperation; the protection of animals, environment and future generations; the information and education of citizens to a global ethics that is respectful of human rights.

The limitation of the Declaration lies in its generality, even though this generality is an indispensable requisite for intercultural and pluralistic dialogue. The Christian-Catholic standpoint integrates the declaration with further specifications, as well as particular reference to the beginning and end of life issues.[20]

As far as the beginning of human life is concerned, it thematizes the intrinsic dignity of human life and the entitlement of fundamental rights from the moment of conception, in contrast with the materialistic-functionalist claims that reduce human life to a mere set of juxtaposed cells. The unborn child is already a human organism with a human nature that begins a continuous development, without qualitative interruptions, but only gradual quantitative complexity.

Regarding the end of human life, it thematizes the intrinsic dignity and rights of the human being in such an existential condition, even if ill, suffering, or close to death. Conditions of life do not exist such that it is not worth living, not sufficiently worthy, in which it would be preferable to die; each phase of human life, even if suffering, incurable and terminal must be respected, helped, assisted with the aim of treating it, taking care of it, relieving pain, accompanying it 'in' dying.

In this sense, the Catholic perspective regarding the dynamic evolution of human rights/bioethical rights, especially with regard to the right to life, right to family, right to sociality/solidarity, expresses strong criticism towards the relativistic interpretation of human rights.

---

[20]The principle texts of Christian-Catholic bioethics: Sgreccia E. (2007) *Manuale di bioetica. Fondamenti ed etica biomedica,* Milano, Vita e Pensiero; Pessina A. (1999) *Bioetica. L'uomo sperimentale,* Milano, Mondadori; Spaemann R., *Sind alle Menschen Personen?*, in Löw R. (hrg., 1990), *Bioethik. Philosophisch-theologische Beiträge zu einem brisanten Thema*, Koln, Communio: 48–58.

The relativistic perspective gives a completely different interpretation of human rights. In a liberal-libertarian perspective, human rights are reduced to subjective claims according to individual self-determination, and in utilitarian perspectives, human rights are identified with social convenience. Human rights, in the relativistic framework, refer to claims for experimental rights or freedom of science; claims for reproductive rights in a negative sense or rights not to procreate, and in a positive sense, rights to procreate, with the use of reproductive technologies; claims for eugenic selection or rights to prenatal genetic selection in order to have a healthy child; claims for the rights to die; claims for family creation according to our owns desire, the so called 'gender agenda' or 'rainbow families'.

In this sense, we may understand the strong tensions, nowadays, in the interpretations of human rights, above all between Christians and relativists. The philosophical root of the relativistic perspective comes from a mechanistic conception of nature, an individualistic notion of man, and a non-cognitivist approach to ethics ("ethics without truth"). Relativism considers the individual will as the source of ethics: individual freedom is unconditionally exalted, without restrictions and limitations.

The separation of ethics from nature and the consequent moral subjectivism lead to a twofold division: the splitting of law from nature and the splitting of law from ethics. Law, separated from nature and subjective morals, or law "without truth", tends to become a merely formal and extrinsic instrument, that renounces the task of proposing content and establishing its obligatory nature, and limits itself to the formal translation of the arbitrary decisions of individuals or to the recording of practice of social behaviour.

The Christian Church offers a critical analysis of the inconsistencies of the foundations of the relativistic perspective.[21] An ethics that is strictly individualistic, absolutizing subjective freedom, means, ultimately, to deny real freedom. The absolutization of freedom for all can only be imaginable and conceivable in an ideal world: in reality it would inevitably lead to an 'all against all' conflict. Absolute and opposing wills that are concurrent and contextual cannot be compatible: the inevitable outcome would be the prevailing of the stronger will over the weaker one, or even the one that is not capable of expressing itself. And this implication goes against the core of the doctrine of human rights itself.

In this sense, the relativistic interpretation of human rights as individual rights is incompatible with the original and authentic meaning of universality of human rights. The ontological recognition of human nature as the source of ethics and law, according to the Catholic perspective on the basis of faith and reason, is a way to overcome relativism.[22] The recognition of the intrinsic value of human nature implies respect that limits behaviour: faced with a value, objectively recognized as

[21] Edward P. Sri. *Whose Rights? The Paradox of Moral Relativism*, "Lay Witness", Nov/Dec 2012.

[22] This is the main content of John Paul II, *Veritatis Splendor* (1993) and *Evangelium vitae* (1995) and Benedict XVI. Pope Benedict XVI (*Light of the World: The Pope, The Church and The Signs Of The Times. A Conversation with Peter Seewald,* San Francisco: Ignatius Press, 2010, pages 50–54) refers to the "dictatorship of relativism".

such in nature, it is not possible to act according to individualistic arbitrariness. The affirmation of the ontological dignity in human nature means recognizing the impossibility of reducing the other to "price", not to be exploited and objectified: it means recognizing a purpose in itself, a subjectivity that is worth protection and respect. In this sense, human rights represent the interconnection between nature, ethics and law, on a rational basis, that may be enforced by faith in the Catholic perspective.

17.5 Article 12 of the Declaration of Bioethics and Human Rights: Respect for Cultural Diversity and Pluralism in the Christian-Catholic Perspective

With particular reference to art. 12 of the Declaration on Bioethics and Human Rights, the Christian-Catholic perspective shares the acceptance of cultural pluralism in a 'just' way. By 'just' recognition of the importance of cultural diversity, it is meant a distancing from the relativist viewpoint.

Relativism demands that the bioethics of every culture is and must be placed on the same level with respect to the bioethics of any other culture, as each culture is equivalent with respect to any other. It is the theory that proposes an attitude of tolerance, understood as the passive forbearance of every bioethics/culture as it is manifested, without expressing any ethical judgement. It is the relativist perspective that, in the viewpoint of the juxtaposition of the many different bioethics, considers that the plurality of bioethics is irreducible to a unit denying the knowability of common values: in this sense multicultural bioethics considers that there is no sense in searching for common values, that it cannot even be hoped to find common values, retaining plurality better than the unit as the expression of wealth and originality, while the unit would be oppressive and suffocating. This is a perspective that can be translated in the formulation of a 'model of separation': every culture is a "closed" world, which establishes within itself its own values and keeps its own traditions and tolerates any other cultural bioethics on the outside.

Such a relativistic vision can be criticized for a number of reasons. The relativist falls into contradiction when he puts forward incompatible claims: on the one hand, he denies the existence and knowability of common values and, on the other hand, he proposes tolerance as a common principle, considering it wrong that whoever lives in a cultural context might judge and interfere with the principles of another cultural context. Furthermore, the principle of multicultural equivalence in the neutral, indifferent, and uncritical acceptance of every culture whatever it may be, considered unquestionable, cannot avoid the historically evident conflict among cultures, which are conflicting and incompatible, contextual and simultaneous: for example between cultures that consider offensive what other cultures consider dutiful, letting the stronger culture prevail over the weaker one. Moreover, equivalence can lead to a self-referential shutting-off of each culture into itself, even though the culture can be criticized only within itself, leading to incommunicability, the renouncing of dialogue in this shutting off and to monologue.

The Christian-Catholic standpoint shares the sense of art. 12 which highlights a criticism of multicultural relativism, appealing to an *intercultural bioethics*. This perspective considers that no hierarchy exists among cultures, but that this does not mean that cultures are equivalent, being all, indifferently on the same level. Every bioethics of every culture can be judged: moreover, there is a duty to express a judgement on the bioethics of different cultures against the relativist thesis of equivalence; not a judgment of superiority or inferiority as ethnocentric bioethics claims, 'imposing' its own vision demanding an assimilation, but a judgement of truth in reference to human dignity, human rights and fundamental freedoms considered the minimum universal value.

Regardless of their cultural belonging, equality must universally guarantee all men the possibility to recognize themselves insofar as men, even before belonging to a certain cultural group, to relate in an inclusive, integrative and unitary logic. To affirm the principle of equality does not mean to ignore or annul or, even worse, to repress differences: to affirm equality means to presuppose difference. Equality is the presupposition for the "recognition" of "differences", which is not understood only as an acknowledgement of diversity, but as a significant interaction among men.[23]

In this perspective the function of bioethics is not to impose one viewpoint as superior, denying and annulling the others, nor even to legitimize every request of every cultural group, resulting in creating a series of separate islands that risk coming into conflict, legitimizing the prevarication of the strongest over the weakest.

The structural reference to human rights assumes undoubted priority in bioethics: human rights constitute that 'unit of sense' in reference to which there can be compatibility *between* the rights of different cultures in the direction of interculturality. This is the way that will make it possible to avoid a number of negative directions: for example the claim of equalitarianism in assimilation, which considers that those from different cultures must become the same as or be standardized to the dominating culture; or the idea of differentiation in separation, which considers that the individuals of different ethnic groups must be guaranteed in the broadest possible conservation of what makes them different. The importance of intercultural bioethics consists in the critical search for a continuous mediation and intercultural integration between human rights and the specific demands of the different cultures, in the attempt to avoid the distortion of affirming the relational logic of diversity in equality. In this sense intercultural dialogue in bioethics would be neither conflict, which cannot but end with a winner and a loser, nor passive acceptance of a pragmatic compromise, but rather the constructive search for integration.

---

[23] Final document of the International Conference 'Dialogue of Cultures and Inter-Faith Cooperation' (Volga Forum), Nizhniy Novgorod/Russian Federation, 7–9 September 2006 (available at www.coe.int/dialogue); Final Declaration of the European Conference on 'The religious dimension of intercultural dialogue', San Marino, 23 and 24 April 2007 (available at www.coe.int/dialogue).

This is also the direction that the Christian and Catholic viewpoint is taking and intends to continue in its bioethical dialogue, along the lines of art. 12 of the Universal Declaration of Bioethics and Human Rights.

Chapter 18
The Dialectical Relationship Between Human Rights and the Christian Faith: A Response to Prof. Laura Palazzani

Kai Man Kwan

I am glad to have the opportunity to read and to respond to Prof. Palazzani's fine paper on "The Christian-Catholic religious perspective: Human rights, cultural pluralism and bioethics." It provides a succinct account of how the Christian-Catholic religion provides the foundation for human rights, and how it views the contents of human rights. By and large I agree with Palazzani's viewpoints. I also find her approach to this matter commendable: "The task of the Christian in today's complex pluralist society is to make himself heard, to dialogue with the non-believers and different believers, to rationally find the common truth together again, but also to not give up the specificity of his faith, to not stop at a generic Christian inspiration of ethical action, to not forget the divine precepts. The Christian must avoid the temptation of privatising faith and moving publicly at the level of reason alone, but must also socially witness values and the Christian announcement."

As a respondent, I need to add something else. I find that Palazzani's paper has articulated why our faith is consonant with the core ideas of human rights but she has not touched upon the tension between the Christian faith and human rights, at least as they are interpreted by the modern secular world. My objective is to provide a wider picture by also reflecting on the potential contradictions between the Christian faith and the secular, liberal understanding of human rights. This is not meant as a criticism of Palazzani, but rather a supplement to her discussions.

K.M. Kwan (✉)
Department of Religion and Philosophy, Hong Kong Baptist University,
Kowloon Tong, Hong Kong
e-mail: kmkwan@hkbu.edu.hk

J. Tham et al. (eds.), *Religious Perspectives on Bioethics and Human Rights*,
Advancing Global Bioethics 6, DOI 10.1007/978-3-319-58431-7_18

18.1 Human Rights and the Christian Faith: From Rejection to Convergence

From the very beginning, the relationship between human rights and the Christian faith is complicated. Let us look at the two foundational documents of modern human rights: the American Declaration of the Rights of Virginia (1776) and the French Declaration of the Rights of Man (1789), and compare their ideological justifications. The American Declaration affirms that all men are *created* equal. It appeals to the *imago dei* (image of God) to ground the 'inalienable' dignity and rights of man. (Even if the faith behind is more deistic than fully Christian, the theistic faith is still unmistakable.) On the other hand, the French document is based more on the rationalism of the Encyclopaedists, which can be traced back to the Classical humanism of Greece. The human rights are a revelation of Reason (which seems to be the secularized God of Enlightenment) which the human nature shares and recognizes in himself. This makes human beings transcendent and the freedom is the expression of the transcendent Spirit. Hence this is the basic right of the human being.

These two traditions, an idealistic humanism of Greek origin and the Hebrew–Christian tradition, in fact speak in different terms: creation versus nature, human brotherhood based on a common Father versus human brotherhood with a common reason, human being as an object of God's love in creation and redemption versus the dignity of a rational autonomous self. However, these two systems interpenetrate one another, and together form the basis for a new understanding of human being. As the idealistic humanism becomes unpopular in the increasingly secular context, many philosophers have attempted to provide different secular justifications of human rights. These diverse theories account for the confusion among theologians' evaluation of human rights. On the one hand, some perceive them as constructs of liberal humanism which have pagan origins and motives. Others even see human rights as expressions of human rebellion and attempts to secure human autonomy. For example, in 1979, Chris Wright, a prominent evangelical, says, "Some fear that the assertion of human rights is derogatory to the sovereignty of God. To them, the whole debate smacks of human arrogance and rebellion. Sinners don't have rights. Others contend that the Bible has little to say about rights but a lot about responsibilities" (Wright 1979, p. 3). Wright was reporting on the not uncommon suspicion about human rights among evangelicals. On the other hand, some claim them as the rightful heirs of the Christian tradition, and genuine expression of the Christian faith. They even passionately commit to the struggle for human rights in practice.

18.1.1 The Catholic Church

Since the 1970s, there are clear signs that the Christian churches are moving towards the embracing of human rights. After centuries of resistance to the language of rights, the Catholic Church has come around to adopt it. As Palazzani points out,

"The reasons for the initial opposition can be traced back to the interpretation of human rights as one of the ways in which the appeal for liberalisation/liberalism and secularisation was expressed in the modern age, understood as de-Christianisation (meaning secularisation as the anti-clerical negation of God and Christ), by means of the explicit exclusion of a religious and theistic foundation of such rights." The pioneer was the famous Catholic theologian Jacques Maritain who builds human rights on the foundation of natural law: "The dignity of the human person" signifies "that by virtue of natural law, the human person has the right to be respected, is the subject of rights, possesses rights" (Maritain 1944, p. 37). He defends a rather standard list of human rights, and claims that "all these rights are rooted in the vocation of the person (a spiritual and free agent) to the order of absolute values and to a destiny superior to time" (Maritain 1944, p. 45).

His views have been influential on the Catholic Church in the twentieth century, say, the Second Vatican Council under the leadership of Pope John XXIII, which "was the occasion of a fundamental shift in the church's understanding of its social and institutional place in a pluralistic world" (Hollenbach 1990, p. 88). For example, the "emergence of human rights as a central concern for contemporary Roman Catholicism is … an astonishing development… In recent years … various groups within the Catholic church have become highly visible on the global horizon as advocates of respect for the full range of human rights… the Holy See has adopted the cause of human rights as a prime focus of its ethical teaching and pastoral strategy in the domain of international justice and peace" (Hollenbach 1990, p. 87). This can be demonstrated by John Paul II's address to the United Nations in 1979: "The Universal Declaration of Human Rights-with its train of many declarations and conventions on highly important aspects of human rights, in favor of children, of women, of equality between races, and especially the two international covenants on economic, social and cultural rights and on civil and political rights- must remain the basic value in the United Nations organization with which the consciences of its members must be confronted and from which they must draw continual inspiration" (Bakalar and Balkin 2001, p. 14).

The construction of a more detailed synthesis of human rights and the Catholic faith has been the major concern of the Catholic theologian David Hollenbach. In 1979, he argued that "[l]ooked at internationally, the Catholic Church has become one of the most visible non-governmental actors in the struggle for human rights. At the base of this action lies the one hundred year tradition of modern Catholic social thought," which has been "formulated in the language of rights" (Hollenbach 1979, p. 1). In contrast with Maritain, he advocates "a *dialogically universalist ethic* rather than a natural law ethic," which is founded on "knowledge of the really existing structure of the dignity of every person and the ethical demands of this dignity" (Hollenbach 1979, p. 131). He also argues that "the rights of the oppressed, those denied both political and economic power, should take priority in policy over privileged forms of influence and wealth" (Hollenbach 1990, p. 98).

18.1.2 Mainline Protestantism

There is also a wide consensus among the Protestants in favour of human rights. In Europe, the mainstream denominations have drafted declarations in support of human rights. For example, the World Alliance of Reformed Churches has sponsored a consultation in London in 1976, and then issued the report entitled *The Theological Basis of Human Rights*. This was substantially founded on the paper presented by the Christian theologian Jurgen Moltmann (see Moltmann 1976). See also "The United Church Pronouncement on Human Rights" (Stackhouse 1984, pp. 295–300), and other similar declarations collected in Miller (1977). People tend to have the impression that the Reformed or Calvinist positions which emphasize total depravity are hostile to human rights. However, according to van Egmond, the "so-called Calvinistic rejection of 'human rights' … is due to their origin within a humanist frame of thought in which humankind itself sovereignly allocates these rights to itself. As far as the rights themselves are concerned, … Calvinists have no objection… The Calvinist tradition itself even provides quite strong arguments in favour of human rights" (van Egmond 1995, p. 197). Of course, some rethinking has been done but the Calvinists would appeal to their "long tradition of common grace" to justify an openness towards "all insights that exist outside the light of special grace in the issue of human rights, and nevertheless to maintain the sovereignty of God" (van Egmond 1995, p. 201).

The enthusiasm of the World Council of Churches (WCC) for human rights is also unmistakable: "The struggle of Christians for human rights is a fundamental response to Jesus Christ. That Gospel leads us to become ever more active in identifying and rectifying violations of human rights in our societies" (quoted in Norman 1979, p. 32). The story of how modern human rights came to be accepted by the ecumenical movement has been told by Jerald Gort. He points out that from the beginning WCC has been concerned about human rights in the broad sense- religious liberty, justice issues, etc. However, it "did not occupy itself with human rights in the contemporary sense of the concept" (Gort 1995, p. 203). The Life and Work movement has done pioneering work towards this direction, but the turning point was the international consultation on Human Rights and Christian Responsibility held in St. Polten, Austria in 1974. Despite some differences in the interpretation of human rights, "St. Polten achieved considerable consensus and thus contributed very significantly to the development of ecumenical understanding of human rights and their advancement" (Gort 1995, p. 210). This consultation further influenced the 1975 Fifth Assembly of the WCC in Nairobi, which affirmed the importance of various rights to life, personal dignity, and the rights of minorities, etc.

18.1.3 Evangelicalism

In view of the aforementioned suspicion about human rights among evangelicals, it may be a bit surprising that evangelicals are also moving towards some doctrine of human rights. I think an important turning point was the *Lausanne Covenant* which expresses a worldwide consensus among leading evangelicals in 1974. In the *Lausanne Covenant*, the evangelicals repent of their negligence of social concern in the past and rededicate themselves to the integration of evangelism with social concern. Wright's book in 1979 represents an early attempt to reconcile the Biblical faith with human rights. He argues that the "Christian view of human rights … locates them within a three dimensional framework with God as both giver of responsibility and guardian of human rights" (Wright 1979, p. 13). Then in 1984, the widely respected and recognized evangelical leader, John Stott, started to write on social issues in his *Issues Facing Christians Today*. He spends a chapter on human rights, and argues that human rights can be grounded in the Christian doctrine of creation: since everyone is made in the image of God, everyone is also endowed with human dignity which cannot be deprived even by the state (Stott 1984). Two years later, another leading evangelical scholar, John Warwick Montgomery, also published *Human Rights and Human Dignity* to defend human rights from the biblical perspective.

Ronald Sider is another famous evangelical scholar who promotes political activism among evangelicals, e.g., concern for world poverty (Sider 1997). In his 2005 article, he first lays down the general biblical framework for the Christian concern for justice and human rights (Sider 2005). Three years later, he points out that at "the end of the twentieth century, strong evangelical support for global human rights (especially religious freedom) led to what some have called a new evangelical 'internationalism' and a stronger emphasis on human rights in U.S. foreign policy" (Sider 2008, pp. 127–128). He approves of this development and concludes that "Christians today ought to be ardent champions of human rights for everyone" (Sider 2008, p. 144). In fact he defends quite a standard list of human rights like the right to life, freedom of religion, the right to fair trial, the right to vote and so on. He also defends the social and economic rights like the right to food and the right to health care. But interestingly he reminds us that the "biblical understanding of the person differs from both secular individualism as well as traditional and modern communalism" (Sider 2008, pp. 130–131). So he tries to achieve a balance of some sort: it is "important to reject radical Western individualism and its inadequate affirmation of obligation, duties, the common good… without denying the profoundly truth about the dignity, worth and freedom of each individual" (Sider 2008, p. 130). We can see that compared to the mainstream Protestants, the evangelicals tend to be more critical of some aspects of the contemporary regime of human rights.

Writing in 2005, Paul Marshall comments, "Paralleling developments in the Roman Catholic Church, most evangelicals now believe that human rights are an essential expression of the gospel, that the language of rights is a good way to express Christian concerns, and that any responsible faith-directed politics must be committed to defending and promoting human rights" (Marshall 2005, p. 307). One piece of supporting evidence for this claim is the declaration by American evangelicals: "For the Health of the Nation: An Evangelical Call to Civic Responsibility" (Sider and Knippers 2005, pp. 363–375). A section in this declaration is "We Work to Protect Human Rights." On the one hand, it states that "governments should be constitutionally obligated to protect basic human rights." On the other hand, it says, "We oppose the expansion of 'rights talk' to encompass so-called rights such as 'same-sex marriage' or 'the right to die'" (Sider and Knippers 2005, p. 373). Similarly, Marshall does not forget to remind us that "though rights may be good, they are not the only good things, and they might squeeze out other good things" (Marshall 2005, p. 310). He also recognizes the concerns of some evangelicals that the whole idea of human rights "smacks of an assertion of human pride and self-will rather than humility… A clamor for rights seems to violate any belief in sacrifice and servanthood… The demand for rights seems to neglect the fact that … the Bible pictures human beings as the clay and God as the potter who shapes our lives as he wills." However, he maintains that "rights need not be tied to an assertion of autonomy or self-will; they can be seen as a gift of God, as one expression of God's abundant grace" (Marshall 2005, p. 311). Besides arguing on biblical grounds, broadly evangelical scholars also provide philosophical arguments for the "Theistic Grounding of Human Rights" (Wolterstorff 2008, chapter 16), and evidence for the historical connection between human rights and Christianity (Stackhouse 1984; Witte 2007).

18.1.4 The Orthodox Church

The above provides a brief survey how human rights come to be widely accepted in the Roman Catholic churches, the mainline Protestants and the evangelicals. However, among worldwide Christianity, there seems to be one exception to this trend: the Orthodox churches are still sceptical about the language of human rights (see Guroian 2005b, chs. 16–17). The Orthodox theologian, Vigen Guroian tries to explain "the important reasons why Eastern Orthodoxy does not invest much of its theological or moral capital in modern doctrines of human rights" (Guroian 2005a, p. 47). For example, he is worried that "sinful human beings" may not be able to "resist turning their claims to human rights into swords of vengeance or into injurious pretexts for self-aggrandizement" (Guroian 2005a, p. 47). His target is mainly secular humanism and rationalism: "Orthodox christology and anthropology do not support theories of autonomous and secular human rights," but in fact he supports "the notion that a normative human nature is concretely manifested in every human individual" as central to Orthodox thought (Guroian 2005a, p. 42). In view of the evangelicals' reservation about individualism, perhaps their divergence is not as great as it appears.

So sometimes it is important to look behind the use of the language of human rights on the surface to ascertain the underlying understanding of human rights. For the Catholics and Protestants who now embrace this language, the essence of human rights is mainly the inalienable dignity of human being and some standard core human rights like the freedom of speech and the liberty of conscience and religion. They are seen to be grounded in the Christian doctrines of creation and incarnation. Moreover, apart from some liberal Protestant theologians who accept almost entirely the contemporary package of human rights, most Christian denominations do try to distinguish the essence of human rights as they understand it from the secular and individualist interpretations of human rights. They want to support the former but adopt a critical attitude towards the latter. The Orthodox position is in fact not very far from the above. Their rejection of the language of human rights does not entail a denial of human dignity but mainly signifies their refusal to accept secularism and individualism, which are seen to be inextricably tied to "human rights." Of course, there are different emphases among different Christian denominations, but concerning certain core understanding of human rights, it is subjected to a rather wide consensus in contemporary Christianity. Moreover, pluralistic interpretations of human rights exist not only in religious circles, but also in secular contexts like universities and courts.

18.2 The Potential Conflict Between Human Rights and the Christian Faith

On the whole I agree with the above development, and regard the defense of *core human rights* as a Christian imperative. To quote John Paul II again, "Every human person-no matter how vulnerable or helpless, no matter how young or how old, no matter how healthy, handicapped or sick, no matter how useful or productive for society- is a being of inestimable worth created in the image and likeness of God... respect every human person, especially the weakest and most defenseless ones, those as yet unborn" (Bakalar and Balkin 2001, p. 13).

Nevertheless, I think we need to be cautious about an uncritical and blanket taking on board of the *prevailing ideology* of human rights. First, there are different and often contradictory formulations of human rights, and proponents of human rights do not speak in one voice. There are also different philosophies of human rights. Some formulation or philosophy of human rights may be more consonant with the Christian faith than others. For example, the current formulations are heavily influenced by liberal humanism, which may lead to an undue emphasis on individual rights. Second, some rights considered on their own, may be perfectly legitimate, but their absolutization may lead to abuses and false representation of reality.

Third, although theologians like to talk about a dialogue between human rights and the Christian faith, often the current understanding of human rights is in fact setting the agenda for the theologians rather than the other way round. As Edward Norman points out, the "adoption by the Church leadership, in each successive generation, of the moral and political idealism of the surrounding secular culture" is not uncommon, and there is the danger of adjusting "traditional understandings of religious doctrine in order to represent the canons of contemporary moral seriousness as exactly embodying the spirit of the Gospels." By embracing the human rights movement, many people have identified the aims of the Church with the goals of western liberalism— "whose transient moral enthusiasms are, in characteristic bourgeois manner, represented as eternal verities. The aims of Human Rights campaigns are being given the authority of laws of God" (Norman 1979, p. 33).[1]

Michael Ignatieff, the Director of the Carr Center for Human Rights Policy at Harvard University, also says, "Human rights is misunderstood … if it is seen as a "secular religion. "It is not a creed; it is not a metaphysics. To make it so is to turn it into a species of idolatry: humanism worshiping itself. Elevating the moral and metaphysical claims made on behalf of human rights may be intended to increase its universal appeal. In fact, it has the opposite effect, raising doubts among religious and non-Western groups who do not happen to be in need of Western secular creeds" (Ignatieff 2001, p. 53). Since even a secular advocate of human rights like Ignatieff warns us of the danger of human rights as idolatry, how much more should Christian theologians seek to elucidate human rights truly from his faith perspective and to provide a critique of the one-sidedness of some formulations of human rights? In fact, as human rights proliferate and become more and more entrenched in the public realm, there are new signs of tension between human rights claims, and faith, such as gay rights, abortion rights, and the marginalization of religious freedom.

Especially in Europe, the European Parliament (EU) is very keen in enforcing gay rights, and this comes into conflict with the policy of some states with strong religious heritage. For example, EU's recommendation to criminalize homophobia in 2006 was a direct reaction to perceived bigotry against homosexual people in Poland and Lithuania.[2] While this resolution was hailed by gay and human rights advocates as a major victory, it was seen as an attack on religious values by others. Aldo Giordano, the secretary-general of the Council of European Bishops' Conferences, told Vatican Radio, "The declaration shows an aversion for certain values of our tradition, notably religious values. Such resolutions risk delegitimizing the European Parliament. It should be clear that certain subjects, especially those relating to the family, are not within the direct competence of the European Union but are the recognized competence of nations." Giordano also observed: "Sometimes it seems there is the domination (within the European Parliament) of a certain ideology of pluralism which sees everything that exists as something good. There really is lacking a reflection on what is truly human, what is human richness, what is good and evil, what is truth."

[1] It has to be pointed out that Norman does not reject the core ideas of human rights. He has a more positive account of human rights in Norman (1980).

[2] The European Parliament has voted to "strongly condemn" homophobia as "as an irrational fear and aversion of homosexuality and of Lesbian, Gay, Bisexual and Transgender (LGBT) people based on prejudice, similar to racism, xenophobia, anti-Semitism, sexism." The resolution passed 469–129 (with 41 abstentions) on January 18, 2006. The resolution called on member states of the European Union to implement—through laws and directives—a ban on discrimination in employment, housing, and a wide variety of sectors, and to implement education against homophobia in "schools and universities, and to consider the use of criminal penalties in cases of violation.

So *some* human rights claims do seem to clash with *some* religious values. In fact some human rights advocates still regard the church as the enemy of human rights, and they won't hesitate to force the church to change by law. Robertson said, "In the twenty-first century the human rights movement will struggle on, against its traditional enemies – armies, churches and states – looking increasingly towards international law to provide a lever against these institutional powers" (Robertson 1999, p. 383).

What are the reasons for this tension? In fact we can get some hints from Palazzani's paper. For Palazzani, "Christianity offers a strong ethics, or a "maximum" ethics. If the right – in particular human rights – is limited to defending (in a horizontal sense) the coexistence of men through justice, Christianity asks something more (in a vertical and transcendental sense), besides the respect of men also the moral involvement towards one's neighbour and the eschatological faith in the providential design." In contrast, human rights represent "minimum" necessary ethics, the ethics of measure and limit, which leaves to the "maximum" moral, transported by Christian thought, the personal search "beyond" the measure, the active and continuous commitment of the individual in view of the complete and concrete realisation of the respect of human dignity and the responsibility towards others."

Ideally speaking, this may be the way that ought to be, but the advocates for human rights are certainly not contented to appeal to human rights only within the realm of minimum ethics. On the contrary, the number of the items of human rights has been continuously increasing. Moreover, human rights are not only used to guard against the abuse of the government's power, but are also used to limit the freedom of citizens. This is particularly clear in various kinds of discrimination laws. In the name of anti-discrimination or equality, politically incorrect views have been censored or marginalized. The contents of education, the practice of counsellors, or the culture promoted by the mainstream media are all regulated or guided by what are regarded as human rights. In this way, human rights are used to promote a particular kind of all-pervading culture or life-style, and the society is reshaped comprehensively. This kind of human rights is in fact another kind of comprehensive doctrine (John Rawls' sense), and is often antithetical to the Christian system of morality. How can they avoid conflicts then?

Palazzani points out that the law "in the measure in which it defends human dignity … is an instrument for salvation." This may well be one side of the coin of truth. However, from the Christian perspective, when the law enforces immorality in the name of human rights, it may be an instrument for social corruption. This would be another side of the coin.

Palazzani has a nice exposition of Maritain's view of human rights. While I also admire Maritain's work, I can't help notice that the prominence of the teleological framework in his work will very likely be rejected by the majority of the secular advocates for human rights. For Maritain, "good (duty) is what is in agreement with the ends of nature; evil (prohibited) is what is dissimilar to the ends of nature. The first absolutely general principle is the principle of finality, on the basis of which everybody acts for an end and the end coincides with good; good is what everything leans towards, and evil what distances itself and deviates from the end." First of all, the language which mentions "good" or "evil" in their singular will make the secularists uncomfortable. They will find the idea of "the ends of nature" unintelligible; they would rather like to talk about various "conceptions of good." For secular advocates for human rights, what is most important is to let people have (almost) complete freedom to choose their *conceptions* of good, and then live accordingly. The emphasis on the conformity to objective ends of nature, in their view, will only stifle this kind of freedom. So this is in fact against human rights *from their perspective*. In short, they will reject a teleological account of human nature.

Maritain's strategy to eschew the search for a common philosophical justification for human rights, and to put more emphasis on "the common principles of action" is helpful. I do not deny that if we remain on a minimal list of practical principles such as the prohibition of torture or the protection of the freedom of speech, both secular and religious people may achieve a practical consensus (to some extent). However, as Palazzani explains, "the material agreement on man's rights is not sufficient. ***A common scale of values*** is indispensable for the hierarchisation, interpretation and application, should there be conflict." Of course, not only that the "same rights can be interpreted, hierarchised and applied differently in the various cultural contexts," they are also interpreted, hierarchised and applied very differently by social groups having different values in the same cultural context. The differences can become so great that culture wars inevitably erupt in the same society, with both sides claiming that they are fighting for "true" human rights. So the ***"common scale of values"*** needed for handling conflicts simply does not exist in our contemporary pluralistic society.

Several specific issues mentioned by Palazzani can serve as illustration. For Palazzani, to protect marriage (as a complementary heterosexual union, lasting in time and open to procreation) is a good. However, for others, this is a kind of heterosexism which is contrary to the rights to marriage possessed by all (which for them means people having diverse sexual orientations). For Palazzani, human rights should include "the intrinsic dignity of human life and the entitlement of fundamental rights from the moment of conception, in contrast with the materialistic-functionalistic claims that reduce human life to a mere set of juxtaposed cells." Of course, most secular advocates believe in these "materialistic-functionalistic claims," and they regard the attempt to ban or limit abortion in the name of the "unborn child" as a violation of the woman's right to reproductive freedom. This is also regarded as the instrument used by the evil male chauvinists to oppress women. Finally, the contention for "the illicitness of euthanasia" will be regarded as the violation of the right to die (or the right to die with dignity). The above disputes over human rights are so familiar in both Western and Asian societies that I do not need to belabour the point further.

So it seems to me that once we go beyond some degree of practical consensus, we find a serious conflict between the secular and the religious visions of human rights, especially over issues concerning marriage, and life and death issues. In Western societies, the secular vision seems to have gained the upper hand, and consequently the religious vision of human rights is widely regarded with suspicion. For the secular elites, this is not only not a genuine interpretation of human rights, but is in fact a corruption of human rights. They also tend to think that the secular side has already won the argument once and for all. Is this really the case? I don't think so.

18.3 The Foundation of Human Rights: Secular or Religious?

While I do not claim that I can definitively refute the secular vision of human rights, I certainly believe that the claim to its intellectual victory is premature. This can be brought out by discussing the intriguing question about the foundation of human rights. Palazzani rightly points out, "There is a divergence in the *foundation* of human rights." While she focuses more on the difference between the Catholic and the Protestant views, I will highlight the differences between the answers provided by the secular worldview and the Christian worldview. In the end, I think it is arguable that the Christian answer is more coherent, rationally speaking, while the secular answers are in general deficient or inadequate.[3] I have provided arguments for my position in a series of books and papers.[4] The following are just fragments of my sustained argument.

18.3.1 Are Human Rights Self-Evident?

The citizens of a modern society usually take the existence of human rights for granted. However, when we seriously contemplate questions like "Why do human beings have rights?", the answers are by no means easy to come by. Some philosophers try to bypass these questions by asserting that human rights are self-evident, e.g., Bernard Williams (Williams 1999, p. 57). However, it is clear from history that human rights are indeed a late "invention", and indeed unheard of in several thousands of years of Chinese history. So for a large part of human history, human rights were simply not self-evident.

18.3.2 Human Rights in a Naturalistic World

Moreover, human rights, self-evident or not, can hardly be some freestanding "truths" independent of our worldviews because the acceptance of human rights seems to have some metaphysical presupposition. For example, as the *Amnesty International Handbook* explains, "the movement's demands are governed, ultimately, in the conviction that *every human being has an intrinsic value*. ... it is affirming a universal value, now inscribed in international law, that every person is entitled to security and dignity- to human rights- simply because he or she is a

[3] Various scholars have argued for this position. For example, see Copan (2013); Menuge (2013); Smith (2009).

[4] See Kwan (2007, 2009). Also see the following Chinese books and articles: 關啟文 (2005, 2006, 2007, 2009, 2011).

human being" (p. 10). But then the question arises, why does every human being possess this kind of intrinsic dignity? In the naturalistic worldview, human beings are only chance products evolved from the inanimate world in accordance with natural laws. They are destined to perish with the collapse of the Solar System. It is hard to find any *telos* or ultimate meaning for human life in this worldview. Basically, human beings are creatures struggling for survival just as other animals do. Why should we think that they have a kind of mysterious intrinsic dignity which is not possessed by other animals or the inanimate world?

18.3.3 Human Rights as the Consensus of the International Community

Some people appeal to documents like the Universal Declaration of Human Rights (1948), and suggest that the consensus of the international community should provide sufficient basis for human rights. However, if this is the case, then it follows that human rights did not exist before the appearance of these documents, and it is not correct to say that the Nazist atrocities have violated human rights because those deeds were performed before 1948. Moreover, if the normative meaning of human rights is founded upon, and exhausted by the consensus, then there is no moral obligation for the countries which have not ratified those international covenants to follow those ideas of human rights.

As Amitai Etzioni says, "The trouble with this approach is that United Nations Charter, international law, and various declarations—in which the globalists find the values they seek to build on—are not widely affirmed. … Typically, they are neither the reflection of a truly democratic process in the international bodies or in the countries represented in them, nor do they reflect the result of a worldwide moral dialogue. Indeed, it often seems that various pronouncements of international bodies are tolerated by many nations precisely because it is known that these resolutions have little legal, political, or normative standing" (Etzioni 1996, p. 236).

18.3.4 Human Rights as Invention Based on Historical Experience

Alan Dershowitz, the Felix Frankfurter Professor of Law at Harvard Law School, proposes an experiential approach to human rights. He said, "I wish I could make an intellectually satisfying argument for the divine source of rights, as our founding fathers tried to do. Tactically that would be the strongest argument" (Dershowitz 2004, p. 4). Of course, he does not accept this theory nor any kind of natural law theory. He believes that human rights "*come from human experience,* particularly experience with injustice" (Dershowitz 2004, p. 8). He candidly admits that human rights "cannot be discovered… nor can they be logically deduced from any external reality or constructed from arguments… rights must be invented by human beings" (Dershowitz 2004, p. 85).

I find this theory far from satisfactory. In plain language, Dershowitz is saying that human rights are not anything real in the world. They are terms invented by human beings just to avoid "the repetition of the grievous injustices of the past." The problem is that human rights are not so much explained as explained away. One may say in general some human rights should be respected to ensure the well-being of the society. But what if I am a dictator or I can take advantage of others without being known by other people? Why should I respect human rights in these cases? So Dershowitz's theory, to have force, needs to presuppose a universal moral framework which is binding on everyone, and this is explicitly what he wants to avoid as a secularist. Even for the decent people, human rights are nothing more than useful rules of thumbs. When we apply them to our situation, there is no guarantee that they are still the best rules to follow. Dershowitz admits that in fact. He wants to define human rights "as something more enduring, more entrenched, more historically rooted, and more institutional than a mere majoritarian preference" (Dershowitz 2004, p. 111). However, in the end he can only say that "the difference between a strongly held preference and a right is not absolute or natural. It is very much a matter of degree, based on changing historical experiences with wrongs… This is all I can do- defend my *preference* for *rights*" (Dershowitz 2004, p. 114).

He is aware of this objection: supposing in a hypothetical situation, the Nazis were destined to prevail over the whole world and all societies which do not agree with their ideas and insist on human rights (say, for the Jews) will be destroyed. In this case, wouldn't experience teach us to ignore human rights? In the end, he wants to "insist that 'suitability' is not the only criterion for evaluating the justice of a society's 'moral reality.' An amoral sociologist would conclude that the moral reality of Nazi Germany was ideally 'suited' to its social structure and ideology- but that would not make it right or just. "There must be an external standard for evaluating a society's morality beyond 'suitability.' The problem is that no such external standard actually exists in nature or in the word of God. The only way it can emerge is if it is constructed on the basis of the broader experiences of the entire world over time, rather than the limited experiences of one particular society at a single point in its history" (Dershowitz 2004, pp. 133–34).

This passage is puzzling. While he insists on the necessity of having some external standard, he seems to deny its existence at the same time. If he is saying that this "external standard" can be constructed on the basis of the broader experiences of the entire world over time, then this standard is clearly inaccessible to finite human beings. Who can know about the past history of *the entire world*, not to mention the point that history is forever open to the future? He also did not make any reply to the hypothetical case about the Nazis: we can now already conceive that the experiential approach to human rights may result in a standard which conflicts with our current standards of human rights. In any case, I am not convinced that we can derive much positive content of human rights just from the need to avoid the gravest mistakes. In the past history, many societies which had no respect for human rights did manage to prosper and endure.

So it seems that the above experiential approach ultimately fails to justify universal rights. The general problems of similar approaches are sharply pointed out by Stackhouse: "if it is so that such ideas are little more than a by-product of a particular historical and social context, it becomes very difficult to argue that they ought to be taken as governing principles when the context has changed substantially… if each ethical or juristic principle is simply a cultural adaptation to those changing conditions, then the 'values' of the Declaration of Independence are ripe for challenge. To insist on them in another time or place or cultural history is simply an exercise in anachronistic cultural imperialism… If human rights are the product of scribblers and sophists only, or even of pioneers and pilots, they will not long endure. Sentiments will change, and other construals will be imagined, other paths found, other channels dug. Human rights will be like civil rights: what is promulgated by one ruler or passed by one legislature can be rescinded by the next. The erosion of the gains for human rights could easily occur, at tremendous human cost, if the idea of human rights is based on nothing more than the changing course of historical experience and discourse about it" (Stackhouse 1999, pp. 13–14).

18.3.5 Transcendent Moral Laws Provide Solid Foundation for Human Rights

I hope sufficient has been said to highlight the general character of the secular justifications, and the kinds of difficulties they face. Hugo Adam Bedau concludes his essay on "Why do we have the rights we do?" in this way, "When I began these remark, I thought I would be able to say why we have the rights we do. I have not done so, and I see that I cannot…. I appear to be in good … company" (Bedau 1984, p. 72).

Bedau holds that we have rights but can't explain why we have them. Louis Henkin, in his reply to Stackhouse, can only say this near the end, "For our time, one can- one has to– justify human rights by some contemporary universal version of natural law, *whether religious or secular,* by appeal to a common moral intuition of *human dignity.* If that is not good enough, it will have to do. May it last!" (Henkin 1999, p. 35). This is, I suggest, highly characteristic of the secular humanist traditions. They are somehow convinced that humans do have human rights but find it difficult to provide an ontological basis for it.

This is not at all surprising to a Christian. That God is dead is a proclamation of Nietzsche and even some theologians. They have not noticed, however, that with the 'death' of God, Man dies too. Nietzsche hoped that death of God would liberate man to be a superman. However the only essence he can find for such type of man is the will to power. Anyway it's difficult to justify human dignity objectively in an atheistic world. It's hard to see how the value of human nature can be derived from the value-free facts of physical nature. If the human person lacks genuine value, it's open for the powerful to exploit them and violate their 'rights'. So we suggest that the secular humanist traditions fail to provide true justification for human rights because they are limited by their naturalistic worldview: they have no transcendent frame of reference, and no ground for the truly human essence (see Pojman 1991, 1992). This inadequate theory has caused some one-sided formulations of human rights, and provides no sufficient resources to ground the universality of human rights.

With all these points in mind, we have some reason to explore whether theology can have some contributions to this problem, and against this background, Stackhouse's claims gain plausibility: "given the evidence of the twentieth century, that domination and ideology are the natural tendency of human experience, unless they are constrained by decisive insights about transcendent moral laws that demand regard for the rights of all. Such moral laws inform us that we are less autonomous beings than creatures under universal principles, not of our own making, and that the arrogant notion that these are nothing more than human products of will and wisdom leads to the worst forms of tyranny and exploitation by those who have the will and think themselves wise, not subject to any pre-given law. Some traditions honor moral principles beyond human artifice, and they offer a stronger account of why human rights, in every context, should be advocated, sustained, and encouraged even where they are not present in the social history of this or that group" (Stackhouse 1999, p. 13).

He further argues that "certain theological principles are indispensable to the sustaining of the idea of human rights… although the idea of human rights involves a quite profound and potentially universal set of implications about human nature, it is not ultimately a fully comprehending idea. It lacks the rationally defensible understanding that we all stand under a universal moral law, and that each person is constituted by a divinely endowed core that is the ultimate basis for the 'right to have rights' before this law… But the 'logos' of 'theos' may well be the most rational ground for holding to human rights in the first place. Indeed, theological ideas are often the unacknowledged and indispensable root of those non-religious universalist philosophies that also support human rights… each person by virtue of being human must be accorded a dignity and a respect that precludes violation of his or her person, relationships, and convictions. Still further, because all peoples and cultures stand under a universal 'higher authority' that humans did not construct and cannot deconstruct, people may seek to change the unjust laws of various nations, the unjust conventions of any cultures, or the unjust practices of any religion that permits or advocates violation of that core… the powers of government should be limited because some things are so sacred that no regime is competent to control their existence…This regulative authority within respectful limits applies, above all, to those institutions where the "metaphysical-moral" presumptions by which people wrestle with ultimate issues, those which no regime can generate or control, are cultivated, celebrated, and propagated" (Stackhouse 1999, pp. 15–16).

"Thus, not only a universal moral law, and not only a sense of a metaphysically and morally grounded understanding of personhood, but also a structural pluralism in society, all theologically grounded, are required for an enduring theory of human rights" (Stackhouse 1999, p. 17). Even if Stackhouse's claim about the "indispensability" of a theological framework can be questioned (he sometimes uses weaker formulations), at least the claim that theism does a better job in providing the foundations for human rights may well be defensible (also see Perry 1998). (Of course much more needs to be said. I would also argue that a theological perspective on human rights can provide some corrections to the imbalance in some formulations of human rights, but that is the subject for another paper.)

18.4 Conclusion

I think the healthy skepticism of Malcolm Evans, the Professor of Public International Law at the Bristol University, UK, is well worth pondering: "human rights and religion do not mix very easily and attempts to make them do so, are fraught with difficulties and dangers. It may well be possible for them to be brought together in a glorious symbiosis, but the experience to date has not been encouraging and one ought not to be deceived by the superficial resonance between them" (Evans 2000, p. 177).

I think Evans is right about the major trends of the human rights movement in Europe but we do not need to regard that as the only genuine interpretation of human rights. In fact, I still believe that the core ideas of human rights (stripped of the more extreme interpretations) and faith can "be brought together in a glorious symbiosis" and there is indeed a deep resonance between them. Even Habermas admits, "Christianity not only fulfilled the initial cognitive conditions for modern structures of consciousness; it also fostered a range of motivations......more than a mere precursor or a catalyst. *Egalitarian universalism, from which sprang the ideas of freedom and social solidarity, of an autonomous conduct of life and emancipation, of the individual morality of conscience, human rights, and democracy is the direct heir to the Judaic ethic of justice and the Christian ethic of love*. This legacy, substantially unchanged, has been the object of continual critical appropriation and reinterpretation. *To this day, there is no alternative to it......Everything else is just idle postmodern talk*" (Habermas 2006, pp. 150–151; italics mine).

Of course, the task to construct and vindicate the "glorious symbiosis" between the Christian faith and human rights is far from easy, but definitely something worthy of our best and greatest efforts. However, nothing in this essay is meant to exclude the participation of non-religious people from the advocacy of human rights. My main contention is only that the religious perspective on human rights should not be prematurely dismissed. People with different convictions, religious or secular, can still work together to promote human rights as a kind of overlapping consensus.

References

Bakalar, Nick, and Richard Balkin, eds. 2001. *The wisdom of John Paul II*. New York: Vintage.

Bedau, Hugo Adam. 1984. Why do we have the rights we do? *Social Philosophy and Policy* 1 (1984): 56–72.

Copan, Paul. 2013. Grounding human rights: Naturalism's failure and Biblical Theism's success. In *Legitimizing human rights: Secular and religious perspectives*, ed. A.J.L. Menuge, 11–31. Surrey: Ashgate.
Dershowitz, Alan. 2004. *Rights from wrongs: A secular theory of the origins of rights*. New York: Basic Books.
Etzioni, Amitai. 1996. *The new golden rule: Community and morality in a democratic society*. New York: Basic Books.
Evans, Malcolm D. 2000. Religion, law and human rights: Locating the debate. In *Law and religion in contemporary society: Communities, individualism and the state*, ed. Peter W. Edge and Graham Harvey, 177–198. Aldershot: Ashgate.
Gort, Jerald D. 1995. The Christian ecumenical reception of human rights. In *Human rights and religious values: An uneasy relationship?* ed. Abdullahi Ahmed An-Naim, Jerald D. Gort, Henry Jansen, and Hendrik M. Vroom, 203–228. Amsterdam: Editions Rodopi.
Guroian, Vigen. 2005a. Human rights and modern western faith: An orthodox Christian assessment. In *Does human rights need God?* ed. Elizabeth M. Bucar and Barbra Barnett, 41–47. Grand Rapids: Eerdmans.
———. 2005b. *Rallying the really human things: The moral imagination in politics, literature, and everyday life*. Wilmington: ISI Books.
Habermas, Jurgen. 2006. *Time of transitions*. Cambridge: Polity. [First published in Germany in 2001].
Henkin, Louis. 1999. Human rights: Religious or enlightened? In *Religion and human rights: Competing claims?* ed. Carrie Gustafson and Peter Juviler, 31–35. Armonk: M.E. Sharpe.
Hollenbach, David. 1979. *Claims in conflict: Retrieving and renewing the Catholic human rights tradition*. New York: Paulist Press.
———. 1990. *Justice, peace, and human rights: American Catholic social ethics in a pluralistic world*. New York: Crossroad.
Ignatieff, Michael. 2001. *Human rights as politics and idolatry*. Princeton: Princeton University Press.
Kwan, Kai-man. 2007. Can Christian theology provide a foundation for human rights? *CGST Journal* 43 (July 2007): 205–228.
———. 2009. Human rights without God: Can naturalism provide the foundation for human rights? *CGST Journal* 47: 157–180.
Maritain, Jacques. 1944. *The rights of man and natural law*. London: Geoffrey Books.
Marshall, Paul. 2005. Human rights. In *Toward an evangelical public policy*, ed. Ronald J. Sider and Diane Knippers, 307–322. Grand Rapids: Baker.
Menuge, Angus J.L. 2013. Why human rights cannot be naturalized: The contingency problem. In *Legitimizing human rights: Secular and religious perspectives*, ed. Angus J.L. Menuge, 57–78. Surrey: Ashgate.
Miller, Allen O., ed. 1977. *A Christian declaration on human rights*. Grand Rapids: Eerdmans.
Moltmann, Jurgen. 1976. A Christian declaration on human rights. *Reformed World* 34: 58–72.
Montgomery, John Warwick. 1986. *Human rights and human dignity*. Grand Rapids: Zondervan.
Norman, Edward R. 1979. *Christianity and the world order*. Oxford: Oxford University Press.
———. 1980. Human rights. In *Essays in evangelical social ethics*, ed. David Wright. Exeter: Paternoster Press. Ch.7.
Perry, Michael J. 1998. *The idea of human rights: Four inquiries*. New York: Oxford University Press.
Pojman, Louis. 1991. A critique of contemporary egalitarianism: A Christian perspective. *Faith and Philosophy* 8 (1991): 481–504.
———. 1992. Are human rights based on equal worth? *Philosophy and Phenomenological Research* LII: 605–622.
Robertson, G. 1999. *Crimes against humanity*. Harmondsworth: Allen Lane.
Sider, Ronald J. 1997. *Rich Christians in an age of hunger*, 20th Anniversary Edition. London: Hodder and Stoughton.

———. 2005. Justice, human rights, and government: Toward an evangelical perspective. In *Toward an evangelical public policy*, ed. Ronald J. Sider and Diane Knippers, 163–193. Grand Rapids: Baker.
———. 2008. *The scandal of evangelical politics: Why are Christians missing the chance to really change the World?* Grand Rapids: Baker.
Sider, Ronald J., and Diane Knippers, eds. 2005. *Toward an evangelical public policy*. Grand Rapids: Baker.
Smith, Christian. 2009. Dowes Naturalism warrant a moral belief in universal Benevolence and human rights? In *The believing primate: Scientific, philosophical, and theological reflections on the origin of religion*, ed. Jeffrey Schloss and Michael Murray, 292–317. Oxford: Oxford University Press.
Stackhouse, Max L. 1984. *Creeds, society, and human rights: A study in three cultures*. Grand Rapids: Eerdmans.
———. 1999. Human rights and public theology: The basic validation of human rights. In *Religion and human rights: Competing claims?* ed. Carrie Gustafson and Peter Juviler, 12–30. Armonk: M.E. Sharpe.
Stott, John. 1984. *Issues facing Christians today*. Basingstoke: Marshall Morgan and Scott.
The theological basis of human rights, Statement of the World Alliance of Reformed Churches Consultation in London. 1976. *Reformed World* 34: 50–58.
Van Egmond, Aad. 1995. Calvinist thought and human rights. In *Human rights and religious values: An uneasy relationship?* ed. Abdullahi Ahmed An-Na'im, Jerald D. Gort, Henry Jansen, and Hendrik M. Vroom, 192–202. Amsterdam: Editions Rodopi.
Williams, Bernard. 1999. In the beginning was the deed. In *Deliberative democracy and human rights*, ed. Harold Hongju Koh and Ronald C. Slye, 49–60. New Haven: Yale University Press.
Witte, John. 2007. *The reformation of rights: Law, religion, and human rights in early modern Calvinism*. Cambridge: Cambridge University Press.
Wolterstorff, Nicholas. 2008. *Justice: Rights and wrongs*. Princeton/Oxford: Princeton University Press.
Wright, Christopher J.H. 1979. *Human rights: A study in Biblical themes*. Bramcote: Grove Books.
關啟文,《是非曲直—對人權、同性戀的倫理反思》, 增訂版,香港: 宣道, 2005。
———,《上帝、世俗社會與道德的基礎》, 香港:天道, 2006年4月。
———,《基督教倫理與自由世俗社會》, 香港:天道, 2007年3月。
———,〈人權的基礎是經驗嗎?——評德肅維奇 (Alan Dershowitz) 的人權論〉,《哲學與文化》, 422期(第三十六卷第七期), 2009年7月, 頁31–57。
———,〈人權的轉化: 基督教自由社群的觀點〉,《中國神學研究院期刊》第51期 (2011年7月), 頁153–182。

Chapter 19
Rooting the Universals of Bioethics and Human Rights in Natural Law: An Islamic Response to "The Christian-Catholic Religious Perspective: Human Rights, Cultural Pluralism, and Bioethics" by Professor Laura Palazanni

Aasim I. Padela

Abstract This chapter considers how a natural law-based, common morality framework might be received within Sunni Islam, and thereby addresses Prof. Palazanni's essay on Christian-Catholic perspectives on cultural pluralism and bioethics. Specifically, I critically examine the notions of moral norms being susceptible recognition by human reason alone and human rights emerging from shared humanity, through the lens of Sunni Islamic moral theology. The first part of the essay describes the tension between Islamic paradigms of moral normativity and rights and those common to universal bioethics and human rights theories, while the later portions introduce concepts germane to Islamic theology that can be used to further dialogues aimed at generating a minimalist consensus around shared ethical values for practical policy ends.

19.1 Introduction

Thought leaders continue to search for moral principles that are common to, or at least can be sourced in, all of humankind's cultural and value systems in order to construct a shared ethical framework that can be used to protect vulnerable segments of society. This quest to find universal elements that can undergird a just social order took on added vigor in the aftermath of World War II when corpses lining the battlefields and interred in concentration camps bore witness to the capacity of humans to dehumanize the "other." In order to appeal to the notion of a singular yet interdependent global society, and with an eye towards preventing future atrocities, the vocabulary of human rights doctrine(s) was fashioned. Beginning

A.I. Padela (✉)
Initiative on Islam & Medicine, University of Chicago, Chicago, IL, USA
e-mail: apadela@uchicago.edu

J. Tham et al. (eds.), *Religious Perspectives on Bioethics and Human Rights*, Advancing Global Bioethics 6, DOI 10.1007/978-3-319-58431-7_19

with the charter of the United Nations in 1945 and closely followed by the Universal Declaration of Human Rights in 1948, successive international declarations and covenants, including the Universal Declaration on Bioethics and Human Rights in 2005, have advanced the universality of human rights schema and attempted to weld together consensus among diverse groups of stakeholders. While different formulations of human rights theory have emerged, for the most part these formulations draw attention to the "human" origins of the theories and adopt a secular lexis to ward off religion-based argumentation. The aspiration for many theorists and policy-makers is a practical consensus around values that must be protected by society in order for humans to live together amicably. As one leading thinker describes it they are drawn towards minimalism in either of two forms. The first form is substantive minimalism where a "thin" theory of what is right, of what is deemed by peoples from across the moral diversity of humankind to be required for human life, is advanced in order to achieve a practical global consensus on the content of human rights. The second form in justificatory minimalism which "aspires to present a conception of human rights without itself connecting to a particular ethical or religious outlook…with the aim of presenting a conception that is capable of winning" global public acceptance (Cohen 2004, 192).

In either case, one of the central ideas within the various permutations of secular human rights theories, and their related universal bioethics frameworks, is that human reason is sufficient for discerning moral truths. While some argue that there exists no underlying metaphysical underpinning to this "secular" claim, others find this assertion to cohere with versions of natural law theory. It is this latter view that appears within Professor Palazzani's paper *The Christian-Catholic religious perspective: Human rights, cultural pluralism and bioethics.*

In propounding a Christian-Catholic view on human rights doctrine and universal bioethics, Prof. Palazzani offers a view of a universal framework for human rights and bioethics that is receptive to religious considerations by adding a "vertical" dimension, a Divine link, to both the fundamental rights advanced and to the process of advancing them. In doing so she largely draws upon the views of the Christian-Catholic theologian, Jacques Maritain. However, in so far as universal human rights and bioethics frameworks advance human reason as sufficient for assessing morality they run counter to traditional Sunni Islamic moral theology. Because the natural law underpinnings of human rights doctrine and universal bioethics discourse run counter to a fundamental tenet of Sunni theology, many Islamic authorities view all attempts at such declarations as disingenuous hegemonic efforts to impose Western values upon Muslims (Abou El Fadl 2002).

In this response to her essay, I aim to shed light on the starkly different moral scaffolding that a human rights and bioethics theory derived from Sunni Islam may possess, and begin by pointing out the areas of agreement between the Christian-Catholic perspective and Sunni moral theology. I next proceed to describe the status and role of reason within Islamic moral theology so as to distinguish between these notions about the capacity of human reason and those that underpin Christian-Catholic perspective Prof. Palazzani expounds. In the subsequent section I comment on the notion of "rights" within the Islamic ethico-legal tradition in order to draw out distinctions between the conceptual vocabulary of the Islamic tradition where humankind is obliged to obey God, and the language of secular human rights discourse where "rights" inhere within man. In the last part of this paper, I reflect on aspects of orthodox Sunni Islamic theological frameworks that open up the possibility for "a practical consensus (vis-à-vis human dignity and protection in biomedical practice and research) for immediate operational ends," a "minimalist" ethics so to speak, among representatives of Islam and Muslims and proponents of universal charters on human rights and bioethics.

19.1.1 The Promise of Something More: A Religious Dimension to Human Rights

The theoretical starting point of contemporary human rights doctrine(s), and the resulting bioethical discourse that is linked to it, is the notion that human beings have rights that accrue to them simply because they are human (Sachedina 2009). Human rights are considered to be fundamental; inhering within humans and belonging to all humans in equal measure. Human rights are not conferred by an authority (divine, state or otherwise) instead they emerge from humans themselves. A just society, accordingly, is one that seeks to protect human rights by assuring that its citizens are not treated as less than human. In the era of nation-states, human rights doctrine offers a conceptual framework needed to "protect the individual from the overwhelming powers of the modern bureaucratic state" (Moosa 2000–2001) and via the conferral of citizenship entitles individuals rights vis-à-vis the state. Moreover, on the international stage human rights ideology serves as the foundation for international law and cooperative agreements amongst nation-states.

Human rights doctrine's preeminent concern is the human, and its purview therefore is fixed upon worldly affairs: rights originate from one's humanity, the human faculty of reason can deduce and specify these rights, the obligation of protecting human rights is part and parcel of being a member of humanity, and humankind's rational faculty, in a sort of global consensus, represents ultimate arbiter of ethical action from unethical action. Hence, Prof. Palazzani states that human rights-based bioethics operates at the "horizontal" level representing the "minimum shareable ethic in a universal sense." Human dignity is protected by a human rights-based bioethics by recourse to the ideal of justice where each human protects the rights of his neighbor in such a way that one protects those rights that he wants others to protect with respect to himself. This golden rule is buttressed by the principles of equality, symmetry and reciprocity.

What religion offers, according to Prof. Palazzani is a vertical dimension or a transcendental component, to human rights-based bioethics. While human-rights based bioethics offers a vision of social order that Catholic-Christians would largely agree with, Catholics would view the coming about of such a social order as part of God's "sapiential plan in the world," and they would judge actions that contribute to bringing out this type of order as part of one's path towards salvation. A religious rationale for human action thereby imbues a further motivation for the protection of human rights. It adds a metaphysical quality to human behavior as well as a *telos* that links worldly actions to the afterlife. Furthermore, Christian-Catholic moral commitments extend the "minimum shareable ethic" by propounding an ethic that suggests that human entitlements accrue at the moment of conception and continue to exist as long as one is alive. From birth until death there exists no condition under which life is not a universal and intrinsic good according to the Catholic tradition. Prof. Palazzani further stresses that the obligation for humans to respect each other's rights gains a further added "vertical" dimension in the Catholic-Christian perspective where the human is an honored and sacred object and is due respect because he represents "the image and likeness of God." In these ways Christian-Catholic moral theology enhances human rights doctrine to build a "maximum" version of bioethics.

From a Muslim vantage-point the adorning of human-rights based bioethics with Islamic theological justifications can also embolden human motivations such that a vertical link to Divine pleasure is added to the horizontal realm of worldly actions. Analogous to Christian-Catholic moral reasoning, Islamic moral theology would also deem actions that pertain to respecting human rights not only as meritorious (in the sense that the actions accrue reward in the hereafter) but also as part of one's obligation to fulfill one's duty to God. Yet, constructing the sort of moral framework that Prof. Palazanni expounds upon in order to enhance a human rights-based bioethical theory presents a challenge for Sunni Islam. A major obstacle for a project that seeks to "find" human rights doctrine within the Sunni Islamic tradition is that Sunni ethico-legal obligations cannot issue forth on the back of human reason alone. The content of, and grounding for, human rights within an Islamic moral framework substantively differs from the Christian-Catholic version presented by Prof. Palazanni.

19.2 Islamic Moral Theology, Human Reason and Natural Law

Islam represents the cumulative guidance provided by God to humankind via sacred revelations to prophets from the beginning of time until the final revelation to the Prophet Muhammad in sixth century Arabia. Each successive revelation reformulated the preceding prophetic message by building upon aspects, and abrogating other aspects, of the Divine message. As such, Muslims hold that the revelation that accompanied the Prophet Muhammad represents not only the last, but the most complete, instruction from God. In Islamic theology the revelatory event that characterizes Islam comprises of a sacred text, the Qur'an, and the Prophetic example, the *Sunnah*. The Qur'an is held to be the literal word of God revealed to Prophet Muhammad by way of the angel Gabriel. The *Sunnah* comprises of the sayings, actions, and tacit approvals of the Prophet Muhammad. The *Sunnah*, therefore, complements the Qur'an and comprises the second component of the Islamic revelation. Both the Qur'an and *Sunnah* are considered divine communications (*wahy*) that serve as the foundational source-texts for all Islamic teachings. Indeed all that can be considered to be "Islamic," whether it be ideas, behaviors or social systems, are indexed to the Qur'an and *Sunnah*.

With respect to ethics revelation occupies a central place within Islamic moral theology. Sunni moral theology[1] is built upon the central tenet that revelation is the primary means through which humans can discern God's will. Human reason, accordingly, is seen as a fault-prone tool for moral assessment and can only confirm or corroborate that which is established by revelation (Qur'an and *Sunnah*). Indeed the Arabic term for reason or intellect, '*aql*, carries the meaning of being attached to something, and for Islamic theologians, the intellect must be tied to revelation in order to discover moral truths. Given the central place revelation occupies within Islam, Islamic moral theologians elaborated a science (*uṣūl al-fiqh*) for deriving normative values from the Qur'an and *Sunnah* to generate a sacred law that has both ethical and legal content. While there are multiple Islamic schools of law[2] that have slightly different ways of deducing ethico-legal rules from revelation they all share in their considering revelation to be the primary source of normative assessment.

Deistic subjectivism is also part of the orthodox Sunni moral universe. Sunni theologians hold "good" and "evil" are not qualities innate to actions, rather they are categories that result from Divine ascription. Consequently actions are good only because God communicates that they are meritorious and vice versa (Brown 1999). This position has profound significance for limiting the ontological role of human reason. Since virtues are not intrinsic to worldly actions and do not exist separate from, and prior to, a divine pronouncement, virtues cannot be rationally known and moral assessment requires revelatory guidance.

The rigid circumscription of reason's ontological authority originates in a Sunni theology that privileges God's omnipotence and infinite wisdom over His other attributes (justice for example),[3] and was a calculated response to neo-rationalist Mu'tazili theology in premodern Islam. The Mu'tazilis held that good and evil were qualities that inhered within acts. Based on this assertion, God's actions must always coincide with the good (for He would never be party to evil). They held that God's creative act was good and therefore all of creation was infused with goodness. Given that God was not in need of creation, the goodness of creation lay in its ends. Accordingly, the natural order of ends was for the "good" of benefiting humankind.

---

[1] In this paper, I adopt Prof. Mohamed Fadel's usage of the English term moral theology to refer to the Islamic science of *uṣūl al-fiqh*. As Prof. Fadel notes in so far as *uṣūl al-fiqh* is concerned with the scriptural sources of moral obligation, the processes of moral assessment, and moral epistemology it is a moral science. And since *uṣūl al-fiqh* is primarily concerned with how God judges human acts and strives to reach the truth regarding moral propositions it is a theological discipline. Consequently the mapping of terms is apropos even if not precise. In Sunni Islam there are two doctrinal schools of theology: the Ash'ari and the Maturidi. These two creedal systems undergird the orthodoxy within the tradition and the extant schools of Sunni law.

[2] The four extant Sunni schools of law are named after their founders who laid the foundations of the particular legal theory and juridical devices of the school: Hanafi, Maliki, Shafi and Hanbali.

[3] Mu'tazili doctrine held God's justice to be His essential characteristic and the lens through which to analyze all of His actions and commandments.

This vision of goodness inhering in actions and being ever-present in nature led to the development of the Mu'tazili position that human reason can deduce and infer moral norms from a teleological understanding of nature. They also considered the Qur'an to be part of creation in effect reducing the epistemic authority it was accorded in their moral theology. Consequently, human reason came to possess the ontological authority to derive moral norms independent of revelation. In effect Mu'tazili theologians had stitched together a "hard natural law" theory that appears to share much in common with the Christian-Catholic analogue that Prof. Palazanni discusses.

Sunni moral theologians who came to represent the Orthodoxy, on the other hand, saw the Mu'tazili position as restricting God's will. Mu'tazili perspectives were untenable because they limited the scope of God's acts such that they must be in accordance with what reason suggests is good, in effect making God's will subservient to human rationality. Instead, Sunni theologians held that God's omnipotence dictates that His actions are unrestrained. He is free to act as He wills and His creation need not benefit humankind (at least not in the temporal realm of worldly existence). Whereas the Mu'tazili view was that God does X because X is good, Sunni theology saw X as good because God says it is. And, according to Sunni theologians, God tells us what is "good" and "evil" through the medium of revelation, the fountainhead of which is the Qur'an. The Qu'ran contrary to being seen as part of creation as did the Mu'tazilis, was viewed by Sunnis as eternal alongside God and part of His knowledge.

These inherited doctrines problematize the construction of a natural law theory comparable to the Christian-Catholic model. For one, it is God's approval that brings into existence the value of "good," and His prohibition the value of "evil." The Qur'an, as the primary source-text of revelation, contains the divinely dictated moral code that expresses how actions are to be labeled "good" and "evil." And the *Sunnah*, as the second component of Islamic revelation, further explicates this code. Hence the moral valuation of actions proceeds from divine communication and is not based entirely on independent rational deliberation. More subtlety, by holding the Qur'an apart from God's creation, Sunni theologians asserted that one cannot assume that God's goodness extends to creation. The Christian-Catholic position that "good (duty) is what is in agreement with the ends of nature; evil (prohibited) is what is dissimilar to the ends of nature" is not a given. Accordingly human reason cannot assuredly discern moral truths by interrogating nature, because the natural order of things need not satisfy a moral order infused with God's goodness.

Notwithstanding these positions, Sunni theology leaves the door ajar for constructing a "soft" natural law theory (Emon 2011). Certainly the Sunni response to Mu'tazili theorizing was to restrict the scope of human reason so that it cannot a reliable guide to moral norms. However, Sunni theologians recognized that it is human reason that connects humankind to divine wisdom. While the Qur'an and *Sunnah* are the only reliable guides to moral truths, both interpreting the message of the Qur'an, and discerning the moral instruction of the *Sunnah* requires human reasoning. Furthermore, while Sunni theology demands that God be free to act as He wills, it acknowledges that God's habit is that His actions bring about benefit for humankind. This habit results from God's grace, and this pattern can be discerned by human reason. Therefore, with revelation serving as its guide, human reason can make moral judgments by drawing analogous causes and ascribing parallel rules. In this way, the Qur'an and *Sunnah*-derived norms are extended to cover additional aspects of life not specifically addressed by scripture. Therefore, Sunni moral theology attaches epistemic authority to reason within moral reasoning and ethico-legal deliberation.

Reason also has another critically important role. When the Qur'an and *Sunnah* are silent concerning a matter, human reasoning is allowed to fill the gap by serving as an ethical guide. In other words, human reason has the authority to distinguish the beneficial from the harmful in light of data gleaned from this world; it can make empirical assessments about morality when the Lawgiver is silent. In these circumstances, however, the reason-based rulings only have temporal jurisdiction as they do not carry moral sanction or reward in the afterlife. Since Sunni theology maintains that only revelation can provide insight into that which God rewards and that which He punishes, a divine obligation does not result in cases where revelation is completely silent regardless of human rationales. Thus human reason can judge apparent good action from apparently bad action, but cannot assuredly assess ultimate good and ultimate evil. These circumscribed functions for human reason come together to form the basis of a "soft natural law" tradition associated with orthodox Sunni moral theology.[4]

The Christian-Catholic addition of a "vertical dimension" to secular human rights doctrine appeals to a version of natural law that differs significantly from Sunni conceptions. Sunni Islamic theology does not hold that the end MUST coincide with the good. The end is just the end, neither assuredly good nor evil, and the good is not the characteristic of an action but rather only a label applied to action after Divine communication. God's reasons for making actions appear to be evil (as viewed by humans) is beyond scrutiny, for that which appears to be evil when empirically assessed may in actuality be good according when the comprehensive reality of things is unveiled in the afterlife. Additionally, the "soft" natural law tradition of the Sunni orthodoxy diverges from the Christian-Catholic stance that "natural law is 'part' of eternal law, that part that is 'imprinted' in man's reason… quantitatively inferior but qualitatively identical." In the Sunni tradition man's reason may contain notions of morality but that imprinting is not one that can be used as the basis of a divine obligation.

Because of these critical divergences convincing Sunni Islamic authorities to sign-on to human rights doctrine and a universal bioethics framework in the same way that Christian-Catholics were persuaded is a challenge; the Sunni conception of natural law may not admit a jus naturalist foundation for human rights.

---

[4] In this context the Islamic ethico-legal construct of *maslaha mursala* deserves mention. This construct refers to considerations of human interests that secure benefits or repel harms from humanity that are harmonious with the objectives of Islamic law but not specifically found within the scriptural sources. For our discussion it is important to note that these considerations (the harms repelled or benefits secured) are "discovered" or "labelled" by the exercise of human reason, and that some schools of law consider the construct of *maslaha mursala* as sufficient grounding for moral obligations and others do not. We see here too that reason maintains epistemic authority within Sunni moral theology.

19.3 Notions of "Rights" in the Islamic Ethico-Legal Tradition

As noted above, the starting point of secular human rights doctrine is that an individual can make claims upon one another, state authorities, and transnational actors, "simply because one is a human being" (Moosa 2000–2001). Belonging to the human race, the shared biology, creates the condition for arriving at fundamental and universal rights. These fundamental rights are also confirmed by something intrinsic to that shared biological existence: the human intellect. Human reason is "the sole criterion for moral cognition" (Sachedina 2009). Secular human rights are thus viewed "as natural" in that they arise from shared humanness, and "as rational" in that they are confirmed by human rationality. Yet, in order to exercise these rights an individual must possess the moral agency to do so. Accordingly, human rights advocates over the past half century have embarked on a mission to engage in dialogue across national and cultural boundaries, to craft charters and declarations, and to enact laws that protect the individual's moral agency.

While these endeavors are noble, grafting the secular roots of human rights doctrine onto the soil of the Sunni Islamic ethico-legal tradition appears to not be a viable strategy. "There is no unequivocal language of human rights per se in Islamic sources" (Sachedina 2009, 85). The center of the Islamic moral universe is the not the human but God. God is the referent of moral agency and the end of the moral life. It is God who labels action as "good" and "evil", it is God's law that adjudicates between man's competing claims both in this world and the next. In light of these notions the Islamic ethico-legal tradition's primary concern is how well an individual comports himself in front of God, and it places the concern for righteous dealings with one's neighbor on the road towards reaching God in a goodly state. Because the Islamic jurist's chief concern is God's reward and sanction in the afterlife, his eyes and ears are glued to the divine communications (Qur'an and *Sunnah*) when he assesses moral actions. Certainly, Islamic law is concerned with setting up a moral social order and there are "rights" that Islamic law bestows upon one's neighbors. However these "rights" are derived primarily through recourse to the duties owed to God as gleaned from revelation.

The Arabic word often used to connote "rights" in modern discourse is *ḥaqq (pl. ḥuqūqq)*. As opposed to corresponding to the term "rights" as understood in human rights discourse, *ḥaqq* carries the meaning of "that which is 'due to God or man" (Moosa 2000–2001) and it is this meaning that is communicated when used within Islamic ethico-legal discussions. Within the Islamic ethico-legal tradition there are three primary kinds of "rights" (*ḥuqūq*): the "rights" of God, the "rights" of humankind, and "rights" that are shared by God and humankind. "Rights of God" encompass those duties that are of a devotional kind (e.g. the 5 pillars) as they have primarily religious ends (Moosa 2000–2001), as well as those that are "beneficial to the community at large and not merely to a particular individual" (Kamali 2003). The "rights of humankind" are those that involve private interests. These involve civil imperatives and rationales such as the "right to own the object (one) has purchased" (Kamali 2003). The main distinction between "rights" of God and of humankind lies in whether the resultant obligation can be exempted by the individual; in the former category it cannot be while in the latter it is possible. The shared rights category is diverse and one where both public and private interests are at stake.

This schema stands in contrast to the secular human rights framework in that "God is the one who confers rights on persons via revealed authority" (Moosa 2000–2001), and rights do not inhere within humankind. Additionally, the Islamic framework begins with the question of man's obligation to God and then proceeds to other individuals, while the secular framework commences by investigating what rights are due to man. Within the Islamic ethico-legal tradition the axiom that humankind is obliged to obey God's command serves as the bedrock upon which a correlative schema between duties and rights with duties preceding rights is constructed. A similar correlation is not mandated by the secular counterpart. Lastly, when searching for rationales upon which to build out the "rights of humankind" Islamic jurists look to revelation before independent reason. Human rights doctrine requires human reasoning to serve as the only source of moral truths. In light of the above, it appears that the secular language of human rights is not easily translated into the conceptual vocabulary of the Sunni ethico-legal tradition.

19.4 Possible Theological Resources That May Assist in the Project for a Common Human Rights Framework and a Universal Bioethics

Up to this point I have suggested that the theoretical underpinnings of human rights doctrine whether seen through a purely secular lens, or argued from the perspective of Christian-Catholic conceptions of natural law, cannot be easily patched onto the moral fabric of Sunni Islam. Some scholars suggest that the solution to this uneasy fit is for human rights advocates to partner with Shia Islamic authorities because Shia Islam, just like both the secular and Catholic-Christian formulations of human rights doctrine, confers ontological authority upon human reason. Others suggest that Muslims should be encouraged to revisit Mu'tazili notions of natural law and thereby seek to reform the groundwork of Sunni moral theology such that it shares more in common with Christian-Catholics and secularists (Abou El Fadl et al. 2004; Sachedina 2009). Both of these approaches are similarly flawed in that they would only appeal to the minority of Muslims.

Shia Muslims comprise between 10 and 15% of the world's Muslims and a wide-scale adoption of Shia moral theology by Sunni authorities is out of the question due to the wide-ranging ramifications Shia theology has for Sunni doctrine related to prophethood, political authority, and ethical pluralism. Similarly, Mu'tazilite sensibilities are so far outside the bounds of the inherited Sunni orthodoxy that individuals who offer such frameworks are immediately criticized, if not ostracized, by traditional Islamic scholars (Emon 2011). Instead of attempting to gain a foothold with the minority sect of Islam, or attempting to foster a Sunni "reformation" a better approach would be to search for the "homeomorphic equivalent for human rights" in Islam (Moosa 2000–2001; Pannikar 1982). Since the goal of the universal declaration on bioethics and human rights is to protect human dignity, it is more prudent to investigate how Sunni Islam satisfies this need than to seek a reconstruction of theological doctrine. While it is important, on the part of Sunni Islamic authorities, to reach the goal of a general commitment to human dignity and certain human rights for "practical ends," it is also critical that these ends authentically emerge from Sunni theological frameworks.

Towards that end I would like to briefly draw attention to two Islamic concepts that can serve as the building blocks of a bridge between Islamic theological commitments and Christian-Catholic or secular notions of human rights. The first concept relates to human nature, *fitra*. A prophetic tradition relates that "No babe is born but upon *fitra*, it is his parents who make him a Jew or a Christian or a polytheist (33:6426)" (Siddiqui 1976). A Qur'anic verse (30:30) uses the same Arabic root (f-t-r) to declare that Islam is the religion that coheres with the *fitra* that God has created humankind with (A. Ali 1999). These and other verses and traditions suggest that humans are born with an inner constitution that inclines them towards "good." The debate among Sunni theologians concerns the nature of these "goods," and more significantly the moral cognitive capacities of this *fitra* state.

The second concept relates to "the good", *al-ma`rūf*. Muslims are oft-commanded in the Qur'an to "enjoin the good and forbid the wrong (22:41)"" (Ali 1999). Lexically the word *ma`rūf* is derived from the root a-r-f which carries the meaning of to know or to recognize, and thus *ma`rūf* connotes that which is generally known, universally accepted or recognized. Exegetes and moral theologians over the centuries have interpreted the *ma`rūf* in varied ways, some considering it to refer to religious duties, others consider it to refer to the *ḥuqūq* categories mentioned above, and others more broadly to suggests that "the good" are actions that are recognizable to all humankind even if Muslims consider them only to be "good" on account of revelation.

These two concepts, *fitra* and *al-ma`rūf*, admittedly complicate the preceding discussion of Sunni moral theology which suggests that human reason does not possess the capacity to discern "good" and "evil" independent of revelation. The narrative grows more complex because there are two streams of theology within orthodox Sunni Islam and their differences can be traced, in part, to their views of *fitra* and *al-ma`rūf*. Of the two Sunni schools of theology, the one most widely written about is the *Ash'arī* school. The other school of theology, *Maturīdī*, is linked to *Hanafī* law. *Maturīdī* doctrinal positions appear to affirm and extend upon the "soft" natural law position of the *Ash'arī* described above.

The *Maturīdī* view is that humans are endowed with the faculty of knowing God as well as limited moral cognition. For *Maturīdīs*, God's sending of prophets with revelation requires that humans in their original *fitra* state must incline towards God (hence they seek news about Him) and instinctively know that lying is evil (hence they affirm that God's prophets speak the truth) (Jackson 2009). Accordingly, human beings must be able to discern some moral truths using their rational capacities "prior to and independent of any revelation" since it is the "very basis upon which revelation acquires its status and value" (Jackson 2009, p 114). As an aside, it is important to note that "good" and "evil" need not be independent qualities of actions. For example, it may be that God's labeling of actions may have occurred before time (the Qur'an relates that God taught Adam the names of all things in verse 2:31) (Ali 1999) and the ability to recognize this labeling inheres within the children of Adam, but it is only fully activated when they come into contact with revelation. Harkening back to the concepts of *fitra* and *al-ma`rūf, Maturīdī* theologians consider the moral assessment abilities of the *fitra* state to be greater than those suggested by the *Ash'arī's*. However with respect to the *al-ma`rūf*, both *Maturīdī* and *Ash'arī* theology advance the notion, although the *Maturīdī's* do so more explicitly, that in the realm of the world human reason possesses the epistemic authority to make moral assessments about good and evil. These judgments cannot contravene guidelines found in revelation and do not carry divine obligation, but are nonetheless necessary for the construction of a moral society.

The fact that both schools of Sunni theology hold that human reason possesses epistemic authority to judge the relative good and evil of actions where there is no revelatory guidance demarcates an area where Sunni Islamic authorities can engage in deliberative dialogue with others about ethics and morality. Such dialogue would not place Sunni metaphysical commitments at-risk and Sunni authorities can work towards a global public consensus with secular and religious counterparts to find areas of moral consensus. Such cooperation has precedence within the Islamic revelation. While reflecting on an alliance he made with tribal elders to prevent oppression and injustice in tribal Makkah prior to his becoming a prophet, the Prophet Muhammad is reported to have noted that if he were summoned to such a pact as a Muslim he would participate.

On the other hand, in those areas where the Sunni tradition finds revelatory guidance, Islamic authorities may still be able to engage in a reasoned dialogue by sourcing their arguments in the maxims (*qawā`id*) and/or higher objectives (*maqāṣid*) of Islamic law. Both the *qawā`id* and *maqāṣid* are gateways into Islamic ethico-legal deliberation that though derived from Islamic revelation, are somewhat analogous to philosophical principles in the case of the former and an ethical prioritization schema for society in the latter. Islamic jurists must use rational arguments when debating which legal maxim is the most appropriate frame for making a moral assessment in a particular case, and similarly conduct reasoned argumentation over the higher objectives of Islamic law when deciding upon which revelation-based rules to apply in a certain case. As such, by using the vocabulary of maxims and objectives Islamic authorities may be able to deliberate over, discuss, and contest ethical values and moral judgments in an interfaith fashion and/or within the secular public square without referring back to the Islamic sacred source-texts from which the *qawā`id* and *maqāṣid* are derived. Indeed many of these maxims and objectives, such as *harm must be removed* (*al ḍarar yuzāl*) and the preservation of life (*ḥifẓ al-ḥayāt*) have analogues within other moral traditions.

In conclusion, "the notion of a common morality known to all human beings is, in the context of human rights language, noncomprehensive, because although the concept of natural rights or duties based on universal reason in Western thought has served as a rationale for a secular universal morality in the Declaration, their cross-cultural application in the context of different religious traditions is seriously contestable" (Sachedina 2009, p 13). The source of contestation from the vantage-point of Sunni Islamic moral theology lies in the theoretical underpinnings of the declaration. Secular human rights doctrine suggests that rights inhere in humans simply because they are human and that human reason is sufficient for discerning moral truths. While Christian-Catholics embellish upon these foundations by suggesting that human dignity arises from God's grace, they also allow for independent human reasoning in moral assessment via recourse to natural law theory. Traditional Sunni theology does not grant similar ontological authority to human reason although it does give reason circumscribed epistemic authority in moral deliberation. Hence further work is needed to sufficiently ground human rights concepts within an Islamic moral universe. The engagement sought by stakeholders that can offer a vision of a universal human rights and bioethics framework requires first recognizing the alienating features of the current philosophical frames used to prop up the dialogue, and then mobilizing dialogues that seek common moral truths and principles that can be framed without, or in spite of, a commitment to a secular or religious metaphysical foundations.

References

Abou El Fadl, Khaled. 2002. The human rights commitment in modern Islam. In *Human rights and responsibilities in the world religions*, ed. J. Runzo, Nancy M. Martin, and A. Sharma, 301–365. Oxford: Oneworld Publications.

Abou El Fadl, Khaled, Joshua Cohen, and Deborah Chasman. 2004. *Islam and the challenge of democracy*. Princeton: Princeton University Press.

Ali, A. (Trans.). 1999. The Quran translation. New York: Tahrike Tarsile Quran.

Brown, D. 1999. Islamic ethics in comparative perspective. *The Muslim World* 89 (2): 181–192.

Cohen, J. 2004. Minimalism about human rights: The most we can hope for? *Journal of Political Philosophy* 12(2): 190–213. doi: 10.1111/j.1467-9760.2004.00197.x.

Emon, A.M. 2011. On Islam and Islamic natural law; A response to the international theological commisson's 'Look at natural law'. In *Searching for a universal ethic*, ed. John Berkman and William C. Mattison. Grand Rapids: Eerdmans Publishing.

Jackson, Sherman A. 2009. *Islam and the problem of Black suffering*. Oxford/New York: Oxford University Press.

Kamali, Mohammad Hashim. 2003. *Principles of Islamic jurisprudence*. 3rd rev. and enl. ed. Cambridge: Islamic Texts Society.

Moosa, Ebrahim. 2000–2001. The dilemma of Islamic rights schemes. *Journal of Law and Religion* 12 (1–2): 185–215.

Pannikar, Raimundo. 1982. Is the notion of human rights a western concept? *Diogenes* 30 (75): 75–102.

Sachedina, Abdulaziz Abdulhussein. 2009. Islam and the challenge of human rights. In *Oxford*. New York: Oxford University Press.

Siddiqui, A. 1976. *Sahih Muslim*. Chicago: Kazi Publications. http://www.usc.edu/dept/MSA/fundamentals/hadithsunnah/muslim/.

Part VII
Monotheistic Religions: Islam

Chapter 20
Human Rights and Bioethics, An Islamic Overview

Dariusch Atighetchi

20.1 Introduction

When the sacred sources (*in primis* Qur'ân and Sunna) and the legal tradition are not clear on a specific subject, for example on recourse to the modern techniques of diagnosis or treatment, the faithful can turn to doctors of the Law (*fuqâhâ'*, *'ulamâ'* and *muftî*) who interpret the sources and issue *fatâwâ* (sing. *fatwâ*), i.e. simple legal opinions, which may well present contrasting thoughts but from a juridical point of view, the faithful are under no obligation to abide by them.[1]

At present, in the attempt to obtain responses that are more adequate to the challenges of modernity, Muslims are increasingly having recourse to the decisions provided by pan-Islamic assemblies, conferences, congresses and academies that bring together jurists and experts from various parts of the Muslim world. These bodies issue documents of progressively legal value: (a) simple opinions; (b) recommendations; (c) resolutions or decisions, which formally have a greater legal force.[2] In all cases, however, the resolutions can be disputed by other juridical subjects (e.g. individual doctors of the Law or academics of Muslim law etc.).[3] It must be remembered that *Sunni* Islam does not have a supreme religious juridical authority or a hierarchi-

[1] See the *fatwa* by *sheikh* Mahmud Shaltut with the significant title: *La fatwa n'oblige pas*, in BORRMANS M., *Fatwa-s algériennes*, in SCARCIA AMORETTI B. – ROSTAGNO L. (Edited by), *Yad Nama*, Roma, Bardi, 1991, Vol. 1, 83–107, 83 note 2.

[2] ATIGHETCHI D., *L'inizio della vita nel diritto islamico*, in ATIGHETCHI D.– MILANI D. – RABELLO A.M., *Intorno alla vita che nasce. Diritto ebraico, canonico e islamico a confronto*, Giappichelli, Torino, 2013, 193–304, 197.

[3] ATIGHETCHI D., *Islamic Bioethics: Problems and Perspectives*, New York, Springer, 2007, pp. 9–11 and 13–14.

D. Atighetchi (✉)
Faculty of Theology, Lugano, Switzerland
e-mail: dario_atico@iol.it

J. Tham et al. (eds.), *Religious Perspectives on Bioethics and Human Rights*, Advancing Global Bioethics 6, DOI 10.1007/978-3-319-58431-7_20

cal religious structure or teaching; the situation in the *Shi'ite* world (which comprises 15% of Muslims) is different since it is historically strongly hierarchized.

To date, Muslim bioethics is not yet an autonomous discipline with a status of its own and a methodology that distinguishes it from all other disciplines. Muslim bioethics still remains, prevalently, a bio-law for at least three reasons: (A) The all-comprehensive role which has been played by Muslim law in the Muslim world for over 1400 years, independently of the diversity of the positions expressed on countless topics; the supremacy historically ascribed to law in Islam has few analogies with other religions and cultures. (B) Historically contraception, abortion and some other classic topics have always been regulated (*inter alia*) by Muslim law (and by extension many other modern bioethical topics are included in this area). (C) The juridical-religious qualification of the acts (compulsory or recommended or permitted or reproachful or prohibited) discussed by bioethics remains the exclusive prerogative of the juridical-religious authorities. Muslim experts on bioethics are playing an increasingly important complementary role, but their theories remain personal speculations. It is not surprising that the states, when they legislate, prefer legitimizing their decisions in health policy by having recourse to legitimization by a religious-legal authority or body. In any case, bioethicists have the aim of developing the thematic present in the Muslim medical, philosophical and legal traditions; their function is limited to providing the religious and the political authority with an updated opinion in order to allow them to promote positions and decisions which are better rooted in the variegated Muslim traditions and capable of facing up to the contemporary challenges.

20.2 Laws, Bioethics, Universalisms and Religions

The deep influence of modern Western-international normative models can be deemed a form of legal-intellectual colonization. The Western influence appears in many different ways and in all the Muslim states. Most of these have imitated modern Western public laws; since the middle of the nineteenth century, juridical acculturation has been discussed in reference to the predominance of models of Roman law (to a lesser extent of Common law as well) in Muslim states. All the states have become autonomous legislators, including Saudi Arabia which nevertheless asserts –in respect of the *Sharî'a*-based approach- that its legislative activity is only an application of the *siyāsa shar'iyya*, i.e. a mere administrative activity aimed at applying the *Sharî'a*, rather than an actual autonomous activity producing legal norms.[4] The partial codification of the *Sharî'a* started in recent centuries as the imitation of codified juridical models from the West, now prevalent in the rest of the world. An imitation of the civil,[5] criminal, commercial and administrative *Western* codes can be seen

[4] CASTRO F., *Diritto Musulmano*, in *Digesto delle discipline privatistiche*, Vol. VI, IV Edizione, Torino, UTET, 1990, 1–66, 14–15.

[5] CASTRO F., *La codificazione del diritto privato negli Stati arabi contemporanei*, "Rivista di Diritto Civile", 1985, I, 377–447.

almost everywhere. For example, the organization of collective courts of law (instead of the traditional *qāḍī*, a monocratic judge); the different levels of jurisdiction; the introduction of a Supreme Court; the introduction of a constitution (a classic institution of Roman law): it is not surprising that Saudi Arabia was the last Islamic country to introduce a constitution into its legal system after a fierce internal debate by Muslim jurists.

Only the laws included in Muslim family law have often remained autonomous with respect to foreign influences. In any case, these transformations have been so considerable that Muslim law, due to external normative and cultural influences, has been transformed from an extra-territorial, personal and confessional law into a state and territorial law.[6]

Today in response to external influences, some Constitutions list the fundamental human rights but, at the same time, specify that some specific rights are acceptable only if compatible with the *Sharî'a*, a mechanism that allows reasserting the primacy of the latter over every other juridical influence (e.g. art. 26 of the Saudi Arabian Constitution: The state protects human rights in accordance with the Islamic *Sharî'a*).

In addition, in parallel with the International Declarations and Documents on human rights, women's rights, children's rights etc., many important Islamic bodies have produced documents on the same subjects aimed at reasserting the Islamic identity and specificity.

Perhaps a new approach to *cultural differences* is urgently needed in the light of two influences that, in the contemporary world, act in synchrony and with incredible efficacy:

1. A universalistic influence which acts on the level of principles, rules, laws and values. Never in the history of humanity has there been such a standardization-imitation-copying of legal codes, laws, languages and concepts from one half of the world to the other as in the past 50 years.
2. A globalizing-standardizing trend that acts on concrete models and life styles, habits, customs, and fashions, going as far as involving technological instruments and medical techniques.

This drive *coincides chronologically* with the enormous pressure-drive represented by the cultural trend of universalization of human rights without disregarding the so-called "global village" effect.

The capacity of penetration of modernity – even limited to the technical and external sphere- is totalizing and strongly invasive, democratizing and levelling regarding the *modus vivendi*.

[6] CASTRO F., *Sistema sciaraitico, siyasa sariyya e modelli normativi europei nel processo di formazione degli ordinamenti giuridici dei paesi del Vicino Oriente*, in BAUSANI A. – SCARCIA AMORETTI..... (a cura di), *Il mondo islamico tra interazione e acculturazione*, Roma, 1981, 165 ss.

Contemporary medicine and the technological means that accompany it, represent fantastic instruments of technological, but also conceptual standardization, to a model/s from a group of culturally specialized areas. The very conceptions on the human body, numerous in past centuries, are increasingly tending to be standardized to the progressive monopoly of some dominant cultural conceptions.

Today, following the joint assault of universalism and globalization, diversities risk being reduced to the survival of *tame and inoffensive* differences, belonging to the categories of socio-cultural-folklore factors, for example: different foods, ways of dressing, prayers, local behaviour and customs. It is not surprising that the universal principles of bioethics are protected from criticism by stating that the *diversities and cultural, religious and social (local) values should be respected and protected* but, paradoxically, this is translated into a condition of protection or implicit recognition of a state of inferiority of the cultures *to be protected* by those *protectors* (the *universalists*) which become paladins of the former (considering themselves morally superior).

In this framework what is the role played by the various universal religions? From the Islamic perspective, Islam is not a version of monotheism *equal* to other versions and worthy of similar respect; in it pure monotheism updates and definitively supersedes the previous Divine Revelations as Islam is the only Revelation based on the direct and literal word of God (Qur'ân) and on the last Law (i.e. the most perfect) given by God to man (the *Sharî'a*). Islam puts the previous monotheisms and religions into a hierarchy, giving them a specific value and role in history.

If the diversities have a concrete meaning, these produce multiple models of universality which cannot be reduced to others. Respecting this approach, it is nowadays fundamental to recover the strong sense of religious and juridical differences.

Of particular importance is the Declaration of Human Rights in Islam approved in Cairo by the Organisation of the Islamic Conference (OIC) in 1990[7] and the Universal Islamic Declaration of Human Rights promulgated in Paris at a UNESCO meeting in 1981 by the Islamic Council of Europe. These are Islamic *universal declarations* that aim to be considered alternative to the secular or religious (Western) declarations. Both the aforementioned Islamic documents constantly refer to the *Sharî'a* as the exclusive source of human rights (see the Preambles of both the Declarations) and as the sole instrument to interpret these Documents (art. 24, DHRI, OIC, 1990). A further difference between the Islamic and non-Islamic universal declarations may lie in the fact that the universality of the Western doctrines of human rights relates to the source of such rights which may coincide with "human nature", "image of God", rationality, etc.; all properties which relate to all human beings. Vice versa, the universality of the Islamic declarations is related to the substance of those rights and to whom they apply, i.e. to Muslims.

It is important to keep distinct lay-secular universalisms from the religious ones. In fact, art. 2 of the 1948 Declaration (UDHR, UN) states that these fundamental rights must be respected independently of every characteristic of individuals,[8] includ-

---

[7] *International Human Rights*, Wien, 1993, 325.

[8] FERRARI S., *Tra geo-diritti e teo-diritti. Riflessioni sulle religioni come centri transnazionali di identità,* "Quaderni di Diritto e di Politica Ecclesiastica", n° 1, aprile 2007, 3–14, 7–8.

ing religion and gender. From the secular perspective, these fundamental rights are *a priori* and independent with respect to religious faiths, religious rights and religious communities. In this framework, religious affiliation is only a *secondary quality*.

To be precise, the anthropological model at the basis of the UDHR (and similar documents) has at its centre a man in whom cultural, socio-economic, religious, political, physical and sexual differences are only added qualities to an ontologically self-sufficient and qualitatively neutral man. Any additional qualification (tall, short, white, black, Muslim, Christian, Hindu, Socialist etc.) appears insignificant and has to remain so, otherwise there is a risk of damaging or limiting the sphere of man's inalienable rights.

Islam immediately perceived this anthropological model as intrinsically non-religious and, as a consequence, gave itself alternative documents to the UDHR. One of the consequences is that if a religious group or a state were to prevent the conversion of its members to another faith, the group or state would violate the respect of human rights. In all these cases the UDHR intends to assert the primacy of the individual conscience and natural individual freedom over the rights and pressures of the religious community. This approach is difficult to accept from those religious laws in which the community has priority over its members.

One significant example is that of apostasy. In Muslim law, apostasy (*irtidād*, the term *ridda* indicates collective apostasy), i.e. leaving the *umma* (community of the Muslim faithful), is not a banal act of personal conscience but an act of betrayal of the "perfect religion" and the Muslim communities (see the expression *Islam is 'Religion and State'* or *dîn wa-dawla*); as a consequence, in Islamic law apostasy is a very severe offence. It is logically unconceivable as well as ethically and legally unacceptable for a Muslim to renounce the last and perfect Revelation (source of every earthly and post-mortem good) opting for non-monotheistic religions or for non-updated monotheistic revelations and ending up by damaging oneself and others, i.e. the Muslim community.

Vice versa, conversion to Islam is not apostasy but a *return to Islam*, i.e. to the natural and original religion of every human being. The result is an ineliminable asymmetry between the UDHR (and similar documents in which all religions are equivalent) and the Islamic conception of *religious freedom*. Historically, when an individual abandoned Islam, all his social and juridical relations were modified, for example, marriage, family relationships, inheritance relationships and criminal rules. Several contemporary Muslim countries, due to the legislative effect of Western juridical models, have moderated to a varying degree the severe legal and social consequences historically associated with apostasy. For example in Morocco, Islam is the official religion and the preamble and art. 6 of the Constitution guarantee freedom of faith. Apostasy is not a crime according to what was established by the Supreme Court of Morocco in 1985 and is not supposed to entail legal consequences.[9] Notwithstanding this, art. 220 paragraph 2 of the Moroccan Criminal

[9]Aluffi R. (2010): Proselytism and the Right to Change Religion in Islam. In: Ferrari S., Cristofori R. (eds.) Law and Religion in the twenty-first Century. pp. 253–259, Farnham, Burlington:Ashgate (2010).

Code condemns anyone who weakens the faith of a Muslim or converts him or her to another religion to a prison sentence from 6 months to 3 years, plus a fine from 200 to 500 *dirhams.*[10] The Government prohibits the import and sale of the Bible in Arabic but allows it in European languages. In 2013, the Moroccan daily *Akhbar Al-Yaoum* published a controversial *fatwâ* issued by the Superior Council of Ulema of Morocco. The text says: "He who renounces his religion is an apostate and must return to his religion. If he refuses, he loses life and the beyond and he must be condemned to the death penalty"…"In no case does Islam allow these people to leave their religion and renounce the social pact that binds them. Doing so is an act of apostasy and disloyalty, and exposes its author to special penalties".

In the wake of these data, different religious laws could represent the last significant alternatives to the triumph of the universalistic influence-aggression (which involves principles, rules, laws and values mainly grounded in European cultures of the last centuries) and of the globalizing-standardizing trends (which involve concrete models and styles of life). Islamic bioethics is subject to the same two conditionings mentioned above. The reactions to these conditionings underscore the Islamic specificity on some cornerstones of the bioethical debate. For example, Islamic thought contests the primacy of the principle of autonomy (characteristic of democratic-liberal socictics) with the consequent redefinition of the principles of Islamic bioethics and their hierarchy. Moreover, it rejects ethical pluralism: of what use is pluralism when the faithful already has the definitive, direct and literal word of God in hand?

It is useful to list briefly at least five topics that challenge Western conceptions and principles. The first two topics come directly within the bioethical debate; topics 3, 4 and 5 are general premises valid in multicultural relations and aimed at protecting Muslim identity also in bioethics: (I) The conception of autonomy; (II) male-female separation in healthcare; (III) assessment of UDHR; (IV) criticism of *Westernization*; (V) criticism of *cultural aggression.*

(I) The different role and significance that the principle of autonomy assumes in North American and European societies compared to any Muslim society, especially when anchored to tradition, cannot be denied.[11] In the former case, the priority given to the principle of autonomy (starting from the hierarchy of the principles of bioethics) is none other than the projection, into the bioethical context, of the importance of the liberal-individualistic matrix characterising the juridical-political culture of the contemporary Western world, despite the strong differentiations within it. Vice versa, in Muslim contexts, the primacy appears reserved for the principle of public benefit (*mas̱laẖa*) and the principle of justice

[10] Article 220, alinéa 2, Code Pénal du Maroc: <<Est puni [d'un emprisonnement de six mois à trois ans et d'une amende de 200 à 500 dirhams] quiconque emploie des moyens de séduction dans le but d'ébranler la foi d'un musulman ou de le convertir à une autre religion, soit en exploitant sa faiblesse ou ses besoins, soit en utilisant à ces fins des établissements d'enseignement, de santé, des asiles ou des orphelinats>>.

[11] See ATIGHETCHI D., *Islam e Bioetica*, Roma, Armando Editore, 2009, pp. 48–54.

as the collective interest takes precedence over that of the individual. For example, the Code of Ethics of the Pakistan Medical and Dental Council (2001, art. 7) states: "If secular Western bioethics can be described as rights-based, with a strong emphasis on individual rights, Islamic bioethics is based on duties and obligations (e.g. to preserve life, seek treatment)…".

Furthermore, the family often remains the decisive subject for the patient's decisions; this can be a limit to the patient's autonomy. Personal identity can take secondary position with respect to the collective family identity; the expression <<You are your family, and your family is you>> is valid here.[12]

In the contemporary period, the countries where informed consent and autonomy are best asserted (obviously in relative terms) are some democratic nations in the West, starting with Germany, Switzerland, Austria, France, Sweden. In other words, the recognition and respect of specific rights of the patient are the result of wider social dialectics within liberal democratic systems in which the protection of the individual's rights has taken on a dimension which has no precedent in the history of humanity. Applying an autonomy similar to that adopted in liberal countries in totally different social, legal and psychological contexts from the former is illogical; otherwise the profound characters of many cultures are manipulated. If this discourse appears clear for men, it can become very obvious as far as women are concerned as their condition (in the case of Islam) is still very often regulated by the institutions of family law of Shariatic origin.

(II) The subject of *male doctors treating female patients*. There are very many documents on this topic. Those published by two of the most prestigious Academies of Muslim law in the world are almost identical[13]: (1) the Fiqh (Muslim law) Academy of Mecca, a body of the Muslim World League (M.W.L.), 8th session (19th–28th January 1985); (2) the Islamic Fiqh Academy of Jeddah, a body of the Organization of the Islamic Conference (O.I.C.), 8th session, Brunei Darussalam (1–7 Muharram, 1414H, 21–27 June 1993). This is the translation of the latter[14]: "[The Academy] resolves as a general rule, if a female specialist doctor is available, then she should be the one to examine the female patient. In the absence of such a specialist, the patient may be examined by a trustworthy non-Muslim female doctor, if not then by a Muslim male doctor, and if not, then by a non-Muslim male doctor; on the understanding that in diagnosing and treating the ailment, the doctor should see only the minimum necessary of the patient's body and to the extent possible divert his look, and that the doctor's treatment of the female patient should be in the presence of a *mahram* (blood relation and certain other persons who, in the eyes of *Shari'a* are ineligible for

[12] Moazam F., Families, Patients and Physicians in Medical Decisionmaking: A Pakistani Perspective, Hasting Center Report, 2000, 30 (6), 28–37, 30.

[13] For an overview of the topic, see ATIGHETCHI D., *Islamic Bioethics: Problems and Perspectives*, op. cit., pp. 31–64.

[14] FIQH ACADEMY, Resolutions and Recommendations of the Council of the Islamic Fiqh Academy 1985–2000, Jeddah, IRTI-IDB, 2000.

marriage with the patient, such as brother and uncle….) or a husband or a trusted woman, to avoid *khalwa* (two persons of opposite sex being together in a remote place)". In addition, the Council recommends that "Due to the insufficient number of specialized female doctors in these fields, and in order to avoid having to resort to rules of exception, health authorities should do their level best in encouraging women to register in medical science studies, in the various branches of specialty, in particular gynaecology and obstetrics".

This approach applies some principles of classic Islamic family law to the doctor-patient relationship. In 2013, some resolutions made by the New Delhi Islamic Fiqh Academy (in theory the most important legal body of the approximately 140 million Muslims in India, the third largest Muslim community in the world, after Indonesia and Pakistan) strongly contested the ultra-Western positions of the Women's Committee of the United Nations on male-female equality: "The Islamic point of view is that nature itself has created differences in the capacities and strengths between men and women, so justice in place of equality is required for consolidation of family system and keeping society healthy. The responsibilities must be assigned to men according to their capacities and capabilities and the same must be the case with women. Then, rights and obligations must be specified for them in proportion to responsibilities and capabilities. For this very reason, Islam has assigned all financial burdens, maintenance of family and its protection to men and women have been exempted from them, but the man has been specified as the guardian of family and his status is as *Authority and Guardian*. All commandments concerning family life are based on this very principle[15]…this ideology of equality with all its nuances is in conflict with the law of nature and whenever a human being violates the law of nature, he faces the wrath of God".[16]

In the end, a document by the International Islamic Center for Population Studies and Research of the University of Al-Azhar (Cairo) reconfirmed the indispensable conditions for a woman to enter the world of work in respect of Muslim law and these conditions can include nursing and health work[17]: (1) before undertaking any work, the woman must have the permission of her husband or legal guardian; (2) juridical Tradition prohibits a woman from using perfume when she leaves the home; (3) a woman must wear decent dress and behave in a decent fashion; (4) she must cover her body with the exception of her face and hands in respect of the Word of God (Qur'ân 24,30–31); (5) in the event that she is eligible for marriage she must not perform work that requires her to work on her own with a stranger as this isolation may lead to undesirable consequences; (6) her work must not induce her to mingle with men in undesirable ways; (7) the type of work must correspond to the female physical and psychological constitution.

---

[15] ISLAMIC FIQH ACADEMY (India), *Juristic Decisions on some Contemporary Issues*, New Delhi, June 2014, in www.ifa-india.org, pp. 309–310.

[16] ISLAMIC FIQH ACADEMY (India), p. 311.

[17] INTERNATIONAL ISLAMIC CENTER FOR POPULATION STUDIES AND RESEARCH, *Islamic Manual of Family Planning*, Cairo, 1998, 64–66.

In the liberal-democratic systems, the principles of autonomy and equality (together with others), strongly foster women's rights and authority as being equal to those of men. This equality and autonomy in making decisions, if mechanically applied to the sphere of health care relations (e.g. in the relationship between a doctor and patient of different genders) in a traditional family-social context (e.g. Muslim), can take on a revolutionary value and risk being rejected. In fact these principles promote, directly or indirectly, a model of a woman free from many forms of legal subordination and "protection" by her husband, male relatives, etc.; a woman who is essentially free from traditional socio-religious constraints.

In the light of these considerations, bioethics (especially of a Western type) appears as an instrument of female "emancipation".

(III) One (of the very many) attempts to articulate the points of contrast between the *Universal Declaration of Human Rights* (UDHR) and Muslim law was made by the Indonesian Council of Ulama with the National Deliberation *Fatwa* No. 6/MUNAS VI/MUI/2000 issued in Jakarta on July 29th, 2000 (Indonesia is the most populated Islamic country with more than 200 million Muslim believers). Similarly to many other Muslim documents, the MUI formally accepts the general principles of the UDHR but, at the same time, puts forward structural objections on its contents.[18]

In the preambles to the deliberation, point (B) recalls that "Human Rights are not applicable in a vacuum space and so far, there has not been any consensus in understanding, the interpretation and the application of Human Rights so that each country is enabled to give its interpretation and comprehension corresponding to its prevailing culture and ethical values and legislation". (C) "...the clauses of the Universal Declaration of Human Rights are impressed to really put rights and individual freedom in priority and ignore the balance between right and obligation, the balance between individual and public interest, as well as the balance between freedom and responsibility". Point D) lists some points of the UDHR that are unacceptable for Islam: ".. (a) Article 16 Clauses 1 and 2 about freedom in looking for couple, marriage and divorce, (b) Section 18 about freedom to change religion; (c) Section 23 about work".

Due to these premises, the Indonesian Council considered it necessary to issue a *fatwâ* (legal opinion) about *the limits to perform Human Rights* dealing with the general conditions to be respected for the UDHR to be accepted:

1. ...
   (a) Appreciating and respecting difference in comprehension and interpretation as well as its implementation based on culture, morality and legislation prevailed in each country;

[18]The Indonesian Council of *Ulama's Fatwa* on Population, Reproductive Health and Family Planning, Center for International Training and Collaboration, National Family Planning Coordinating Board, 2010, Jakarta, ISBN: 978-602-8068-52-9, pp. 15–20.

(b) The … implementation of Human Rights must notice the following points: (1) The balance between individual rights and individual obligations; (2) The balance between individual rights and public rights; (3) The balance between freedom rights and responsibilities.

2. Due to Clause 16 Article 1 & 2 and Clause 18 of UDHR the Moslems must abide closely to Islamic teachings because the freedom to practise religious teachings is a part of Human Rights.
3. Obliging Government and the Moslems, … to socialize the Human Rights corresponding to the values of religion, culture and ethics among the society as well as the prevailing legislation in Indonesia.

(IV) So-called *Westernization* is denounced by Resolution No. 38 (13/4) concerning the Recommendations of the Fourth Session of the Council of the Islamic Fiqh [Muslim law] Academy, Fourth session, Jeddah (Kingdom of Saudi Arabia), (February, 6 to 11, 1988)[19]:

FIRST:
RECOMMENDS......

c) That practical plan be worked out to safeguard the authenticity and Islamic Heritage; abort all attempts at Westernization, imitation and elimination of Islamic identity; to face all forms of challenges, to combat intellectual and cultural invasion which does not conform to Islamic principles and ethics...

d) The education must be Islam-oriented; that all sciences be taught from an Islamic angle; that religious subjects be basic subjects at all stages and all specialties; in order to uphold the Islamic doctrine and root Islamic ethics in spirit and enable the *Ummah* [Islamic community] to constantly remain at the vanguard in all fields of science.

e) That the Muslim family be raised in a sound manner; ... always propagating and upholding Islam; that women be trained to undertake their role as mother and housewife; and that an end be put to the growing phenomenon of resorting to foreign governesses, in particular non-Muslim governesses.

THE COUNCIL FURTHER RECOMMENDS:

d) That the history of science and knowledge be reformulated to lay emphasis on their development and the contribution made thereto by Muslims, as well as to clear them of eastern and western theories that infiltrates into them to deviate the course of right; that the classification of sciences and research curricula be reviewed from an Islamic angle, through Islamic scientific centres and institutes and centres for Islamic economy, in the various Islamic countries.

e) That sciences which research the universe, man and life have their relationship with these fields must view them as the product of a wonderful divine creativity and perfection of his work.

f) That the controlling devices and rules emanating from Islam, or in consonance with its objectives be the principles governing all science; that the shortcoming of western curricula be stressed...

[19] FIQH ACADEMY, Resolutions and Recommendations of the Council of the Islamic Fiqh Academy 1985–2000, Jeddah, IRTI-IDB, 2000.

(V) The Resolution N° 69/7/7 concerning *Cultural Aggression* issued by the Council of the Islamic Fiqh Academy [Academy of Muslim law], Jeddah, Saudi Arabia, May 1992[20]:

RECOMMENDS THE FOLLOWING:

Second	That education and instruction curricula be purified and promoted so as to build generations on contemporary Islamic foundations and to give them the right training that would enlighten them on their religion and immunize them against all forms of cultural invasion.
Fourth	That the mosque be given its interacted educational role in the life of Muslims so that they may be able to stand up to all forms and effects of cultural invasion and to have a full and sound knowledge of their religion.
Fifth	That the doubts created by the enemies of Islam be refuted with sound scientific methods and with the believer's faith in the perfection of this religion without resorting to weak defence justificatory methods.
Twelfth:	That action be undertaken to emphasize the aspects of Muslims unity and complementary at all levels and to solve their differences and disputes through peaceful means in conformity with the well-known provisions of *Shari'a*, thereby thwarting the designs of cultural invasion aimed at fragmenting the unity of Muslims and surveying differences and disputes among them.
Thirteenth:	That action be undertaken to build Muslims strength and economic as well as military self-sufficiency.

Conclusion

Regarding the principles of bioethics and the conceptions of universal human rights, there are *at least* two trends in the Muslim world. (1) One trend that passively accepts the main concepts of the Western declarations of the last century, restricting itself to looking for their presence in the Sacred Texts. (2) A critical approach which tends to Islamize the language of the documents and introduce specifically Muslim and non-negotiable fundamental concepts.

[20] FIQH ACADEMY, Resolutions and Recommendations of the Council of the Islamic Fiqh Academy 1985–2000, Jeddah, IRTI-IDB, 2000.

Chapter 21
General Considerations About Islamic and Universal Bioethics

Nouzha Guessous

Abstract Muslims have shown great diversity in understanding and practicing Islam from very early after the Revelation to nowadays. Consequently, the way they implemented Islamic values in their daily life has been diversified and deeply changing over time and space, according to the contexts and needs of Muslim societies. Islamic Bioethics, like Islamic human rights and Islamic feminism; is increasingly claimed to be new approach for research, debates and advocacy in the specific contexts of Muslim societies. It aim to develop and promote culturally accepted rules, laws and practices based on common principles of Islamic and universal human rights. This is very possible if it is based on the contextual reading and understanding of the Qur'an that show a global coherence of the founding principles of Islam with the principles stated in the 2005-UNESCO Universal Declaration on Bioethics and Human Rights.

Muslims have shown great diversity in understanding and practicing Islam from very early after the Revelation to nowadays. Consequently, the way they implemented Islamic values in their daily life has been diversified and deeply changing over time and space, according to the contexts and needs of Muslim societies.

Taking the legal changes in Moroccan family law as a case study,[1] I will argue that the issue of cultural/religious specificities versus universal framework of human rights poses more or less the same dilemmas and controversies that it shows while dealing with bioethics. Thus, I will take advantage of my theoretical and practical experience in advocating and acting for changing laws and mentalities concerning women in Morocco and more widely in countries with Muslim majority in the discussion of Prof. Atighetchi's paper of on Islam and Bioethics.

This paper is a contribution to the discussion of the paper on "Bioethics from Islamic perspective" presented by Dr. DARIUSCH ATIGHETCHI during the Third International Conference on Bioethics, Multiculturalism and Religion (HK, 3–5 December 2013)

[1] Nouzha Guessous, "Women's rights in Muslim societies: Lessons from the Moroccan experience", Philosophy and Social Criticism, 2012, 38(4–5), pp. 525–533.

N. Guessous (✉)
Hassan II University, Casablanca, Morocco
e-mail: nouzhaguessous@gmail.com

J. Tham et al. (eds.), *Religious Perspectives on Bioethics and Human Rights*, Advancing Global Bioethics 6, DOI 10.1007/978-3-319-58431-7_21

21.1 Diversity Among Islamic Societies and Cultures

Although the statements of legislative nature (commonly called "*Shari'a*" statements) do not exceed 5% of the *Qur'an*, Islam is commonly presented as dealing not only with spirituality of Muslims but also as organizing all aspects of their individual and social life including in the fields of economy and politics. This is why it is usually qualified as "Religion and life" (*Din wa Dounia*) or religion and state (*Din wa Dawla*). This is to say that although it is derived from the *Qur'an*, *95%* of the so called "Islamic law" or "*Shari'a* based law" supposed to guide individual and collective Muslim practices as well as state legislations, is *of human origin* and reflects the understanding of particular human scholars in particular time, place and context. These understandings have been very diverse and subject to very important and interesting debates among scholars from the death of the *Prophet Muhammad* (PBUH) up till the present day.

It is important to remind that, as Prof. Atighetchi wrote, "The *Shari'a* had never been codified" (*page 1, 1st paragraph*). Furthermore, there is no consensual Islamic Supreme Authority for all Muslims. This contributed historically to a large variety of opinion among religious and legal scholars (*Ulema*), as well as among Muslims in general. From very early eighth century various schools of jurisprudence (*Fiqh*) emerged to reflect the diversity of cultural environment and they have been revising and developing their views according to the evolution of their local societies and needs. Consequently, except for the rules of practicing religious rites (prayers, fasting, pilgrimage etc.), there is a large diversity among Muslim countries not only between *Sunni* and *Shiaâ* but also among Sunnis according to the followed school of Fiqh. Thus, Muslim states have been revising and adapting their laws over the centuries. For example, in the seventh century the Caliph Omar Ibn Khattab suspended the hand amputation penalty (which is cited in the Holly *Qur'an*) because of the famine, and this suspension has been maintained up till now except in very few Muslim countries (Saudi Arabia, Iran, Sudan, Nigeria, Afghanistan and Pakistan). The situation is similar for other penalties called "*Hudud*" (literally "limits") set by the *Qur'an* that are no longer applied in the majority of Muslim countries (e.g. flagellation).

On the global level of the evolution of the Islamic thought, it may be relevant to mention that many Muslim thinkers and scholars made a great attempt to develop "*al-Fiqh al-maqãsidi*" starting from the eleventh Century with *al-Ghazali*, followed and developed in the fourteenth Century by *al-Shatibi*. By seeking the comprehensive underlying objectives of *Shar'ia (maqâsid)* and through an innovative reading (*Ijtihad maqâsidi*) of the Islamic frame of reference, they attempted to rationalize both theology and law in order to act in the (best) interests of humankind. This approach allowed important changes in the application of penal rules derived from the Qur'an or the *Sunnah*. Modern thinkers from early twentieth Century[2] have fol-

[2] Mohammed Iqbal, "The Reconstruction Of Religious Thought In Islam", 1930, Oxford Edition, ISBN 8171510817.

lowed and developed this approach, notably in the issue of individual rights and especially women's rights and family law, showing a clear convergence with universal human rights set out in international instruments. Through this inductive reading of scripture, it is possible to set up some general values and principles to be implemented in norms compatible with current social needs.[3]

The social transformations induced by the industrial and technological revolution in the twentieth Century, have deepened the gap between the still dominant "traditional" beliefs, discourse and culture on one hand, and the "modern" daily life on the other hand. Without questioning their religious Islamic references, most of Muslim countries have implemented to some extent "secular" public law in criminal, commercial, administrative and civil domains (the greatest controversies and resistance are found in family laws issues). This has been promoted by the emergence and spread of universal human rights philosophy and law, driven and powered by the globalization of communication and technologies in general. Although I fully agree with the cultural impact of the globalized new technologies, I do not share the idea of Prof. Atighetchi that this evolution is a "Western universalistic aggression/assault" or that the main consequence of this is the "occultation and disappearance" of cultural diversity.

21.2 Bioethical Issues in Muslim Societies and Cultures

In Bioethics, like in human rights in general, one of the most conflictive questions is the compatibility between universal and Muslim religious/traditions/culture-related values. As said by Abdulaziz Sachedina and Nageen Ainuddin "there is a common widespread 'misconception' that follows common Islamic opinions and beliefs to say that as bioethics is dealing with life and death issues, it should be exclusively driven by religious expertise, and that Islamic Bioethics is a sub-field of the Islamic jurisprudence (*Fiqh*)."

In fact, ethics is more concerned with the moral reasoning and assessment of an act in terms of its benefit or harm for the patient, for the society, for the environment and for future generations. Bioethics as conceived by Potter (1970) is a multidisciplinary approach aiming to make a "bridge" between "Scientific Facts" and "Moral Values" that can be identified amongst all peoples and societies, and that are based and promoted by religions, cultural traditions and history. This is to say that, although religious values are the sources of bioethical principles and norms, bioethical deliberation needs to take into account the risk/benefit of a medical decision or a scientific technology both on individual and social and humanity levels, as well as the moral values at stake. In other words, bioethical issues in the Muslim context cannot be exclusively driven by the *Fiqh* since both scientific knowledge and technology as well as moral values are constantly evolving.

---

[3] "Gender and Equality in Muslim Family Law. Justice and Ethics in the Islamic Legal Tradition" 2013, Edited by Ziba Mir-Hosseini et al., I.B.TAURIS, ISBN 978 1 84885 922 7.

Islamic Bioethics (like Islamic human rights and Islamic feminism) is increasingly claimed to be new approaches for research, debates and advocacy in the specific contexts of Muslim societies, aiming to develop culturally accepted rules and practices based on common principles of Islamic and universal human rights. As mentioned before, distinguished Muslim thinkers have made alternative approaches, based on the founding principles and ethics of Islam.[4] By a contextual reading and analysis of the *Qur'an* and by searching for the objectives aimed at by its statements of legislative dimension, they endorsed the Universal Human Rights philosophy and the UN Corpus as globally compatible with Islam.

In most majority Muslim states, legislation, research and debates on bioethical issues remain very recent. The UNESCO Cairo Office conducted a survey of national regulations in ten topics of bioethics and genetics from September 2007 to May 2009 in 17 member states of the UNESCO Arab Region, concluding that there was a lack of awareness combined with lack and/or inefficiency of existing regulations.[5]

It seems to me that the diversity of sociological, legal and political situations has more impact on the way Muslim societies face the dilemmas brought by the developments and globalization of science and technologies than the common "Islamic heritage," although they are using the same sources of regulation, i.e. the *Qur'an*, the Prophetic *Sunnah* and the *Fiqh*. It is not unusual to observe that what is legal in one Muslim country may be illegal in another. For instance, regarding research on embryonic stem cells, Iran as a *Shiî* Muslim state has more "liberal" views and guidelines than *Sunni* states and is even more liberal than many Western countries.

Most recommendations on biomedical questions are produced by the Islamic Organization of Medical Sciences (IOMS) and the OIC-Islamic *Fiqh* Academy, aiming to keep the general trends of Islamic Medical Ethics in step with scientific progress as long as public benefits and fundamental Islamic principles are not endangered. From an inside observation, I would say that these recommendations are usually seen as not binding on either Muslim practitioners or patients, and that their impact is limited on Muslim State's stakeholders. At individual and small community level, a specific opinion of a religious scholar "*fatwā*" may even be more important.

Finally, I think that the impact of the biomedicine market at the international level may even be more important.

---

[4] Abdullahi Ahmed An-na'im, « Islam and the Secular State, Negociating the future of Shari'a", 2008, Harvard University Press.

[5] Ethics and Law in Biomedicine and Genetics: *An Overview of National Regulations in the Arab States UNESCO Cairo Office 2011 –EG/2011/SS/PI/01 – ISBN 978-92-3-104211-9.*

21.3 Building Islamic Bioethics on Islamic Values and Principles

This has been the approach of UNESCO. The International Bioethics Committee (IBC) with other organizations have worked on identifying bioethical principles derived from universal human rights philosophy that can be implemented more concretely in different cultural and social contexts. This ended in October 2005 with the adoption of the *Universal Declaration on Bioethics and Human Rights* by UNESCO member states including those where Islam is the dominant religion. Fifteen principles derived from universal human rights philosophy have been proclaimed as universal principles of bioethics, and as such, they should be implemented in all member states with respect for cultural diversity (Article 12), More, respect for cultural diversity cannot be invoqued to infringe upon the other principles, like non-discrimination and non –stigmatization setted in article 11.[6]

The four bioethical principles of autonomy, beneficence, non maleficence and justice are supported by Qur'anic verses and thus have been legitimized by many Muslim jurists as falling into the sphere of Islamic principles. They have subsequently become the foundational spirit underlying most versions of the *Oath of the Muslim Physicians* and thus dictate the conduct between a Muslim physician and his or her patient.

A holistic approach to the Holy *Qur'an* shows values and principles underlying Islam's spirit that are and should be called upon by Muslim bioethicists. Several verses of the *Qur'an* call on human dignity (*Al- Karama Al- Insaniya*) as the foundation for the sanctity of human life and the duty of preservation of health, equity and justice (*Al- A'dl*) with clear reference to distributive justice and solidarity, equality and non-discrimination, love and compassion (*Mawadda wa Rahma*), individual autonomy and responsibility, solidarity (*Attaâoune*) and respect for environment as a common will of all living organisms. Based upon these values and principles, several methodological maxims and tools have been developed by Muslim scholars for producing rulings (*ahkâm*) by deduction from the sacred text or the *Sunnah*. As examples, I will mention the duties of beneficience (*Al Ihsan, Al Istihsan*), nonmaleficence (*La Darar wa la Dirar*), avert probable harm (*Dafa'e al;-darar al muhtamal*), priority to necessity (*Addarura tubih al mahzurah*), and public interest (*Al Maslaha*), etc.

Using this holistic approach of the spirit of Islam, it is quite possible to agree on a core of universal principles of bioethics that are deeply compatible with Islamic principles.[7]

---

[6] Nouzha Guessous, In "Non Discrimination and stigmatization, in Handbook of Global Bioethics", 2014, pp. 139–151, Springer Publishing.

[7] Abdullahi Ahmed An-Na'im, "On the incompatability of Islam and human rights" 2010, ABC Religion and Ethics, http://www.abc.net.au/religion/articles/2010/07/06/2945813.htm

Nevertheless, the challenge will remain in implementing them practically through laws, guidelines and practices according to the specific contexts and needs of each Muslim society or group. In other words, we must recognize that despite the fact that all Muslims believe in the same religion, there is much diversity among Muslim societies and that this must be taken into account.

Chapter 22
Response to Darius Atighetchi's Paper on the Islamic Position

Gonzalo Miranda

Darius Atighetchi's paper is connoted by "fear": fear that Islam could be "colonized" by other cultures; and specifically fear for the danger of corruption of Islam because of the paradigm of "human rights" as a product of Western culture. The text begins with the complaint of "Western-international colonization" and it ends by quoting the same concern, clearly and loudly expressed by some major Islamic organizations.

Speaking of "colonization", I would like to say that the concept indicates an active and voluntary attitude to dominate a population, politically or culturally. It is different from the phenomenon of the influence a civilization exerts over the others. Possibly, some people or groups have a truly "colonial" attitude, but this is not always the case.

There has always been "contamination" or influences among cultures. The classical Greek philosophy came to the West via the Arabs (for example, through the contribution of the school of translators in Toledo, Spain). This mutual influence is today much stronger, because of the modern phenomenon of globalization.

It is not always true that all and every element imported from another culture transmits its values and principles. Atighetchi says: "I would like to recall that a computer, a plane, a car, a shirt, a syringe, a Computer Assisted Tomography (CAT) etc., instruments are not neutral." Europe received gunpowder from China, without receiving a profound influence on its culture. The use of powder changed many things; but if it had come from Africa instead of China, it would not have made a different cultural impact.

The same can be said about many inventions and instruments coming from different cultures. I honestly do not know how the computer can be a religious and even a cultural vehicle of the United States to the rest of the world. Again, it has changed many things, but it has not been a contaminated the world with American identity.

G. Miranda (✉)
School of Bioethics, Ateneo Pontificio Regina Apostolorum, Rome, Italy
e-mail: g.miranda@arcol.org

J. Tham et al. (eds.), *Religious Perspectives on Bioethics and Human Rights*, Advancing Global Bioethics 6, DOI 10.1007/978-3-319-58431-7_22

We must understand that human beings always seek and use the best things we invent or discover: the wheel, agriculture, the use of horse carts, cars, gunpowder, and technological advances. It is impossible to avoid this phenomenon. And there is no good reason to avoid it.

Something similar could be said about concepts, ideas, principles and values. Atighetchi seems to link the progressive cultural dominance of the West to its economic and technological strength. We should ask whether it is not also due to the greater perfection of some of its principles (human rights, democracy, equality for all, equality between men and women, etc.). There may be principles, traditions and laws that are more responsive to the essential tendencies of all human beings, and therefore they take root, flourish and spread.

In fact, Atighetchi seems to admit this when he says: "There is a cultural evolution which makes some cultures […] prevail over others apparently condemned to be absorbed or disappear. In a theological vision of history, this is all part of a divine plan."

Atighetchi seems to think that the recognition of cultural diversity in art. 12 of the *Universal Declaration on Bioethics and Human Rights* is only motivated to avoid criticism, as if it does not express a real conviction of those who wrote and reviewed the text. If so, I disagree. I believe—based also upon personal experience with the revision process in Paris (2004–2005)—that the text of Article 12 expresses the deep conviction of many participants.

Nor do I agree with him that Article 12 expresses an attitude of considering other cultures as inferior, for the very fact that it says different cultures must be "protected." Before saying that cultures must be protected, the Article says that they must be "respected." Something must be respected because it has a value; and something must be protected because that value may be at risk. The Article does not say that the strongest or highest cultures should protect the weaker or lower ones, but rather establishes that we should protect a culture from possible invasion of others.

With regard to the claim that Islam is not a monotheism "equal" to others and that is a "superior" religion, because it's the last and final revelation, let me make a brief comment. Neither does Christianity consider other religions to be equal or superior. Christians are convinced that the other religious traditions are missing something essential, since they do not know that God became man and saved humanity by the incarnation and sacrifice of Jesus Christ. However, Christians are convinced of the equality of all human beings and their right to the same respect. Respect is not due, strictly speaking, to religious or cultural elements, but to persons of whatever religion or cultural background. One can quote here the answer that G. K. Chesterton gave in a public debate in England. When his opponent told him that he had to respect his ideas, Chesterton answered, "Your ideas deserve no respect. I respect you, not your ideas."

If it is the case that the principles, values, customs and laws of Islam are most perfect, there should not be fear of cultural contamination or domination: they will win on their own.

To say that there are "many universals" is the same as saying they are no universals. I do not think that we should deny that there are truly universal values or principles, valid for all human beings, even if we always have a partial understanding of them. Therefore it is possible to dialogue and seek common elements. First, we should discuss the elements already recognized as common. Next, we should confront the elements in which we diverge, recognizing that, through discussion and argumentation, we could eventually reach a common understanding.

One important point, I believe, is that we should recognize the human dimension of religion. God gave us the ability to understand and choose. Revelation does not remove that capacity and necessity. In fact, various interpretations of sacred texts are possible, which shows that there is always human mediation.

Yesterday, Professor Aasim Padela explained in his paper that there are different "schools of theology" among the Sunni Islamic believers, and they are different from the Shia Islamic theological schools. In fact, whenever a Muslim talks about bioethics in Islam, he or she stresses that they do not have a "Magisterial teaching" or a unified school. In other words, there are several interpretations of many points. This, I think is simply inevitable, and it happens in all faiths and religious traditions, as well as among secular thinkers.

I think that the problem of "fear" reflected in the text of Atighetchi and in the documents he cited, is partly linked to the understanding of religion as a totalizing reality that goes beyond religion (cfr. the expression "Religion and State" quoted in his text). If religion gets back to its essentials (faith in God, understanding the ultimate meaning of existence, profound values, search for the moral good, etc.), then it can adapt to different cultures, environments, and technological developments, etc. It may also be open to the paradigm of "human rights."

This does not mean that we should assume and accept all the so-called "rights" in a naïve way, without any criticism. On the contrary, each person must be open in a "critical way" to the proposal of human rights, and to any specific rights presented as such. And if it should be the attitude of every single person, it should also be the attitude of every human community, including every religious community. This dynamic critical attitude can help us all to look for the truth while engaging in an open and frank dialogue.

Part VIII
Monotheistic Religions: Judaism

Chapter 23
Between Humaneness and Human Rights: A Jewish Perspective on Modern Bioethics

David Heyd

23.1 Right-Based vs. Duty-Based Morality

At a first glance it seems that rights and duties are mutually dependent, or in the language of philosophers – "correlative": if I have a duty to tell you the truth, you have the parallel right (against me) not to be told lies, and vice versa; if a doctor has a duty to treat people even if they do not have money, the poor have a right to be medically treated, and vice versa. But this correlativity is obviously not universal. For example, I may have a duty to procreate (as is the case in the very first commandment in Genesis 1: 28), although there is no parallel right of non-existent people to be born; or I may have a natural right to property, even if I live on a desert island with no one having a duty to avoid transgressing my holdings, let alone provide me with a piece of land. Furthermore, even if there is some correlation of rights and duties, the direction of dependence of the one upon the other demonstrates that rights and duties are not simply two sides of the same coin. Thus, the duty of the government not to restrict my expression is *derived* from my right to free speech (rather than the other way round, i.e. it is not the case that the right to freedom of speech is derived from the duty of governments not to intervene in speech)[1]; on the other hand, the right of individuals in the Lockean state of nature to punish those who violate the laws of nature derives from the duty of individuals to avoid violating these laws (rather than the other way round, i.e. it is not the case that the duty of individuals to stick to the laws of nature is derived from the right of others to punish them for doing so).

[1] Despite the disagreement regarding the source of this right – whether it lies in our inborn nature, our autonomy, a hypothetical contract or human dignity – all philosophers who recognize the right of free expression would deny that this source is the duty of the government to avoid interfering with people's expression.

D. Heyd (✉)
The Hebrew University, Jerusalem
e-mail: david.heyd@mail.huji.ac.il

J. Tham et al. (eds.), *Religious Perspectives on Bioethics and Human Rights*, Advancing Global Bioethics 6, DOI 10.1007/978-3-319-58431-7_23

Ronald Dworkin coined the terms "right-based" and "duty-based" normative theories to characterize the significant difference between two opposite approaches to the justification of norms.[2] What makes the difference is which of the two terms – rights or duties – is *fundamental* and justified by reasons other than the other term. For example, right-based Kantian or Rawlsian contract theory or constitutional law are justified in terms of the value of *autonomy*; duty-based religious ethics is based on the value of *obedience to God*. Accordingly, the reason for the right of civil disobedience, for instance, is not the duty of the state to tolerate it, but some independent principle (like the principle of individual conscience). But the duty of the state to abstain from interfering with the individual's faith or private life *is* based on the right of the individual. Or, the reason for the duty to follow the Ten Commandments cannot be derived from the right of God to be obeyed, because God cannot be said to have "rights". It must be the independent principle of the created being obedient to the creator, recognizing his authority. Thus, the two alternative ways of reasoning about the justification of norms – starting with rights and deriving correlative duties from them, or starting with duties and inferring rights from them – are not only methodologically different from each other but, as we shall see, in potential conflict with each other.

I want to claim that religious and modern (often called "Western") bioethics stand in sharp contrast to each other as duty-based vs. right-based normative systems. Religion in general, and the Jewish religion in particular, are founded on duties and commandments which derive their authority from a metaphysical, divine source. Interestingly, the Hebrew word for religion, DAT (דת), means *law* in its original Persian source (going back to Sanskrit) and is associated with the Latin "datum/data" (given).[3] Religion, in other words, is a system of laws which are given to human beings rather than legislated by them. The Jewish religion has no official theology or dogmatic thinking. Its core content is constituted by commandments (*mitzvoth*) which cover all aspects of individual and social life and following them is the core expression of a person's religious commitment. Of course this does not mean that the commandments relating to behaviour towards other people are arbitrary or independent of the status of those to whom they are owed. They definitely tally with the conception of human beings as having been created in the image of God and hence deserving of respect and dignity. However, these values differ from natural rights in the modern sense which are constituted by the essential property of being human (i.e. being free and autonomous) and serve as the basis for *claims* made by individuals on their fellow beings.

Modern medical ethics, at least as we know it from the past 50 years, is a subfield of ethics which is typically (even if not exclusively) right-based, relating to *rights* such as informed consent, control over one's life and body, privacy,

---

[2] Ronald Dworkin, *Taking Rights Seriously* (Cambridge, MA: Harvard University Press, 1977), pp. 171ff. Dworkin applies the distinction to political theories, but it can be equally employed to characterize moral theories, as I will do here.

[3] See The Oxford English Dictionary ("datum") and *The Book of Esther* (in the Hebrew Scriptures), 3: 8.

confidentiality, procreative freedom, etc. The development of this field in the 1950s was particularly focused on the practices of experimentation on human subjects, abortion and euthanasia and were normatively driven by the newly raised role of the patient's consent, the respect for the patient's will and the general constraints imposed by the treated person on the manner in which she is treated. These so-called patient's rights challenged the traditional paternalistic model of doctor-patient relationship as well as the principle of the sanctity of life that is independent of the will of the individual. This is was a reversal of the traditional medico-ethical approach in which the duties of the doctor were justified in terms of either religious commandments, the good (of the patient or of society), or of the integrity of the profession itself (as typically expressed by the Hippocratic Oath), which later has become associated with the virtue-ethics approach to bioethics.

23.2 The Development of the Jewish Attitude Towards Medical Practice

Jewish medical ethics is, accordingly, typically duty-based and we will explore later on the tension created by the challenge of modern bioethics which is typically right-based. But even the duty-based view of medical practice was for centuries a matter of controversy. In the Hebrew Scriptures (i.e. the Old Testament), the sole "doctor" is God himself. Although there are some stories of human intervention in cases of malady, it is usually undertaken by prophets (Elisha and Isaiah), that is to say, under God's power and instruction.[4] Medicine is not recognized as a separate profession and ordinary people trying to cure illnesses are suspected of transgressing the sovereignty of God.[5] It should be noted, though, that the Torah does have a notion of health which underlies prescriptions and proscriptions relating to purity of the body, particularly in sexual activity and food consumption. In modern eyes these could be interpreted as a kind of preventive medicine.

Later on, under Stoic influence, Jewish views of illness and cure in the Talmudic literature (in the first few centuries of the Christian era) consider illness as either a matter of divine providence, or of fatalistic necessity, or of materialistic deterministic causation – none of which can be controlled by human beings. The Talmud's hostile attitude to medicine is encapsulated in the famous saying that "the best of

---

[4] Most typical is the story of Na'aman, chief commander of the King of Aram's army, who was afflicted by leprosy. The prophet Elisha instructs him to bathe seven times in the river Jordan and the plagued general is completely cured. The divine nature of Elisha's therapeutic capacities is highlighted by his refusal to get any remuneration for his medical advice: "As the Lord lives, whom I serve, I will not accept anything" (II Kings, 5: 16). The prophet is just a mediator between God and the patient. He has no medical skills of his own.

[5] "In the thirty-ninth year of his reign, Asa suffered from an acute foot ailment; but ill as he was, he still did not turn to the Lord but to physicians". II Chronicles 16: 12. (The following verse tells us that Asa died 2 years later, but there is no hint whether the timing of death had to do with his appeal to physicians rather than to God).

doctors deserves hell".[6] This peculiar proverbial aphorism is almost universally interpreted by later commentators in much more qualified and less negative terms (for example, that the saying applies only to physicians whose motivation is malice, or that doctors who cause death due to a mistake are not liable in civil or criminal court but only before God). As can be understood from the following passage, there is a transition from the general prohibition to heal to a more permissive attitude.

> On going in to be cupped one should say: 'May it be Thy will, O Lord, my God, that this operation may be a cure for me, and mayest Thou heal me, for Thou art a faithful healing God, and Thy healing is sure, since men have no power to heal, but this is a habit with them'. Abaye said: A man should not speak thus, since it was taught in the school of R. Ishmael: [It is written], He shall cause him to be thoroughly healed. From this we learn that permission has been given to the physician to heal.[7]

From a plain prohibition on human healing, which is considered a transgression, we move to the first a sign of a more conciliatory attitude towards the human "habit" (of getting such healing services as a matter of human psychological need), and then to a straightforward principled permission to practice human healing as a delegation of divine power. Furthermore, in the debate between the rabbis about whether to feed someone who says he does not need food though the doctor says he should eat, the tendency of the rabbis is that "he should be fed according to the experts" (namely, the physicians) rather than follow the wishes of the patient.[8] And even those who say that one should follow the patient's choice justify their view by an appeal to a quasi-medical argument, viz. that the patient's inner feeling should be trusted. It is not anymore a theologically grounded hostility to human medical intervention as such.

The development of the positive attitude to medical treatment was gradual, and the debate about the legitimacy of medical practice ended only some time in the high middle ages. Ibn Ezra (twelfth century) rules that the doctor may only treat external injuries (rather than internal syndromes), and Nahmanides holds a peculiar position that the doctor is permitted to treat but the patient is prohibited from undergoing treatment. But ultimately, the doctor is conceived as the delegate of God which grants him not only a permission to heal but imposes on him a positive duty to do so. The view of Maimonides, the famous philosopher and interpreter of Jewish law (1135–1204), is that since God's intentions and design are expressed in the world through the laws of nature, the use of science to cure illness by understanding and manipulating natural causation is not only allowed but also the ultimate religious acknowledgement of divine providence.[9] And together with the physician's duty there is a positive duty of the patient to seek medical treatment.[10]

---

[6] *Babylonian Talmud*, Tractate Kiddushin, 82a.

[7] Tractate Berachot, p. 60a.

[8] Tractate Yoma, p. 83a.

[9] For a good exposition and analysis of this Maimonidean view, see Noam Zohar, *Jewish Bioethics* (Albany: State University of New York Press, 1997), pp. 29–31.

[10] For these stages in the development of post Talmudic medical ethics, see Julius Preuss, *Biblical and Talmudic Medicine* (Jerusalem: Magnes Press, 2012), chap. 1. [This is a Hebrew translation of the original 1911 book published in German].

The growing appreciation of the medical art is primarily motivated by the fundamental value assigned to human life. The basic term in this context is *pikuach nefesh*. Its origin is the early debate whether it is permitted for a Jew on the Sabbath (in which all work is prohibited) to uncover an individual buried under a pile of stones which have fallen on him so as to save his life. The answer is positive and the rule is that it is not only permitted but also a duty due to the sanctity of life which overrides even the holiness of the Sabbath. The idea is that one should live by Torah law rather than die for it. The particular example of the removal of stones is then extended to all circumstances of saving lives and particularly to medical practice, and its scope widened so as to apply to any significant risk of losing life or undermining its prospects. This opens the way to a full endorsement of medical treatment as obligatory also from the religious point of view.

> The [laws of] the Sabbath are suspended in the face of a danger to life, as are [the obligations of] the other mitzvot. Therefore, we may perform – according to the directives of a professional physician of that locale – everything that is necessary for the benefit of a sick person whose life is in danger.
>
> When there is a doubt whether or not the Sabbath laws must be violated on a person's behalf, one should violate the Sabbath laws on his behalf, for the Sabbath laws are suspended even when there is merely a question of danger to a person's life.[11]

Nowadays there are only very few and marginal remnants of the old hostile attitude to medical intervention, but the support of medical treatment on the basis of the principle of life's sanctity has become so widely interpreted that it covers also the permission of IVF treatment, PGD, abortions that serve to save the life and health of the mother, and even – although it may sound paradoxical – some limited forms of euthanasia in extreme terminal cases.[12] Medicine should not only be allowed to save life but also to positively promote it.

23.3 From Duties to Rights

Despite its current highly pro-active attitude to medicine, Jewish bioethics is still typically duty-based. The sick person ought to seek treatment while the doctor's duty is to apply it. There is no general right to health and patients have no particular rights against their physicians. There is nothing surprising in this absence of the

---

[11] Maimonides, *Mishneh Torah* (trans. Eliyahu Touger), Shabbos, chap. 2, article 1. Maimonides goes out of his way to emphasize the principle of the sanctity of life in declaring that even a hundred Sabbaths should be violated in order to save one life.

[12] Pain and suffering have no religious meaning in the Jewish view and hence not only should be relieved even when this involves a violation of another commandment, but also totally avoided in extreme cases by allowing for example a woman whose anguish of further births is particularly great to get contraceptive pills, or for a dying person to get no treatment which would just prolong his suffering. See Immanuel Jakobovits, *Jewish Medical Ethics* (New York: Bloch Publishers, 1959), chap. 8.

language of rights from religious discourse. Rights as we understand them are the product of seventeenth-century philosophical culture in Europe. It is a modern concept. But beyond that, even after its integration in modern liberal worldview, it has not been easily incorporated in religious thought in general and that of Judaism in particular. For rights are claims that human beings have against each other, or against the state; but it would be absurd to make claims against God. Rights particularly call for the protection of the interests of an individual from competing interests of other individuals (or the state); but God has no competing interests against which a human being must be protected. Rights are not derived from duties but rather *impose* duties on others.[13] Obviously, human beings cannot impose duties on God and hence can have no rights against Him. Rights are characteristically mutual, that is people have at least the same human rights against each other. But this reciprocity cannot apply to the relation between humans and God. There is something intrinsically alien in the concept of rights in the sphere of religious, duty-based ethics.

Furthermore, even within the relations between human beings, such as doctor and patient, rights do not serve as a normative basis for the conduct of the two sides. The ultimate ground for medical practice is the value of human life (and health) – not on the individual's preferences and desires. In other words, the starting point in the traditional, duty-based conception of medical practice is the objective value of life and health rather than the free choice of the individual, namely her *autonomy* or her liberty to plan her life as she sees fit. Consent plays a major role in medical treatment and is an almost absolute constraint from the liberal point of view. Hence, there cannot be from that perspective any general duty to subject oneself to medical treatment, even under life threatening circumstances. This of course cannot be accepted by religious medical ethics, especially in the Jewish tradition which puts such a premium on life itself and its preservation. Autonomy is anchored in voluntariness which is the core of individualism. But these principles lie outside the religious framework which does not recognize the individual and his will as a source of intrinsic value.

With all its modernization and sophistication, the current religious literature in Jewish bioethics avoids almost completely the notion of rights. Although the word used to designate rights in modern Hebrew, *zechut*, is an old Hebrew word, it originally meant something else – moral credit or merit. It is only with recent liberal political and jurisprudential discourse that the term has become to be used to refer to right in the sense of claim. This change of meaning seems to express a deep transformation in ethical view. For merit or credit are essentially *differential*, or even elitist, while claim rights are essentially egalitarian and universal. There are contemporary Jewish thinkers who try to show that Judaism leaves an essential place for human autonomy and responsibility since the nature of God can be described only through the mediation of the *human* endeavor to recognize God. But even in their attempt to reconcile liberal autonomy with traditional Jewish theology, the ultimate approach is duty- rather than right-based, since the ultimate goal of this

[13] Joseph Raz, *The Morality of Freedom* (Oxford: Clarendon Press, 1986), p. 181.

attempt is a matter of value rather than of right.[14] However, in medical ethics this shift of meaning in the term "right" is of less ethical consequence, since, as I wish to argue, the difference between the duty-based and the right-based bioethical norms is not as significant as one might think from abstract theoretical reflection. In other words, my understanding is that in bioethics the Jewish religious approach, despite its different discourse from the secular-liberal one, can more easily integrate modern secular principles than in other spheres of social and political life (such as those pertaining to constitutional rights and the democratic procedure, education, or gender equality).

In his comment on my paper Hans Ucko expresses doubt as to the very usefulness of the project of involving religious and inter-religious thought in contemporary bioethical discourse. For he claims that religions have no answers to dilemmas which have risen only in the very recent past. There is a sense in which he is obviously correct: no religion could have thought about genetic enhancement or cloning, organ donation and brain death, vaccination of whole populations and heroic measures of prolonging one's life. However, religious thinking is rich in general principles and reflects systems of values with which it might be intellectually fruitful to engage even from a secular point of view. After all, liberal thinking has not had any more chance to develop principles for dealing with those bioethical issues than theological thinking. Furthermore, it may be politically unwise to ignore religious thinking about bioethical matters since social regulation of medical practice should take into account the beliefs of significant sectors in particular societies. As we shall see in the last section of this article, the universal point of view of human rights cannot disregard particular cultural and religious norms and values even if they compete with the universal right-based approach.

Coming back to so-called Jewish bioethics, I propose the following explanation for its adaptability to current ethical standards of Western democratic countries and international forums. The fundamental view of human beings in the Jewish tradition is originally egalitarian: all human beings are created in the image of God, a fact which grants them all with a basically equal moral standing. Every human being has dignity which is derived from his or her pure "human-ness", i.e. belonging to the privileged species in nature. Distinctions between people of different religious status come only after the fundamental dignity of human beings as such has been recognized and respected. And since life is the basic starting point, medicine is more easily accepted as a universal practice than practices and institutions which are concerned with more particular values than that of life itself. Thus, although the Jewish religion has little place for the idea of human or individual rights, the principle of *humaneness* plays an important role in it. Humanity stands at the pinnacle of creation. Beyond its particularistic character expressed in the special duties imposed on those belonging to the Jewish people, the overall value of human existence lies in the universal ideal of spreading God's image through the procreation of human beings. Pro-creation is the closest human beings can get to the act of creation.

---

[14] Lenn Goodman, *Judaism, Human Rights and Human Values* (Oxford: Oxford University Press, 1998).

According to my interpretation of modern Jewish bioethics, we might refer to the relation between the autonomy- or right-based liberal approach to medical ethics and the religious, duty-based approach in terms of what philosophers call "extensional equivalence".[15] This means that there is an overlap in the *content* of the norms guiding the practice of medicine in at least many of its fields and circumstances, although the *grounds* or justification of these norms lie in completely different sources. Bioethics is a most interesting test case for this phenomenon. Take for example abortion. The permission to get an abortion is justified by liberal bioethics in terms of the right of the woman over her body, while the orthodox Jewish approach justifies it in terms of the danger to the physical and mental health of the mother. Or take organ donation. Liberal bioethics grounds the practice in terms of the autonomy of the person to decide what to do with her body after her death, whereas many Jewish religious authorities are happy to accept the norms and regulations of organ donation on the basis of the priority of the value of life over that of the integrity of the corpse. Or, a third, interesting example is reproductive technologies such as sperm donation, IVF and even surrogate motherhood, which have been lately endorsed by mainstream Jewish rabbis on the basis of their potential contribution to the increased chance of procreating, whereas the standard liberal reasoning appeals primarily to the desire of the prospective parents to have a child, or to fulfill their own life plans which include parenthood.

Note that this equivalence or overlap is in our context only partial and contingent, and hence fragile (because it is not "principled"). The religious approach to abortion and euthanasia may be much more restrictive in scope and hence only partly overlap that of liberal attitudes, and hence, as we shall see, the specific legal regulations of the medical practice may still be contested also on the substantive level and may call for compromise. Nevertheless, the relation between the two perspectives is dynamic in the sense that they constantly influence each other. Traditional religious judgment is tempered by the beneficial prospects of new technologies as well as by liberal culture, while the autonomy principle is constrained by values which lie beyond individual choice and often are derived from religious tradition. Liberal thinkers often resort to traditional values in fixing a "wedge" in a slippery slope which is created by a new technology (like genetic manipulation which is so far allowed only through screening for serious hereditary disease but not for the purpose of enhancement).

I could go on with many more examples of such convergence or equivalence of actual acceptance of new norms in medical practice which originate in radically different reasoning and justifying principles. For this convergence can be generalized to duty-based and right-based norms in doctor-patient relationship across the board. The right of the patient to get medical help overlaps with the duty of the doctor to lend such help. The duty of confidentiality, derived from the physician's Hippocratic Oath, is the other side of the coin of the patient's right to privacy – at least in terms of the *content* of the sphere of secrecy. But the surprising thing in extensional

[15] The term was originally coined in the context of distinctions between two versions of utilitarianism by David Lyons in his *Forms and Limits of Utilitarianism* (Oxford: Clarendon Press, 1965).

equivalence is that despite the convergence in the actual norms accepted by the two parties, the general principles underlying this acceptance might not merely be different but straightforwardly contradictory or incompatible. For example, autonomy might be regarded as a human hubris by religious views while obedience to a transcendent authority may be considered by liberals as lacking rational and hence moral justification. This is why the convergence itself remains shaky.

In their comment on my paper, Jonathan and Adina Halevy rightly hail the spirit of compromise which characterizes much of the process of regulation and legislation on bioethical matters in Israel. I nevertheless want to distinguish between *compromise* and convergence (or extensional equivalence) because both are relevant to the prospect of partly bridging the gap between the religiously committed and the liberal, secular sectors in society. Convergence cannot be intentionally created. It is either there or it isn't. It may be the outcome of a long process of mutual impact of two ideologies, as I believe is the case in the Judeo-Christian tradition of the last centuries, but it is a given. Compromise, on the other hand, is a pragmatic choice of people who cannot reach a principled agreement but share the interest to form a fair and effective solution to a problem of policy or regulation. Unlike the "cultural" (ideological) nature of convergence, compromise is typically political. Now, although there is an ad hoc nature to compromise, it may be grounded in the general phenomenon of the more systematic convergence. Thus, the general agreement on the importance of organ donation may drive the two sectors to compromise on the particular rules of the way to decide brain death (such as the involvement of a religious authority in the decision). Or, if there is some shared view about the futility of suffering of the dying patient, a compromise may be struck about the scope of the cases in which stopping treatment on the request of the patient might be legitimized (as in the Israeli law, which includes in this scope terminal cancer patients but not Alzheimer patients). So although extensional equivalence or convergence is deeper and relatively more stable, compromise is a fruitful and effective complement.

23.4 Universal Human Rights and Multiculturalism

The tension between the religious, duty-based perspective in Jewish bioethics and the liberal, right-based approach is manifest in contemporary Israeli society. Israel is a typically multicultural society with a large sector (among other sectors) of religiously committed Jews who follow the Halakhic law and have strong influence on legislation and regulation. It is an interesting test case for the problem of forming bioethical guidelines within a democratic constitutional framework which would be nevertheless acceptable to all sectors. As I have tried to show through the idea of convergence or extensional equivalence, the closeness in content of the two points of view makes the accommodation of religious sensitivities in secular state legislation somewhat smoother in the sphere of medical practice than in other contested normative issues (such as the regulation of the Sabbath in the public sphere, the framework and content of school education, or the laws of marriage and divorce).

From the other direction, it is also easier for the religious sector to accept some of the new bioethical regulations since many of them fall within the values of that sector too. As I mentioned, it is striking how easy on the whole it was to pass laws in Israel allowing technologies of assisted parenthood, including controversial practices such as surrogacy or stem cell research, with little religious resistance – the simple reason being that these technologies proved so effective in the promotion of reproductive capacity of previously barren couples.

In a way, the very success of multicultural society is constituted by the ability to bring people to converge on some core institutions and second-level rules, without conditioning it by some shared value system or substantive normative view. This is an aim which goes beyond simple compromise or mutual toleration.[16] It satisfies different sectors in society without forcing them to adopt a particular normative point of view (typically that of the majority). But of course this is only a political ideal and in reality the tension between systems of values may not always be resolved in such convergence and the debate will not only revolve around the forms of justification of practices but also about the content of the practices. In those cases there is no alternative to compromise, at least in a democratic society. This often involves the adoption of solutions which seem to all parties to the debate as *second best* (defined as not the best, on the one hand, but better than no agreed solution, on the other). Thus, the law of surrogacy in Israel expressed a consensus based on the convergence of the views of different parties on the value of assisting couples in reproducing; but then, when it came to the question *who* would be eligible to such assistance there was no convergence of attitudes. To avoid stalemate, the parties had to compromise: unmarried (but stable) couples would be eligible; same-sex couples would not. Both sides to the debate preferred legalizing surrogacy to having *all* their conditions met. The same two-tier method of reaching agreement on controversial practices in medicine can be illustrated in the way the issues of abortion, euthanasia, and organ donation were solved on the regulatory level in Israel. And of course this leaves other debates unsolved. For instance, neither convergence nor compromise is possible in Israel regarding active euthanasia, which is both legally and ethically prohibited (despite some people who strongly believe in its moral legitimacy).

But on the more general level of the clash between human rights and multiculturalism I find that there is some deep chasm that cannot be easily bridged. The best way to examine it is through a close reading of Article 12 of the UNESCO Declaration on Bioethics and Human Rights (2005):

> The importance of cultural diversity and pluralism should be given due regard. However, such considerations are not to be invoked to infringe upon human dignity, human rights and fundamental freedoms, nor upon the principles set out in this Declaration, nor to limit their scope.

---

[16] It would be interesting to compare this notion of convergence with John Rawls' idea of "overlapping consensus", developed in his *Theory of Justice* (Cambridge, MA: Harvard University Press, 1971). Rawls seems to be a little more ambitious in the characterization of the overlap, which extends beyond the content of the agreed upon practices to some form of common commitment to formal rules of the political game, i.e. fairness.

Here, we are taking one step up in moving from multicultural plurality *within* a given society to cultural diversity and pluralism in the world as a whole. This step uncovers a serious conceptual problem in the accommodation of multicultural plurality in the framework of universal human rights. The whole idea of human rights is based on the *individual* as the fundamental moral unit, as the subject of autonomy and freedom and as the object of dignity and respect. These are all explicitly mentioned in the preceding articles of the Declaration. Now, multiculturalism refers to *cultures*, that is to say, to a community of people rather than to individuals. Multiculturalism wishes to preserve the pluralism of whole systems of values and ways of life – not just the pluralism of individual preferences and choices. But this creates an inevitable tension between the rights and dignity of an individual and the value of maintaining the culture in which this individual happens to live. For respect for the rights of an individual may conflict with respect for the system of norms of the culture or sector to which the individual is subjected. Thus, from a human rights perspective, informed consent is a basic principle in medical ethics which should (with some well-known exceptions) be routinely adhered to. But from a religious or other traditional point of view, the welfare of the patient should be the guiding principle in doctor-patient relationship. And as we know, the autonomous decision of the patient may very well conflict with her real interests or objective welfare, let alone with the values of the community to which she belongs.

Now Article 12 is a bit vague and does not specify the kind of force the consideration of cultural diversity should have in the creation of normative bioethical rules. But the value of diversity as such cannot be interpreted as a right, for there is no particular individual it protects. And the Declaration explicitly demands that consideration of pluralism should not "infringe upon" human rights. But in the multicultural debates the argument is often raised that there is something partial, not universal, in the very culture of rights and that there are societies in which rights do not play a major role (as my paper has shown regarding religious Jewish culture). The question is then raised about the possibility that the Western liberal culture of rights just forced its own values and principles as if they were universal. From the point of view of societies which do not share the principles of individual autonomy and which uphold communal or family values or norms there is nothing sacrosanct about liberal ethics or bioethics.[17]

There is no easy answer to this challenge. Historically speaking, the 1948 UN Declaration of Human Rights could be called "Universal" since most of the member states of the institution at the time belonged to roughly the same cultural tradition. But in 2005 the awareness of multicultural heterogeneity has become acute and the adjective "universal" more difficult to apply. For it is the often heard that the concept of human rights itself can be extended to apply to claims by societies to be permitted to stick to their values and norms in which there are often practices that

[17] There has been an intense debate whether liberalism itself is just one "parochial" political view among others and that it consequently has no particular standing on the cosmopolitan level and cannot claim universality. This has often been the argument against liberalism put forward by communitarians such as Michael Sandel and Michael Walzer.

are incompatible with individual human rights. This is a shift of meaning of rights from the individual to whole communities. This changes the basic sense of the concept itself. Article 12 seems to be aware of that problematic shift of meaning and insists that despite the respect owed to diversity of cultures, this cannot serve to limit the scope of human rights, let alone infringe upon them.

Summing up by returning for a moment to the Jewish approach to bioethics, one should note that despite the reluctance to adopt a rights point of view in medical ethics, the religious sector often does appeal to rights in the multicultural sense of the autonomy and freedom of a particular community within the larger society to maintain its traditional norms (and of course the ways of reasoning about them), even if from the liberal, right-based morality, some of these norms infringe upon the rights of individuals. It is the weakness of liberalism that it cannot fully respect individual rights and at the same time respect cultural autonomy. But modern Jewish bioethics may serve as an example of an attempt to create some tense but tolerable co-existence between the two approaches and gradually adapt to each other's point of view even without fully accepting it.[18]

[18] I wish to thank an anonymous (and meticulous) referee of this article for having suggested to me some important nuances in the reading of the Hebrew Scriptures on both the general conception of rights and on the nature of medical treatment. Equally helpful were comments of two referees of the whole volume.

Chapter 24
Response to Professor David Heyd's Paper Entitled: "Between Humaneness and Human Rights, A Jewish Perspective on Modern Bioethics"

Jonathan Halevy and Adina Halevy

24.1 Prominent Issues in Professor Heyd's Paper

Professor Heyd argues that modern bioethics, being rights- based, stand in sharp contrast to all religion based bioethics which, by definition, are duty-based.

Until the mid- twentieth century, medicine in general and the doctor-patient relationship in particular, were paternalistic, with little or no account paid to the wishes and beliefs of the patient. Modern medicine and modern medical ethics are based on the patient's autonomy over his body and the doctor's duties are created, or at least formed and limited, by patients' rights; today's norm of "informed consent" requires that the patient be a full partner in the decision-making process relating to his diagnosis and treatment at every stage.

Heyd claims that the rights of the individual do not exist in religions in general and, in particular, not in Judaism. The whole concept of individual rights (or human rights) is relatively modern, originating in the seventeenth century and bringing with it the inverse concept that An Other (be it a fellow human being, society or state) then has duties towards the individual. From the point of view of religions, however, it is clear that individuals cannot impose duties on God. Therefore, in that context, the rights of the individual do not exist.

Nevertheless, Heyd goes on to maintain that, despite the axiom that the rights based autonomy approach and duty based Jewish religious approach stand in contradiction to each other, the field of medicine actually does make possible a bridge between the two.

J. Halevy (✉)
Shaare Zedek Medical Center, Jerusalem
e-mail: halevy@szmc.org.il

A. Halevy
Psychotherapist, Jerusalem

J. Tham et al. (eds.), *Religious Perspectives on Bioethics and Human Rights*, Advancing Global Bioethics 6, DOI 10.1007/978-3-319-58431-7_24

Heyd explains in terms of "extensional equivalence" the fact that both the rights-based modern bioethics and the duty-based religious approach can reach the same norms from completely different ideological bases and principles. Heyd brings abortion as an example – allowed by modern bioethics based on the autonomy of the woman over her own body, and allowed under certain circumstances (danger of life for the mother) by the Jewish religious approach based on the sanctity of life. A further example is living organ donation, such as kidneys. Modern bioethics allows this based on the autonomy of the individual over his own body while the Jewish religion allows it based on the view that the sanctity of life of the recipient supersedes the injunction of not harming the body of the donor. Similarly, assisted reproductive techniques such as IVF which, again are allowed by modern bioethics because of individual autonomy, are allowed by the Jewish religion because of the prime importance of procreation.

However, according to Heyd, this convergence is shaky because of the opposing principles it is based upon and it does not reflect tolerance of the opposing viewpoint.

Heyd concludes that Jewish medical ethics as implemented today may serve as an example of an attempt to create tense but tolerable coexistence between the disparate approaches of religion and modern bioethics, at least in practice if not in ideology.

In this paper, we would like to demonstrate that Jewish ethics have long recognized that absolutism does not hold in real life, which is subject to compromise and practicality. And, contrary to the view of Prof. Heyd, there is today a strongly growing, not a shaky, convergence between the rights-based and duty-based approaches to medicine.

Thus, in practice, the claim of the individual's complete autonomy, the cornerstone of modern bioethics, is not strictly upheld. Abortion and euthanasia even in the most liberal and free-thinking countries are not automatically permitted "on request". In Holland, for example, assisted euthanasia is regulated by laws that require confirmation from two senior physicians that the patient is suffering from an incurable disease and has less than 6 months to live, and that the quality of life in this period will be intolerable. Theoretical modern bioethics has been refined from a black and white view to recognition that society must enforce some limitations to the absolute autonomy of the individual.

Israel, a Jewish country with largely secular laws (except in matters of family, marriage and divorce being regulated by traditional Jewish religious law known as Halakha) has reached a modus operandi between the rights of the individual and the upholding of the norms of Jewish culture in many fields. Thus, for example, when travelling is forbidden on the Sabbath according to Jewish law, government-funded public transport does not operate in most cities out of respect for those who wish to keep the Sabbath fully in the manner ordained by Biblical edicts. In the field of education, legislation allows for diverse streams – secular, modern orthodoxy, strict orthodoxy, Muslim and Christian minorities – a non-absolutist approach necessitated by recognition of the multicultural nature of the state.

Heyd himself points out that the field of medicine lends itself even more easily than other fields to a compromise between right-based and duty-based religious methodologies. Despite different principles, there is clear convergence in practical norms.

As a prime demonstration that real life is a matter of compromise, not a choice between absolutes, we would like to trace the enactment in Israel of three highly significant pieces of medical legislation – The Patients' Rights Law 1996, The Dying Patient Law 2005 and The Brain/Cardiac Death Law, 2008 – and to show the evolution that is taking place in Israeli society regarding the convergence of modern bioethical concepts and the principles of traditional Jewish medical ethics.

Passed in 1996, The Patients' Rights Law defines the right of every individual to receive quality medical care with dignity, with no discrimination of gender, ethnic origin, age or religion. The original intention was to include an article (article 10) which would also establish a legal right "to die with dignity". However, the legislative body of the Knesset (Israel's Parliament) could not reach consensus on this point, mainly because of the opposition of the religious parties and the law was passed without resolving this specific matter.

Seven years later, after much further deliberation in the Knesset and in public media, a committee of 59 physicians, nurses, social workers, psychologists, rabbis, philosophers and lawyers was convened, headed by one of Israel's leading bioethicists. Following 2 years of intense discussion, The Dying Patient Law 2005 was enacted. I would like to quote its opening Chapter:

> Goal and Fundamental Principle
>
> Goal
>
> (a) This Law regulates the medical treatment of the terminally ill patient based on an appropriate balance between the value of the sanctity of life, the value of the individual's autonomous will and the importance of quality of life.
> (b) This Law is based upon the values of the State of Israel as a Jewish and democratic state and on fundamental principles in the realm of morality, ethics and religion.
>
> Fundamental Principle
>
> In prescribing the medical treatment of the terminally ill patient, his medical condition, his will and the degree of his suffering are the exclusive considerations.

This law, which forms a comprehensive legal guide to all physicians who attend the dying, makes a practical compromise between rights-based and duty-based ethics. Rights-based, the patient's autonomy is held in high regard, advance medical directives are respected (indeed, a registry for such documents has been established by the Ministry of Health). However, the patient himself cannot "order" his own demise; his condition must be assessed by two senior physicians and it must be determined that he has less than 6 months to live because of an incurable disease which greatly erodes quality of life. Although active euthanasia is not permitted, medical care-givers are not required to implement the duty-based ethic of the sanctity of life and impose upon the dying patient an existence of misery and suffering. We may justifiably regard this law as a firm embodiment of the convergence of the two ethical approaches.

A further Israeli law of significance to our argument is the Brain/Cardiac Death Law of 2008. The law is intended to promote cadaveric organ donation, which is possible only from cadavers where the circumstance of death is brain death. Pronouncing brain death is based on the Harvard Criteria (1967)– a situation where extensive and severe brain damage is well-documented at both clinical level (characterized by deep coma with no response to external stimuli, no spontaneous breathing, no pupillary and corneal reflexes, support of heart and circulation by artificial means) and at laboratory level (flat EEG indicating no electrical activity of the brain, no electrical activity under stimulation, no blood supply to the brain on ultrasound Doppler).

This relatively new law again reflects compromise and convergence. Most Jewish law authorities have joined with modern science in recognizing brain death but, in acknowledgement of duty to the sanctity of life, extremely strict assessment of the patient's condition is legislated – only certain doctors who have undergone special training on the matter of brain death may determine whether this is such a case, and all confirmatory laboratory tests (stimulus of the brain and demonstrating no blood supply) are mandatory. In Israeli hospitals, the family of a brain-dead patient may choose the option of donating organs, entailing the cessation of support systems. However, should they choose against this, frequently because they do not recognize brain death as death, the medical staff is committed to continue supportive measures until cardiac death occurs.

Thus we see that this law reflects the convergence of the individual's autonomy, sacred to modern bioethics, with the religious views of that segment of the population i.e. the ultra-orthodox (chiefly Jews but also of other religions or secular), who do not recognize brain death. By respecting the wishes of both parties, the organ donor pool in Israel is not significantly reduced (the ultra-orthodox comprise about 10% of the general population), while, on the other hand, the religious principles deeply rooted in this section of the population are preserved.

It should be noted that considerable public debate arose as to whether those who do not recognize brain death should be "punished" for their refusal to donate organs, based on the principle – if you do not give, you will not receive. Once again this resulted in a compromise which reflects respect prevailing for the multicultural nature of Israeli society: those who do not donate may certainly receive organs, but among those waiting for a transplant, a slight preference is given to those who have themselves signed on an organ-donor card. This is seen not as a punishment singling out a segment of the population, but also addresses the sadly large majority of non-orthodox citizens who have not joined the pool of prospective donors – the aim is simply to encourage more people throughout the entire religious/secular spectrum to become donors.

The implementation of the Brain/Cardiac Death Law epitomizes the manner in which the conflict between individual rights and the norms of culture of a specific segment of the population are in practice accommodated in Israel. It is true that it may be claimed that the decrease in the donor pool that stems from the objection of some of the population to recognize brain death and sign donor cards infringes on the individual rights in the rest of society. However, after public debate and debate in the Israeli legislative body, it was determined that this infringement was de facto and numerically insignificant enough to be tolerated by society as a whole. We would conclude that this is a fine example of the convergence between individual rights, multiculturalism and religious principles and a source of great optimism for the future.

We would like now, to look a little more closely at the attitude toward medicine in Jewish thought (Encyclopedia of Jewish Medical Ethics, compiled and written by Avraham Steinberg, Feldheim, 2003). In his article, Prof. Heyd depicts the attitude of the Old Testament as a straight forward belief that God is the true healer, and man's only active role in the preservation of his health is to follow the precepts God has laid down in the Torah. This is supported by verses such as "And I will remove sickness from your midst"(Exodus 23:25), "I kill and I make alive, I wound and I heal and none can escape My hand" (Deuteronomy 32:39), "And He said, if you diligently hearken to the voice of the Lord your God and do that which is right in His eyes and give ear to His commandments and keep all His statutes, I will afflict you with none of the diseases with which I afflicted the Egyptians, for I am the Lord, your healer"(Exodus 15:26).

We are in full agreement with Heyd's view that the Jewish attitude to medicine has since undergone great changes. The Talmud already upheld the position that, unlike all other professions, there is specific permission for men to engage in healing implied in the Biblical statement "He shall surely heal" (Exodus 21:19). By granting humans the intellectual power to diagnose and treat illness, Talmudic scholars argued that God has made it clear it is His will that physicians act as His representatives in healing. Although both doctor and patient must still place their faith in God. It becomes the active obligation of the doctor to employ his God given skills to save life, just as the sick are obligated to seek healing from physicians.
The following is brought by the Midrash, (Midrash Shmuel 4:7) the ancient Jewish rabbinic method of Torah study, to illustrate the regard in which the physician's role is viewed by later Rabbis:

> Rabbi Ishmael and Rabbi Akiba were questioned by a sick man in Jerusalem as to how he could be cured. When they replied with various instructions as to how this could be achieved, the sick man challenged them he had been afflicted with his disease by God, therefore the rabbis were interfering in God's wish by attempting to relieve his suffering. The rabbis drew the parallel between the intervention that the sick man himself in his profession as a tender of vineyards had made to improve the natural vineyard established by God and the work of the doctor. Without man's active participation in weeding, fertilizing, pruning and ploughing, the vineyard could not flourish and yet all this was not considered to be interference in God's initial design. Similarly the lore and medicine of the physician, far from being forbidden, were a necessary part of God's ultimate desire that man should do all in his power to preserve life.

Thus, medicine came to be viewed as a noble profession and Jewish spiritual leaders often served simultaneously as Rabbis and physicians. As it is not only permissible for a physician to heal but it is in fact a commandment to do so, medicine is held to be engaging in the fulfillment of Torah law.

In conclusion, while we do not subscribe to Prof. Heyd's sharply black and white view of the clash and distinct contradiction between rights-based modern bioethics and duty-based Jewish medical ethics, we are in agreement with him that despite their differing principles, the two approaches may converge, especially in the sacred field of medicine. We hope that real-life examples that we have brought from modern Israeli legislation illustrate the manner in which this is already being implemented.

References

Deuteronomy 32:39
Encyclopedia of Jewish Medical Ethics, compiled and written by Avraham Steinberg, Feldheim, 2003
Exodus 23:25
Exodus 15:26
Exodus 21:19
Midrash Shmuel 4:7

Chapter 25
Response to the Paper, "Between Humaneness and Human Rights"

Hans Ucko

While reading "Between Humaneness and Human Rights", I found myself more than once nodding in agreement. And I began asking myself how to provide a reply from a Christian perspective, when much of what I could say had already been said, and better, through the presentation of what was referred to as the Jewish tradition. Should my Christian presentation just echo what was said or should I look for anything uniquely Christian in relation to bioethics and as being different from what could be said in other religious traditions? And is this really possible?

When thinking of the affinity that I sensed, a sentence attributed to the educator and religious thinker Ernst Simon came to my mind: "The people I can pray with, I can't talk to, and the people I can talk to, I can't pray with." You're in dialogue with someone of another faith and you suddenly realise that there is something that reverberates in you that you had not really expected, not least because it is labelled as belonging to another religious tradition. Simon actually gives voice to the experience of many engaged in interreligious dialogue: You may suddenly feel surprisingly closer to a person of another faith than to people of your own religious tradition. And you realize that the dividing line doesn't go between religious traditions but within religious traditions. Such an experience is definitely valuable also in a context, where we from different religious traditions are solicited to reflect on issues as diverse and controversial as bioethics. I appreciate the affinity between people of different faiths on these issues and I know that it is not a given that I find this like-mindedness with people of my own faith. And I therefore wonder about the added value of mirroring one religious tradition after the other on one bioethical issue after the other, trying as it were to crystalize a Jewish point of view, a Christian position and a Muslim stance. Where are we supposed to end up? What is the purpose of a confessional definition and refining? Do we end up at a point, where we can say: "This is it"? And what is it? We try to sharpen a Christian perspective, a

H. Ucko (✉)
Interreligious Relations and Dialogue of the World Council of Churches, Geneva, Switzerland
e-mail: hansucko@gmail.com

J. Tham et al. (eds.), *Religious Perspectives on Bioethics and Human Rights*, Advancing Global Bioethics 6, DOI 10.1007/978-3-319-58431-7_25

Jewish perspective, a Muslim perspective but must ask ourselves if our religious traditions just like that are providing the tools we need to face the black holes of ethical problems arising from biological research and its applications in fields such as organ transplantation, genetic engineering or artificial insemination. I wonder about the wisdom of having us look at bioethics using only glasses polished by a particular religious tradition. Isn't there a risk of othering the other by having a Jewish, Christian, Muslim, Buddhist or Hindu perspective displayed one after the other? To make complicated problems to be gleaned above all through my particular religious affiliation carries with it the risk of narrowing my understanding. Are we not taking a step back when going to our religious traditions asking them to find the handle to a religious response? Isn't there a risk of essentialism, that the bioethical issue so to say would have a set of characteristics, which makes it what it is and that religion would be the main key to open it up or the other way around that religion could be reduced to be the interpretative key that unlocks the bioethical issue? We know that bioethics is probably the place, where we will not find an answer and yet at the same time fully aware of that bioethics is intimately connected to our own life or the life of our parents and children. It is a whamming insight.

What is important, it seems to me, would therefore be to take note of our topic as first of all calling for **humaneness** because of our shared humanness. This is not minimizing the contribution of each religion but to be realistic about our religious traditions: they do not offer a "vade mecum" for addressing issues of cloning or how to solve the overpopulation of our planet.

Could we recognise first of all our shortcomings as Hindus, Buddhists, Muslims, Jews and Christians in getting a particular handle to the bioethical challenges overwhelming us? I would therefore rather take David Heyd's hand saying: "Excellent; *kol haKavod*! And now, where do we together go from here?" Together we should sit down in honest deliberations as to what it is that we need to explore, what we possibly could say it and how we possibly could say it.

When I participate in interfaith events, listening to our listing of our religious ideals but more seldom to the religious realities as they played themselves out in history, I often think of what the ordinary man and woman thinks of us. Many would say: "Leave religion out of such complex issues all together!" They would refer to many examples in history, when religion has not been a useful guide. The footprints of religion are often frightening. We need to bear this in mind, as we explore the contribution of religion on issues such as bioethics and similarly human rights. We must ask ourselves whether religions more than in a very general way can provide moral or ethical resources to deal with bioethics. There is more the risk of hovering over the issue than daring a real touchdown. Our religious traditions offer a sentence, a verse, a theological assertion but do these really answer the complexity of moral or ethical dilemmas of bioethical realities? Can e.g. *pikuach nefesh* from the Jewish tradition be the versatile tool for every situation of bioethical dilemmas? I know that it means that one should live by Torah rather than die for it. And yet? Can it alone carry every situation?

Christians will often refer to what in my Protestant tradition is called the Little Bible (John 3,16) as the interpretative key to an ethical understanding of life in all its complexities. The Bible verse may sound nice but is the meaning the same in every situation? We hold as religious people a compass for which way to go but isn't it also true that we often end up in situations, where the compass needle is nervously oscillating between contradictory directions? The question of abortion comes to mind, where the dilemma is that there is not **one** answer.

When we as religious people are gathered in interreligious dialogue, we sometimes paper over the complexities of peace, development, poverty, human rights, bioethics or whatever it is that brings us together draped in our religious resources. Is what we have enough? Here is a Jewish response, a Christian claim or a Muslim declaration. But do they suffice or do they only temporarily silence our worry that we are unable to answer that which has so many dimensions to it that one answer is simply not sufficient.

The expertise needed to fathom the consequences of genetic screening or gene-therapy is not immediately coming out of our religious traditions or Holy Scriptures. The answer to ethical questions, questions of right and wrong in decisions and rules of conduct in scientific research or behaviour arising in the relationships in bioethics, in life sciences, biotechnology, medicine are not really immediately at hand for theology. Considering the fundamentalist or equivalent streak in religious life today and a tendency towards religious defensiveness, I am weary of religious answers to various issues in society. The religious identity today seems often to perceive itself as under threat and the reaction seems to be to portray religion as having the answers irrespective of the question. When saying that this or that issue in bioethics is answered through this or that quote from this or that Holy Scripture or religious tradition, I have a feeling that the hand of our religious traditions is forced beyond its own intention. I do not think that we in the New Testament or in any other holy scripture will find a response to what to think about cloning or genetic engineering. Religion is not in these and other matters an immediate a priori arbiter of right or wrong; the answer is not prima vista in religion and religionists need before answering interact with people with hands-on experience or knowledge of the issues at stake: abortion, euthanasia, cloning. To familiarise oneself with the issues, religion must join company with people not necessarily coming at the issues from a religious perspective, which does not mean that they are without human ideals or hopes for a better world. Irrespective of religious affiliation or illiterate as to religious language or outside any religious framework, they may nevertheless witness to an unyielding commitment to the enhancement of human life, the protection of integrity and dignity of all persons.

There are for sure religious resources that we could tap but we all know that religion today is not only a tool for peace but also a weapon for conflict. My concern is therefore that our thoughts and opinions in ethical matters are not pontificating. These can be the source of knee-jerk automatic responses like" "I am a Jew, so I think X" or: "I am a Christian so I think Y" or "I am a socialist so I think Z" etc. The more complex issues of e.g. bioethics are the more some religionists are likely to present simplistic assertions.

Our main task today in our religious communities is "understanding". This must be an increasingly central objective: harder, deeper and more enduring than merely "being right." Such an objective is independent of whether we are religious or agnostic. We may be driven by what is really the common source of all human beings, perhaps of all creation, non-human as well. If anything can be the source of genuine cross-cultural global bioethical communication that is at the same time interreligious, it will have to come from a shared attitude of seeking understanding, an Anselmian principle for our time, the "fides quaerens intellectum".

The moral crisis of our time, which includes but goes beyond dilemmas in bioethics, is sometimes discussed in terms of a loss of bearings or a loss of meaning. And religion provides direction. But a loss of bearings or a loss of meaning doesn't automatically mean that we have to rediscover those lost bearings as if they were all still lying there in the past. Our responses cannot be a matter of finding again the snow that melted already last year but of interpreting anew from within each particular situation. Jews, Christians and Muslims invoke the God of Abraham and Sarah, Isaac and Rebecca, Jacob and Rachel but should also make sense of what it would mean that God is **our** God in our time and in our generation. We cannot face the challenges of a new era simply by promoting the return to how we used to behave. Paradise lost is really lost.

David Heyd's distinction of right-based and duty-based categories plays out the difficulty of religion in our society, at least in the Western hemisphere. These categories are voices in a duet, differently sung in the Renaissance, Reformation, Enlightenment and Secularization, each in their own way giving an emphasis to the role of man and woman in society and the world. Religion sees humankind in relation to the Divine not as autonomous but as dependent. Human beings are in every religion seen to be on the way, not standing and waiting at a transcendent or apocalyptic bus stop. We are on our way and this is the way it is. We are not there yet. We have to know the way and the task of religion is to help us get going. It comes across in all religions; religion is about walking. The first Christians referred to themselves as belonging to the Way and the Way is Christ. Halakhah is the path that one walks and the way is paved with the *Jewish law.* Sharia is the pathway to be followed by every Muslim. *Shinto* is the way of the gods. *Tao* signifies way, every one well knowing that the Tao that can be mentioned is not the real Tao and that the sense moral is to get lost in Tao. Every Buddhist knows that the Dhammapada is the path of the teaching and Bhakti Yoga is the path of pure spiritual devotion to the divine. It is intrinsic to religion to walk along a given path; any discourse on humans endowed with given rights is never seen in splendid isolation but if at all subsumed under duty.

Not least as a consequence of the Renaissance, Reformation, Enlightenment and Secularization, our time has given birth to a rights-based language. Nowhere is this more evident than in the way our time looks upon children. The Convention on the Rights of the Child introduces a new framework; the child is not the property of anyone. It has a value not only because it is the extension of its parents or family or a link to the future. It has a value not only once it has learned what we want it to know, a value as a prospective adult. Already as a child, irrespective of what it has received, it has a right in itself and this is something new in our time.

I find inspiration in the Jewish reading of the Ten Commandments. They do not begin with the commandment as it were “ex nihilo”: “You shall have no other gods before me” The commandments are a response. Because “I am the Lord your God, who brought you out of the land of Egypt, out of the house of slavery”, your response is to have no other gods before the Lord, your God! How do we find back to a response that is not only duty but responsibility and even gratitude? We cannot forego the right of rights to be a dominant factor in our building of society: in relations between children and adults, between men and women, between human rights and animal rights, in environment concerns and a holistic world-view. But rights need more than rights to be nurtured. When the emphasis of our rights eclipses the interrelationship of responsibility and rights, a vital dimension of being human is lost. How can we retrieve responsibility as a ground-setting value to interact with our concern for rights as the dominating constituent in the building of community? André Malraux expresses this dilemma: « Je pense que la tâche du prochain siècle en face de la plus terrible menace qu’ait connue l’humanité, va être d’y réintégrer les dieux. » (I think the task of the next century facing the most terrible threat humankind has ever known, will be to reintegrate the gods). What does he mean and to what extent is this possible or even desirable? How could we create space for that dimension that we label divine? We are today autonomous and emancipated. We shoulder what it means to be a human being. Can we go back to a situation, where we abdicate from what we have achieved? How could we reintegrate a space for God, gods, the divine, the ultimate, without handing back the rights we so long have fought to obtain and where we still have not reached our goal? And yet, we need this dimension of always being called to a response, like in the Jewish understanding of the Ten Commandments: Because we were set free, we will be responsible.

One of the problems often held up in relation to the Universal Declaration of Human Rights is that it seems to be overemphasising rights as an overarching value. The Valencia Declaration or “Declaration of Human Duties and Responsibilities” tried to address the issue. The preamble states categorically: “The effective enjoyment and implementation of human rights and fundamental freedoms is inextricably linked to the assumption of the duties and responsibilities implicit in those rights.” But this declaration didn’t really catch on. We need today to recall the intention of the Universal Declaration of Human Rights. The emphasis was to finding a universal language, addressing all people, irrespective of religion, where the even stress was on **HUMAN** and **RIGHTS**. Our common task is to retrieve that even stress and the best way to get there would be the intentional embrace of our common **HUMANENESS** as our strongest and at the same time most vulnerable characteristic. From there on there is a possibility to balance human rights and human responsibility.

Chapter 26
Lessons Learned

Joseph Tham

After reading all these very interesting papers, the reader might find the relationship between universal human rights and local cultural diversity to be more complex than first meets the eye. In this chapter, we will attempt to give an overview of the different positions of this relationship, from the perspectives of the major world religions and in reference to certain bioethical themes.

We begin with a quick summary of the positions expressed within each of the seven religious traditions. This makes evident how time and again, cultural diversity is inseparable from the religious identity of the localities. Each religion faces challenges from their engagement with the global concept of human rights, from the interpretation of the religious response, and from the interaction between religion, culture and science.

Second, we reflect on the cause of this tension, which is in fact an intersection of debates on different planes—cultural, political, philosophical, theological, and ultimately metaphysical. They range from the debate on a maximalist versus minimalist approach to ethics, the emphasis of duties contrasted with rights, the priority of religious against secular views, the tension between individual and societal rights, the relationship between faith, reason, and science, the question of nature versus nurture, and ultimately a metaphysical question regarding one versus many.

26.1 Religious Perspectives on Rights and Duties

First, we will look at the monotheistic religions which have a longer history of engagement with human rights, especially that of Western Christianity. As Palazzani notes, the relationship between Christianity and human rights has been uneasy at

J. Tham (✉)
School of Bioethics, Ateneo Pontificio Regina Apostolorum, Rome, Italy
e-mail: jtham@legionaries.org

J. Tham et al. (eds.), *Religious Perspectives on Bioethics and Human Rights*,
Advancing Global Bioethics 6, DOI 10.1007/978-3-319-58431-7_26

best. The Church's acceptance of the human rights language was relatively recent, and it was only after the Second World War that it has become commonly accepted in the West as compatible with Church teaching. Jacques Maritain, a Catholic metaphysician, laid the groundwork for it in the Universal Declaration of Human Rights. Even though he was instrumental in arguing for its formulation in international politics, he was aware of its lack of a solid philosophical basis. As a neo-Thomist, he recognized the need to orient human rights towards finality, especially the goal of true human flourishing. Within this framework, Christian authors (Palazzani, Chang, Yeung, Kwan) employ natural law reasoning with an emphasis on the centrality of the human person. This vision of personhood is founded ontologically and not functionally, thus defending against the discrimination of human life from the very beginning (embryos) to the very end (comatose) even in the absence of functional manifestations. In this light, human beings are not reduced to the autonomous self as bearer of rights. Personhood also implies a relational dimension: towards others in solidarity, brotherhood, and an extension of charity towards the Other. The transcendental dimension of man also shows his openness towards God. Thus, according to the natural law tradition, reason and faith are not opposed. Palazzani quotes especially the International Theological Commission (ITC) document *The Search for Universal Ethics: A New Look at Natural Law* (Commission 2012), which as the title suggests, has specially relevance for our discussion.

Even though there is recognition of the basic tenants of human rights, Christians are nonetheless wary of its secular and liberal turn today. We already see this in some of the points mentioned above. The secular version of human rights is less concerned with finality, ontology, and personhood, but instead exalts individual choices and rights. Palazzani rightly points out that the human rights discourse is a minimalist approach, concerned with what the minimal requirement to restrict actions contrary to the human good are. However, Christian ethics is maximalist, concerned with the substantial and integral good of the human person and society. Kwan, following Palazzani, elucidates the discordance between these two visions. He notices that the secular version of human rights runs the risk of abuse precisely because it lacks teleology (finality), anthropology (personhood), a proper scale of values, and the common good.

We now turn to Judaism, which with its history of the *Shoah*, is quite sympathetic to the human rights discourse. Heyd analyzes the binomial of rights and duties, and finds that while modern bioethics begins with rights and derives duties from it, religious Judaism begins with duties which then points to their correlative rights. So while modern right-based ethics emphasize autonomy, equality, and universality, duty-based approaches sees man as an image of God and human dignity as the foundation of an ethics with a paternalistic bend. Heyd traces the Jewish religious thought of God as healer to a gradual acceptance of human interventions in medicine as God's instrument. Yet there can still be tension between duty and right based ethical approaches. In the state of Israel, Jewish bioethics reveals a coexistence of these two visions through convergence and compromise. While convergence means a substantial agreement on shared values between the two, compromise points to pragmatic solutions that accommodate the different interest groups involved. Here, the Halevys see more examples of convergence than compromise, but the examples they offer on patients rights, end of life issue, and brain death seem to confirm that legal solutions are compromises among different stakeholders.

Like Judaism, Islam takes a similar approach to bioethics in their reliance on interpretations of revealed truths. However, their reliance on the role of reason in ethical analysis is very limited. According to Atighetchi and Padela, the source of ethics cannot be found in reason, but in revelation. Since nature and goodness reside in the mind of God, Islam affirms the superiority of revealed truths over human reasoning. For this reason, both of them have reservations regarding human rights, since God's revealed plan trumps all human demands and rights. Atighetchi in fact complains of a type of colonization of western liberal ideals of human rights in Muslim countries, generating unease and discontent. Guessous, on the contrary, is quite sanguine that human rights is compatible with Islam based on the reading that there is not one Islamic culture, and that traditional religious views are evolving towards greater acceptance of rights. This contrast of opinions is fascinating because while Atighetchi and Padela are both men residing in non-Islamic countries, Guessous is a feminist scholar from Morocco. This shows once more the strains that exist in many Muslim countries as religious traditions confront science, human rights, and modernity. This tension can be boiled down to the question regarding the interplay between faith and reason in accessing truths. While the West has historically confronted this dilemma since the Enlightenment, Islam is still in the process of finding an adequate response. The problems with a voluntaristic approach to God's will, fideism, fundamentalism and their degenerate and extreme manifestation in terrorism, is on everybody's minds. The Regensburg address of Pope Benedict XVI puts the finger on this sore spot, which generated much reaction and reflection among Islamic scholars (Benedict 2006). Hence, Padela's proposal of a soft version of natural law reasoning in the Sunni legal hermeneutics as a possible approach to dialogue is both novel and laudable.

The aforementioned antagonism between traditions and modernity is also noted in India, home to over a billion Hindus. As Desai notes and Tarasco emphasizes, human rights is foreign to Hinduism because one of its basic tenants states that everyone is created unequally, with contiguous doctrines reflected in *dharma*, reincarnation, and the acceptance of caste systems. Likewise, Tarasco shows that the emphasis of duties in *dharma* would be incompatible with human rights. At the same time, the Constitution of India has guaranteed equality of all citizens since 1949 and adheres to the principles of human rights. This difference in local religious culture and the ideal expressed in the law is something that has coexisted in India, with resultant friction and occasional violence. Lunstroth sees human rights as a Trojan horse of science and liberal ideology which infringes on the more cultural and local beliefs of the country. In spite of this glaring incompatibility, the debate regarding equality, rights, and duties is much less pronounced than in Islam. In part, this is due to the nature of Hinduism that Desai describes: a polyphonic religion, less centralized and dogmatic in its beliefs, and capable of incorporating new ideas by absorption and syncretism.

Buddhism inherited the doctrine of dharma from Hinduism and similarly puts an emphasis on duty rather than the language of rights. In addition, the rights language posits humans as individuals with claims, an atomic concept of man that is very alien to Buddhist values. Zhang believes, and Hongladarom agrees, that Buddhism may permit the concept of human rights through a juxtaposition of duties as negative rights. Zhang furthers analyzes the meaning of freedom and individual choices in this perspective. With this rearrangement, choices should be responsible, in view of the greater common good. This communitarian approach will emphasize the interconnection and interdependence of all beings. However, in this vision, humans will no longer be considered special with respect to other life forms. In contrast to ontological inequality of beings in Hinduism, Buddhism acknowledges the concept of radical equality of all lives. This latter position poses a problem of considering humans as bearers of rights because of their unique dignity, especially when contrasted with the monotheistic notion of *imago dei*.

Similar to Buddhism, Daoism has an exalted notion of nature that includes all beings, animate or inanimate. Humans form a part of this web within the Daoist cosmology. Hence, according to Bidlack, Chia, and Palmer, Daoism is not concerned with human rights, while at the same time not necessarily opposed to it. Ethics therefore regards movement towards a state of harmony of people with themselves, with others, and with the rest of nature. This drive for oneness and perfection does not depend on fixed ethical norms or principles. The concept of *ziran* and *wuwei* means that one should strive to go with the flow of Dao, as one cannot easily foresee a clear-cut dimension of good and evil in particular choices. Palmer adds that human rights, like other ideals outside Daoism, in so far as they could facilitate the goal of perfection and oneness, may be undertaken as a worthy means to an end.

Together with Buddhism and Daoism, Confucianism forms the common heritage of all Chinese people. Whereas Buddhism and Daoism place a larger emphasis on spiritual progress, strictly speaking Confucianism is not a religion but a philosophy of life based on elaborate ethical and political hierarchies. As in the other Eastern religions, the emphasis is on duties instead of rights. Whereas duty in Buddhism is directed toward all life and in Daoism toward unity with the cosmos, the more pragmatic Confucius and his followers emphasize duty to the immediate family and the state above all. In this sense, individual needs and rights are secondary to societal or familial ones. Confucian scholars like Chan, Fan, and Zhao are therefore quite critical of human rights as manifestations of the liberal ideal of individualism. However, Fan and Zhao think that precluding this substantial liberal notion of self, there can be room for Confucian rights which are based on the virtue of *ren* and oriented towards the family. Accordingly, in an ideal Confucian society where members cultivate the virtue of *ren* interdependently and harmoniously, there will be no need for human rights claims. However, in the imperfect world, human rights can be instruments that foster the forming of a virtuous society. Yeung likewise agrees that personhood not grounded on autonomy but on human nature is compatible with human rights in Confucianism. Furthermore, he posits a possible convergence with Christianity through a theoretical horizontal extension of *ren* to all human family alongside with a vertical relation with a transcendent God through rituals (*li*).

26.2 The Tension Between Universal Human Rights and Respect for Cultural Diversity

We now consider the difficulties encountered in this debate more deeply. The issue is multifaceted, reflecting many shades of the complex dilemma facing the modern world. It is a broad subject that has occupied scholars across several disciplines—political theorists, sociologists, philosophers, theologians, ethicists, and religious scholars to name a few. In this book, different authors have touched upon certain feature of this dilemma. Though by no means exhaustive, the multi-religious perspective shines a special light upon it. The particular applications in bioethics have provided some real examples of why this question is relevant, even though most of the discussions have centered on theoretical aspects. While the enquiry may appear at first glance to fall under the realm of ethics, on deeper analysis we are brought back to the anthropological issue regarding what human nature is.

The ethical debate of universality of rights can eventually be banded into two general camps: thin vs. thick approaches, minimalist vs. maximalist ethics, rights vs. duties language, secular vs. religious convictions, and the tension between universalism vs. particularism. These divisions are necessarily broad generalizations, and there are definite overlaps as well as deficiencies. Nonetheless, delving into these categories can help us penetrate more profoundly into the problem.

The thin approach is not very concerned with finding a foundation for human rights. It is more pragmatic in orientation, content with the usefulness of the rights language that can garner sufficient consensus in the political and international circles, so that inhumane atrocities could be condemned, restrained, and persecuted. Guessous, ten Have, Ucko and Heyd are optimistic in finding some substantive agreement on human rights that could be shared. However, as Palazzani and Lunstroth worry, and Kwan convincingly demonstrates, rights language unmoored from any firm foundation easily becomes the victim of partisan and ideological manipulations. In the long run, rights could be employed to justify any action, and fall prey to the proverbial "might is right." Hence, we can comprehend the uneasy protest of religionists, and those who like Atighetchi are anxious of Western and liberal colonialism and ethical imperialism. Related to this is the fear that when human rights are not rooted in something substantial, they can fall into moral relativism. Ironically, those who espouse the liberal relativist stance often raise the banner of plurality of religions and multiplicity of cultures as a proof of the impossibility of a common morality. Thus, multiculturalism is translated to mean diversity of the human race, without a common nature, and ethical compromise can only arrive through negotiated consensus (Engelhardt 1996). As we will see, this is a disingenuous instrumentalization of religion by secularists, only to discredit the possibility of a common or global ethics.

We now turn to the camp of thick or substantive approaches, which as we have seen from different authors, tends to be religiously inspired or metaphysically grounded. They tend to be more centered on duties than individual rights, since traditional religions all focus on personal responsibility towards those in need.

Confucians sees this duty as a virtue that everyone must develop towards his kin, family, and state to attain familial and societal harmony. Judaism derives human equality from *imago dei*, and according to Heyd, there is a duty to extend humaneness to them all. Christianity conceives this supererogatory duty as charity towards God and neighbor, and personal salvation hinges on its fulfillment. Hinduism, while eschewing radical equality of all human beings, nevertheless attributes duties proportional to each person's state of life. Buddhism relates duties to compassionate response to the interrelated whole of all life, especially those who are most vulnerable and who suffer. Garcia et al. traces this thick narrative.

Religious thick approaches also have strong views about the nature of the human person. This is so because religions have traditionally provided questions regarding the meanings of suffering and death, life and the afterlife. Thus, ethical input is often shaped by certain anthropological and cosmological presuppositions. However, as religions enter into modernity, many of these traditional answers are now proffered by science, whereas technology seems to have alleviated many aforementioned sufferings and inconveniences. Hence, world religions are facing the challenges of secularism, modernization, science, and hence, the questions of globalization and global ethics. Miranda has critiqued Atighetchi about the excessive preoccupation of colonialism from the West against Islam, unfairly conflating science and technology with human rights. Yet Lunstroth is also wary of the imposition of a scientific and positivistic viewpoint on indigenous cultures, with human rights and modern bioethics representing this ethical hegemony. As we have seen, the question regarding the relationship between faith and reason, and science and faith are dealt with differently in different religions, based on their socio-historical past. As various authors have shown, the question of human rights in ethical reflections is caught up in this discussion.

Regarding the interplay between faith and reason, there is a certain reaction against reason encroaching upon faith to the detriment of the authority of revealed truths. At the same time, pure reason and rationalism has not been able to resolve the challenges facing humanity, as the failed Enlightenment project has demonstrated. Without doubt, all authors in this volume are sympathetic to a balanced approach where faith and reason work together, and where both extremes of rationalism and fideism are avoided. As Padela's proposal of soft version of Islamic natural law has shown, this is not just a Catholic imposition, even though the Catholic tradition has always been a strong advocate of the *fides et ratio* binomial. This is further confirmed in the famous dialogue between Cardinal Ratzinger before he became pope with the liberal political philosopher Habermas, when they both concurred on the dangers of rationalism and fideism. The danger of fideism ignoring reasonable input can degenerate faith into fundamentalism and hence terroristic acts. Yet, the danger of scientism as the only source of knowledge can be equally damaging to ethics. Ratzinger points out that secularization, which marginalizes the place of religion in society and politics in the West, is in fact an anomaly compared to the rest of the world. He believes that secular rationality without any boundaries or limits is incomprehensible to a majority of the world's citizens (Ratzinger and Habermas 2007). In the already mentioned Regensburg address, he recognizes that faith and reason can purify each another from extremism. Hence, a healthy tension between faith and reason, avoiding the extremes of fideism and rationalism, can take on an intercultural dimension as the debates within Christian, Buddhist, Hindu, and Islamic cultures become more frequent.

In the field of bioethics, the rejection of religious input is manifested as "secularization of bioethics" which I have written extensively. A historical overview of bioethics will demonstrate that early pioneers of American bioethicists had theological training and religious sympathies. However, due to historical and sociological circumstances, the different spheres of politics, culture, science, education, and philosophy have undergone secularization. Ethics was the last casualty, with the rise of a secular bioethics that is sometime conflated with modern bioethics. At the root of the marginalization of religion is an uncertainty about its place in democracy, and of situating religious ethics in public ethics (Tham 2008). This prejudice continues to the present day. One such example is found in a Timothy Murphy article claiming that bioethics should avoid religious input in its normative analysis (Murphy 2012). Murphy's position is consistent with the Enlightenment bias which considers religious input as detrimental to the well-being of society. Fortunately, the inadequacies of secular and irreligious bioethics have precipitated a reexamination of the possible contribution of religion and theology in ethics (Tham 2013a).

The relationship between universal human nature and the presence of diversity of cultures is a vexing philosophical question. How is it possible for human beings to have a common nature when there is such a proliferation of religious and cultural manifestations? Would cultural diversity negate the fact that there is sufficient commonality to guarantee a common set of rules for behavior, a universal or global ethic? There are those who would make such a negation to the possibility of global ethics, and hence human rights and the Declaration of Human Rights and Bioethics (Engelhardt 2006). Others, as we have seen, prefer to put the emphasis on diversity as a value to the exclusion of commonality which is portrayed as ethical imperialism. Still others see the value of difference a good thing, advocating a form of syncretism of religious practices and ethical relativism.

Ten Have offers a possible middle way to these two extremes. He speaks of a cultural heritage which is common for all humanity but is local. More precisely, these local customs: food, sites, arts etc., are valuable for all humanity because they contain values that are universalizable, transcending their local origins. Analogously, global bioethics expressed in the language of human rights can be such a common heritage whose content is shareable with all peoples. In this way, we can acknowledge cultural diversity while at the same time insisting on universal values. In place of multiculturalism, which describes the plurality of cultures, he prefers interculturality which is also the preferred language of ITC document on universal ethics.

26.3 Bridge Concepts from the Thin Approaches

In order to move forward, certain bridge concepts may further advance this dialogue between human rights and cultural diversity. Coming from the thin approach of human rights, we can examine the nature and types of dialogue itself, with proposals about convergence, compromise, and dialectics. From the other end, the thick approach offers reflections on human nature, natural law, humaneness, and relationality. Roughly speaking, they correspond to the traditional division of ethical methodology into teleology and deontology, with their respective strengths and deficiencies. The thin and teleological approaches of human rights seek consensus in a changing world by adapting to the local situations and contexts and then projecting these globally. Thick deontological approaches prefer to start with the metaphysics of the human person and derive ethical principles, duties and rights from it. The weakness of the former is that a consensus language of rights does not seem to give ethics a firm base and is open to whims of cultural change. On the other hand, the latter methodology is considered top-heavy and inflexible in adapting to the changing contextual and cultural needs of the times. But if we study these two approaches more carefully a rapprochement can be found.

Corresponding to the thin approach of rights, ten Have proposes a method of dialectic evolution. He sees it as an effort to bridge the divide between universalism and particularism. Globalization does not mean homogenization of cultures, but rather a greater interconnectedness both in perception and deed. Human rights are therefore not considered as set in stone, but serve as action guides that are still evolving until proven to be wrong. Hence, a dialectics approach acknowledges human fallibility, and is never satisfied with a finished product. There will be movements towards convergence and divergence in this vision. This process of globalization, according to ten Have, is seen in the evolution of bioethics during the period 1970–2010 where we move from the four principles of principlism to 15 in the Declaration of Bioethics and Human Rights.

The question of dialectics in ethics is not new. Gustafson (1996) proposes a dialectic method of doing ethics in order to stay relevant by contextualizing theology to presumed modern needs. This dialectic approach is considered vital in a pluralistic culture where justification of ethics must take up the task to include all human experiences—science, history, philosophy, psychology, sociology, and culture, etc.—in order to be credible to the non-believers. The dialectic plea to modify religious justification revolves around the question of whether human nature is static and fixed or dynamic and evolving as noted in the contraceptive debate. As a result, Gustafson proposes that each new scientific or cultural breakthrough will call for a theological revision in this ethical dialectic to reflect and often accept the latest behavior accepted by our society. Unfortunately, he was unable to overcome the criticism of relativizing theology with this methodology.

Palazzani also observes the presence of both deductive and critical dialectic approaches in the ITC document. This document traces the historical development of natural law from Greco-Roman sources, especially their legal tradition, its enrichment from Christian thought, and finally the contribution of Catholic magisterium. Roman laws, Francisco de Vitoria, and Grotius made important contributions to the notion of natural rights that prepared the way for modern human rights. It also recognizes the presence of natural reason in "the wisdom traditions and religions of the world"—*Dharma* and *Ahisma* in Hinduism; the five ethical precepts or *sila* of Buddhism; the Tao or the Way in Daoism; the harmonious virtues indicated by the way of Heaven (*tian dao*) of Confucian thought; the ethics of life in traditional African religions; and the morality of obedience in Islam. At the same time, the document also engages the dialectics of universality and particularism. It proposes rationality as the common ground to deduce the universal basis for human rights and dignity, thus avoiding the danger of consensus ethics on the one hand, and the danger of equating multicultural and multi-religious settings with ethical relativism on the other. It warns that without a firm acknowledgement of human nature, human rights in the absence of duty and limits can be abusive. Grounded on our natural capacity to reason, it can concurrently counteract the claims of cultural relativism while permitting intercultural and interreligious dialogue (Tham 2013b).

The question of consensus in ethics with regard to relativism needs further comment. Heyd talks about the difference between convergence and compromise in the formulation of biolaws. Convergence means that there are true agreements on the principles, whereas compromise means the disagreements are overlooked but accepted in the process of negotiation. But whether convergence is superior to compromise is not discussed, and one is still left with the doubt of relativism. In our previous volume, *Religious Perspectives on Human Vulnerability in Bioethics* (Tham et al. 2014), I amply exposed the theory of MacIntyre who offers a solution that allows for the expression of cultural diversity and yet eschews moral pluralism. According to him, different moral traditions can confront each another on equal footing. In this engagement of culture and traditions, it is possible to enter the conversation with intellectual honesty and "maximal vulnerability" without hiding one's own defects. In this pain-staking, slow, and difficult process of soul searching, exchanges and comparisons would allow the rival traditions to see their weaknesses and strengths, and rationally recognize their own incoherence and the superiority of their rival, with the possibility of abandonment of their own tradition (MacIntyre 1989). In a similar vein, Durante (2015) presented a paper in a subsequent workshop proposing different levels of agreements in interreligious dialogues. He proposes "dialogue despite diversity" among the different religious traditions as an attempt to provide a framework of discussion. This seminal paper is a proposal that is not only informative, clearly stating what each religion believes, but also aims to engage the different traditions in a serious manner. He conceives a three stage approach: (1) consensus building, where different religious traditions freely expound their ethical visions as an on-going conversation in search of "bridge concepts." Relativism is avoided since one can see the reasoning behind such justifications without agreeing upon a truth. (2) Accepting interpretive diversity. When there is sufficient unanimity for some ethical reasoning to be considered universal, this universality does not imply uniformity but allows for indigenous pluralism. (3) Agreeing to disagree, when there are incommensurable differences. The stance is that of tolerance which is a last resort practice and not a principle. All these are different attempts to reconcile the demands of universal rights and cultural diversity without falling into relativistic reasoning.

As a last comment on the thin approach, Lunstroth's introductory paper is quite critical of human rights as a negation of cultural and religious diversity. He parallels the history of American bioethics with the drafting of the Declaration, both of them prone to the same defects of being drafted by naturalist lawmakers and politicians who kowtow to scientists. This description is akin to the thesis of sociologist Evans (2012) on the "thinning" of bioethical arguments. Similar to my account on the secularization of bioethics, he demonstrates how the successful overtake of the theologian's traditional competency in the area of ethics by professional bioethicists is signaled by the shifting of the debate from substantive or thick questions of the ends to one of a thin formal rationality of the means alone. Thick theological questions on human ends were ignored by the bioethics profession which became the legitimate voice that "gave cover" to the scientists and acted as an agent of the bureaucratic state through the governmental commissions. Without significant discussion on the ends of scientific research, scientists gained control of the conversation. The locus of debate has purposefully been shifted from the public to the bureaucratic state, to the detriment of the democratic process. Evans notices that the bioethics profession is incapable of saying "no" to the scientists, of being a real critique of technology and the industry. Lunstroth's critique of the human rights movement is similar in that the general populace with religious convictions is not well represented in the drafting of these international soft laws of human rights. Hence, both of them propose a greater democratization or participatory model of decision making process. Thus in place of naturalists, scientists, and politicians acting as representatives of the public opinion, with each new technology and their corresponding ethical concerns, the public should be able to participate in the debate on the messier thick questions of human goods and ends through their political representatives. In a way, this is compatible with ten Have's view on human rights and bioethics as an on-going unfinished product that requires dialectic evolution. The difference is whether this dialectic occurs at the higher levels of expertise and decision-makers, or that they should happen at a more grassroots level.

26.4 Bridge Concepts from Thick Approaches

We now turn to the thick approach of human rights in our analysis of bridge concepts. Here we again face the question of common morality that can provide a solid foundation for human rights that can be shared by different cultures and religions based on the collective human condition. We have seen natural law could be a possible candidate for global ethics, but it also faces many challenges (Pontifica Academia Pro Vita 2010). First, there is the opposition from modern and postmodern deconstructionist philosophy that denies the existence of objective truth. Scientific or logical positivism denies any source of truth outside of empirical science, whereas legal positivism places truth at the mercy of societal consensus. Natural law has unfortunately been misconstrued as equivalent to the laws of nature, i.e. physical or biological laws. This "physicalist" interpretation leads to the accusation of committing the naturalistic fallacy of G.E. Moore or the *is-ought* problem of David Hume. Second, a related complication is that natural law language has become unintelligible in contemporary culture. The word "nature" is not comprehensible for many people today because they understand it empirically, and no longer metaphysically. This is due in part to the preeminence of evolutionary theories which make it difficult to discern the presence of rationality within nature today. In other words, it is difficult to see purpose and finality (teleology) if nature has evolved and constantly evolves, and when these occurrences are contingent, casual, and random. Finally, there is the question of the historicity of natural law. The specific question here concerns the application of universal norms in particular situations both geographically and historically. Some critics of natural law highlight the fact that certain practices such as usury, slavery, and the death penalty have been justified by natural law reasoning in the past but are now shown to be untenable.

There are also challenges to natural law from religious sources. Human rights are based on the radical equality and dignity of members of the human race, which is sometimes coined human exceptionalism. This notion of equality may not be present in all religions, especially the Eastern ones. Zhang realizes that in Buddhism, due to a belief in reincarnation, humans do not occupy an "absolutely privileged position" but are in continuity with other sentient beings. Thus, animals also have dignity and even rights. Without further exploration, this concept of animals having rights is also present in many contemporary Western thinkers and movements due to Buddhist influence and the fading of *imago dei* theology. Likewise, we can intuit the same problem with Daoism, where dignity is extended to all of nature, and human beings are only a small part of the whole. Desai and Tarasco also point out that the caste system in Hinduism would be a hindrance to human rights. In Islam, the challenge to natural law is epistemological. Fortunately, Padela offers a possible acceptance of natural reasoning through reason's role in interpretation of sacred texts.

Heyd proposes, and Ucko seconds, humaneness as another bridge concept that can appeal to our commonality. Even though this concept originated in the theology of *imago dei*, it can be easily accepted by other religions or even the irreligious. Humaneness elicits the sense of duty toward compassion and mercy, or as Emmanuel Levinas famously proposed, seeing the Other in the face to face encounter is the basis of all ethics. Chang apparently takes on this intuition in the concept of relational self derived from both the Aristotelian-Thomistic and Confucian traditions. He argues for a robust ontology of the human person that is at the same time intrinsically relational. Hence, it is an attempt to overcome the dichotomy between individualistic propensity of human rights and the communitarian duty to care (*ren*) for others. He sees the shift from the autonomous self to the relational self as a theoretical solution to the tension between universalism and particularism. Furthermore, he foresees the possibility of extending this relationality to a greater interconnection of humans with the rest of nature, thus addressing the problems of plurality of cultures. This new relational framework extends even to the ecological spheres. There will be a greater awareness of our interrelatedness with all beings, without diminishing the unique dignity of the person. This is a novel and praiseworthy effort to combine monotheistic *imago dei* doctrines (Judaism, Islam, Christianity) with Eastern ideals of harmonization with nature (Hinduism, Daoism, Buddhism). Lastly, Yeung may wish to supplement this Confucian concept of relational charity to our relationship with God through worship.

26.5 Conclusion

The philosophical question of the "one and the many" has plagued philosophers since antiquity. What we have seen in this debate reflects the different manifestations of this inquiry: between being and becoming, between universality and particularity, between common human nature and diversity of cultures, between global ethics and local customs, between common and individual good, and between absolute principles and situational applications. It is certainly a generalization that Western philosophical tradition has sought the unifying principle of being, essence, and truth whereas non-Western cultures are more at home with a changing and mystical reality of harmony in diversity (Bernstein 1991).

While most United Nations documents and declarations are explicitly non-religious, they claim universality because of a political consensus. However, as we have seen in this book, the claim to universality of human rights and cultural diversity cannot be easily made. A purely secular approach is unable to give an adequate answer to the problem, and in fact seems a bit schizophrenic when it tries to appease pluralism and universalism simultaneously. On the one hand, having turned its back on religion, postmodern culture finds it difficult to accept a universal ethic which smells too much like totalitarianism and authoritarian religious ideology. The fragmented moral tradition prefers the language of diversity and tolerance. On the other hand, there is a need to affirm human rights which can only make sense if it is universal in its scope. Secularization has made engagement with other cultures difficult, since secular liberalism is broken within and antagonistic to religious input. Too often, the liberal West has been identified with secularism which does not do justice to its religious past. Hence, we can see the importance of religious input into this problem. The papers in this book have made a significant contribution to thicken the discussion precisely because consensus-based universalism on cannot escape its own vicious circle. The contributions in this volume show that engagement is possible when both reason is open to faith and faith-based assumptions are open to the critique of reason. In this way, thus faith and reason can purify each other from possible excesses.

References

Benedict XVI. 2006. Faith, reason and the university memories and reflections. Retrieved from http://w2.vatican.va/content/benedict-xvi/en/speeches/2006/september/documents/hf_ben-xvi_spe_20060912_university-regensburg.html.

Bernstein, R. 1991. Incommensurability and otherness revisited. In *Culture and modernity: East-west philosophic perspectives*, ed. E. Deutsch, 85–103. Honolulu: University of Hawaii Press.

Commission, I. T. 2012. *In search of a universal ethic: A new look at the natural law*. London: Catholic Truth Society.

Durante, C. 2015. Dialogue despite diversity: Sharing norms when our moralities differ. *Studia Bioethica* 8 (1): 7–17.

Engelhardt, H.T. 1996. *The foundations of bioethics*. New York: Oxford University Press.

———. (ed.). 2006. *Global bioethics: The collapse of consensus*. Salem: M & M Scrivener Press.

Evans, J.H. 2012. *The history and future of bioethics: A sociological view*. New York: Oxford University Press.

Gustafson, J.M. 1996. *Intersections: Science, theology, and ethics*. 1st ed. Cleveland: Pilgrim Press/United Church Press.

MacIntyre, A. 1989. *Whose justice? Which rationality?* 1st ed. Notre Dame: University of Notre Dame Press.

Murphy, T.F. 2012. In defense of irreligious bioethics. *The American Journal of Bioethics* 12 (12): 3–10. http://doi.org/10.1080/15265161.2012.719262.

Pontifica Academia Pro Vita. 2010. *Bioetica e Legge Naturale: Atti della Sedicesima Assemblea Generale dei membri, Città del Vaticano, 11–13 febbraio, 2010*. Rome: Lateran University Press.

Ratzinger, J., and J. Habermas. 2007. *The dialectics of secularization: On reason and religion*. San Francisco: Ignatius Press.

Tham, S.J. 2008. The secularization of bioethics. *The National Catholic Bioethics Quarterly* 8 (3): 443–453. http://doi.org/10.5840/ncbq20088329.

Tham, J. 2013a. A response to irreligious bioethics. *Studia Bioethica* 6 (2–3): 12–19.

———. 2013b. The challenges of bioethics in Asia: A natural law perspective. *Asian Horizons, Dharmaram Journal of Theology* 7 (4): 55–61.

Tham, J., A. Garcia, and G. Miranda, eds. 2014. *Religious perspectives on human vulnerability in bioethics*. New York: Springer.

FSC www.fsc.org
MIX
Papier aus verantwortungsvollen Quellen
Paper from responsible sources
FSC® C105338

If you have any concerns about our products,
you can contact us on
ProductSafety@springernature.com

In case Publisher is established outside the EU,
the EU authorized representative is:
Springer Nature Customer Service Center GmbH
Europaplatz 3, 69115 Heidelberg, Germany

Printed by Libri Plureos GmbH
in Hamburg, Germany